S0-ADX-003

The Bad City in the Good War

THE AMERICAN WEST IN THE TWENTIETH CENTURY

Martin Ridge and Walter Nugent, editors

The Bad City in the Good War

San Francisco, Los Angeles, Oakland, and San Diego

Roger W. Lotchin

INDIANA
University Press

Bloomington & Indianapolis

FLORIDA GULF COAST
UNIVERSITY LIBRARY

This book is a publication of

Indiana University Press
601 North Morton Street
Bloomington, IN 47404-3797 USA

http://iupress.indiana.edu

Telephone orders 800-842-6796
Fax orders 812-855-7931
Orders by e-mail iuporder@indiana.edu

© 2003 by Roger W. Lotchin

All rights reserved

No part of this book may be reproduced or utilized in any form or by any means, electronic or mechanical, including photocopying and recording, or by any information storage and retrieval system, without permission in writing from the publisher. The Association of American University Presses' Resolution on Permissions constitutes the only exception to this prohibition.

The paper used in this publication meets the minimum requirements of American National Standard for Information Sciences—Permanence of Paper for Printed Library Materials, ANSI Z39.48-1984.

Manufactured in the United States of America

Library of Congress Cataloging-in-Publication Data

Lotchin, Roger W.
   The bad city in the good war : San Francisco, Los Angeles, Oakland, and San Diego / Roger W. Lotchin.
       p. cm. — (The American West in the twentieth century)
Includes bibliographical references and index.
   ISBN 0-253-34143-4 (cloth : alk. paper) — ISBN 0-253-21546-3 (pbk. : alk. paper)
   1. World War, 1939–1945—California. 2. Cities and towns—California—History—20th century. 3. California—History—20th century. I. Title. II. Series.
   D769.85.C2 L68 2003
   940.53'794'091732—dc21
                                        2002010943

1 2 3 4 5 08 07 06 05 04 03

FLORIDA GULF COAST
UNIVERSITY LIBRARY

This book is dedicated to Phyllis Morris Lotchin

CONTENTS

ACKNOWLEDGMENTS

I would like to acknowledge several persons and institutions that have contributed to the completion of this book. I owe a great debt to the librarians at the Reference Department at Davis Graduate Library at the University of North Carolina, who patiently dug up one rare government document after another until the book could hold no more. These people include Ridley Kessler, Jennifer Pendergast, Tommy Nixon, Cindy Adams, Donna Cornick, Hugh Singerline, Robert Dalton, Suzanne Lankford, Barbara Levergood, Rita Moss, Maureen St. John-Breen, Mike Van Fossen, and Linda Lloyd. Their help has been invaluable. So has that of Susan Bales of Circulation, who aided my work at several points. I owe another debt to my secretary, Rosalie Radcliffe, and to all the History Department staff—Pamela Fesmire, Linda Stephenson, Mattie Hackney, Wanda Wallace, and Nadine Kinsey—for facilitating my work in more ways than I can count. Special thanks are also due to the staff of the Bancroft Library, present and past, especially to Bill Roberts. The Institute of Governmental Studies at the University of California was also extraordinarily helpful. The Huntington Library granted me several leaves to research this and related books and invited me to organize a 1995 conference that probed and illuminated the impact of World War II on California. Several scholars participated in that conference and the ensuing book, which helped me to understand further a very complex subject. These included Gary R. Mormino, Arthur Verge, Jacqueline Braitman, Linda Harris Mehr, Ronald D. Cohen, William Issel, Paul Rhode, Sarah S. Elkind, K. Scott Wong, Kevin Allen Leonard, Steve Erie, and Greg Hise. Robert C. Ritchie, Director of Research at the Huntington Library, enthusiastically supported both the conference and the book and patiently saw the conference through to conclusion. George and Marylou Boone made the conference possible through their generosity. Several journals supported previous versions of this research, particularly the *Pacific Historical Review,* the *Western Historical Quarterly,* the *Journal of the West, Urbanism Past and Present,* the *Journal of American History,* and the *Georgia Historical Quarterly.* Special thanks to editors Norris K. Hundley, Clyde A. Milner II, Bruce Fetter, Robin Higham, Martin Ridge, and John Inscoe.

I am also most grateful to the San Diego Historical Society, especially to Sally West, Rick Crawford, and Susan Painter. The oral history collection of the Society is invaluable to anyone who hopes to understand the contribution of that wonderfully congenial city to World War II. I owe an equal debt to the growing number of scholars and laypersons who have written enough about the homefront to both whet one's appetite for it and sharpen one's insights into it.

My department granted me several leaves to write this and a companion volume, and the University of North Carolina supported the work with several grants. Carol Kennedy ably edited and corrected the manuscript and saved me from many errors.

I owe a special debt to my editors, Martin Ridge and Walter Nugent, who offered encouragement and sound advice and good-naturedly suffered through many delays in the completion of the book.

Kendra Stokes efficiently managed the ebb and flow of various drafts of charts and text, and Indiana University Graphics Services ably reconstructed the charts. Bob Sloan exercised infinite forbearance with the author and equal judgment in choosing the photographs. His enthusiasm and support made the author's job much easier.

My greatest debt is to my wife, Phyllis Morris Lotchin, who shared the adventure of World War II in California cities and who encouraged me to construct *The Bad City in the Good War* and to deconstruct the early versions of its grammar. This book is dedicated to her.

The Bad City in the Good War

Introduction
The Bad City in the Good War

Riders were very appropriate to a western war, but these horsemen were a diverse bunch, some looking like remnants of the Old West and others like modern cosmopolitan gentlemen. One group patrolled the ocean-front of San Francisco after dark. While the residents of the nearby Sunset District and Seacliff huddled around the radios in their living rooms, curtains pulled and blinds lowered, listening to war news or to *One Man's Family,* other residents rode the beaches. Mounted on their own ponies, the men of the San Francisco Polo Club labored through the sands of China Beach, Baker Beach, and Ten Mile Beach, looking for Imperial Japanese intruders. Far to the south, guns on their hips, another group of riders wound along the paths of the "famed 'Green Verdugo Hills' lying between La Crescenta Valley and the aircraft production area of Glendale and Burbank." These cowboys from the Onondarka Ranch, "realizing the ever-increasing threat of sabotage" in the hills, served as the night patrol for the county sheriff and the forestry department. Still farther south, the celebrated Buffalo Soldier horse cavalry of the United States Army rode the trails along the Mexican border. They carried guns with the triggers lashed down and barrels stuffed shut to avoid incidents with the Mexican troops across the international boundary from them. Anywhere else they would have seemed out of place and time, but in the West they seemed fitting.[1]

With the news of the attack on Pearl Harbor, the border troops were ordered to hasten to Camp Lockett to reinforce the defenders there. This they did in good order and strict military style, riding their horses seven minutes and walking them three. In and beyond the city, everything was apprehension and uncertainty. Thousands of people streamed out of San Diego over the mountain road, fleeing the beleaguered city. They had been told that all nonessential military personnel had to leave, and they were not certain that they would be safe in this southern Navy citadel if they stayed. But they certainly meant to come back. As the mobile columns met on the mountainside, the white occupants of the retreating family caravans leaned out their car windows, yelling to the horse-borne advancing black troops, "Go get 'em, Boys! Go get 'em!"

These episodes could not have been more symbolic of the California metropolitan areas in the Good War. Separated by space, race, class, and occupational barriers, normally the aristocratic polo men, cowboys, and black soldiers had very little in common. But in World War II that changed. The war created a very strong sense of community, participation, and shared experience in something larger than the individual or group.[2] It was an extraordinarily participatory conflict that brought disparate peoples together to protect and abet the homefront endeavor. The diverse peoples that "fought" the war in California cities had their disagreements. Some of these quarrels were quite substantial, and the opposing parties did not forget them during the conflict. Yet their fear of totalitarianism united them in a greater effort. Americans have traditionally been very skeptical of their cities and often downright hostile to them, but cities and city people would contribute markedly to the overthrow and containment of totalitarianism. The "bad city" came in very handy in the "Good War."

In this book I intend to illustrate this argument by stressing cities. This includes the impact of the war upon cities, the impact of cities upon war, the way in which cities were mobilized to fight the war, and the fate and contributions of groups within cities.

For Americans, World War II was perhaps the most nearly universal experience of the twentieth century. Hardly anybody was unaffected by it. Whether fighting in Europe and Asia, migrating to a defense center, writing to service personnel at the front, building war machines in the arsenals of democracy, giving pennies at school for war bonds, saving scrap material, or pounding a civil defense beat, most Americans participated in this momentous conflict. And their participation was immediate, constant, and unrelenting. Although many participants worked in formal settings such as offices, factories, bureaucracies, and barracks, the wartime community also included volunteers. The nation state grew, as historians have stressed, but its growth was matched by a vast renaissance of voluntarism.

A number of excellent studies of the larger picture of the war have appeared, but these are not specific to the state of California, which this book hopes to be. However, they have been broadly conceived and as comprehensive as the research literature has allowed them to be.[3] Yet the cutting edge of research history has not been; most specifically, the local history of the homefront war has not usually been written from such a comprehensive viewpoint. Instead, the history of the urban domestic front has been highly fragmented. Historians have studied Japanese relocation, women who worked in war industries, African Americans, Mexicans, Hollywood, and prisoners of war, but the vast majority of Americans do not appear in these segmented studies. There have been several notable exceptions to this rule in books by Arthur Verge, Marilynn Johnson, Beth Bailey, David Farber, and Marc Miller. Still, it is generally true that the war itself has had a broad focus, but the recent research by historians has had a narrow one.[4]

Topics such as economics, labor, specific geographic homefronts, and a few other matters are treated episodically. However, a great deal of the human experience of the war has yet to find its research specialists. Farmers, for example, who made up a large and crucial part of the war effort, are virtually ignored. Any number of ethnic groups—Italians, Irish, Germans, Scandinavians, English, Chinese, Filipinos, French Canadians, white Southerners, Cubans, Slavs, Greeks, Jews, and almost everyone else besides African Americans, Mexicans, and Japanese—have become homefront nonpersons. They are the invisible men and women of the Second World War. The same is true of homefront topics other than specific groups of people. Matters such as politics, technology, agriculture, science, and values, all matters central to American history and culture, are equally as, if not more, neglected. One book cannot rectify all of these deficiencies, but it can at least address some of them in order to restore a part of the wholeness to the story of the Second World War.

A few topics that need to be addressed require explanation. I omitted the subject of politics both because the literature on California urban politics during the Good War is practically nonexistent and because the topic is too large to squeeze into this manuscript. I dealt with city planning in an extensive article in the *Pacific Historical Review,* which appeared in May 1993. It too is too long to shoehorn into the present project. Finally, I covered urban rivalry in a preceding book, *Fortress California,* so that topic too seemed unnecessary to this project.

Probably the most famous group slogan of the war was the African American "Double V." During the First World War, African Americans had subordinated their domestic reform agenda to the greater good of the war effort. In doing so, they felt that they had been shortchanged because the war ended without significant modifications in the system of segregation. In World War II, black leaders again backed the war effort, but, unlike in World War I, they insisted on immediate progress on the homefront as well. Thanks to the many books and articles on the subject, their struggle is now well known to historians. It is less well known that nearly every other group had the same kind of Double V agenda, although they did not necessarily call it that. Liberals wanted to win the war but extend the power of the nation state in the process. Conservatives wished to win the war but stalemate the growing power of the state. Business hoped to win the war but maintain control over its own economic operations. Labor desired to win but to increase its membership and legitimacy while keeping new in-migrant members at bay. Catholics strove to destroy fascism but wanted to keep Catholic women out of the factories and in the home. Italian Americans wanted to win but to dissociate themselves from fascism and Mussolini in order to gain full legitimacy in the United States. Hollywood wanted to defeat the Axis but keep up its profits and control of movie subject matter. The media hoped to destroy Hitler but to maintain freedom of expression unrestrained by the censor's pencil. Colleges wanted to aid the victory but to retain enough of their male students to stay open. And the government censors wanted to preserve freedom of expression but not at the expense of the war effort. Every group had its own Double V. The war presented them simultaneously with threat and opportunity.

It is precisely this universal Double V that is not fully acknowledged by historians. Professor Cynthia Enloe has captured the tenor of this history by the title of her article on homefront women, which asks the question "Was It a Good War for Women?" That is the same question that is asked in various ways by and about all of the groups. "Was it a good war for us?" ask blacks, Okies, women, Japanese Americans, Mexican Americans, towns like Lawrence, Massachusetts, and unions.

One genre of this homefront literature, women's history, can serve to illustrate the prevailing approach. For example, Esther MacCarthy criticizes the male Catholic hierarchy and Catholic women for not "changing either the [National Catholic] Welfare Conference's ideology on war or its attitude toward women." Maureen Honey faults war propagandists for appealing to middle-class people in one manner and to working-class ones in another, which was calculated to keep them in their place. Susan Hartmann complains that traditionalists took advantage of the war emergency to redefine sex roles in a manner detrimental to female progress by harping on their obligations to returning veterans. Cynthia Enloe charges that the war reinforced racism and sexism. And Deborah Scott Hirshfield objects that the war did not allow women to keep the wartime jobs in the postwar era. Richard Santillan is one of the few women's historians to highlight the importance of women in winning the

war, or to put it more precisely, to emphasize both sides of the Double
V. He takes pride in Mexican American women's contributions to the
homefront, while still asserting the importance of female gains during
the conflict.[5]

Still, the "Was it a good war for us?" approach certainly asks appropriate questions. They are proper questions in the 2000s, and they were
proper questions in the 1940s. If a war cannot withstand the scrutiny
of a democratic people, it should not have been fought. Yet this impact
approach ignores, or at least minimizes, the other wing of the Double V.
Every one of the groups, towns, businesses, or institutions that hoped
for gains or tried to preserve or advance their own agendas *also wanted
desperately to win the war.*

And it is well that they did. World War II was one of the most important wars in the last one thousand years of western history.[6] Had
Hitler won the war or gained a stalemate or had Stalin occupied Western
Europe, the world would have been an infinitely worse place for most
people in it. So winning the war was uncommonly significant, and the
contributions of women, African Americans, Mexican Americans, cities,
business, labor, seniors, the unemployed, children, cities, and towns were
extraordinarily important.

Groups were only one part of California cities' contribution to the
homefront. At the beginning of the conflict, cities possessed remarkably diverse assets that could be useful in winning a war. Many years
ago, Robert Merton advanced the idea of "latent functions." Applied to
politics, the concept stressed the not-so-evident advantages of machine
politics. Although one may quarrel with the idea of latent resources as
applied to political machines, it is certainly a viable way to look at cities at war. Wars are won by industries, labor, natural resources, values,
transportation networks, and so forth, but they also are won by the
advantages cities provide to the military effort. Both cities' physical structures and nearly every other urban quality contributed to this outcome.
The concentration of people and things in a small space provided many
external economies (advantages) for war.

Cities are among the most neglected topics of homefront history,
so studying them will help fill one of the major gaps in the story of the
conflict. But investigating the city is important on at least two more
counts. The current research literature emphasizes the parts more than
the whole, with very little sense of how the various fragments fit together
beyond their roles as victim and victimizer. So restoring the city to its
proper role will help to surmount the fragmented character of homefront
research history and help us to understand how the whole operated and
how the parts related to each other. An emphasis on the city allows us to

see the homefront more holistically than does an emphasis on the parts and on groups such as blacks, women, and Japanese Americans. Perhaps more significantly, urban areas played an enormously important role in winning the Second Great War, so an emphasis on cities will also help us to understand how the war was won.

The homefront literature has tended to neglect the war itself. Many of the studies look at the war's impact and keep the war at arm's length. Historians discuss whether the defense effort was discriminatory toward African Americans, whether it reinforced class consciousness, and whether it was fair to give the best postwar jobs to men instead of women as if the homefront were self-contained and not connected to the tides of battle. This emphasis undermines our ability to recapture the ambience of the war. Much that happened did so in response to the ebb and flow of battle at the front. For example, the wartime housing crisis went through several stages, each triggered by developments on the fighting fronts.

War militarized cities in diverse ways that urbanites could not ignore. War and defense were everywhere about them, from the bunkers and pillboxes along the coast to the carousing sailors downtown to the model airplanes in their children's bedrooms. War is one of the important influences on twentieth-century cities, and cities are an important element in modern war. Cities become its production, transportation, and administrative centers; their streets teem with workers and warriors; their space is the focus of group concentration and conflict; their infrastructure absorbs an extraordinary pounding, even behind the lines; and their people suffer loss. Putting the subject of cities at war onto the agenda of urban, California, and western historians is important in and of itself.

In a way, the traditional historiography of war in the West has been an extension of the "What has the war done for us?" approach. That is so because this historiography posits the notion that the Second World War transformed the West from a colony of the East to a pacesetter for the nation. This question is an appropriate one, but the conclusion seems overstated. In many ways, the war dragged California cities in contradictory directions. In other ways, it accelerated traditional lines of development. In still others, the conflict stimulated regression. In short, the conflict had a complex impact on California cities. Above all, the war did not deflect Golden State cities from their projected path. It was not transformative, nor revolutionary, nor comparable to a Second Gold Rush. It was both more and less; the whole was more complex than the sum of its parts.

1. Limping to Vallejo
The Martial Metropolises at War

The family of Barbara Schillreff of La Jolla Shores learned the seriousness of the war in the customary unusual manner. On December 8, 1941, "Mother opened the blinds and we had ten eyes looking up at us because our house was about four feet off the ground . . . so it was [a] very lovely eye level," Schillreff remembered. "These [eyes] belonged to five soldiers manning a machine gun in our front yard, dug in behind the palm tree that was right outside the window next to our dining room table." Her experience was typical. War rapidly changed California cities into citadels.[1]

Fortress California came of age in World War II. Although there had been a massive buildup of military resources before the Imperial Japanese made their colossal blunder at Pearl Harbor, the war outdid even this impressive concentration. San Francisco became the "American Singapore," to use the contemporary phrase, and San Diego became the "Gibraltar of the Pacific"—a designation also bestowed on the Bay Area concentration of warriors and weaponry. Although San Diego ultimately secured a larger proportion of the Navy and kept it beyond the great demobilization of the late 1980s and early 1990s, San Francisco had as much—perhaps more—military wherewithal. It certainly did during World War II.

Historians have not paid much attention to the fact, but American cities had not been fortified since the Civil War. Therefore, it is worth taking a look at how they achieved that condition.[2] Their first line of defense was also the most eccentric. Initially, the government did not have enough commissioned military boats to patrol the seas against Japanese submarines, explained Albert Eugene Trepte, a member of the San Diego Yacht Club. To remedy this defect, Washington seized all the suitable yachts in California harbors. They equipped the boats with sonar and sent them one thousand miles offshore to hunt Japanese subs. Blimps manned by military personnel flew overhead. As the yachts sailed quietly along, if the crew heard a noise, they radioed it to their blimp partners, who made further inquiry with their own sonar and, if appropriate, dropped depth charges. California citadels were further protected by a tugboat fleet, also linked to a line of blimps, which patrolled the ocean for hostile sea and air craft.

Catalina flying boats formed another line of defense. In the Bay Area, before the planes took off, a boat swept the channel in the bay for driftwood, and then the channel was illuminated by a string of portable lighted buoys. Next the great planes labored up the channel and flew out over the Golden Gate Bridge to their lonely vigil.[3]

The war also created a tremendous new need for both short- and long-range ocean transport. The nation state partially met this challenge by commandeering the tuna fleets of San Diego, Monterey, and other cities. The Navy prized these boats highly because they often contained refrigeration units. Re-christened YP, or yard patrol, boats, these craft plied coastal waters and those of the Santa Barbara and San Pedro channels to deliver food and equipment to the military personnel on the Channel Islands. The military sent many of the larger boats to do similar service close to the fighting fronts and used others to patrol well out to sea.[4]

On shore, the scene was just as odd and much more crowded. Only a plane ride over the Bay Area could convey the enormous amount of martial materiel in that metropolis. Along the southern tip of Marin County, curving around under the Golden Gate Bridge, artillery bristled out of bunkers at forts Barry, Baker, and Cronkhite, protecting the military cornucopia within the Bay. Eventually, anti-torpedo-boat guns replaced the heavies as the threat of torpedo boats replaced that of battleships and cruisers. An anti-submarine net stretched across the Golden Gate Strait, and sentry boxes stood at the highway approaches to the bridge. On the south shore of the strait, Fort Point (originally Fort Winfield Scott) rested, literally, below the bridge. Anti-torpedo-boat guns protruded from historic Fort Winfield Scott to prevent an attack through the Gate. Down the oceanfront of San Francisco other guns peered out of pillboxes, and machine-gun emplacements awaited the enemy.[5]

East of the Pacific front stood base upon base. San Francisco contained Fort Mason, port of embarkation for the island infernos, Hunters Point Naval Shipyard, the Presidio, and Fort Funston. At Hamilton Field in Marin County planes stood ready. Benecia had the Arsenal, and at nearby Vallejo was the senior Bay Area Navy yard. Contra Costa County factories turned out huge quantities of ammunitions, and sailors at Port Chicago, the principal loading facility for the Pacific, anxiously dispatched them to the 1,650,000 servicemen departing from Fort Mason. The Richmond Tank Depot (formerly the Ford assembly plant) produced most of the tanks for the Pacific Theater, and other factories fabricated "military vehicles, bomb trailers, and tractors." In the East Bay the Army supply depot in Oakland shipped other supplies to the forces, and the naval air station in Alameda protected the supply depot. On the San Francisco Peninsula, Moffett Field at the U.S. Naval Air Station, Sunnyvale, housed blimps to patrol the seas against submarine or surface raiders. In San Mateo, the Coyote Point Merchant Marine Training School prepared seamen for one of the war's most dangerous tasks. Adjacent to Yerba Buena Island was the Treasure Island Naval Training Station. At Berkeley, University of California laboratories worked feverishly to produce weapons-grade material for the atomic bombs, and the engineering school hastened to improve the welds on Liberty ships and the superchargers for plane engines. Hardly any point on the great bay named for the peaceable St. Francis was far removed from war.[6]

Shipyards abounded: Marinship next to Sausalito, the Mare Island Naval Shipyard at Vallejo, the Kaiser yards at Richmond, Moore Dry Dock Company in Oakland, Western Pipe and Steel at South San Francisco, the yards of Bethlehem, Moore, and Scott, and United Engineering and Dry Dock Company in San Francisco, the city built of steel. Strange as it seems, Barrett and Hilp Construction built concrete vessels on reclaimed Marin marshlands. Smaller yards rose at Napa, Richmond, San Francisco, Oakland, and Alameda. Subcontractors flourished to service these producers.[7]

The Los Angeles region bristled with weaponry and bases as well. In the harbor the Navy maintained the naval operating base and Roosevelt Naval Air Base, both at Terminal Island. The naval reserve armory, where Hollywood made many films, nestled in Chavez Ravine. Fort MacArthur stood on the Palos Verdes Peninsula. At a huge Army air base in Santa Ana, fliers received preflight training, preparatory to more advanced experience. They learned to fly at night at March Field, Riverside. At "the far flung" Camp Haan, a secret base in the desert, adjacent to March Field, men matured into anti-aircraft artillerists, firing at plane-drawn balloon targets. In another part of the desert, near Indio, George Patton drilled soldiers in tank warfare at the famous Desert Training Center. North and west of there, Army Air Corps bombers worked out tactics and test pilots flew planes, including the Bell Aircraft SP-59A, the first American jet, from Muroc Air Force Base and from Rogers Dry Lake (then called Muroc Dry Lake).[8]

The Los Angeles area saw more shipbuilding than one might imagine. Calship (California Shipbuilding Corporation) built Liberty cargo ships at its Terminal Island yards, and Los Angeles Shipbuilding and Dry Dock and Consolidated Shipbuilding Corporation at Wilmington produced other vessels. Fellows and Stewart Boat Building Company at Terminal Island constructed subchasers, and Western Pipe and Steel Company at San Pedro built various boats, including icebreakers (in sunny Southern California!). Calship converted others, and Bethlehem repaired and built still more. The naval dry docks on Terminal Island could handle any ship in the world. Others from Long Beach to Newport–Balboa Bay produced diverse smaller vessels.[9]

But Southern California's real specialty was plane manufacture. Douglas produced aircraft at Long Beach and Santa Monica airports and at El Segundo; Lockheed-Vega fabricated them in Burbank; Vultee churned them out in Downey and Long Beach; and North American manufactured others at Inglewood, including the famous P-51 at Los Angeles Airport. Subcontractors all over the Los Angeles area furnished parts for these major assembly plants. Timm Aircraft of Los Angeles even manufactured the plywood gliders that would carry men into battle beyond Normandy Beach.[10]

Schools abounded to train pilots to man these craft. At Los Alamitos and Oxnard, flight schools taught men to fly the motored craft coming off the L.A. area assembly lines, and at Twentynine Palms another school taught them to handle the gliders built at Timm. At Cal Tech, scientists tested aircraft in its wind tunnels. Others labored to improve rocketry, joined by engineers at the Jet Propulsion Laboratory when it was established. On college campuses, servicemen studied everything from culture to languages to shell velocities.[11]

San Diego presented the same martial appearance. The *Los Angeles Times* claimed that "of all Southern California cities, the atmosphere of war most extensively pervades San Diego," and it is hard for the historian to disagree. Across the mouth of the harbor, between North Island and Ballast Point, the Navy stretched one submarine net, with another about one-half mile inland. These were raised and lowered as the occasion demanded. For example, each morning at daybreak, the nets were lowered to allow authorized travel out. Virtually all civilian traffic, except for fishing boats, disappeared from the harbor. Radar scanned the horizon for boats and planes; eventually sonar equipment attached to buoys

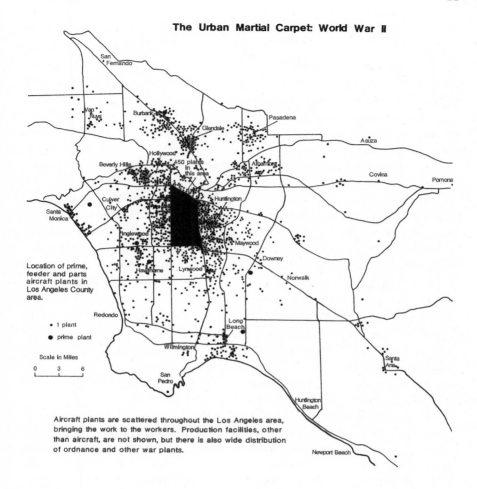

The Urban Martial Carpet: World War II

Location of prime, feeder and parts aircraft plants in Los Angeles County area.

• 1 plant

● prime plant

Scale in Miles

0   3   6

450 plants in this area

Aircraft plants are scattered throughout the Los Angeles area, bringing the work to the workers. Production facilities, other than aircraft, are not shown, but there is also wide distribution of ordnance and other war plants.

searched the seas for sounds of vessels, and men atop the Point Loma Lighthouse peered some thirty-five miles out to sea for ships or signals. At Fort Rosecrans communications teams stood ready to sound the alarm when it was passed on from ships at sea or the coastal blimps.

Crash boats at the mouth of the harbor were on alert to rescue the pilots of the many aircraft that had unsuccessful takeoffs from North Island. As soon as the planes splashed down, water-going giant cranes lumbered to the crash site to fish the planes out of the sea. At night, searchlights (made in Germany for General Electric!) played over the skies, the waves, and the Mexican border. Out in the sea, beyond the harbor mouth, three lines of boats patrolled the waters to challenge any mysterious callers.[12]

Fortifications, installations, and men crowded the land. Shortly after the attack on Pearl Harbor, the Utah National Guard occupied the coast from San Diego to Escondido. In addition, the 19th Coast Artillerymen peered anxiously into the Pacific from their own pillboxes at Fort Rosecrans. These structures were every bit as impressive as those that the GIs encountered on the French coast on D-Day. The roof was made of six feet of reinforced concrete with a "strike face" fifteen feet thick. Another twenty feet of soil was piled on the top. The big guns in these monster bunkers belched flame and projectiles from Point Loma onto dummy targets bobbing in the ocean behind a tugboat tow.

At night, the residents of the Azure Vista Housing Project on Point Loma were entertained by the air bursts of anti-aircraft artillery practicing from Kearny Mesa. Elsewhere, on Ballast Point near the lighthouse, 37mm cannons and .50 caliber machine guns lay in wait for enemy aircraft. Ninety-millimeter radar-controlled cannons hovered nearby. Bases choked the smaller San Diego Bay as they did San Francisco Bay. South of the entrance, North Island Naval Air Station stood at the mouth of the Harbor of the Sun, and north of it on Point Loma was the fortified U.S. Military Reservation, including Fort Rosecrans. The latter packed lots of firepower, including Battery Ashburn and another 16-inch gun battery intended for targets up to twenty-five miles away.[13]

Smaller cannons lurked in other bunkers, waiting for meaner targets, and .50 caliber machine guns anticipated the approach of torpedo boats. Other 155mm howitzer emplacements ran down the Silver Strand. Observation towers studded the coast, here on a water tower on the Silver Strand, there in a field in La Jolla. Guns were everywhere: machine guns bristled out of the roof of the naval hospital in Balboa Park and anti-aircraft guns sheltered beneath the camouflaged roof of Consolidated Aircraft Corporation; 16-inch guns, 10-inch guns, 8-inch guns, 6-inch guns; 155mm howitzers, 90mm guns, 37mm rapid-fire cannons; mortars of several descriptions; .30 caliber and .50 caliber machine guns; and one mammoth cannon seventy feet long. Each of the batteries was named—Ashburn, Whistler, Cabrillo, McGrath, Gillespie, Zeilin, Woodward, Grant, and, inauspiciously, Fetterman. Bomb shelters stood ready to protect men whose barracks were under attack. In fact, the oceanfront was honeycombed with underground bombproof plotting rooms, bunks for the gunners, underground kitchens, sunken searchlight emplacements, depressed passageways, and tunnels. Until 1943, much of this destructive array was hidden by camouflage from the naked eye. At night the entire city lay hidden under a different, more somber canopy. Except for blinker lights, flashing signals to and from ships at sea, San Diego was virtually without light, and not just during a blackout.[14]

Around the harbor to the east stood the U.S. Navy Training Station, and adjacent to it was the Marine recruit depot alongside Lindbergh Field, itself a military base during the war. Directly south of the airport, between Broadway and Market, sat the U.S. Naval Supply Depot. To the south, from about the north boundary of National City to 28th Street, stood the naval station, and with it, the destroyer base. On the narrow neck of the barrier island, between Imperial Beach and Coronado, rested the Navy's amphibious base. The military sprinkled "lesser" installations between and beyond these larger ones. Point Loma and Chollas Heights had impressive radio stations; another, which became the Navy's famous sonar school, nestled southwest of the naval training center. Balboa Park housed the Navy hospital. As in the Bay Area, lots of munitions crossed these militarized docks. At the 32nd Street Pier, longshoremen stacked ammunition into civilian ships, and service personnel loaded ordnance onto Navy vessels. Other sailors loaded explosives from North Island, and marines packed in theirs from the foot of Broadway.[15]

To the north were many more installations. North of La Jolla on the Pacific was the Army's Camp Callan on Torrey Pines Mesa (where anti-aircraft artillerists trained), with the Navy's Fallbrook Ammunition Depot nearby. Other installations stood further out from the city. Camp Pendleton Marine Base near Oceanside was one of the foremost of these. At Bing Crosby's race track in Del Mar, marines "set up camp on the race grounds" and trained in the surf for the deadly Pacific island beaches that awaited them. And at Camp Elliott, atop Kearny Mesa, just northeast of the city, marines received combat training. Camp Lockett, which housed California's only horse cavalry post, rested on the Mexican border, as did Border Field, a gun range where marines and Navy men fired their weapons. Along the railroad between there and San Diego, we had "guns and patrols on all the tunnels and bridges," recalled a Buffalo Soldier.[16]

Both repairs and new building abounded. The U.S. Naval Repair Station on the eastern shore of San Diego Bay patched metal ships, and the Concrete Ship Company at National City constructed masonry ones. Consolidated-Vultee and Ryan Aeronautical built planes at Lindbergh Field, and Solar did so nearby. In Chula Vista, Rohr turned out others.[17]

Barrage balloons—tethered balloons designed to thwart low-flying air attacks—protected the welders, boilermakers, and shipfitters and streamed out of many other "vital military objectives" above coastal cities and fields, in what the press called the "greatest installation of its kind ever attempted." "The balloons went up all over San Diego," recalled resident Frank Antonicelli, "Point Loma, Mission Hills, North

Park. They made a circle around Consolidated Aircraft." A number even floated above San Diego from its cemeteries. Sometimes they broke loose, creating spectacular electrical showers on the high-tension lines.

From all kinds of improbable places, such as the El Cortez Hotel in San Diego, radar searched the skies for unidentified planes. When one was spotted, searchlights illuminated the skies till the plane was recognized.[18]

And during the day, whole sections of the cities simply disappeared from view. The Palace of Fine Arts in San Francisco vanished under a canopy of camouflage. Hollywood set designers "replaced" the aircraft factories of the Los Angeles region with tracts of simulated suburban homes. In San Diego, Consolidated Aircraft Corporation and Ryan Aeronautical "vanished" from Lindbergh Field—and so did the airport itself. Eerily enough, planes coming into that city's airport were visible until they got to the netting and then were miraculously swallowed up by the faux urban fabric. The plants languished under a net of chicken wire filled in with the painted feathers of this unfortunate, inoffensive bird, to the everlasting merriment of city residents and endless discomfort of the workers, who had to cope with the falling plumes and fluff. Elsewhere, some camouflage was more real than faux. On Point Loma, the government used diversely painted houses for barracks. Instead of spotting recognizable barracks on the ground below, an enemy plane crew would see only more tract homes—this time the real thing, except that military personnel lived in them.

Transportation presented one of the most changed aspects of city life. Trolleys, city buses, trains, and airplanes were choked with men in uniform. Train travel was supposedly set aside for servicemen, or at least they had preference. Civilians also traveled about, but the service presence was overwhelming. And even when one was not riding in a crush of warriors, the transportation stations were martial. Long Beach Municipal Airport housed the Ferrying Command: "Practically all planes made for the Army come to this field from their factories and are flown by Army pilots to various points of delivery." The government found equally good use for Oakland Airport, as storage for planes awaiting shipment. To protect them from the weather, the planes had to be wrapped. Thus the field appeared to be one vast mass of brown paper hiding the aircraft, with women on scaffolds, five to a side, furiously packaging the newly arrived craft into their tan mantles.[19]

The ship traffic on San Francisco Bay provided other new sights. No one had to remind the men and women at the Vallejo Navy Yard of the horrors of war, but now others learned as well. Accustomed to seeing

1 6 2 7 1   1 0 - 6 - 4 3
CONSOLIDATED   VULTEE
EAST ADDITION TO BLDG.
NO. 7
CONTRACT NO. 1-7

Camouflage nets help hide the Convair aircraft plant in San Diego.
Courtesy San Diego Historical Society, Photo Collection.

whole tankers, destroyers, liners, and tugs confidently plying the Bay, residents were shocked to see crippled ships hobbling into port. And limp they did, with every kind of injury imaginable. "Boy did they bring ships in here blown up!" remembered Vallejo welder Effie Walling. This melancholy pageant of ships included the wounded vessels from Pearl Harbor, such as the destroyer *Shaw*, which had lost its bow. And after them came hundreds of others, with shell-torn superstructures, gaping holes in the bow, and guns torn asunder—blasted ships limping to Vallejo.[20]

Actually, the melancholy pageant to the Bay Area for repairs began long before the United States even entered the war. The Lend Lease Act of 1941 allowed "public vessels of the British Empire to be repaired in U. S. shipyards." The sixty-first ship to be repaired in the United States was HMS *Orion*, injured nearly fatally on May 29, 1941, evacuating troops during the Battle of Crete. It literally staggered eighteen thousand miles, with several stops, to the Golden Gate, still carrying some of its dead, sealed into compartments by the explosions that crippled the vessel. *Orion* entered the harbor at night and sneaked up to Mare Island Navy Yard, where it was repaired and sent back into action. During repairs, the last remaining dead were removed from the ship, taken back to sea in a tugboat, and buried off the Golden Gate.[21]

With U.S. entry into the war, service personnel were everywhere. One observer remembered looking down from his multi-story office building on the "sea of sailor hats" floating along the streets of San Diego. Unless he was colorblind, he must also have noticed the working women in "their blue aircraft uniforms [who] lend color to the mass of humanity during shift change hours at the Plaza." Not only did the war own the sidewalks in the central parts of town, but the military used others for training. For example, Army Air Corps clerks marched morning and evening through Flower, Grand, and 8th Streets in Los Angeles.

The scenes were not always so edifying, however. The thousands of service personnel retreating from the gin mills often navigated no more smoothly than the limping ships. Resident Phyllis Burns remembered coming home from her late-night job at the U.S. Post Office in downtown San Diego, lurching from side to side on the transit, while the even less well anchored sailors swayed too, often emptying their guts on the bus floor. Drunk or sober, uniformed men filled the cities.[22]

Everywhere the war kept intruding into people's consciousness. Modern city dwellers can usually keep the unpleasant parts of urban experience at arm's length. They can avoid certain neighborhoods, turn off the television or radio, forgo the frightening parts of the newspaper, and confine their contacts to a circle of predictable friends. World War II did not allow this protective personal quarantine. Immense billboards exhorted one to do one's duty. Aircraft companies' outdoor advertising begged pedestrians to please help build planes, and equally prominent signs pointed the walkers in the direction of the plants. To ensure against losing a single precious worker, company representatives met the trains to collect employees before they disappeared into the urban wilderness instead of through the factory gates. On the streets, autos with loudspeakers or men using megaphones begged for more war workers: "Women were [are] badly needed for the war effort," they pleaded. "Please come." "We have got to keep the boys flying," exhorted the plane factory loudspeakers. "We have got to keep those bombers going overseas." Newspaper boys reinforced the message by calling out the latest good news from Guadalcanal or bad tidings from Kasserine Pass. And radio broadcasts kept up the staccato drumfire of war information, appeals, exhortations, and tributes.[23]

Wartime advertisers, short of products to sell to the public, sold the war instead from every medium available. Vibro-insulators from B. F. Goodrich protected the battleships from the shock of their massive guns; Coca-Cola provided soldiers and sailors with the "real thing," no matter how far they strayed from home; Life Savers in helmets marched into battle (thus explaining their absence from the drugstore shelves and candy counters); and Mobilgas reminded its frustrated customers that the gasoline they could no longer buy was doing a more important job moving a tank remorselessly toward victory on a Pacific atoll. And if all of this chaos of communication did not remind citizens that "there was a war on," people were rousted out of their houses and apartments by the tumult of cannons' test firing, which the residents sometimes mistook for an attack.[24]

Occasionally, the reminders were momentous. April 2, 1942, broke clear and bright to reveal a large naval task force heading out of San Francisco Bay. The group included several destroyers, two cruisers, a tanker, and a great ship of this war, an aircraft carrier. The thousands of defense workers streaming across the Golden Gate Bridge to work at Marinship or farther north at the Vallejo Naval Shipyard must have been surprised and puzzled to see an aircraft carrier because the United States had only four in the entire Pacific Theater at that moment. They must have been even more puzzled to see B-25 bombers tied and chocked to the decks instead of the fighters that carriers customarily conveyed. Only later did they learn that the *Hornet* and Task Force 16.2 carried the planes that Colonel James H. Doolittle would lead in his historic raid on Japanese cities on April 18, which, ironically, was the anniversary of the great San Francisco earthquake and fire.[25]

Sometimes the reminders were not so puzzling. In August 1942, golfers on the Lake Merced and Lakeside golf courses in San Francisco looked up to see a derelict Navy blimp floating overhead. It dipped down, dug out a divot of earth, rose and wandered aimlessly on toward Daley City, minus its two-man crew, scraping rooftops and fouling telephone and electrical lines, its radio blaring away amidst the accompanying electrical showers. It finally came to rest, depth charge and all, in Daley City and collapsed in exhaustion over a couple of autos. A crowd of two thousand people swarmed around before the craft could be quarantined by firefighters, civil defense, and military personnel. Other thousands had "watched the sagging blimp float in from the sea." In another incident, during a parachute exercise near San Diego, a jumper's chute became entangled in the tail of the plane from which he had leaped. People watched in horror as the aircraft flew back and forth just off Point Loma, madly trying to find a way to get the hapless jumper untangled.[26]

These experiences were quite new to most Californians, and so were the incoming people themselves. The human procession seemed to be both endless and remarkably varied. One resident remembered fondly the many different people that she met at her San Diego housing project. Welder Effie Walling recalled encountering a great number in her job at the Mare Island Navy Yard. She was then forced to meet many more when she or they were unceremoniously shifted to a different department. There were "people that traveled all over the world, people that had never been any place," Walling remembered. "You name it and they were there." Mary Jean Potts recalled, "I met more girls in that short [span] of time than I would have for years and years." Others experienced the same sensation. When Marinship opened to build ships in 1942, it scoured Southwestern cities for workers. In Santa Fe the recruiters signed up Ray Silvertongue, a full-blooded Indian. In Dallas they recruited the Zacchini brothers, circus performers who went from being shot out of cannons to welding them onto the decks of Liberty ships. Manual and Delfino Maes left their cattle business to weld boats. Ting Chu Chang, an electrical engineer from San Francisco, helped to plan the ships that the cowboys, Indians, Mexicans, and Italians built. Whatever else it might have been, the war was a remarkably cosmopolitan experience for its participants, whether civilian or military.[27]

But just as certainly, all these new acquaintances kept leaving. People bonded together emotionally in a defense job to help win the war, to experience life in the exciting defense centers, to care for the children of new-found friends, to share the melancholy certainty that one of them was going off to those dreadful islands to face the possibility of death, or perhaps even to encounter the death of one of their loved ones. Then they were gone. The men at the naval shipyards volunteered for active service duty; people quit their jobs to find better; the officers at last Saturday's dance were abruptly shipped out to Tarawa; women left the shipyards to help out in the aircraft factories. Individuals were forever going "home" to Wisconsin, Alabama, the Southwest, or just back to El Centro or Woodland. Young people met at an aircraft factory dance, but then the warriors left for the grisly struggles on Pacific atolls. It was a time of goodbyes for these uprooted, incipient cosmopolitans.

Perhaps none were sadder than those goodbyes said in San Francisco by some of the women evacuated after the Japanese attack on Pearl Harbor. After spending several apprehensive weeks waiting to be sent home, often with small children in air raid shelters, two wives who were close friends got shipping to the West Coast at last. Finally on shore, Wilsie Orjas got separated from her friend Louise. She searched for a phone to call Missouri 3600 for Helen Lewis, who was taking them in. After replacing the receiver, Wilsie turned into the fog and walked to the taxi stand. "I never saw Louise again," she noted plaintively.[28]

The unending farewells heightened the uncertainty of the period. Uncertain too were the everyday lives of people who stayed put. People searched endlessly for housing. Others shopped for day care. Still others hunted for loved ones. Even the most mundane affairs were shot through with uncertainty. Resident Herman Silversher remembered wistfully the service dances from which the dancers kept leaving. Dance or no dance, when a hospital ship with wounded marines entered San Diego Harbor, "the nurses and doctors would immediately rush to the hospital . . . and they often worked 72 hours at a stretch." The "doctors and nurses, they really had fun, lived it up, drank a lot," he recalled ruefully. "They didn't know what [to expect] next." No one else did either.[29]

Fearing the worst, they sometimes got it. Wounded servicemen were far more numerous than the mangled ships hobbling into port. Medical personnel from places such as Letterman Hospital in San Francisco or the naval hospital in Balboa Park, San Diego, saw the worst of it. Men dead on arrival or nearly so, men broken to pieces by shellfire or gutted by grenades, men burned and blinded all came in by the thousands because the California ports got a disproportionate share of the military traffic. Those merely wounded by rifle fire were often the lucky ones. And just as the taxi drivers spread the news of Pearl Harbor through San Francisco, the hospital workers passed stories of ghastly wounds and death around every California citadel.

And so did the fighters themselves. The cities abounded in posters urging each person to "Zip Your Lip," but many became unzipped in the gin mills. The cities' central business districts in peacetime were information centers for business; in war they were the centers for war information. *San Diego Union* reporter John Spencer Held recalled that thousands of sailors, marines, and defense workers invaded the Plaza nightly to drink, dance, and unburden themselves. Thousands of tipsy youthful warriors are not the safest guardians of information, and time and again, Held learned the truth from which the authorities wanted to shield the population. In his nightly forays into the area for stories, Held once ran into a man who had been flying above the aircraft carrier *Wasp* when it was torpedoed by a Japanese submarine. Horrified, the flier watched the whole affair for two hours as "hundreds of men went over the side" and the vessel sank under the waves. After two of the fiercest battles of the Pacific war, Eldon Foster at Fort Rosecrans got a phone call from a relative. His brother-in-law had been serving on the ill-fated carrier *Lexington,* and over a drink Foster soon found out about the battles of the Coral Sea and Midway.[30]

Perhaps the fear was worst in gendered work situations because of their critical mass. The post office service was heavily female, since the draft had claimed the young men, and the war plants, the older ones. For example, Phyllis Burns worked with eighty women and one male. "Now you've got to realize that the women in the post office were nearly out of their minds with fear and anguish, because they had sent their marine husbands off to the South Pacific," she reminisced. Legally or not, they read as many Navy postcards as they could, hoping to glean some information about the location and severity of the fighting that their bridegrooms, boyfriends, and brothers might be facing.

There were simply too many sources of information to keep the public totally in the dark. These "leaks" repeatedly frustrated the efforts of the government's censors. People may not have learned the full story of the war exactly when it happened, but they fully understood a lot of the chapters.[31]

And death was omnipresent. Newspapers carried military obituaries in special stories. The dead and wounded were trumpeted into the consciousness of the cities. Perhaps worse still were those reported wounded or missing and then later reported dead, with the accounts first raising expectations and then dashing all hope of their survival. Arthur Verge has noted the sudden hush and emptying of the courtyard houses of Los Angeles when the Western Union man appeared. Usually his presence could mean only one thing, because most of these people did not receive telegrams for any other reason. And when the little yellow paper arrived, another icon went up in the window of an additional "gold star mother." A silver star signified the wounding of a warrior, and both were abundantly visible to the passersby on the street.[32]

In short, death was always a presence. One read of it in the papers, witnessed the visit of the Western Union man, heard it from the returned servicemen, discovered it from the medical personnel, got it from the taxi drivers, or even witnessed it with one's own eyes when trainers crashed in taking off from North Island Naval Air Station. Seven hundred thousand Californians went into service out of a prewar population of 7 million. Many more shipped out from the Golden Gate, and their mothers, sisters, and sweethearts migrated from out of state to be with loved ones and stayed for the duration. Hardly anyone's anxiety was vicarious.[33]

Even the civilians themselves were in danger. From colonial times onward governments had insisted on the storage of powder and other explosives in areas remote from crowded urban areas. However, in World War II that regulation had to be suspended. The urban docks were already in existence, and the shipping was right there to handle the munitions so desperately needed in New Guinea, Saipan, and Okinawa. So the government ignored the rule regulating explosives in crowded cities and sling-loaded away. Longshoremen and sailors loaded ammunition from four different sites in San Diego alone. As Charles Forward, the former San Diego harbor master, explained, his port handled as many as 340 munitions ships in one month. As he laconically remembered, this work was fraught "with a good deal of danger." That was putting it mildly. At Port Chicago, on Carquinez Strait, the Navy found out just how monstrous the danger was when two ships exploded in 1944. More than three hundred men, 200 black and over 100 white, died in a blast that leveled Port Chicago. Had that explosion occurred at the 32nd Street Pier on San Diego Bay, a good bit of National City would have similarly disappeared, with even greater loss of life.[34]

Given the uncertainty, people seized the moment. Robert Wright of San Diego remembered that people "lived for the day and that's the way it was. A lot of these guys went overseas and saw a lot of combat, a lot of the sailors never came back." One person remembered that a kind of desperate gaiety prevailed. This was partly responsible for the sense of excitement that captured so many people. Part of the explanation stemmed from the war, part from their youth, and part from the new-found urban experience. "Well it was very exciting for a boy coming from northwest Arkansas," recalled Harris Wright. "I find I was exposed to a lot bigger place than I knew about."[35]

Cities have rhythms of their own, just like individuals or countries. Chicago boomed on the railroad industry and the opening of the Midwest; San Francisco exploded into being from the Gold Rush; and New York thrived on the great tides of immigration, to mention just a few. Global conflict imposed a different set of rhythms on California cities, one based on the ghastly music of battle. For example, when the Pacific campaigns heated up in the final stages of the war, men flooded into San Francisco, Oakland, Long Beach, and Los Angeles, awaiting what might be their final trip. When great naval battles such as Midway or Savo Island occurred, damaged ships, armadas of the damned, thereafter came sidling into port for repair. When hospital ships came to port after island struggles like the Battle of Iwo Jima, the Red Cross blood bank issued an emergency call for all possible whole blood in San Diego, San Francisco, and Seattle, and people jammed the donor centers to help. The next time it might be an emergency call for hands to harvest the crucial farm crops in a time of labor shortages. And when the Japanese Americans were unceremoniously uprooted and relocated into camps, "Thousands of local people, white people, went down to see them off when they left San Diego." On a more mundane level, with the great crush of military and defense plant people in San Diego and the twenty-four-hour work day, the rhythms of city life moved in tides of humanity responding to the shift changes. The last shift of sailors and defense workers gravitated to the downtown for a beer to unwind while the next shift moved inexorably to the shipyards, bases, and aircraft factories.[36]

There was also an unending quality to life in the urban arsenals. New York is thought of as the city that never sleeps, but any city is such to a certain extent. There are always air, bus, and rail terminals, late-night clubs, early-morning coffee stands, newspapers, bakeries, hospitals, police stations, freeways, produce markets, and the restaurants that cater to them which operate late at night or even at all hours. The war added many other all-hours activities. Many weekending servicemen simply could not find places to sleep and thus just partied all night until time for their bus ride back to March Field or Camp Roberts. Many others did not intend to sleep even when they found a place. Movies often ran twenty-four hours a day to accommodate the heightened demand of workers. And the three-shift day dumped workers, especially from the 3:00 to 11:00 P.M. (12:00 or 1:00 A.M. with overtime) swing shift, onto the city at odd hours. So thousands got off work to eat and recreate just as others were thinking, hopefully or resignedly, of bed. This schedule kept the day rolling on into the night. As one irate San Diego temperance reformer noted, the "real show" at the many clubs "doesn't begin until nearly midnight." Gigi Sanders, a riveter at Consolidated Aircraft in San Diego, was typical. When her shift ended at 11:00 P.M., she and her boarding house chums, male and female, headed home to clean up and then go out to eat. Afterward they searched for recreation. One night it was all-night dancing at the Mission or Pacific ballroom. The next night they might attend a movie at the nonstop theaters, and the next night they would skate at the ice rink on 32nd Street. If they stayed "home," the boarders often played cards "till dawn." As they finally tumbled into bed, the workers on the 11:00 P.M. to 7:00 A.M. graveyard shift hit the town to let their own "good times roll," in Paul Casdorph's wonderful phrase.[37]

And California cities provided vast outlets for good times. The mostly male soldiers and sailors required lots of entertainment, whether they were destined for the grisly battles on Pacific Islands or simply rusticating in a Riverside cantonment. Perhaps the best known "recreational" event of the war was caused by the sailors' presence in East Los Angeles, which triggered the Zoot Suit Riot of 1943.

Yet that event should not be allowed to overshadow the cities' more positive entertainment contributions to the war effort. From San Francisco's Barbary Coast to Hollywood to the central business district of

San Diego, the purveyors of diversion, sometimes legal, sometimes not, responded with a will. One observer looking from a tall building upon the San Diego business district likened it to a sea of white sailor caps floating between the gin mills. Movie houses, bars, dance halls, YMCAs, Knights of Columbus halls, Protestant churches, beaches, parks, and city recreation departments vied with each other to provide a last bit of fun to men who would soon enough be facing the machine guns of the Imperial Japanese. Prostitution thrived on the market of rootless, lonely men. San Francisco certainly provided more than its share of vice. That city was the acknowledged center of prostitution recruitment for the Pacific Coast and the entire Pacific theater.[38]

As Ronald Cohen and Lewis Erenberg have shown us, music was at the center of this wartime effort. Every name band of every race and culture played the California urban scene. Nat King Cole urged the migrants to get their "Kicks on Route 66," and Bob Wills and his Texas Playboys regaled the Southwestern whites with "Steel Guitar Rag." The black and white big bands offered the signatures that made them famous—"One O'Clock Jump," "Getting Sentimental over You," "Song of India," and "Stomping at the Savoy." These venues were joined by perhaps the greatest group of popular female singers in American history—including June Christy, Billie Holiday, Peggy Lee, Helen Forrest, Ella Fitzgerald, Kay Starr, Jo Stafford, the Andrews Sisters, Helen O'Connell, and Anita O'Day. They offered their own signatures, ranging from Peggy Lee's "Why Don't You Do Right?" to Billie Holiday's "Trav'lin' Light," at places as diverse as the South Central Los Angeles night spots, Venice Pier, the Trianon Ballroom, and Dreamland in San Francisco. Wherever Mexican migrants landed, so did their music; where the Okies stopped, country melodies, the "white man's blues," stopped with them; and wherever African Americans alighted, so did their own version of the blues. For example, in Oakland, Craby Joe's Big Barn and John's Half Barrel featured barn dances, and disc jockeys such as Cactus Jack provided the same sounds to people who could not get to the dance halls. Southwestern blacks added to the musical diversity just as southwestern whites did. In West Oakland, Harold "Slim" Jenkins's "premier nightclub" purveyed jazz to southern black migrants, and performers at Minni Lou's in Richmond sang the blues. Given the upheaval and loneliness of the war, there was plenty to sing about.[39]

Despite arguments to the contrary and ex post facto investigations concluding that there was plenty of sugar and gasoline, many shortages existed during the war. In San Francisco, ten thousand students rode streetcars and buses to school. However, the war put a premium on getting defense workers to work and back, so the students, who often traveled long distances to schools and to social and athletic events, were told to walk to nearer ones. With so many people rooming or too harried to cook, restaurants had a large clientele, but the trick was getting a seat. John Spencer Held, the *Tribune* reporter who "ate out every night" and spent his evenings downtown, remembered that "I went to a lot of different restaurants. You had to stand in line frequently outside. . . . You had to stand in line for everything." Scarcity created closet inflation. The Office of Price Administration set prices, so in theory they did not rise much, but the butchers found a way around the regulation. They simply reclassified their lower-grade cuts of meat as higher-grade ones and sold hamburger at the price of ground chuck.[40]

Other shortages existed as well. Historians have noted the recreation boom that accompanied the war. However, the boom of commercial recreation was accompanied by the cessation of many community recreations. People gave up their travel vacations for outings closer to home. Stanford stopped its football program. Pasadena lost the Rose Bowl in 1942, and when it returned in 1943, it was without the storied Rose Parade. And many of the less famous cities and towns suspended their community festivals as well. Alhambra deferred its "famed Storybook Parade," San Fernando sacrificed its "Mission Fiesta," and Holland-derived Clearwater-Hynes postponed its "annual Dutch Hay and Dairy Fiesta," a mixed metaphorical event if ever there was one.[41]

Partly due to shortages and rationing, improvisation was also the order of the day. For example, a high school band leader, Edward Ortiz, could not get new instruments, nor parts and oil for his old instruments. He improvised the oil from kerosene, perfume, and iodine crystals. When the government lagged in constructing buildings for the Linda Vista Housing Project school where he taught, the athletic department carved niches out of the hill to practice on and the shop department built a stage at the bottom of the canyon. "The drama and music departments put on their programs there. The students sat on the side of the hill," he recalled. "We just used the natural amplification of the canyon."

The military had to improvise, too. Soldier Pete Cutri remembered the exceptionally cold winter of 1943. Lacking blankets and coal or wood for fuel in the Old Point Loma Lighthouse, he and his mates had to burn the old guest registers at the lighthouse and to use huge old wool American battleship flags to wrap themselves in while they slept.

One of the most interesting improvisations of the war occurred at the historic Santa Anita racetrack in Arcadia. While a military threat persisted, the government discouraged some crowd activities and banned others. One was horse racing. Bay Meadows at San Francisco Bay closed for a time, and so did Santa Anita. The track was first used callously to incarcerate the Japanese Americans, who were then relocated to more permanent camps in various western states. That left Santa Anita without a purpose, but the Army soon found one. The large, open space was ideally suited for training tank corpsmen. Army Ordnance quickly moved in and transformed Santa Anita Race Track into Camp Santa Anita, where General Sherman tanks belched exhaust fumes and churned up the ground "on the same track where once famous horses pounded into the homestretch." Brigadier General Julian S. Hatcher claimed that Santa Anita was becoming the "Aberdeen [Proving Ground] of the West Coast." All this mechanized activity was perhaps not appropriate for a town named Arcadia, but no one seemed to note the irony.[42]

"The Playground of the World" provided one of the most novel improvisations. In order to free up space for the Navy in Port Hueneme, the Maritime Seamen Training School moved to Santa Catalina Island. To accommodate these mariners, the government converted the famed Avalon Casino "from a dance hall into a classroom" and transformed the "spacious front lawn, once an emerald green, . . . [into] a well trodden drill ground." And at the internationally known multi-million-dollar St. Catherine Hotel, "Where movie stars and blue book figures once paid $25 and more a night to sleep, apprentice seamen—oiler, wiper, deck hand, or steward—now bunk."[43]

Other sights were merely incongruous or odd. At the top of the list was the city hall at Manhattan Beach. Like their Great Plains ancestors, the Manhattanites built a sod house and heavy board wall all around the city hall. They added a concrete "shatter proof room, partially underground" to house emergency communications. Another oddity was the dilemma of servicemen encountering female officers who outranked them. The men did not like it, but men saluting women occurred all over town. And residents of Palos Verdes, one of the most fashionable suburbs in the L.A. area, repeatedly witnessed Douglas dive bombers swooping over their peninsula, dropping sacks of flour. It turned out that this rain of vegetable matter was a practice exercise coordinated with the anti-aircraft crews of the area. California itself was incongruous to the newcomers who passed through. Richard Markham "pulled into LA" after leaving Kansas in a blizzard. "The grass was green and beautiful. Man, that was a good sight." Others, awaiting endless sunlit days, found only rain and fog.[44]

And some visitors and residents, expecting a city, found extensive agriculture instead. Victory gardens blossomed everywhere, especially in San Francisco, where North Beach vintner and agricultural economist John Brucato led the outstanding San Francisco Victory Garden Council. Aptos Junior High had ten thousand square feet under cultivation, and Parkside Grammar, Balboa High, and James Denman Junior High were also furrowing away. Naturally, classes on gardening sprouted along with the lettuce at San Francisco Junior College. To facilitate the process, the city government relaxed its health and nuisance regulations "for the duration" to allow the raising of rabbits and chickens, but drew the line at roosters, who remained under the ban.

Nor was the Southland entirely outdistanced in this agrarian competition. Beverly Hills and Pasadena stood out. The former surveyed all the vacant lots in the city, ploughed them, opened them to any gardener, and even supplied hose connections where needed. East Los Angeles sprouted 6,800 plots, and "flat-dwellers are raising tomatoes in tubs and flower pots, lettuce in window boxes or hanging baskets" all over the area. The Office of Civilian Defense actually constructed a master plan "under which each block would have its block captain to aid and encourage gardeners." The number of gardeners in Los Angeles County alone reached 120,000 by mid-war. As their products matured, the price of tomatoes in the shops slipped markedly, from five dollars to two dollars per crate. The gardens not only provided food to supplement that available to families from their rationing coupons, but also served to check inflation, which existed despite price controls.[45]

World War II was a very unusual time in California cities. They gave up their normal peacetime appearance and their normal peacetime tempo of activity. During the conflict, everything inevitably got back to the gruesome battles in faraway places, which touched people's jobs, their recreation, their vocations, their habits, and their souls. City residents had to confront appalling events in an alien world, meet new people, share burdens, confront uncertainty in everything, improvise even the smallest tasks, accept war's discipline, face death and departure, live with the tension of excitement and depression, and sacrifice. In addition, not being certain of the future, they had to live for the moment. The Second World War was a most unusual interruption of their existence. Whether they willed it or not, or even knew it or not, everyone "marched to the sound of the guns."

2. Dunkirk at the Marina
War and the Renaissance of
Urban Community

San Franciscans learned the reality of war in a most dramatic manner. The news reports of Pearl Harbor shocked the city, but first accounts of casualties tended to minimize the damage. However, shortly the correct news came out, and it did so in a typically urban way.

The military sent the Pearl Harbor wounded to San Francisco for treatment, and the flotilla carried widows, orphaned children, vacationers, and others from Hawaii as well. "No public announcement was made in advance of the convoy arrival," explained the *San Francisco Chronicle*, but a group of camouflaged ships is difficult to hide coming through the Golden Gate Strait and under its storied bridge in a city where numerous hills and ocean and bay viewpoints abound. Instantly, "the city saw it moving in the Gate." Suddenly, "there was a rush toward the waterfront," by families, onlookers, and friends, which the military authorities halted two blocks from the docks. There, mothers, wives, and friends stood in a drizzling rain awaiting word of their loved ones. Officials placed an emergency call for trained nurses, and vacationers, evacuees, and wounded began to debark.

Far from being a handful, the injured servicemen completely swamped the ambulance service dispatched to transport them. To make up the deficit, the Yellow Cab Company was pressed into service. The cabbies got the wounded to the hospitals and in the process got a clear picture of how badly the Japanese had mauled the American fleet at Pearl Harbor. Once the news entered into that urban information network, word moved swiftly about the city. At the same time, evacuees and vacationers spread out to hotels, homes, or the houses of friends, and children of servicemen went to various Christmas parties held in their honor. Through all of these media, the news expanded like a Southern California brush fire.

Los Angeles too learned of the magnitude of the disaster in a curious way. Mayor Fletcher Bowron had been informed that the defeat had been minor and believed that estimate until he went out to the airport to pick up a distinguished visitor. Eleanor Roosevelt soon set him straight on the matter. From that point onward, the City of Angels, like its northern rival, knew the worst.[1]

As it turned out, neither city suffered that extremity, but anxiety and perhaps panic gripped both. The exact extent is still in question. Although both California and national historians have claimed that the onset of the war plunged the West Coast into a state of "hysteria," that conclusion seems far from obvious. Certainly some California urbanites suffered from a state of fear, but was there really a general state of hysteria? The relocation of the Japanese, such incidents as the nonexistent "Battle of Los Angeles," the many supposed "sightings" of enemies in the air, on the sea, and in the bush, and the sometimes wild pronouncements of politicians and soldiers have all been used as evidence of a disordered state of mind in California cities during the early months of the war. Some of the participants in these events have even seemed to confirm the worst. Fletcher Bowron, in confessing his sins against the Japanese Americans before a congressional investigating committee in 1954, referred to the "widespread hysteria" prevailing during these critical months.[2]

Yet in 1941, the mayor and many other prominent Californians went to great lengths to disclaim the presence of hysteria in their cities. Bowron did so repeatedly. In fact, months before the war commenced, the *San Diego Union* claimed that any hysteria that existed centered on the top of the federal structure in Washington rather than at the bottom among the people in the cities. Mayor Bowron would reiterate this charge throughout the war with more than a little venom. In truth, much of the hysteria that has been attributed to California's cities and much of the supposedly ludicrous conduct of people in these places is traceable to the policies or the pronouncements of either the military, civilian officials of the national government, or California politicians. Well into 1943, long after the Japanese had been put on the defensive, the government continued to assert that an invasion or an attack upon West Coast cities could occur at any moment. Beyond pointing to the hypothetical peril of such actions, the services repeatedly created alarm by sounding the air raid sirens. "Since Pearl Harbor," said Mayor Bowron in early 1943, "there have been twenty three official air raid alerts signaled by the Army."[3]

Sometimes military officials assured the newspapers that enemy planes had actually been over the cities in question, although those claims appear to have been unconfirmed. In addition, the military created many other anxious situations. The Army or the Navy forced cancellation of the Rose Bowl, ostensibly to protect the massed spectators from aerial attack, and arrested Japanese fishermen on very slight pretexts. The federal officials also issued a maze of often contradictory regulations and instructions, many calculated to frighten by their implications. They handled the Japanese situation about as badly as possible, vacillating over the decision for months while issuing orders piecemeal in such a way as to alarm both the Japanese Americans and everyone else. Almost immediately after the attack on Pearl Harbor, federal officials froze all Japanese nationals' bank accounts; then they pushed them out of sensitive harbor areas; then they raided the Japanese colonies for suspect persons; and then they unfroze the frozen accounts![4]

Even the best-intentioned government action could cause legitimate fright. When the Bay Area experienced its first blackout, the cars and commuter trains on the Bay Bridge were forced to halt. "We were frightened," remembered resident Mary Jean Potts, "we really were."[5]

Local and national politicians enhanced the alarm. On June 23, 1942, two weeks after the outnumbered American fleet routed the Japanese armada at Midway and after the removal of Japanese Americans, Earl Warren, running for governor, spoke to a meeting at the Palace Hotel. The "Japanese have been removed completely from San Francisco but this city still houses a real and powerful fifth column which will attempt to defeat us behind the lines in the event of enemy invasion," Warren asserted. As the election campaign wound to a close in late October, well after all threat of Imperial Japanese action had passed, Warren promised that one of his highest priorities as governor would be to create an "effective and fully trained sabotage prevention organization for California."[6]

Kilsoo K. Haan, "representative of the Provisional Korean Government," assured Angelenos that the Imperial Japanese would invade California in mid-April. Not to be outdone by the Koreans, nor to be deterred when their predicted invasion failed to occur, in late May Secretary of War Stimson promised the Pacific Coast that an air "attack is a moral certainty to pay us off for our raid on Tokyo." In March, the Navy issued orders to "shoot to kill" violators of the blackout on the San Francisco waterfront. A taxi driver learned the hard way that the Navy meant it when a sentry's bullet crashed through his window after he failed to douse his lights and halt.

Admittedly, California residents and their city governments added to this sense of alarm. For example, right after Pearl Harbor, the San Francisco police arrested a Japanese person, recently arrived from Hawaii, because he had used a "large camera" to photograph Twin Peaks. That well-known tourist landmark must have been photographed by Caucasians and Asians at least a million times before that without any sinister motive being attributed to the photographer. In mid-1942 great controversy had been generated over the Italian American mayor, Angelo Rossi. To still the ruckus, the San Francisco Board of Supervisors had to pass a resolution of support for this faithful public servant in order to overcome the "hysteria and prejudices with which the human mind may be pervaded, particularly in war times."[7] And, at about the same time, the Downtown Association was assuring its readers that it must pass the civil defense measures on the ballot because "ENEMY AGGRESSION MAY COME AT ANY MINUTE. THIS IS WAR! IT'S RIGHT AT OUR FRONT DOOR." On the day of Pearl Harbor many civilians fled from San Diego. One of the Buffalo Soldiers, advancing to take up positions of defense at Camp Lockett, remembered that as his men and cavalry horses struggled breathlessly over the mountains, "people were leaving San Diego in droves."[8]

In one notable instance, on February 26, 1942, inexperienced defenders shot the sky full of anti-aircraft shells at planes that were apparently not there. The incident became derisively termed the "Battle of Los Angeles" or the "Great Los Angeles Air Raid" and is often cited as an example of the buffoonery that suffused the war effort in the state. But the planes easily could have been there, and the Angelenos were by no means the only American military and civil defense personnel who were jittery gunners in the weeks and months after Pearl Harbor. Such anxious reactions were no argument against the military and civil defenses that the government put in place in California metropolitan areas during the war. It is true that the defense and civil defense personnel never had to deal with a live enemy. Nonetheless, they needed to be ready to do so. If an enemy attack of any significance whatsoever had been allowed to penetrate the defenses of the Pacific Coast and devastate unprepared urban areas, especially after the example of Pearl Harbor, the death and destruction would have been substantial. In addition, the subsequent political firestorm would have wrecked both civilian and military careers, as the Pearl Harbor debacle ruined the careers of Admiral Husband Kimmel and General Walter Short over their decisions in Hawaii.[9]

For a people supposedly in the throes of hysteria, these urban Californians tackled the work of organizing for defense and civil defense in a very rational, clear-headed, and determined way. And if some of them feared invasion, many did not. For example, the late Herb Caen, the legendary San Francisco columnist, went about his humorous business, poking fun at the war situations as impartially as he had previously at peaceful ones. If some people were inclined toward Japanese bashing, others, including newspapermen, were inclined to defend their rights publicly. If military men or downtown businessmen had a vested interest in spreading alarm and therefore encouraging mobilization in the population, others such as the Chamber of Commerce had a vested interest in trying to calm the public's nerves. If a hysterical picture of Los Angeles, San Diego, and San Francisco became certified, it might hurt the tourist trade; worse still, it might induce the federal government to move some of its defense plants from such a panic-prone and endangered area. Finally, widespread apathy accompanied whatever panic there was. The *San Francisco Chronicle* had to scold the city's "scoffers" publicly in a front-page editorial for not becoming *more alarmed* at the war. At yet another time, the paper noted that only a few people were fleeing the city to Oakland or such exotic places as Reno, and they predicted that these misguided refugees would soon be back. They urged air raid precautions, but noted that "we are very far from them [the Japanese] and far from the scenes where they need their warplanes most." As the *Chronicle* calmly put it, "Heaven is as near to San Francisco as to any other spot." And if "droves" of civilians retreated from San Diego, they were told to. A former school teacher noted that "we were told only that a lot of unnecessary people should leave because San Diego was an important port and liable to be attacked."[10]

The behavior of the commuters trapped atop the Bay Bridge in the first Bay Area blackout is equally instructive. As Mary Jean Potts noted, she was scared. However, instead of rushing out of the trains and autos onto the bridge and running, in a movie-style mob, for the Yerba Buena Island tunnels for shelter, the passengers stayed put. Soon the conductor passed through the cars, saying, "Don't be alarmed, everybody. This is a black-out. Roosevelt has said to practice." Another woman's conduct in the same blackout reinforced the point. When her carpool was halted on the Bay Bridge by the sirens, she simply got out her knitting and went to work. In short, a lot of cool heads existed alongside the hot ones. To date, hysteria has been assumed to exist rather than being methodically investigated. Without comprehensive study of wartime hysteria by people who have some training in psycho-history, we should be skeptical. Until that study is done, we should not use the excuse of a genuine national emergency to heap contempt upon these harried urbanites.[11]

Perhaps we should also be more sensitive to the very real dangers under which urban Californians lived and labored. There was nothing fanciful in the fear of enemy activity against coastal cities. Counting

Coastal defense, California style?
Courtesy Huntington Library.

inlets, bays, and peninsulas, California has a coastline of some 1,264 miles, which would have been easy to penetrate. Its great cities stand right on the edge of that coast, and these cities were indeed martial metropolises, thickly studded with military installations, factories, barracks, headquarters, and parked airplanes. By 1943, for example, there were 866 subcontractors in the Los Angeles County airplane industry alone, not to mention the hundreds of businesses working for other branches of the military. The War Department had designated each of these arsenal cities as combat zones. Many were within easy shelling range of the sea, and all were within easier flying range of carrier-borne aircraft. One has only to remember the famous Doolittle Raid on Japan in retaliation for Pearl Harbor, launched from American carriers several hundred miles out at sea, to realize that an attack on the West Coast was eminently feasible. If we did it in 1942 with our inferior naval forces, surely they could have done it with their superior ones. The possibilities of a battleship, cruiser, or carrier coming at the cities from out of the heavy Pacific fog seemed rather good.[12]

The danger wasn't just theoretical. Imperial Japanese submarines actually operated off the coast and even sank American merchant shipping within sight of onlookers on shore. In fact, at one time six Japanese subs were stationed off the California coast awaiting their prey. One of the Japanese submarines, the I-17, was a football field in length. It was big enough to carry a catapult plane and had tried on at least two occasions to firebomb the forests in Oregon. Later the Japanese tried to set the Pacific Northwest forests on fire by sending incendiaries via balloons. With the Great Tillamook Burn still a fresh memory in the minds of coastal residents, no one dared to underestimate the potential of these actions.[13]

Nor did the one shelling of an oil refinery at Goleta and the shellings of the Oregon Coast, near Seaside and at Estevan Point in British Columbia, remove their suspicions. The shooting into the air during the Battle of Los Angeles did not take place in the absence of any potential for the Japanese to put planes there. In retrospect, it is surprising that the Japanese did not exploit these military possibilities more fully. Part of the reason that they did not was the American pressure exerted against them, starting at Guadalcanal, which forced the Imperial Japanese to reduce the submarine strike force of subs intended for the West Coast.[14]

One of the best arguments against the hysteria hypothesis is the manner in which the cities prepared for the possibility of military damage. In this effort city dwellers contributed markedly to the eventual victory. Although isolationism declined after Pearl Harbor, not everyone in the country was automatically ready to shoulder the burdens of war. Countries going to war have to mobilize their civilian populations, and much of this responsibility fell onto the shoulders of California urban leaders and ordinary residents.

Civilian defense, while never put to a military test by the Japanese, nonetheless worked wonders in giving civilians a sense of participation in the conflict and a stake in its outcome. It also helped to combat one of the central problems of urban life. Cities, by their nature, seem to create individualism, and these individuals are often isolated from the larger urban whole, anonymous in large degree to it and each other. They suffer from the lack of a sense of community in the larger sense. As historians such as Richard Wade, Zane Miller, and Samuel Hays have noted, cities contain both disintegrating and integrating forces, decentralizing and centralizing influences. War turned out to be one of the chief ways of overcoming the disintegrating tendencies of the metropolis by enhancing its sense of community.

Not since the Progressive Era had the name of "community" been
evoked as often or as insistently. Nor was this renaissance of community
an afterthought or sidelight. Urban leaders saw the need for a sense of
belonging and participation as a means to win the war, and they set out
consciously to create that sense. At first, the impulse toward community
struggled against heavy odds. "Amid the tranquility and security of
Southern California's sunshine, and with the normal routine of our daily
lives," warned Mayor Bowron in a rebuke to both capital and labor for
stoppages in local defense industries, "the conflict across the seas may
be won or lost, the future course of civilization may be determined, right
here in our own community."[15]

Despite a landscape bristling with martial paraphernalia, it took
some time for Californians to learn that lesson. Civil defense, begun in
1941, limped along, and apathy continued. In August, Bowron scolded
his constituents again. The mayor favored American intervention into
the Asian war in the event of a Japanese descent upon the Dutch East
Indies. He already saw the war as one against Nazism and feared a Japan
loaded down with the riches of Southeast Asia and turning out goods
with cheaper labor. Soon they would be "underselling our manufacturers, taking our foreign markets, breaking down our living standards,
building up wealth and power." Americans must stop their domestic
bickering, he thought, and face up to the threats from without. Yet, till
forced to quit, they went right on feuding.

It is sometimes easy to overlook the divisions within American society when the war broke out, of which the interventionist-isolationist split
was merely the most famous. Labor fought capital; racial, religious, and
national rivalries smoldered; reformers fought what they thought was
municipal corruption; housewives and restaurant owners fought rising
food prices and the men behind them; everyone chafed under government
edicts; and cities competed with each other and with their suburbs.[16]

Recent historians have challenged the image of the so-called "Good
War" by citing the many conflicts that occurred during the struggle.
Certainly war generated hostility from whites, and from Asians such as
Filipinos and Chinese, toward the Japanese Americans. This hostility
subsided with relocation, but then resurfaced when the Japanese were
released and tried to return to their homes, now occupied by African
Americans. Race triggered other conflicts, as when blacks tried to break
the Boilermakers Union's hold over shipyard jobs. Blacks also urged the
government to provide more public housing and neighborhoods, and
"Nimbys" (Not in My Back Yard) before their time strove to keep these
projects at arm's length. Men took offense at women on the job, and

wives of male workers resented even more the presence of women around their husbands. Cities fought each other for military installations, and corporations competed against each other for laborers. People from every group resisted government restrictions on consumer goods by resorting to the black market. The old settlers disliked the migrant war workers, whom they blamed for transforming their California paradise into just another urban megalopolis.

Any able-bodied-looking man walking about the streets incurred the wrath of hordes of passersby, who thought that all who could do so should be with the colors. Mexicans strove to overcome their traditional burdens by breaking into new work and housing situations. Sailors resented the wearers of zoot suits, who, Nimbys in their own way, in turn resented the presence of the military in their neighborhoods. Landlords sought to increase rents against resisting tenants and an unsympathetic federal government. Union men fought management, staged so-called hate strikes against the employment of minorities, and even bucked their own union leaders, such as Harry Bridges, who was willing to sacrifice hard-won unions gains in order to speed up the war effort. The war did not recreate the United States in the image of a pre-serpentine Garden of Eden.[17]

Yet this disunity was not about the war itself. Every group had its own version of the Double V. Each wanted to win the war while maximizing their gains within the war effort, or at least minimizing their losses. But while various interests could struggle to promote or protect their own interests within the war effort, hardly anyone openly opposed the war itself. Even the longshoremen, when defying the orders of the left-wing leadership of the longshoremen's union, often had sons at the fighting fronts and were proud of their own contributions to helping keep them safe. They just were not willing to be pushed around in the process. Differences of opinion about the composition of a sling load did not imply dissent about the "Good War."

Still, those advocating community and unity had their work cut out for them. They approached it by both individual and community acts. Politicians and citizens called on labor and capital to calm down. At first, at least, politicians, citizens, and newspapers advocated toleration for the Japanese and throughout emphasized toleration for every race, creed, and color. And they participated in civic events designed to draw them closer to each other as communities and to the war effort as well. In May, San Francisco celebrated Citizenship Week, culminating in "I Am an American Day," which emphasized the necessity of eschewing racial, creed, and color distinctions in the name of winning the war. San Francisco followed this up with a massive demonstration at Kezar Stadium reminiscent of the metropolitan-military fetes of the 1930s.

Thousands watched as participants conducted ceremonies appropriate to General MacArthur Day (L.A. went them one better and named a park for him) and also put on the standard sham battle. Tragically, one of the projectiles loosed during the spectacle killed Marion Livingston, the wife of a prominent insurance executive. Other than this "unfortunate incident, it was a wonderful day," commented Supervisor Jesse Colman. San Francisco went on in May to stage a mass urban prayer on Mother's Day for "the mothers of the United States and for victory in our war." To blot out the influence of the outside world on the community, the radio industry agreed to "shut off this city from the outside world of general broadcasting" to allow people to participate in a five-minute mass urban prayer. In San Diego, comedian Red Skelton ended his routine on a more somber note. He asked that all lights in the stadium be doused and that everyone light a match. "What an impressive sight," said Robert Wright, "to make us impressed that we were all in this war together."[18]

War and urban community could hardly have been more commingled, and they were again in a series of civic observances of the anniversary of Pearl Harbor. San Franciscans staged a "One Year After Parade," which they hoped to be the "largest parade ever to be held" in the Bay City. Army, Navy, Marine, police, fire department, civic, and fraternal contingents marched to remind citizens of the tragedy of Pearl Harbor. From the steps of city hall, Fletcher Bowron, by radio, led Los Angeles in a similar commemoration. Against a backdrop simulating the sounds of bombs, machine guns, artillery, and screeching planes, the mayor resoundingly denounced the "cowardly stab in the back at Pearl Harbor." In the same tone, he spoke of the young men "murdered in cold blood by a conscienceless, unscrupulous national neighbor turned foe." The crowd listened to taps, pledged allegiance to the flag, sang the national anthem, and heard it sung above their own voices by Hugo Kirckhofer and several other singers. Angelenos in their cars, factories, streets, and homes took part by radio. Nobody had yet invented the term "global village" to describe the influence of media in bringing diverse peoples into a larger community, but surely the California cities employed the radio to unite their own disparate elements on such occasions.[19]

These mass urban observances were supplemented by other activities designed to unite every organization, group, sex, age, and institution into a remarkable web of community. No matter how small, offbeat, seemingly insignificant, or obscure, there seemed to be *something* that everyone could do to help *their city* win the war. Civil Defense might not have had to cope with enemy bombing of their home towns, but it certainly got people ready to face the prospect and to feel that they had a hand in the just application of bombing to the foe.

The foremost urban concern on the Pacific Coast was the possibility of air attack. Initially, some air-power advocates refused to countenance the implications of their new technology. In January 1941, as the air war over European and Asian cities mounted, Fletcher Bowron praised "the belief of the peoples of the United States that the civilians, the elderly people, the women and children of an invaded country, should never be made the defenseless targets of total war." The mayor was appalled at the "ghastly description" of the air war, but thought that Americans could not stop "this repugnant spectacle of madness," except to produce "more and better engines of destruction" to enable the Allies to win the conflict. He took some comfort in the fact that the planes that Los Angeles factories were building would be employed by Anglo-Saxons, who would use them "upon military objectives rather than upon defenseless civilians for the purpose of creating terror." Of course, at that moment British air-power theory was changing to emphasize the very terror, or area, bombing that the city's chief executive deplored. By year's end, however, after Pearl Harbor, Bowron himself no longer regretted it, believing "laying Tokyo and the gardens of the Makada [*sic*] in waste," to be a "just retribution" for Japan's bombing of an "open city." San Diegans underwent a similar evolution. "The actions of the Japanese have not changed our abhorrence of the bombing of unarmed civilians and cities . . . [but] sometimes it is necessary to fight fire with fire. . . . The Japanese have indicated the type of war they want to fight. . . . And now, when the proper time arrives, they need not be surprised to feel the full fury of the hatred and bitterness they have inspired."[20]

Thus, urban Californians came to expect terror bombing against their own homes and those of their enemies. Because the military held out the possibility of such raids at least through 1943, they expected them momentarily. Therefore, the coastal cities solemnly set about preparing for them. Air raid precautions constituted the earliest and single most important activity of civil defense. In most of the cities, civil defense limped along from its initiation in early 1941 until Pearl Harbor. Probably most agreed with a news story out of New York City that belittled Japan's air power. Unfortunately, the *San Diego Union* chose December 7, 1941, to print that story. Whatever the resulting damage to the reputation of the city's leading newspaper, the benefit to civil defense was marked. Within two weeks of the Japanese bombing, San Diego civil defense enrollments rose from four hundred to eighteen thousand, with a target of forty thousand. By the same point, San Francisco had enlisted forty-five thousand on the way to a target of sixty-five thousand, and Los Angeles boasted of eighty-three thousand by March 1942.[21]

These volunteers cut their spurs on the cities' first blackouts, held shortly after the war began. Although later historians and even contemporary observers charged that a severe case of hysteria gripped coastal cities during these months, people conducted themselves very well under blackout conditions. It may help us to gain perspective by reminding ourselves of much less threatening, but just as somber, urban circumstances. For example, in 1979, New York City suffered a power failure, which triggered widespread rioting and looting. Yet under much more threatening wartime conditions, the supposedly hysterical residents of San Francisco, Oakland, Los Angeles, and San Diego acted with discipline, humor, composure, and courage. Perhaps the best evidence of this statement was the nearly complete lack of violence that accompanied the blackouts. The police reported precious few outbreaks, and those related directly to the blackout emergency. In San Diego an irate person kicked out the lights of an automobile when the owner refused to turn them out, and in San Francisco several people broke store windows in order to get at the light switches. Beyond that, "Runt" Meyer, a San Francisco burglar, took advantage of the gloom to commit a couple of thefts, but given Runt's criminal record, he might have committed them anyway. Few others emulated him or the window breakers.[22]

Like many of the civil defense exercises, the blackouts were community events. For example, when the sirens sounded at 7:32 P.M., five days after Pearl Harbor, they immediately halted the normal life of the entire San Francisco Bay metropolitan area. From San José in the south to Napa in the north and from the breakers on the Great Highway in San Francisco many miles into the East Bay, most lights went off, the power went out, civilian transportation ceased, and people settled in somewhere in the great metropolitan region. On the Great Bay Bridge linking San Francisco and Oakland, the cars and commuter trains stopped, suspended in mid-air above the bay. In San Francisco, riders alighted from stalled streetcars to wait out the darkness in doorways of adjacent buildings. Passengers in motor cars had to pull to the corner, douse the lights, and find shelter. Pedestrians groped their way along the sides of buildings on the way home. Patrons of cafes and restaurants, in the best San Francisco tradition, simply stayed put, eating, drinking, laughing, and singing their way through the candlelit gloom. Market Street movie houses were a special haven, accommodating the many pedestrians on that street who were caught short of their destinations and needed a place to sit down. One enterprising proprietor of a newsreel movie house entertained the blackout victims with scenes of actual air raids in less fortunate lands. Other movie patrons simply stayed to watch the feature over again. On Geary Street, three hundred residents "struggled" into the Curran Theater. Undaunted by the gloom, an actress, "Miss Katherine Cornell, walked through the darkened streets from her Nob Hill hotel suite, accompanied by her Dachshund" (admittedly an inappropriate pet for this war), and "at the theater the rest of the cast assembled, . . . [and] the show went on." Not all the lights were doused, but gradually residents in all cities perfected the technique.

Seldom do urbanites share such common experiences. Perhaps modern sports spectacles, such as the World Series or the Super Bowl, or the tragedy of the September 11, 2001, bombing of the twin towers of New York City's World Trade Center, come closest to paralleling the blackouts, but no contemporary civilian event did. Suddenly over a million people were without auto lamps, door lights, billboard signs, street lights, window displays, home lighting that might have shone on the streets, neon signs, bridge illumination, flashlights, monumental lighting, illuminated building fronts, and even power to drive the streetcars. For two hours and forty minutes the darkness of war and the experiences within it joined a disparate urban area together. Before it ended, war would do so again many times.

In the meantime, residents set about perfecting the blackout procedures. San Diego allowed pedestrians to carry special kinds of heavily shielded flashlights. The San Francisco Board of Supervisors advocated the adoption of daylight saving time to give defense workers and others time to get home from work without having to drive during blackout hours. San Diego merchants agreed to a uniform closing time of 5:00 P.M. to the same end, and San Francisco stores began a "shop in the forenoon drive" to get its own people off the streets by dark. San Diego church leaders urged adoption of a similar policy to abstain from holding church services after 6:00 P.M. The regional weather bureau in San Francisco even blacked out all weather information to deny Japanese pilots knowledge of climatic conditions over their targets. Finally, to make all of these sacrifices endurable, a Stanford professor invented a low-intensity indoor lamp. Said to put out one-tenth as much light as the moon, it would ensure that life inside homes and stores would be darker than that outside, although the skeptic may well wonder what good that did.[23]

By late February, San Francisco had experienced seven blackouts, but had not yet perfected the technique. A nineteen-minute response to an unidentified aircraft on February 19, 1942, revealed that householders obeyed the blackout to the letter, but that the downtown area did not. The city's newly organized nerve center in the basement of city hall functioned properly, with the city government assembled there, ready to carry on when the bombs hit. However, quite a few downtown lights remained on for longer or shorter periods, including stoplights, a huge neon advertising sign on the Bay Bridge approach, skylights atop buildings, the famous Mark Hopkins Hotel, and comically, for a time, the lights on the second floor of the city hall. Meanwhile, the city's other air raid precautions moved ahead. Los Angeles had even more trouble getting the lights in the commercial district doused. However, in time, they too learned to curb their lights.[24]

Precautions against air attack had to be quite numerous and complex. Either civil defense or the military required air raid wardens, block captains, plane spotters, fire watchers, auxiliary firefighters, instructors, casualty stations, nurses, first-aid specialists, plotters, telephone operators, ambulance drivers, bureaucrats, and more. Each performed a key role in the division of defense labor. Catalina flying boats took off from the waters of bays and harbors and ranged hundreds of miles into the Pacific, providing the first line of defense. Next came the spotters, listeners, and plotters. For example, by January 3, 1942, people manned sixty-one hilltop posts in San Diego, women by day and men by night, except for weekends, when Boy Scouts relieved the women. At a typical post everything centered upon the watching, the telephone for reporting planes, and the clock, for helping to plot their course. Like other aspects of the war, these jobs tended to bring together people who might not ordinarily have had such contact. One San Diego station had eleven different nationalities working its phones and braving the "cold atop these wind tormented hills." Volunteers, most of whom had full-time jobs during the day, supplied their own phones. If the ground spotters failed to pick up the aircraft, volunteer civilian airmen provided a backup. These men flew, often in their own planes, over the metropolitan areas, making the same kinds of checks that the ground observers did. When either group picked up an aircraft—friendly, enemy, or unidentified—they relayed the information to a filter center, which plotted all planes on a map and identified them. Volunteers staffed these posts as well.[25]

In case an enemy broke through these defenses and the military planes went up to stop them, grim preparations had already been made to deal with the resultant bombing. Incendiary, especially magnesium, bombs seemed most likely to be dropped on California's heavily wooden and dry cities. To cope with their descent, each city maintained a small

army of air wardens. Los Angeles boasted thirty-three thousand volunteers by 1942; San Francisco, over twenty thousand; and San Diego,
about ten thousand. Each city aimed to have one fire warden per block to
confront the flames and take charge of all operations in their block. Fire
watchers, perched atop city buildings or hills, supplemented the wardens,
scanning the cities for air raid fires. The fire wardens were usually organized by proximity, so the organization was ordinarily a neighborhood or
block one. Each had a casualty station stocked with medicine to treat the
injured. To back them up, the cities possessed an emergency air raid or
civil defense ambulance service in addition to its regular corps. If worse
came to worst, an emergency clearance and rescue squad stood ready to
clear away the damage. And an auxiliary firefighting service stood ready
to help the regular department combat the flames.[26]

Householders waiting for bombs or fire had already been instructed
by civil defense authorities on how to help themselves in the interim. The
newspapers carried extensive stories on how to recognize the wailing of
the air raid sirens, how to get the kids home from school before the attack,
how to spot Japanese aircraft, where to hide from the bombs, how to recognize an incendiary, how to extinguish it, what kind of auxiliary water
pump to use (a stirrup pump) in case the regular one broke down, how to
respond to a gas attack, what kind of medicine to have on hand for burns,
and how to contact the fire wardens. Schoolchildren received a similar
set of instructions. Administrators conducted air raid drills, evacuating
children into the schoolyards, where trenches had sometimes been dug
for them, or into basements or interior halls, preferably with sandbags
at the windows or exits. Some districts preferred to send children home
between the warning and the actual beginning of the raid; others hoped
to hold onto them and discouraged their parents from coming to claim
them. To make doubly certain that no one was lost, the San Francisco
city government provided over fifty thousand identification tags, like GI
dog tags, one for each child in the public schools.[27]

Anyone caught in the open or downtown was directed to get into
a shelter, because most of the deaths in London had been caused by
bomb fragments, flying glass shards, splinters, and similar objects hit-
ting residents who were out in the open. Therefore, downtown had its
own shelters, preferably located in the basements of tall buildings, which
the London experience had again shown to be the safest places in the
city. Civil defense rules even provided for the emergency care of pets,
especially city dogs. The dogs had to be tagged, kept from running about
town, provided with special caches of food to last the duration of an
emergency, kept out of the public shelters, and kept away from smoke,

which could easily suffocate them. In Los Angeles, justly famed for its elaborate pet cemeteries, civil defense sent out a circular prescribing the proper drugs to be administered to the animals in case they panicked—sodium bromide for mild anxiety, Nembutal for more serious fear, and others still in case of terror. San Francisco provided just as comprehensively. Apparently ungrateful for all these efforts, the canines of that city promptly subverted civil defense measures by polluting the heaps of sand piled around to douse the incendiaries.[28]

Evacuation presented the authorities of the martial cities with one of their thorniest problems. The very notion of evacuation seemed to be a demoralizing idea. Moreover, initially at least, San Diego defenders did not think that evacuation could be carried out because the fleeing refugees would have to use the same roads as the advancing (hopefully) or retreating military personnel. Beyond that, they had no place to put the thousands of potential refugees. As yet, they had not witnessed the great Hamburg, Germany, raid of 1943, which routed 1.2 million people out of a city of 1.8 million.[29]

San Francisco figured differently. Not only did they count on an evacuation succeeding, but they did so well into mid-1943. Apparently inspired by the British evacuation of Dunkirk in 1940, which saved the Island Kingdom's last available ground forces from capture, the San Franciscans intended to evacuate many by boat themselves. So serious were they about this plan that instead of "the annual water parade and aquatic celebration customarily held on May 2nd," they planned to evacuate 1,500 civil defense air wardens from the Marina District and Aquatic Park to Pier 60 as a readiness test. The owners of "small boats, yachts, power boats, and other types of watercraft" were to assemble off the shores and, after Red Cross, auxiliary police, and evacuation officers had processed them, carry the evacuees to the Navy-controlled Pier 60. This "Dunkirk at the Marina" was elaborately planned and impossibly bureaucratic. Still, if that many Marina District and Aquatic Park boat owners participated, it says something for both the lingering fear of air attack and the widespread desire to further the war effort. So does the tentative proposal to evacuate Alcatraz of its residents. Civil defense planners feared that an air raid might disrupt the penal island and loose its infamous inhabitants, such as Al Capone. However, they could think of no easy way to get the three hundred desperadoes off the "Rock" and into some other safe prison while under Japanese attack.[30]

The threat of air war also meant that San Franciscans, San Diegans, Oaklanders, and Angelenos would have to give up an impressive list of things close to their hearts. The Army banned both the Rose Bowl and the East-West games because the assembled throngs might present too tempting a target for Japanese aviators. The West Coast took some consolation from the fact that Oregon State beat Duke University in the "exiled" Rose Bowl of 1942, but the game in Durham, North Carolina, was just not the same as in Pasadena. Santa Anita and other horse racing went the way of postseason football, and so did the cities' lighted night-time playground activities. In fact, the authorities sought to minimize any kind of after-dark outdoor play, encouraging home recreation instead. Indoor night-crowd recreation such as the opera, movies, restaurants, or other similar activities did not fall under the ban, and a few crowd activities were permitted on college campuses in daylight. To keep defense workers' morale high, professional baseball, even that played at night, was not immediately banned. But college dances were shunted to the East Bay in the San Francisco region to make them less vulnerable to Japanese air power.

Loose gossip fell under the same ban, as authorities staged campaigns urging one and all to "zip your lip." Bartenders and cosmetologists were critical in this effort since they came in contact with so many service persons and war workers trying to drown their loneliness or fatigue or restore a "factory face" to its normal beauty. For example, a "dramatic 3 A.M. meeting of the men who mix San Francisco's drinks," in March 1942 signed up 1,200 bartenders to monitor the conversation of the bars. They were to listen for seamen who "pop off," particularly about the names of ships, the types of cargo, their time of arrival, and "talk about morale and the nature of their work by defense workers." The barmen promised to turn in to the shore patrol or the military police any persons with "loose lips," which could "sink ships." Amateur radio operators had lost their right to be on the air even earlier, one day after the war began.[31]

The world of high culture shared the deprivations of popular culture. Shortly after December 7, 1941, the director of the vulnerable Palace of the Legion of Honor art museum, which sat beside the ocean in Lincoln Park, acted to protect its "priceless art treasures." Some were removed, and all were numbered (in order of value) for quick removal to vaults in case of emergency. Additional watchmen, measures to strengthen the roof, piles of sand, and "complete blackout control" quickly followed.[32]

The communication, as well as the organization, of civil defense demonstrates that the war, though it bore down hard on them, did not disrupt cities. Civil defense messages went out over a diverse network. Especially in the early days of the war, the press carried masses of civil defense information. The *San Francisco Chronicle,* the *Los Angeles Times,* and the *San Diego Union* nurtured the war effort in every way, right down to suggestions that their readers overdose on vitamin A in order to combat the night blindness they might experience in case of combat. Radio played a major role as well and provided a particularly effective medium for leaders to communicate with a part of their communities that the newspapers did not reach. Fletcher Bowron, of forward-looking Los Angeles, made particularly good use of the radio to urge ethnic pluralism, to laud the city's war effort, to urge participation, to praise the military services, to warn of possible enemy attack, and to evoke the emotions of war on behalf of community. In addition, each of the cities generated civil defense bulletins ad infinitum—perhaps more than were required. Anyone missed in these larger efforts could get the word through service clubs, veterans' organizations, schools, school support groups, and other associations. And those overlooked this time around received information through newsreels and the movies, some of which were designed in consultation with Mayor Bowron to teach the civil defense message.

Information also spread through neighbors, by phone, and in the parks. For example, the San Francisco Fire Department explained how to "put out incendiary bombs in Hamilton Square Playground," Rossi, and other playgrounds and parks. Los Angeles, with its proximity to the dramatic influences of Hollywood, went them one better and staged civil defense pageants in the playgrounds, employing children as actors.[33]

More remarkable still was the organizational structure through which these messages were circulated and implemented. Civil Defense Councils and some other associations were new creations elicited by the war. However, most civil defense measures were performed through the existing organizational structure of the city. Each institution, in turn, helped to mobilize another constituency for the war effort. When it became necessary to train air wardens, the public schools contributed the space, and various professionals around the city donated their time as teachers. When the city government needed kiddy dog tags, it paid for them and the Parent Teacher Association distributed them. When the city appealed for advice about air raid planning, the architects and engineers formed an air raid precaution advisory committee to help form policies for buildings and other structures. When it became relevant to hear "Singapore Joe," an operator of a theater string in that city, tell how the Japanese took his town, the Commonwealth Club of San Francisco provided a ready-made forum. When San Diego airplane spotters required telephones and house rent, the Encanto Club, or some other organization, paid the bill. When defenders of the Bay City wanted to test their evacuation capabilities, the Inter-Bay Yachting Association helped the Coast Guard to plan the operation and also furnished the boats for the test. As the terrific pace of war industrial activity became a health hazard, the San Francisco County Medical Society offered a "free industrial health service" to conserve "civilian manpower by removing needless illness and accident hazards."

When the air raid wardens began creating casualty stations in West Los Angeles, the Brentwood Golf Club, the Venice Post Office, the University of California at Los Angeles, Pacific Palisades Gas Station, and Venice and Hamilton high schools volunteered rooms. In the harbor area, Admiral Leigh Gymnasium and San Pedro Hospital provided rooms; in the San Fernando Valley, North Hollywood High School did; and elsewhere in the city, the Southeast Nursing Station, Union (railroad) Station, Blessed Sacrament School, city hall, the Elks Club (B.P.O.E. No. 99), the Forum Theater, Los Angeles City College, the Southern California Auto Club, St. Paul's Cathedral, and Wilshire Methodist Episcopal Church School did too. Casualty stations proliferated in San Francisco as well; even the Cosmetologists Association Inc. appealed to its members to "turn beauty parlors into improvised first aid stations."

As the San Francisco Red Cross and Emergency Medical Service matured, civil defense leaders turned to the Chauffeur's Union, Local 265, for skilled drivers and to the city's merchants for converted "light trucks, delivery cars, and station wagons for use as ambulances and emergency vehicles." When Los Angeles authorities mounted the "EVENING-AT-HOME" campaign, they could count on the public libraries to "feature displays of books on home games, hobbies, etc." When the mass demand for first aid broke out with the war, the Red Cross promptly increased its classes from seventy-nine to five hundred and prepared to train twenty-five thousand additional people to cope with the casualties of Japanese air power. When the Army and Navy required model airplanes to be used "for aircraft recognition and gunnery practice classes," school and youth groups began whittling away on the models, for which they supplied the wood, glue, and paint, receiving the specifications from the military. When the services needed additional fliers and planes to help spot, individuals stepped forward. Even night club and theater owners tried to help, the former by incorporating exit instructions into their acts and the latter by training their ushers and usherettes in first aid, air raid drills, and other precautions. Finally, when pet owners fretted over the air raid fate of their dogs, the Society for Prevention of Cruelty to Animals stepped in with drugs, care, leashing, and other instructions to see the pets—and their worried owners—through the emergency.[34]

When police chief and San Francisco Civil Defense Council (SFCDC) co-director Charles Dullea called for 4,000 fire-fighting volunteers, the International Longshoremen's and Warehousemen's Union organized a voluntary brigade of 1,500 members to suppress fire on the waterfront. When the Army and Navy requested model airplanes for military training, the Chinese Playground in San Francisco volunteered the services of many youngsters already skilled in kite making. When the block club movement caught the attention of the city, the *San Francisco Chronicle* stood ready to publicize the movement and the Group Work Council of the Community Chest, to organize it. On the Sunday following Pearl Harbor, the city was still unprepared to counter the threat of Japanese air power, so San Francisco scavengers, Italian Americans to a man, spent all day "bringing sand (to quench fires) from the ocean beach to all parts of San Francisco."[35]

And when an organization or group of volunteers did not exist, one often sprang, almost miraculously, into being. John Wright, the air raid warden for a part of the Upper Mission area in San Francisco, learned this truth when he had to survey his district. In order to help, his wife Betty had to hire a babysitter for their infant son, Colin. When she returned home, the sitter refused payment for her services, saying that "this was her contribution, her bit" to the war effort. The girl then suggested that her friends would be willing to do this sort of thing to help other neighborhood wives attend "ARP [Air Raid Precaution] classes and first aid classes and the like." Mrs. Wright then proposed that the girls organize, and the "Vickies," or Volunteers for Victory, came into being. The movement soon spread to other portions of the city. Not content with simply minding the kids, the Vickies worked to develop their childcare skills. For example, Mrs. Josephine Gardner of the Golden Gate Story League visited the Vickies "every Saturday morning to help them perfect their story-telling techniques." The girls went on other days to watch Mrs. Wright bake bread, and on still others to Mrs. Rizzo's home to "watch how she cares for her 3-months-old baby."[36]

The same spontaneous outburst of community occurred all over the city. For instance, atop Telegraph Hill, a couple of days after Pearl Harbor, Mrs. Morse Erskine began circulating among her neighbors, inviting them to a meeting. The gathering produced an emergency council, contact between otherwise disparate peoples, and an information survey that revealed the names of the block wardens and physicians and the locations of first aid stations, shovels, garden hoses, and firefighting equipment. Leaflets were put out in Italian, English, and Spanish to inform the other blocks on the hill and delivered by members of the Telegraph Hill Boys' Club. Besides civil defense cooperation, a part of the plan was to "know your neighbor to guard against espionage and sabotage." This movement spread rapidly throughout the city, partly by spontaneous combustion and partly through the auspices of the Group Work Council of the Community Chest. Sometimes a neighborhood improvement association (for which San Francisco was famous), sometimes a property owners organization, and sometimes a playground club took the lead, but everywhere this was supplemented by the spontaneous creation of block clubs.

Clubs elected officers, designated air raid wardens, set up subcommittees on organization and evacuation, created block headquarters stocked with cots and first aid supplies, took charge of the sand piled around by the scavengers, and aggressively got to know each other. The *Chronicle* assigned reporter Bill Simons to cover them. The editor noted that the earlier pioneers and village dwellers had a keen sense of neighborliness. "As the American Nation sprawled out over a vast continent, the village inherited strength of neighborly mutual responsibility, to be finally swallowed in the mighty cities that have arisen as signposts of the great Nation," he argued.

> As the people have been brought into closer physical proximity the immediate tasks of the day have obscured the spiritual sense of mutual reliance. As America has grown stronger in mass, [it has become] weaker in realization of individual responsibility. Now the ordeal of war is reviving this first principle. . . . It is a spontaneous combustion. . . . If all Americans know their neighbors in the truest sense of the words we shall not have met our present ordeal in vain. In these little groups, by block and by district, a power peculiar to and typical of America is being brought back into vitality.[37]

Patterned on such model neighborhood block clubs as the one in the Sunset District bounded by 25th and 26th Avenues, Lawton and Moraga, the clubs proliferated. By mid-March, two hundred had organized and by mid-April, three hundred. How much residue of this martial organization survived the conflict is not known, but it is very likely that it contributed further to making San Francisco the collection of neighborhoods that it was already famous for being. San Diego also adopted the block plan for its 5,300 city blocks, and Los Angeles followed suit. The same spontaneity and dedication appeared in those two cities as well. Everywhere women played a disproportionately important role in this movement.

The same voluntary initiative combined with institutional support can be seen in the Oakland model airplane program, designed to provide models to train military personnel to spot friendly and enemy aircraft. A tool designer named Harvey S. Robbers, who had been a flying sergeant in the First World War, got a Navy contract to provide the planes. He then turned his house into a factory. In it, he produced perfect replicas of the aircraft, using his entire family as a workforce, together with eighteen members of the Oakland Cloud Dusters Club, "a model plane group of which Robbers is president." Next he recruited the Oakland school system to provide students to mass produce the models built in the Robbers' factory-home. Finally, to popularize the idea, he organized a model plane exhibit at Oakland Municipal Auditorium co-sponsored by the Junior Chamber of Commerce and the schools. The Prop Busters, the East Bay Aironeers, and the Bay City Model Airplane Association cooperated as well.

In short, everyone wanted to serve somehow, in some way, in the war effort. This popular demand actually became an embarrassment to one city government. The block club seemed the best way to mobilize the entire city populace, to help the air wardens, and to assist the war effort in any way. It would give "each neighbor a part of the nation's war effort." This would have meant a network in every city block, of which San Francisco alone had 5,500 and Los Angeles, infinitely more. Los Angeles embraced the idea and organized right down to the level of the block mother. But as late as mid-1943, the San Francisco supervisors still vacillated, despite Mayor Rossi's insistence that "a fuller participation of all citizens" is "vitally needed by our fighting forces and for civilian protection on the home front."[38]

Yet citizens were almost diabolically clever at finding ways to involve everyone, regardless of age, sex, race, condition, or other designation, in these manifestations of war and community. For example, all cities conducted the usual scrap and bond drives. With the cruiser USS *San Francisco* audaciously engaging the enemy at the naval Battle of Guadalcanal, it was inevitable that Los Angeles would organize a bond campaign to finance a cruiser bearing its own name. In this event it raised sufficient money to build a cruiser and four destroyers to boot. And if one could not afford a cruiser, one could purchase a less expensive piece of equipment. Pearl Harbor hit Alhambra High School especially hard. The Japanese aviators killed six graduates of that institution on December 7, and on the same day the students pledged to get even. They began a campaign to buy a bomber to be named "Alhambra's Answer," which "may do its share in the destruction of Tokyo." Within a year, the students collected

$30,000 of the necessary $175,000. And if a plane cost too much—San Diego tried unsuccessfully to purchase a bomber—one could still buy a bomb. Therefore, Southern California theaters led a drive to buy 500-pound bombs, which donors could sign in return for their support.[39]

And the participants were endlessly publicized, positively or negatively. The names of killed and wounded were published in the newspapers, and the names of those serving were also posted in public places. For example, Hamilton Junior High School in Long Beach maintained an honor roll of over five hundred names of graduates who were in service and added to it every day. In case anyone forgot, the entire school periodically paraded in front of the honor roll to be reminded. The papers also regularly published stories of individual men and women serving at the fronts. And when people did not serve, the newspapers remorselessly reminded the community of that act too, through the publication of their names.[40]

These individual or group displays were often supplemented by massive public ones. When the battered cruiser USS *San Francisco* hobbled through the Golden Gate on its way to Mare Island Navy Yard for repairs, the crew was landed for what turned into a "tumultuous tribute." San Francisco may not have been as economically successful as Los Angeles, but few cities knew better how to evoke the spirit of community. The one hundred survivors of the Naval Battle of Guadalcanal were paraded down Market Street, San Francisco's great ceremonial way. The jeeps carried the "new skipper of the ship that bears the city's name, and Bruce McCandless, who wears the Congressional Medal for bringing the ship through to victory after his superiors [including Admiral Daniel Callahan] had been killed," noted the *Chronicle*. "Then came 10 others, enlisted men, wounded, in bathrobes, carrying canes and crutches and scars of battle." The others followed, the men sitting "quietly, stiffly, ill at ease in the little Army cars, looking straight ahead, for the most part." The sidewalks were packed three deep, where people fought to glimpse the sailors, while thousands of others "packed fire escapes and office windows. . . . There were whistles, cries and endless thunder of clapping hands" from the estimated one-hundred-thousand crowd.[41]

But the Southland too knew how to stage a parade and acted on that knowledge often. One stands out in particular. In January 1943, the Rose Bowl game returned to Pasadena, but not the Rose Parade. Instead the "Crown City" organized a Bonds Parade. As the *Times* explained it, "instead of buds, this year it's bonds. Instead of beauty, this year it's battle—an odious metamorphosis made necessary by the treachery of America's enemies." And instead of a pleasant entertainment that all the country listened to over the radio, the event became a national competition between cities to determine which could collect the most money for the war effort. Houston won the grand prize, and the contestants together collected $85 million. A United Nations Parade replaced the Rose Parade. The procession featured people from all countries on the Allied side of the struggle, from American cowboys to Russian Cossacks. The Chinese marched, together with ten thousand Czechs, Canadians, Aussies, Scots, Englishmen, Russians, Danes, Norwegians, Greeks, Dutch, Koreans, Poles, and others. They stepped out to the music of the Monterey Park American Legion "girls drum and bugle corps," which alternately regaled the crowds with "Mademoiselle from Armentieres" and "Praise the Lord and Pass the Ammunition."[42]

The war effort in urban California amounted to a great deal more than disruption and hysteria. The Second World War initiated a renaissance of community there. Perhaps the examples of war theater are enough to demonstrate that a lot of community integration occurred. The war unleashed opposing forces, drawing people together and distancing them from each other, but fortunately the influences that drew them together predominated. By one means or another, people were drawn into conflict and community, and thereby their lives assumed a public significance that they never had in peacetime.[43]

And even more importantly, this renaissance effectively mobilized the cities to fight the war. Historians have emphasized that, lacking the actual death and destruction of war itself, Americans had a less realistic sense of participation in the conflict. Unlike the residents of London, Manchester, Berlin, Stalingrad, Nanking, or Tokyo, who had to pick their way through the rubble and bomb craters to get to work, most Americans had to fight the war with their imaginations. These community observations and efforts helped sensitize those imaginations to the very real dangers that would come much closer if the Allies did not win.

3. Al Capone and Alcatraz
The Latent Military Resources
of Urban California

It must have been the "Nation's Strangest 'Assembly Line,'" just as the article entitled "San Quentin—A War Plant" claimed. One thousand men, five hundred on the day shift and five hundred on the swing shift, labored to produce United States Government ration book number three, soon due to replace books one and two. The convicts all were volunteers; they completely organized and supervised their own work, and they guarded the finished product. In fact, even Warden Clinton Duffy himself could not get into the storage area at night without the permission of the convict guarding it. "Major" John Hendricks, the director of the prison band, "doing the book [a life sentence] for a murder rap," organized and directed the entire operation. As columnist J. Campbell Bruce put it, Hendricks and his assistant Earl Keyes had put together "the strangest roster of employees a personnel manager ever saw—murderers, thugs, robbers, burglars, embezzlers, bad check artists, swindlers, and thieves of every category."

The work was organized on a true assembly-line basis, minus heavy mechanization, with each convict performing one task: opening request letters, stuffing, licking envelopes in the "bundling" section, and so forth. The prisoners made very few errors, as compared to the applicants for the ration books, 30 percent of whom goofed. The men liked their work, and some of them volunteered for both shifts. Besides the 1,000 men making ration books, another 1,500 worked on other defense projects. As the journalist noted, with tongue very much in cheek, San Quentin was an ideal war plant. There housing was not a problem, nor was transportation, absenteeism, or wage disputes. In order to replace the Hendricks system, the government would have had to provide 30,000 feet of floor space; 2,500 volunteers or paid workers; gasoline, rubber, and tires or other transportation for those working; and armed guards to protect the precious ration books.[1]

From that point, the San Quentin war effort dramatically expanded. They produced textiles for the Mare Island Navy Yard, military desks and small furniture, jute bags, mattress covers (40,000), burlap, and metal beds, and they wove the submarine nets that protected the harbors from enemy penetration. In mid-November 1942, they were starting on an order of seventy-one "troop landing boats."

Not to be outdone by their counterparts at San Quentin, the hard-core inmates at Alcatraz mobilized on December 7, 1941. Their convenient island location and background in laundry made them ideal for doing the wash of the merchant marine, but they also cleaned the linens of the military posts, garrisons, and Army transports. We don't know if public enemy number one, Al Capone, scrubbed the sailors' socks, but his fellow prisoners washed them by the boatload. They also produced deck mats for warships and made and cleaned uniforms for the Quartermaster Corps. The San Quentin and Alcatraz experience reminds us that metropolitan areas are vast repositories of excess resources, which can easily be turned to some other account.[2]

Robert Merton has posed a theory that big city political machines had latent functions, not easily evident even to the eye of the trained observer. These, he said, accounted for the longevity of those machines. That theory can also be applied to cities' military resources. Cities have a much greater capacity to serve a society at any given time than is evident or than they are usually called upon to use. For example, with the exception of freeways, expressways, and downtown streets, modern urban transportation routes are usually not crowded. Neighborhood streets park endless rows of unused cars and provide limitless surface capacity that is seldom driven on. Streetcars and buses run half-filled to empty most of the day, and amusement parks douse the lights at midnight. With the exceptions of central business districts, neighborhood business districts, and malls, most pedestrian areas have few if any people on them most of the time. Parks often draw a large crowd only on weekends and at night. Most oceanfronts and lakefronts are equally empty or underutilized. For example, San Francisco's famous Ten Mile Highway usually has hardly anyone on any given stretch of road or beach, and on weekdays neither does Chicago's matchless twenty-five-mile lakefront. Both downtown hotels and suburban motels are empty for half the day, and in the slack season more than that.[3]

Cities such as Las Vegas and Reno have more hotel and motel capacity than they have residents, and the rooms wait for the Fourth of July or Memorial Day weekend to fill them up. Huge football amphitheaters stand empty till the weekend, and then host only one or two games for a few hours on one or two days. Baseball stadiums remain unused half the time. Movie houses run only from one to eleven; schools hold forth from eight to three; restaurants are busy at only three rush-hour periods. Office space in the downtown and other clusters is often 10 to 15 percent in excess of what is rented at any given time. Housing is frequently in the same condition. Excess tidelands and harbor space abound, as do derelict neighborhoods, often partially or mostly abandoned by their residents. Some contemporary New York City areas have suffered such losses that the residents are raising vegetable gardens in the empty spaces. Churches and temples operate only a few nights a week and on their sabbaths. These enormous unused capacities were also present in earlier cities—latent resources waiting for a war to activate them.

These latent military resources are not confined merely to the physical structures of cities or the built environment, either. They exist in every other urban realm. There are more lawyers, more teachers, more brains, more techniques, and so forth than are being used at any one time under ordinary circumstances. This has been true of large parts of cities for at least the last two hundred years. Thus a modern city by its very nature is a place that concentrates a vast number of people and institutions that do not run at anything close to capacity. Yet war asked them to do so, and fortunately, they could.

That was particularly true of World War II. Wars in that era were fought much more effectively from cities. War also required rural production, but modern war is pre-eminently an industrial operation for which cities are well suited and for which hamlets and farmsteads are inadequate. The booster axiom that "bigger is better" is greatly disputed by the modern critics of urbanism, but it is the thesis of this chapter that *during World War II* the boosters were correct.[4]

It might be helpful to begin with some contrary examples. The South provides a cardinal example of the inefficiency of fighting a war from a small city, town, hamlet, or rural base. For example, Pascagoula, Mississippi, and Mobile, Alabama, both saw significant action on the homefront. Neither could provide schools, parks, sewers, ration quotas, housing, transportation, nor most of the other assets that the war required. Each was staggered by the war effort, and each had to be bailed out by a huge effort on the part of the federal government, which wasted resources that in more urbanized areas could have been devoted solely to the war itself. Consequently, both places greatly taxed government resources because of their underdevelopment. By contrast, California cities, because of their overdevelopment, offered maximum support to the modern nation-state war effort.[5]

One urban scholar recently labeled Los Angeles "the capital of 20th century hubris." As Stephen Erie, Arthur Verge, Mike Davis, Martin Schiesl, David L. Clark, and other historians have demonstrated, the epithet is eminently apt. Los Angeles had few reasons for being a great city in the first place, lacking many of the resources necessary for nineteenth- and early twentieth-century urbanization, such as water, a harbor, coal, timber, centrality on the West Coast, closeness to migration routes, proximity to national markets, and a nearby source of excess population. It did have oil, climate, scenery, open spaces, and an ocean beach. But so did many other places not poised to become the largest metropolis in the United States. What Los Angeles had and other places did not have was leadership. These boosters created the resources, material and spiritual, that nature neglected to put into this far southwestern desert.[6]

The critic perhaps understated the case when he accused Los Angeles of hubris. The dictionary defines that term as "wanton insolence or arrogance resulting from excessive pride or from passion," and the boosters of L.A. met most of these criteria. They built a city where few expected one to be, one that has continued to prosper despite the repeated predictions of its critics that its demise is imminent. No other California city quite matches the "wanton insolence" of Los Angeles in succeeding where it was supposed to fail, but most of them share the quality of hubris to an extraordinary degree. Even today, when growth control may be just over the horizon in the Golden State, people there still act economically as if bigger is better.

And in World War II, bigger *was* better. The overbuilt, overnight, jumped-up, "improbable" California cities were an enormous asset to the American homefront. Nobody planned it that way, but when the Japanese attacked Pearl Harbor, California cities were ready to resist, even if they did not yet know it. Military historians have frequently pointed out that American forces lacked very few material resources in their fight against fascism. That is something of an overstatement, but the homefront not only supplied the American services, but contributed significantly to the British and Soviet forces as well. Historians have sometimes assumed this prowess instead of examining it, so an explanation is in order. The complex causes of this success included natural resources, capital, industrialism, labor, and American culture. But another important reason for homefront productivity was the asset of cities, largely because of their prodigious latent military resources.[7]

These assets were of many kinds, including infrastructure, transportation, recreation, housing, other buildings for training or headquarters, health, education, communications, mobilization of public opinion, water, and a labor force. With the influx of the military, families, and war workers, housing was an especially perplexing problem. The government constructed housing in Oakland, Richmond, Vallejo, Los Angeles, San Francisco, and San Diego, and it allowed private enterprise to build some as well. But there was never enough to go around. The latent military resources of cities made up the difference. The cities were simply turned into huge dormitories for war workers, largely through sharing the existing housing stock. One of the most important sources of housing was vacancies. Just as it has excess office space, every city has unoccupied housing. For example, in 1940 the Los Angeles area alone had 67,008 vacancies. That amount represented 70 percent of the total new housing subsequently constructed in the area by the government between 1940 and 1944.[8]

"Vacancies" were sometimes less formal than an empty apartment or house. Elderly San Francisco parents rented the rooms of their sons who were absent at war. Across the bay, housewives let spare rooms to shipbuilders. As Marilynn Johnson put it, "During the course of the war, thousands of East Bay households responded to these appeals [for housing] particularly in blue-collar neighborhoods near the waterfront." San Francisco had the same experience. There the city's population jumped by 100,000 in just over two years. The foolish relocation of Japanese Americans freed up spaces for 5,000; the government built public war housing for another 14,000 people at Hunters Point; and San Francisco completed five city public projects.[9]

Even these facilities were insufficient, so by 1945, many people doubled up. A housing survey of Los Angeles County estimated that the county lacked 133,000 family units; so 75,000 of these families had to live doubled up. At five persons per family, that would have meant 375,000 people; at six persons, the total would have been 450,000. Hotels and motels housed others, sometimes for shorter periods, sometimes for longer. People rented basements, extra rooms, garage lofts, back porches, and anything else that a human being could fit into. To pare expenses and combat loneliness, servicemen's wives moved back to a family home, thereby freeing up additional rooms for in-migrant war workers. Crowding often resulted. Robert Wright remembered that his aunt and uncle in San Diego squeezed his mother, his sister, and himself into one room and then rented another room to a sailor and his wife. And when *newly employed residents*—women, seniors, children, and African Americans—trooped into the factories, they thereby alleviated both the labor and the dwelling shortages. This allowed the government to avoid diverting resources to house more in-migrant laborers who otherwise would have had to fill these jobs.[10]

The government also found new residences by the standard urban device of conversion. Non-housing structures were refashioned into residences, and large single-family homes were transformed into apartments. Fittingly, in the Los Angeles area this program began in the coastal areas and in Inglewood, where factories were furiously fabricating ships and planes. The *Times* explained the savings to the war effort: "An objective is the providing of additional living quarters with minimum use of critical materials and location within reasonable transportation distance of war plants." Others rented bunks on the hot-bed system. San Francisco reminded observers of one immense worker barracks. The Bay City housed many of the workers at the Bethlehem Shipyards in San Francisco, the Marinship ways in Sausalito, the Navy works at Vallejo, Moore Dry Dock and Shipbuilding in Oakland, and the yards in South San Francisco.

These latent housing resources benefited military people, too. In 1944, after Los Angeles had become an official point of embarkation and as the war in the Pacific reached a crescendo, ever more servicemen arrived in the Southland. It was quickly overrun by lonely men "celebrating" a last night on the town, a problem San Francisco and San Diego had experienced even earlier. Thus cities had to house increasing numbers of personnel on a temporary, usually weekend, basis. Every migrant serviceman wanted to see Hollywood, so that community bore an unusual housing burden. Due to shortages of materials and time, it was not possible to build shelter for all of these men. Instead, the government relied on the unused resources of cities. Young men found themselves sleeping in all-night theaters and hotel lobbies or just walking the streets and not sleeping at all.[11]

In response, beginning with the Congregational Church and followed by Hollywood Methodist, one institution after another provided beds, often in church basements. These included American Legion Post 43 (225), Bethany-Lutheran Church (14), B'nai B'rith (142), Christian Service Center (63), First Methodist Church (157), Hollywood-Beverly Christian Church (87), Congregational Church (100), Guild Canteen (850), Hollywood High School Gymnasium (767), USO (200), YMCA (119), Knights of Columbus (120), Lutheran Service Center (154), and

Temple Israel (257). And where the demand for these subterranean berths outran the supply, the bunks marched right upstairs and into the aisles and open spaces of the sanctuaries. "Never did a church hear such utterly blissful snoring," quipped *Times* writer Alma Whitaker. Hollywood alone housed over 3,000 of the 13,000 people who visited the Los Angeles area. Another 4,600 per night slept in area hotels, including an average of 1,000 in the Biltmore alone. To cope, the county even adapted its Patriotic Hall and "Pilgrimage Play Theater" in Hollywood for weekend housing. And where they could not provide a roof over these heads, tents or temporary quarters sprouted in public spaces. Failing even that, the men camped in the parks. Serviceman Gordon Wagenet remembered thousands of weekending sailors sleeping in Balboa Park.[12] Still, despite this temporary discomfort, cities housed enough workers to win the battle of production and mobilization, which was infinitely more important than the temporary discomfort of the employees.

When the supply of even this makeshift housing seemed to be running out, the cities found further resources to increase it again. In early 1944, fearing a local labor shortage, the Citizens Manpower Committee of Los Angeles staged a drive to induce war workers to "Stay on the Job." The Committee took advantage of the great Army and Navy show at the Los Angeles Coliseum to stress the need for housing. Like so many other institutions in the area, the Los Angeles Coliseum was built by city boosters. It arose in 1923 and was increased in size in order to lure the 1932 Olympics to that city. The Coliseum well illustrates the kind of hubris that Los Angeles's detractors cite, but it also gave the homefront popularizers of the war effort a magnificent urban space in which to persuade defense workers to "Finish the Job" and landlords to keep renting to transients. Time and again, the sporting arenas of the cities, like the Rose Bowl and Kezar Stadium, hosted these huge homefront morale- and participation-building spectaculars.[13]

This anxiety about workers arose because American entry into the war created a huge labor shortfall. The cities also helped abate this dearth. The conflict greatly increased the demand for products, while taking 12.5 million persons out of the workforce at the peak of the fighting. So these workers had to be replaced, and another 5 million paid workers were needed to expand the workforce enough to meet the requirements of war. The 425,000 prisoners of war (most of whom were not available until mid-1943) and braceros and other immigrants did not begin to make up this total, so again the country turned to other sources. Women, African Americans, Mexican Americans, southern whites, farmers, seniors, children, and the unemployed trooped into

American plants. In the San Francisco Area, even prisoners headed to jail and those already in San Quentin and Alcatraz became a part of the Good War workforce.[14]

Historians of the homefront have produced a considerable literature about some of these groups, particularly migrant blacks, factory women, and, recently, Okies. However, these studies have usually not recognized the military significance of nonmigrant workers, those who already lived in Urban California. Yet whether the residents were women, children, Okies, Mexican Americans, blacks, or seniors, they were much more valuable to the defense effort than were transients. Migrants used up gasoline, rubber, and train space getting to Urban California in the first place, and they consumed more still when they sent for their families. And once inside Fortress California, they had to be supplied anew with various services. Nonmigrants already had housing and day-care arrangements, and their children had a place in the schools. Even short-range travelers, like those who commuted from Sonoma or Woodland to the Vallejo Naval Shipyard or from San Bernardino to the Los Angeles aircraft factories, consumed precious tires and automobile parts, five and often six days a week. Resident workers, such as those in West Oakland, Hunters Point, or Wilmington and San Pedro, often walked to work from houses that were already constructed. So the *resident* black, Mexican American, southwestern white, female, child, and senior defense workers saved precious building materials, auto tires, rubber, and parts.[15]

In addition, unlike single women, whose employment often was "exploratory" and who contributed to high labor turnover, married women were more dependable and did not add to the pressing problem of labor turnover. Leonard J. Maloney, employment manager of Consolidated Aircraft Corporation in San Diego, noted the difference between home-grown married women and migrants in 1943 when he said that the former "represented the only new source of labor supply in this area, due to the inadequate housing for 'imported' new workers."[16] He might have added that they were also better trained, since one-third more metropolitan Californians had finished high school than had people from the southwestern states from which most migrants hailed. That education was a critically important matter for an industrial workforce heavily involved in aircraft manufacture.[17]

Some who probably had not finished their schooling nonetheless contributed as well. For example, in November 1942, San Quentin paroled five hundred men "to enter defense industries." In June, San Francisco became the first city in the country to begin emptying its city jail by putting prisoners on work probation. This domestic, or resident, part of the workforce perhaps amounted to as much as 40 percent. So quantitatively these people made up a very large portion of the workforce, and qualitatively they were its most valuable component. Nor was this efficiency inconsequential. William L. O'Neill has shown that by war's end, American fighting forces faced serious materiel shortages, which created markedly adverse strategic consequences. Every tire or gallon saved at home helped curtail those deficiencies and the attendant strategic repercussions abroad. More could certainly be saved in a city with a 40 percent resident workforce than in places like Pascagoula (which grew tenfold) and Mobile, where almost everyone came from somewhere else.[18]

Child-care arrangements were required to bring women into either defense work or other positions that opened up when job holders moved into war work. The government and business built a few day-care centers, but most women had to fend for themselves. They did so creatively by drawing on other latent resources of cities. School girls, stay-at-home neighbors, and relatives tended children. Other women shared babysitting. One tended the kids of a friend on the day shift, then shuttled them back to the day-shift worker while she hurried to her job on the swing shift. These child-care arrangements were critically important because they freed female labor for defense work. Again, residents had a big advantage over migrants because they already had established networks of relatives and friends. Contemporaries were regaled with horror stories about babies left in parked cars at the factory gate, but most kids were parked elsewhere. The nation state has been justly criticized for not providing enough day care, but women deserve major credit for improvising for themselves without it. Their concentration in cities helped them do so.[19]

Besides providing qualitatively superior workers in quantitatively impressive numbers for steady jobs, the cities often supplied others to meet particular crises. For example, since the war uprooted so many Americans from their homes, the mails took on a greatly added significance. To ease this crisis of absence, during the Christmas rush of 1942, the swamped Los Angeles Postal Service begged for volunteers to keep the mails flowing. The response was gratifying. "An army" of five thousand women, high school girls and boys, and "gray-haired veteran clerks" answered the call, a number equal to the entire number of full-time postal employees.[20]

Another crisis recurred at harvest time and was met in a similar manner. Between the draft and the high-paying defense industries that lured workers, such as Central Valley Southwesterners, from the low-paying farm sector, the war created a severe labor shortage in the countryside.

The relocation of Japanese Americans, one of the prime agricultural entrepreneurial groups, to detention centers worsened the situation. Almost before the gates closed on the ill-fated Japanese, cultivators were complaining of a scarcity of help. Machines, Mexican immigrants, military personnel furloughed from bases like Camp Roberts, prisoners of war, and other sources made up some shortfall, but harvest time always required more hands. Nor did the men laid off from defense industries after war production peaked take up this work. The answer? "It all boils down to the simple fact confronted last year and the year before and in all the war years," noted the *Call Bulletin,* "that the men and women and boys and girls of the towns and cities, not ordinarily employed in farm work but available for it at various times and in varying degrees, must give [lend] a hand."[21]

These hands usually belonged to young women and housewives, who helped for a week, a weekend, or the duration of the harvest. Predictably, the latent military resources of California towns and cities were called into service. When the 1943 Sonoma apple crop ripened, female pickers, in rolled-up jeans, tied-up shirtwaists, and bandanna-knotted hair, attacked the orchards. They bivouacked in the high school gymnasium and rode to work on school buses. These buses even transported the temporary workers from San Francisco to the Sonoma apple front. At other times, the workers were boys from San Francisco high schools or university students from Cal. By 1945, the numbers had grown to be quite impressive. In 1943, 93,445 of these volunteers and 40,000 Mexicans harvested a record crop. By September 1944, that number had risen to a record 99,482 volunteers who participated in the Emergency Farm Labor Project. Grapes and tomatoes claimed the largest numbers, but many other crops benefited, too. The shortage of pickers led to widespread crop losses in 1942, but in 1943 the volunteers and others brought in a record harvest without loss.[22]

Some jobs were equally crisis driven but more eccentric. Just after Pearl Harbor, the United States frantically dispatched troops to the southwestern Pacific to hold the advancing Japanese. New transports required fifteen thousand "crew berths to be used in ships carrying our troops to Australia." This necessitated 140 miles of rope, but as "expert splicers were not available, sea scouts were excused from the Oakland schools." In seventeen days they completed the berths.[23]

Throughout the war, President Franklin D. Roosevelt feared for public morale. In the wake of Pearl Harbor he worried that defeatism might take hold, and then when victory seemed assured he suspected that overconfidence might lead to a slackening of the war effort. Cities had vast resources to manage morale and keep the population in the fight. These included the press, radio, and much else. Union newspapers, business newsletters, block organization handouts, club bulletins, and movie houses added to the bracing stimulus. So did the sports stadiums, often built with public monies, in which civil defense volunteers staged vast military sham battles and other war theater to keep the populace keyed up for the contest. The communications networks of cities served another important purpose as well: they greatly helped to mobilize the work force. Newspaper ads flooded readers with job possibilities; radio programs began and ended with exhortations to get a job and help the cause, and telephones enabled job seekers to contact the most likely employers. The contrast with underdeveloped American areas is downright stark. In California metropolitan counties, household telephone ownership reached a level of 85 percent. In the Southwest, whence most migrant workers hailed, the highest figure, which was in Texas, was only 37 percent. Thus anyone in the California arsenal cities was much better able to respond to defense work opportunities than someone in Arkansas (which had a telephone ownership of 17 percent).[24]

And in Fortress California, this workforce could be mobilized on a greater variety of transportation forms. California cities had a much higher per capita ownership of autos than other parts of the country, and despite rationing many owners continued to ride their balding tires to the defense plants. Historians and contemporaries have rightly emphasized that, especially in Southern California, a large majority of workers commuted to work in their cars. However, those whose tires had worn out or who were too poor to own an auto could still get to defense plants on mass transit. Both the Los Angeles transit systems—the Los Angeles Railway and the Pacific Electric—and the Market Street Railway in San Francisco had seen better days, yet those, the San Diego trolleys, and the Municipal Railway of San Francisco lumbered along, hauling millions of passengers to and from the defense sites. Even the limping, wounded transit in Los Angeles carried 1,000,000 passengers *daily,* and that in Long Beach and surrounding cities, another 115,000. San Diego trolleys alone conveyed 353,000 daily. The Bay Area had modernized its auto traffic by opening the Bay Bridge and then the Golden Gate Bridge just before the war broke out. A revival of the ferries supplemented these assets. So, for example, workers from San Francisco could travel by car to the Richmond shipyards, by bus to the Moore yards in Oakland, and by trolley to the Hunters Point Shipyard in San Francisco.[25]

Again, it may be instructive to think about the opposite case. For example, women in the southern countryside or hamlets where defense industries did not cluster were kept from contributing to the war effort by the transportation bottlenecks of their areas. Women who had children or other family obligations and could not migrate for the duration to the war centers could have *commuted* to Norfolk, Mobile, or Wilmington defense centers if transportation had been available. However, with few cars and a serious gasoline and rubber shortage, these potentially useful employees were grounded at their farms, hamlets, and towns.[26] This was the case despite the availability of good urban jobs and the critical labor shortages.

And autos carried many more than just the driver and regular passengers. Especially on weekends, servicemen needed rides to town, and hitchhikers were almost invariably rewarded with a lift. Empty trucks halted to load servicemen aboard. When they did not stop, serviceman Gordon Wagenet remembered, a California highway patrolman might pull them over on some frivolous charge while the hitchhiking servicemen piled aboard. This impromptu carpooling probably carried hundreds of thousands.[27]

One of the greatest urban transportation assets to fall into military hands was the harbors. The war in the Pacific required a huge logistical effort for which large cities were ideally suited. These seaports, whether state or municipally owned, were public assets that had been patiently built up over the years to serve the imperial dreams of their cities. Obviously, nature took a hand in providing harbors, especially that of San Francisco. However, even the great natural harbor of San Diego had to be dredged extensively before the Navy could use it. Los Angeles–Long Beach harbor had to be constructed largely de novo. And whether natural or artificial, all the harbors had extensive manmade onshore works, particularly in San Francisco, Oakland, and Los Angeles.

Among other assets that the cities created were the extensive artificial land areas that the port facilities stood on, created out of submerged or tidal lands. These were very considerable in Los Angeles and San Francisco and also important in Oakland, Alameda, and San Diego. The City of Los Angeles alone had invested some $60 million of its own money in its port by the time the war broke out, not to mention other tax moneys recycled to the city through federal rivers and harbors improvements. The State of California put another $86 million into the port of San Francisco and had "1,912 acres of facilities at the Embarcadero."[28]

Of course, harbors were crucial booster projects. In Oakland and Los Angeles, the city builders had championed the move to acquire the waterfronts from the railroads and then led the struggle to improve them. Los Angeles boosters often considered their harbor as more responsible for the growth of the "improbable city" than any other asset, and San Diego, Oakland, and San Francisco esteemed their ports equally well. The federal government operated much harbor space during the war, to its own very marked advantage. As with the housing of resident war workers, the embattled nation state did not have to build docks, warehouses, berths, and beltline railroads anew. As L.A. mayor Fletcher Bowron explained, the government, "desiring possession of facilities to make possible the establishment of a Port of Embarkation at Los Angeles and feeling that *time would not permit the construction of new facilities*, negotiated with the Harbor Commission a plan for utilizing very substantial areas at the port" [emphasis added]. A contemporary observer captured the value of such latent military assets when he noted, "During the early months of the war, San Francisco cleared more military supplies than all the other ports combined."[29]

In the case of airports, the interaction was more equal because airports were not yet an overwhelming presence in cities. In addition, the government built them up somewhat during the war. Yet even before these wartime improvements, the airports could accommodate DC-3 and Boeing 247 planes, so they were a considerable asset before the military enhanced them. And the government did not invariably extend airport facilities. It did those of San Francisco, but it purposely retarded those of Los Angeles for a time. The "sky harbors," as the boosters originally called them, allowed the government to expand and quicken its communications greatly and to shuttle its personnel around much more rapidly than it could by train, auto, or ship. Airports supplied other needs as well. Some coastal surveillance, Coast Guard, and military planes were based there, and Lindbergh Field and the Santa Monica and Los Angeles airports were also aircraft manufacturing sites. While awaiting shipment to the fighting fronts, the planes were stored at Oakland Airport and Long Beach Airport, which housed the Army Ferrying Command. Of course, airports were some of the boosters' proudest works, genuine economic multipliers that would spin off factories, hotels, and real estate bonanzas.[30]

Water was an even more precious resource in the often arid and desert climates of California cities and just as much a booster achievement. This was true even of Northern California cities, which nature supplied better than those of Southern California and the San Joaquin Valley. The Owens Valley Project had taken from 1905 to 1913 to build and to secure water rights, federal permission, public electoral backing, and financial support. This system was enhanced by linking it to the creeks that supplied Mono Lake, an extension completed in 1940. In order to underwrite the development of the rest of the Southland, Los Angeles also joined the movement to dam the Colorado. In 1931, the Metropolitan Water District of Southern California, which Los Angeles dominated, voted $220 million to build an aqueduct from Parker Dam to convey the water to Riverside for distribution in that city and to the remainder of the Southland. Despite its arid natural state, at the beginning of the war the area boasted a vast surplus of water. At the time of its completion, the Colorado River hydraulic system was not yet crucial to the Los Angeles area. Between the groundwater at places like Long Beach and the San Fernando Valley and the Owens Valley–Mono system already in place, Los Angeles and its neighbors had plenty of water. Except in Santa Monica, "the [Colorado] water is a stand-by supply that is sometimes used," asserted the *Times*. [31]

The experts estimated that the Colorado supply was enough to provide for an extra 2 million people. Los Angeles had laid the groundwork for war well because that conflict brought nearly 400,000 civilians and thousands more military personnel to use their water. San Diego added another 100,000 plus, but that city did not keep pace with hydraulic works of its own. Consequently, the Navy's heavy demands during the war nearly made the Border City hydro-bankrupt. However, when the Navy subsidized San Diego's efforts to secure fresh supplies, that city also tapped into the Riverside terminal of the Los Angeles–financed Colorado Aqueduct. [32]

The most spectacular Angeleno liquid contribution came not from its downtown gin mills, but from the establishment of a training center in the high Mojave Desert. Realizing that American troops would soon see action against Germany in North Africa, the Army sought a geographic area similar to that terrain. Because the Colorado River Aqueduct ran right by the site, the abundant urban water supply enabled the Army to create the enormous Desert Training Center, renamed the California-Arizona Maneuver Area (CAMA), at Shavers (now Chiriaco) Summit, some thirty miles east of Indio. General David C. Henley noted that "CAMA was the world's largest military installation, both in size and population." Starting in 1942, over one million men and women trained there, with 191,620 at one time in 1943. General George Patton located, created, and initially commanded the center. Given his achievements in armored warfare, the center must have served him and his troops well. [33]

Oakland and the East Bay joined together in the East Bay Municipal Utilities District (EBMUD) in 1923. Their system, based on the Mokelumne River, was completed between 1923 and 1929. It required twenty years for San Francisco to finish the Hetch Hetchy Valley waterworks, which was opened in 1934 at a cost of $100 million. Subsequently extended, it eventually supplied several peninsula cities and San José besides providing for San Francisco.[34]

The impossibility of mounting a war effort in a desert like Los Angeles or San Diego without a well-developed water supply is clear. Both San Francisco and Los Angeles have been perennially denounced for the manner in which they acquired their original long-distance supplies of water, but without the public aqueducts of EBMUD, Hetch Hetchy, the Owens Valley, and the Colorado, the war simply could not have been fought out of those geographic sites. It took six years to build Boulder Dam, nine years to construct the Colorado Aqueduct, six years to finish EBMUD, seven years to construct the Owens Valley system, and nearly twenty years to complete Hetch Hetchy. These complex hydraulic works could not simply be instantly improvised like paving the streets of Pascagoula or throwing up wartime temporary housing in Mobile!

In addition, both the Los Angeles and San Francisco aqueducts generated power in their fall from the mountains to the sea. Those cities' contribution of power, unlike water, was not as great as that of the private companies in the Bay Area. But in Southern California, which benefited from both the Owens Valley system and Boulder Dam, the reverse was true. This windfall of plentiful, cheap power aided the arsenals of democracy, especially the aircraft industry.[35]

Public open spaces contributed another advantage. Although urban areas are by their very nature comparatively congested, American cities from the mid–nineteenth century on provided considerable public open spaces for municipal recreation. These fields came in the form of both small playgrounds and large parks. California cities built both, including the magnificent Griffith Park in Los Angeles, Balboa Park in San Diego, and Golden Gate Park in San Francisco. These spaces were handy for the military. It used them for cantonments, with the dry climate allowing servicemen to camp in them, considerably alleviating the need to provide other housing. Before long, tents sprouted in the smaller parks and public spaces of San Francisco, such as Funston Park in the Marina District and the Civic Center. Other canvas went up in Exposition Park next to the Coliseum in Los Angeles. In fact, San Diego went the whole way, giving the park over to a full-fledged marine installation, Camp Kidd. The Navy Hospital was already located in Balboa Park. Beyond the zoo, much of the park was a military area for the duration. Even the most unusual urban open space proved useful. In a San Diego cemetery, the Army established a base, which sent up barrage balloons whenever there was an air raid alert. And, of course, the government snapped up private open space as well.[36]

Not the least contribution was the urban infrastructure. Public roads, sewers, overpasses, and culverts absolved the government from building these crucial works, which it could not have done without and could not build in time. In particular, the war impacted heavily on sewers, streets, and roads. As Lawrence Kinnaird has noted, Bay Area city streets deteriorated from heavy wartime truck traffic. The military spent some money to improve streets, but cities picked up the remainder of the bill. Nor could treatment plants handle the added load generated by increased populations. Cities simply had to dump raw sewage into the ocean and bays, polluting and closing beaches to swimming at a time of optimum demand for recreation. Municipalities could not obtain scarce materials and priorities to build the new plants that they desperately needed. After the war, every city faced expensive referenda to remedy the situation.[37]

Schools also had a vast latent war capacity. Even before the schools delivered any military education, they made other crucial contributions. They were ideally suited for rationing centers because they were housed in already running buildings; they were within walking distance of those who would be rationed and therefore saved gas, rubber, and transit wear and tear; and they had a corps of "loyal, kindly" teachers who could staff the system and who knew the legitimate needs of their neighborhoods. In addition, the conflict created a great need to learn new skills, and the public school systems taught many of them. Block wardens wanted to perfect first aid; high school males and adult women must learn welding; and servicemen needed to master languages and understand the history and cultures of the lands they would liberate. The regular school kids went home around three o'clock in the afternoon, and from then, sometimes until midnight, the educational task of winning the war proceeded. All over Urban California schools housed the training centers used to prepare unskilled women and minorities for the production lines. The Los Angeles Negro Victory Committee understood this clearly when it insisted on the establishment of training centers near black homes and conducted a demonstration at the city school board to get them. Schools promoted both arms of the Double V.

And even when the government constructed new schools, as it did for some housing projects, such as Linda Vista in San Diego, the latent resources of cities played a role. Anxious to expand production in San Diego aircraft companies, the government built public war housing first. However, they took another full year to construct the schools. "Consequently, we taught in houses until the schools were built," recalled

Edward Ortiz. Sometimes the schools simply altered their regular offerings to accommodate the military. Twenty-four hours a day the Samuel Gompers Trades School trained adults, both for civilian jobs such as sewing machine operation in the garment industry and for skilled labor in industry; high school boys who wanted to earn a degree and a trade at the same time; and even service personnel. Each morning a gray bus from Treasure Island unloaded sailors at the Mission District school to master trades from engine repairs to Morse code.[38]

Colleges tapped out the same message. The war threatened to depopulate the universities because their "workforce" was heavily draft-age, young, and male. By subcontracting to train servicemen, the universities salvaged some of their operation by bringing the college boys back, and the government received services without constructing new schools. Under this arrangement, the University of Southern California offered seventy-six courses under the "engineering, science, and defense management training program of the U. S. Office of Education." Best of all for the individual trainee, the government paid the tuition. To the north, higher education found yet another mission. On December 21, 1942, Santa Barbara State College graduated its first class of "aircraft engine mechanics and machine shop workers after months . . . of intensive training." And Stanford University trained civil defense volunteers to cope with the incendiary bombs favored by the Imperial Japanese.[39]

A slightly more idiosyncratic school system operated in the prisons. San Quentin's "war training classes" taught the cooks who prepared food on the convoy ships. As the *Chronicle* reporter tactfully put it, "When graduation and parole dates arrive [Jean] Tigare [the master chef] enrolls his proteges in the high-paying jobs with the Marine Cooks and Stewards' Association." So "successful are the . . . culinary classes that the War Manpower Commission has requested enrollment of 500 more pupils," said Warden Clinton T. Duffy. San Quentin taught others to weld, type, take shorthand, and use business English "as preparation for defense jobs."[40]

The built environment proved to be another boon to the government. In the wake of Pearl Harbor, the Navy, Marines, and Army moved into vacant office space and even on occasion evicted civilians from theirs. Various headquarters units found space in the skyscrapers of downtown San Francisco, and other buildings proved equally useful. For example, the famous Fairmont Hotel, Nob Hill survivor of the 1906 earthquake, became a transient officers quarters. The Navy took over the Globe Theater in San Diego's Balboa Park, and other elements occupied private mansions on Point Loma for military research. Downtown, the government moved a filter center into the Spreckels Building, and when that facility became obsolete, they put the new radar control center in the Fox Theater building. On occasion, the military even rented civilian housing, as in the case of the first six female marines sent to San Francisco, who were "bivouacked" in a local boarding house.[41]

Besides these big categories, there were myriad other ways in which the latent resources of the city promoted the nation state's war. These ranged from garment shops to junk heaps. Jane Jacobs, Betty Smith, and David Nasaw have reminded American urbanists that a city, among other things, is a world-class junk heap. Trash can be very useful either to poor kids selling scrap or to Japanese automakers buying it. Scrap collection for the war is well known, but some kinds of junk particularly illustrate the vast range of uses for trash. As Northern California cities abandoned their trolleys, tons of high-grade scrap in the form of abandoned steel rails became available to the war effort. These alone were enough to supply the steel for 175 medium tanks. Before the advent of full services in Los Angeles, wood-burning potbellied stoves were used "by the Fire Department . . . when outlying fire stations were without gas." Twenty-five of these were discovered by city councilman Delamere McCloskey, who turned them into a defense asset, though "it took him nearly four months to unwind the red tape" necessary to lend them to the Red Cross. Ultimately, they ensured that "soldiers occupying isolated searchlight posts in the San Fernando Valley could keep warm on winter nights."[42]

If these examples seem unduly eccentric, it must be remembered that California cities uncovered literal mountains of other scrap in the regular drives as well. By mid-1942, the Southland alone had unearthed 13.8 million tons of scrap, including "vast quantities" in "auto graveyards," and had "set a quota for the second half of the year at 17,000,000 tons." World War II Essex Class aircraft carriers weighed 27,100 tons, so the yearly total could provide the steel required to build several complete carriers at a time when there were precious few of them. At mid-year, when the 13.8 million tons had been collected, the U.S. had just won the decisive Battle of Midway. After it, the Navy had only two remaining carriers in the entire Pacific! To provide further context, during World War II, the United States outproduced the Imperial Japanese in carriers by a score of 104 to 14, so there must have been some other cities that were doing their part, too.[43]

Sometimes the junking was good riddance, and sometimes it was not. When the earthquake and fire of 1906 decimated the San Francisco central business district, merchants moved west to Fillmore Street to begin anew. The merchants and property owners of that area hoped

Removing the governor's cuffs to conserve fabric.
Courtesy Huntington Library.

that the transfer would be permanent and mark their street instead of Union Square and Market Street as the center of town. To make their neighborhood more appropriate to its hoped-for glorious future, the merchants constructed and lighted fourteen arches over the street. The merchants paid for the arches, and the city supplied the lights. Thirty-five years later, their dreams of business grandeur had long since been dashed by the renaissance of the central business district in its former location. With their lights "extinguished to keep down 'sky glow'" that might guide attacking planes and "the metal needed for armaments," the merchants sadly consented to the removal of the Fillmore Arches for military scrap. No such sentimentality accompanied the contribution of one hundred thousand "pounds of old metal" from San Quentin. As an observer put it, probably with considerable understatement, "convicts joined the [scrap] drive with gusto yesterday, tossing cell bars from an abandoned steel dungeon onto the scrap heap."[44]

Stockton raised the linkage of waste and warfare to its ultimate level. Overnight, on the derelict Banner Island landfill site in the San Joaquin River, Guntert, Zimmerman, and Higginbotham Brothers created a shipyard. Although the patriotic sanctification of Stockton's rubbish cannot be said to have been a watershed equal to El Alamein or Midway, the yard produced vital small vessels and sixty-ton cranes for ports.[45]

The established charity institutions coped with other derelicts. Susan Laughlin, women's counselor for Lockheed-Vega, often found herself with employees who were actually in need. As Laughlin put it, "Ivy Grace with the Salvation Army was fantastic. She would do anything for us. If we sent somebody to her, she always said, 'We give soup, soap, and salvation in the order that it comes.'" That sustained, scrubbed, and perhaps saved a soul. It also kept the war effort rolling by solving employee problems that could otherwise lead to absenteeism.[46]

The economic and industrial prowess of the United States and the importance of industrialism to American success has been much written about. For example, Harold Vatter makes the critical point that the United States won the Second World War with only modest additions to the industrial capacity that it had possessed in 1929. That was one of the most remarkable facts of World War II. However, cities made a singular contribution as well; and without the increasingly high degree of urbanization, even industry would have been hampered in its response to the war. To an extraordinary degree, boosters built California cities and created them much larger than any natural law of urbanization would have sanctioned. For example, due to the lack of water, Southern California had a very limited capacity to urbanize under technological conditions existing in the first half of the century. Without the boosters, it would have remained a much smaller place. That is another way of saying that without the boosters, the Second World War military would have had to build endless miles of roads, highways, bridges, sanitary and storm sewers, open space, docks, berths, breakwaters, aqueducts, power plants, housing, educational plants, recreational venues, and other requirements of war. Expending those resources would have made the war much less efficient. Not only did the presence of large cities allow the nation state to avoid these expenses and the attendant time delays, it also enabled the government to evade many of the costs of war, such as damaged streets and polluted beaches, which the cities had to assume and their residents had to endure.[47]

To date, California homefront historians have been loath to recognize this major contribution. Fittingly, much has been written about the industrial prowess of California firms who created the shipbuilding and aircraft-building miracles. Beyond that, it could perhaps also be said that California and most other local homefront history has been recorded as a story of impacts, whether written from a radical, liberal, or traditionalist point of view. Each assumes that the most important story is about the impact of the war on either their groups or their sections. Thus some historians are disappointed with the outcome of the war because the conflict established the conditions for a ghettoized future for minorities such as Mexicans and blacks. Others praise the progress of women, African Americans, and Hispanics, but point out realistically that the progress stopped well short of equality. Still others look to the impact of the war on the West per se and posit great change because of the contest. These points of view have been endlessly productive, but focusing only on the impact of war on society implies that society had no impact upon war. That is another way of minimizing the importance of cities. Even those writing general histories of the homefront, although painting a much wider canvas of the conflict, omit the urban dimension.[48]

This is not to argue that the cities did it all. Obviously, the federal government contributed substantially long before, just before, and during the war. Washington lent the moneys to build the Bay Bridge in San Francisco, used public moneys to fashion Treasure Island, helped Los Angeles obtain the water rights to the Owens Valley, allowed San Francisco to dam up the Hetch Hetchy Valley, and lent the moneys to the Colorado Compact states to build Boulder Dam. It also improved some streets, ports, and airports during the conflict. San Diego benefited especially from this largesse. And the war emergency ultimately elevated the Los Angeles Airport to a top priority that belatedly allowed the city to obtain the materials to complete parts of that facility.[49] San Francisco Airport received similar stimuli. City politicians like Mayor Fletcher Bowron of Los Angeles ultimately came to believe that the federal government did not contribute its fair share of the defense costs imposed on cities, but it clearly did pay some. Yet the government usually did not supply the impetus for such major prewar projects as the bridges, dams, and hydraulic works. Los Angeles actually elbowed a federal Bureau of Reclamation project out of the way in order to eliminate a competitor for the Owens Valley water.[50]

The government lent moneys, but was no more responsible for the outcome than private lenders, who lent the moneys to build the Golden Gate Bridge. And as with a loan from a private bank, in the case of Boulder Dam every cent was repaid to the national authority. The concentration of these assets in cities constituted the latent resources that helped win the war. And even when the government did grant, lend, or authorize projects, these projects almost invariably originated at the local level under booster leadership. With the exception of naval expenditures that also benefited cities, the local public works were usually in no way an outcome of national public policy. The locals initiated them and paid for them with private moneys or those recycled to them as their share of the taxes spent for local public improvements around the country. And even when the federal government did pay for some of these, it was merely financing the local imperial projects, such as the Bay Bridge or Treasure Island, of city boosters, who wrested public financing from the government to guarantee their position within the projects. And these same people also fashioned much national legislation, like that to aid airports, which came down from Washington.

Americans have traditionally exhibited much hostility to their cities. Historians disagree somewhat over the depth of this antagonism, but it seems evident enough. Whether the animosity is a majority view or a minority one, American aversion to cities is very deep. Perhaps western cities have come in for more abuse, possibly because they do not always resemble eastern ones. Los Angeles has been a special target. Carl Abbott discovered one such anonymous detractor, who called the City of the Angels "topless, bottomless, shapeless and endless . . . random, frenzied, rootless, unplanned," a "violently aggressive organism." The same is said of San José, "the Los Angeles of the North," and other California cities.[51]

Whatever the case may be today, *during World War II*, California cities contributed markedly to the war effort. The latent military resources of Golden State cities far outweighed the diseconomies, such as crowded housing, inadequate day care, overburdened infrastructure, discrimination, and crowded schools. Because it was far from the fighting fronts, rapid urbanization did not create the disecomony of congestion that would heighten cities' vulnerability to military attack. Well out of harm's way, California urbanites could concentrate on production rather than defense. Of course, the nation state could have conducted the war in the Pacific even if the West Coast had not yet been urbanized. However, it was a lot easier to fight the war with so many advantages built into the jumping-off points. The government did not have to divert enormous amounts of either time or resources to creating these assets. Cities allowed the war effort to be conducted with much more efficiency than if cities were not so "endless." Had California cities not been "violently aggressive organisms" and had they not indulged in urban aggrandizement, they would have been much smaller and less useful in the campaign against Japanese and Nazi imperialism. The country was lucky to be a nation of cities, and California was luckier still. Had the Golden State been a Jeffersonian idyll with few cities or even rural like the American South, winning the war would have been infinitely more difficult. *In this case,* bigger was better.

4. Tijuana Breakfast
Learning from the Women of
Rancho San Rafael and Wake Island

"Help Wanted"—"Help Wanted"—"Jobs"—"Jobs"—"Jobs": Juanita Loveless remembered the entreaties swimming around in her brain. "If you're an American Citizen, come to gate so and so; at Lockheed or at the shipyards in San Pedro," she recalled, "they were begging for workers." Not only was she "bombarded" by movie newsreels and newspaper articles demanding, cajoling, imploring people to come to work in defense industries, she was subjected to high-pressure recruiting while she was actually at work: "Every day someone came in saying, 'Do you want a job?' My head was going crazy," she recalled. "I was having people approach me six to ten times a day." The war must have seemed like the promised land to people like Loveless, starved by the Depression, broke, "no experience, and I was under age." Like so many other Californians, she came from the scorched Southwest, Texas, and Oklahoma. She first worked in agriculture at Indio, and from there she visited Hollywood and Los Angeles; remembering them after she went home, she decided to return. In what amounted to a carpool of migrants, who rented a ride in a private automobile, back she went to the Golden State. Once in California, she was astonished by the demand for workers. At home, she had been begging for work. In California, it was the other way around. In the words of a historian of black migrant women, "Word of employment was everywhere, electrifying the atmosphere of streetcars, markets, theaters, diners, and dance halls."[1]

From the beginning, even before entering the defense factories, Loveless was doing work that was non-traditional for women. She started by setting pins in a bowling alley. That job lasted for two days, and then she pumped gas at a filling station. Another recruiter wooed her away from that "situation" on the outside of the car to one as a grease monkey below, which lasted six months. She also took a second job during that time. But the patriotic and monetary pressure to join the defense effort was so intense that Juanita finally succumbed and went to work in the "cavernous" Vega Aircraft Plant. However, she did not abandon her moonlighting during her stay at the Lockheed subsidiary; she continued her work at other war-related, but not strictly defense, jobs. One was "for a record cutting company; we'd cut records and make tape recordings for the servicemen to send back home."[2]

> I also worked for a fellow in Glendale who had a storage garage. As the young men were going to war, they would store their cars with him. He hired me to come over and take each car out every other day or so and put a few miles on it to keep up the engine and I'd check the water, check the tires, check the oil, and sometimes lubricate them. He wasn't paying me very much, but I got gas coupons and I'd take a car occasionally to work.

In 1944, she quit Vega, disillusioned with the war; yet her story illustrates both the impact of the war on women and the impact of women on the war. Their role was vastly greater than the famous "Rosie the Riveter" paradigm would indicate.

Although the topics of women in wage-labor, gender, and discrimination have largely dominated the thinking of historians of women in World War II, most women did not work for wages. Either they stayed at home and contributed or they worked in volunteer activities. Thus to gain an understanding of urban women at war, we must address these experiences. In addition to assessing the variety of paid work that women did, we must look at both their unpaid and volunteer experiences. Many women combined both roles, worker and housewife, and many had been doing so for some time. In early 1943, at a time when thousands of females worked in Pacific Coast shipyards, Marinship in Sausalito compiled a profile of women workers in their own yards from their application blanks. Nearly 60 percent were married and nearly all, 83 percent, had worked previously as waitresses, housekeepers, and low-income factory workers. Marinship employees were most often blue collar and usually had no children, but they were married, so they had houses to manage. So did those who moved into their jobs as they moved into defense work. The war presented real problems to both.[3]

One solution was willing husbands. Most of the World War II literature emphasizes women's crossing of gender boundaries in work, but men did so also in order to help their wives with housework. Helen Studer remembered of her husband, "We were equal. And he always helped me whenever he was around. And I never had to ask him. . . . He just automatically did what had to be done." Charlcia Neuman agreed: "My husband helped me a lot with the housework. . . . He was very strong and could do his work and then help me with some of mine, too."[4]

Otherwise, they coped as best they could. Child care plagued all women, defense workers or not. The Lanham Act provided day-care facilities for 130,000 children in the country, a paltry number compared to the need. Female leaders fought for Lanham centers, and from 1943 onward the government created 25,566 places in California, not sufficient to care for defense children. State, management, and union aid was minimal, so mothers looked elsewhere. Most relied on families, husbands, sisters, older children, and especially mothers. For example, single parent Marye Stumph's mother moved in to care for the kids, and Mom then branched out to mind children of other defense mothers. Helen Studer, like many others, chose the night shift so as to be home with her daughter during the day. Some relied on the "Vickies," others on commercial day care. There were six thousand day-care centers in the state, some costly, some scandalous, but altogether too few. Given the shortfall, it is puzzling that women, precocious at creating voluntary organizations, did not found them for day care too. In any case most mothers associated public child care with welfare and refused even to use the existing centers. Although women's spokespersons then, as have modern historians, emphasized the need for public child care, white mothers flatly opposed it, and 83 percent depended on family and neighbors. So did African Americans.[5]

Women's work shifts often left them little time for the supermarket. The government did not emulate the British policy of "released time" to shop. Nonworking sisters shopped for some women, others had husbands who did the shopping, and many squeezed their buying between quitting time at the factory and closing time at the store. The successful consumers often had deals with the grocers, who slipped them an extra bit of sugar or coffee when they had it. That expedient was unsatisfactory because by quitting time many scarce items had been cleaned off the market shelves. So women often had to take time off from work to catch up with the store. Nonworking wives had a distinct advantage here.[6]

Child care affected the hours that women worked. Many periodically took days off to cope with child care. Others worked the swing shift so that they might be home during the part of the day when their children were in the house. Susan Laughlin discovered another rationale of swing shifting: "We found that an awful lot of women whose husbands were gone liked that swing shift because [during] the hours when they would most miss their husbands, they were occupied. . . . We recommended it finally to girls who were pretty unstrung."[7]

Recognizing the need for female workers came very early in the conflict. Before the war was even four months old, the National Industrial Conference Board was calling for the registration of "all American women to determine the number available and qualified for industrial war work." Government agencies issued "long lists of workers desperately needed," while pressure was applied to schools to train skilled workers and professionals.

And women immediately began entering the workforce to meet these demands. It would appear that some joined the workforce in a multi-staged process. First they took non-defense jobs, such as pin setter, grease monkey, and filling station attendant, when men vacated those positions to take higher-paying defense jobs, especially in aircraft and shipbuilding. Then as better-paying, but not premier, industrial jobs, such as those in textile plants, manufacturing cloth and bags, opened up, women occupied these. Finally, as the services sopped up the young male draft pool, women made the next step into the prime industrial positions, which were 40 percent higher paying than the usual female work. Soon there were no young men in these positions, though the wives of young men abounded. Sometimes women entered the better-paying sector through traditional female work such as cooking and waitressing in the cafeterias at the aircraft factories and shipyards. When the men left the production jobs for war, the women moved up and over within the airplane and shipbuilding companies. Charles Wollenberg explained that the "breakthrough at Marinship came in the summer of 1942, when the company began hiring women craft workers." The largest category of women workers was in welding, first on the less demanding jobs and then on heavier, more dangerous ones. The breakthrough for women draftsmen (as they were called then) in shipbuilding began as an anticipatory program even before the war began.[8]

The percentage of women at Marinship rapidly rose to 23.3 percent by the end of 1943 and remained over 20 percent through the end of 1944. In aircraft, the figures sometimes reached 40 or 50 percent. One historian estimated that the California aircraft women amounted to one-third of all workers in that industry in the United States.[9]

Working conditions were often disagreeable and dangerous. Welders in the Vallejo yard had to wallow in grime to get to parts of the ships. Others had to use blowers to evaporate rainwater and then lie on their backs and weld. Once Lockheed "was building airplanes in the open" and it was pouring rain. The girls' hands would get so cold, remembered Susan Laughlin, that she protested to Cyril Chappellet, the executive in charge. He explained that they were building a structure around the outdoor work space but it was not completed. In the meantime, the planes had to be assembled, so the women stayed in the cold and built them. Women suffered fewer accidents than men with the exception of the shipbuilding industry. There they experienced more injuries, more severe injuries, and longer recovery periods than men.[10]

In California, the most famous working women labored in the aircraft and shipbuilding industries. Both were novel experiences. First came the training programs. These were crucial both for the war effort and for the psychological well-being of the women. The responsibility of getting the job right and avoiding rewiring "was very frightening to me," explained Helen Studer. Failure in their work could cause great frustration, which sometimes left the women in tears. Male teachers or coworkers were often indifferent or unhelpful. However, many, including some in top management, were very constructive. Lockheed stood out in this respect. They tested every position in the factory by putting female workers in the jobs to see which ones suited them best. Sometimes the training was very high-powered. In the Bay Area, the University of California trained 3,500 women as draftspersons, especially for shipbuilding and aircraft, which required lots of detailed drawings.[11]

Bernice Hubbard May, an administrator of another program, remembered that in all the testing to determine the suitability of women for a given job, the officials tried the process out on her first. If she could perform the function, it was assumed that all women could. Women were also examined for emotional stability. For example, the Engineering, Science, and Management War Training (ESMWT) program at Berkeley did all of the testing for emotional stability for Lockheed and others as well. "If the tests showed that they were emotionally stable, then we sent them to Lockheed, but if they didn't pass, we sent them to Douglas," she wryly recalled. At first, the requirements for admission were rigorous: "trigonometry, mechanical drawing, solid geometry and so on," May recollected. "Later the pressure [of the labor shortage] was so great that we began asking applicants, 'Can you add your bridge score?'"[12]

If they could, the next hurdle was the dress code. In the white-collar jobs, the secretaries established the canon, so draftswomen dressed as they did. In the factories and plants, more practical rationales prevailed. Hairnets and slacks or overalls were mandatory for safety reasons. No loose-flowing tresses or dresses could be tolerated close to dangerous, high-speed machinery. In the aircraft industry women wore hairnets or bandannas, but the shipyards frequently required a hard hat. "It could never be off our heads," reminisced Mary Jean Potts, "they were very strict about it." Mare Island female welders were into heavy leather long before it became fashionable. Leather gloves up to the elbow replaced genteel ones; leather clothing supplanted skirts and sweaters. And every welder had to wear a hood. Women felt foolish in these clumsy getups, but safety dictated their use.

They felt funnier still when they were told to wear protective plastic brassieres, but the women were game. They went into the changing rooms, tried them on, and howled with laughter. Effie Walling recalled:

> You should have seen them. They were plastic and no give. Absolutely no give at all. . . . Well, we couldn't wear them. . . . We put them on and stood there until we were hysterical. Then we took them out and told the men "Sorry, they [the authorities] made a mistake."

Leather gloves and pants, steel-toed shoes, and hard hats they would accept, but plastic bras . . . "There was no way." In the shipyards, badges replaced brooches, and depending on the work, women supplanted their ornamental belts with tool belts, heavy with contraptions. Jewelry, rings, and earrings fell under the same ban as dresses. Excessive makeup did too, and some supervisors at Moore Dry Dock even barred fingernail polish to minimize distractions to male workers.[13]

Then there was the noise, which was monumental. Gigi Sanders remembered that "you just heard it . . . drills, rivet guns, all the racket going on." "The noise was absolutely terrible," remembered Helen Studer. And the hours were long and often not voluntary or predictable. As Gigi Sanders remembered her overtime work, "They [the foremen] said, 'you and you will stay over tonight so many hours,' and we did. Everybody wanted to." If it rained in Vallejo, the welding had to go on anyway, puddles or no. Besides sharing jobs, women also shared considerable danger. Welding flashes burned the eyes, heat prostration threatened workers dressed in such heavy clothes in the summer, burns multiplied, and "galvanized poison" fumes threatened the welders working on the galvanized metal in the turrets.[14]

Historians have accurately emphasized the novelty of security checks and the work itself, but often the work spaces were even more novel. Mary Jean Potts remembered that "it was just very exciting to go on a ship for the first time, because I had never been on a big ship of any kind. . . . We had to climb down the ladders of the decks, which was the most amazing thing for me, because I had never done anything like that before," she recalled. "It was like being an acrobat!" Plant size amazed even more. "I was awed, really awed," Helen Studer said; "it is [was] so huge."[15]

Then there were the oddities and patriotic overtones, not normally associated with factory work. One was the beautiful inspectors. Female employees remembered that the working women were older and average looking, but the "lady" inspectors were always young and stunning. Factory lore had it that only the gorgeous women could get those relatively untaxing jobs. Katherine Archibald minimized the presence of prostitution in the yards, but other contemporary observers thought it thrived in the lower depths of the ships and elsewhere. Other pastimes occurred more in the open. Since people worked six days a week and often ten or twelve hours per day, the war shortchanged their recreational lives. So another set of volunteers had a solution for this deprivation as well. Astonishingly enough, stars from the amusement industry appeared to entertain the workers at lunch and dinner chow breaks! There was a big stage at the Convair plant on which the USO presented shows for the wartime working stiffs. "There was one night and I'll always remember this," Gigi Sanders said in awe, "Sophie Tucker came" to perform.[16]

A ceremony accompanied the launching of ships or the completion of landmark airplanes. At the Vallejo Naval Shipyard each ship had to be christened, sometimes by the wife of a Bay Area notable, sometimes by one of the female shipyard employees. In late 1944, Marinship went them one better by launching a ship with an all-female cast of participants, from the speakers to the dignitaries to the color guard. Upon completion of its five-thousandth plane, Convair at San Diego held a "big dedication." All of the men and women who had worked on the craft climbed into the cockpit and signed the log book, and the supervisors signed their names on the outside.

Other memorable moments were not so festive and more impromptu. One learned about them the hard way. When older workers arrived looking grave and were asked why the long faces, the men replied, "Well, my son. . . ." "Several of the fellows that we worked with, the older men, their sons were killed in the service and I tell you, that was trying," remembered Effie Walling.[17]

Sometimes breakthroughs in employment for women came easily. The Long Beach post office encountered no opposition when it hired thirty-five female employees and planned to add more. But progress often required a struggle against both employers, reluctant to hire women, and unions, reluctant to work with them or allow them into traditionally all-male jobs. Gradually the men came to accept, or at least tolerate, female

The explosion of jobs in defense industries
meant an expanding role for women in the workplace.
Courtesy Library of Congress, Prints & Photographs Division, FSA-OWI Collection.

coworkers, and management such as Marinship's and Lockheed's went to considerable lengths to counsel both genders in order to break down bias. Counseling seemed to work well. So did training. Some Lockheed supervisors would not do a single thing to help women adjust to their new surroundings, but the Lockheed Corporation itself went to considerable lengths to test women in every job and put women in the ones where they could perform best for the war effort. It also mounted a considerable public relations campaign to explain the need for women workers to their communities.[18]

Men have often been described as hostile to working with women, but both men and women seemed to cope pretty well. Effie Walling noted the absence of a battle of the sexes. She thought that men accepted women after a while as work partners and did not try to show them up by greatly outperforming them. In the aircraft factories, they quite frequently worked as teams. "Bucking" rivets was heavier work than riveting, so men often "bucked" the rivets on the outside of the plane and women "shot them" home from within. That was a rational division of labor, as was the custom of women's working in confined spaces because they were smaller than men. Walling also remembered that most of the women did not try to compete with the men. Katherine Archibald noted that men treated women with the utmost respect, as they would their wives, mothers, or daughters. However, she felt that underneath, men seethed with resentment at the presence of women in the yards. Others noted an initial anger, which receded as men understood the necessity of women workers. Commentators have often emphasized that men came to accept women workers "for the duration" only, but it would seem that most women also wanted to be there just "for the duration." Effie Walling remembered that both she and most women at the Vallejo Navy Yard wanted to quit once the war was over. In any case, many women and men seemed to get along famously, despite the age disparity in the factories. And romances blossomed all over the cavernous aircraft plants amidst the chattering rivet guns and wailing power hoists. Effie Walling found the same phenomenon in the Vallejo Navy Yard, as did Katherine Archibald at Moore Dry Dock in Oakland.[19]

War plant "amour" was the prime motivation of one of the groups most stubbornly opposed to women at work. Wives feared that their husbands would be tempted by the presence "of the adventure-seeking woman and the vastly experimental unmarried girl." Other women objected because they thought that working women neglected their children. Susan Laughlin, women's counselor at Lockheed, tried to explain women in the workplace to the public in a series of meetings, and she found audiences made up of mothers who wanted women *in* the home. Sheila Lichtman found skepticism of women workers by female counselors and personnel supervisors but noted that "oldtime craftsmen also resented new male workers, often distrusting them as much as or more than they distrusted women." The gender map was very complicated.[20]

Supervisory work illustrates the point. The glass ceiling seemed a reality to some women, but that issue requires much more research. Women held numerous supervisory positions, yet even that issue is complicated by seniority, skill, productivity, danger, and other matters. The issue of pay is equally complicated. Women's historians emphasize discrimination, although some women actually working in the war industries claimed that the pay for men and women was equal for comparable work. Historians of women at war argue that the pay differential had narrowed markedly in new plants by the conclusion of the conflict. Certainly government and unions were committed to the principle of equal pay for equal work. Other experts argue that women earned more during the war, but hardly enough to live on, and that the gender gap actually increased. However, by this same testimony women accepted their pay status and were glad to earn the higher wages.[21]

No matter how that question is sorted out, another equity issue is usually ignored. The government remunerated service-men and -women much less than civilians earned in defense employment. When the war broke out, Uncle Sam paid privates $21.00 a month. Women earned vastly more in the martial industries. For example, Effie Walling earned $6.50 a day by war's end, or $156.00 per twenty-four-day month (that is, four 6-day, or 48-hour, work weeks). In other words, in three days her pay almost equaled the monthly salary of a private at the beginning of the war. Mary Jean Potts received $.92 an hour, or $7.36 a day, or $176.64 per twenty-four-day month. In her case, three days yielded *more* than a serviceman's entire *monthly* check. Gigi Sanders earned $.85 an hour when she began in 1944 and $1.15 per hour in 1945 when the war ended. She and her co-workers often put in a ten-hour day, six days a week. Not counting overtime, that would amount to $51.00 or $69.00 for a sixty-hour week at the beginning and ending rates. On a monthly basis, their pay would have been $204.00 and $276.00 per month.[22]

In August 1942, trainees for sewing machine jobs in San Francisco's low-paid garment industry, hardly the salaried elite of working persons, could expect between $15.00 and $35.00 compensation per week, or $60.00 to $140.00 per month, three to seven times more per month than a soldier. Of course, civilian males often realized even more. Merchant seamen could earn $750 to $1000 a month. Admittedly, that was a dangerous job, but so was the "work" of the marines on Guadalcanal. Service pay rose, and servicemen received room (when not in combat), food, and clothing, but compensation never caught up with civilian defense workers. By mid-war, service pay was only $50.00 per month, and many risked their lives in the bargain. So while some men did receive more than women working in the same plant, both received more than the 12.5 million military personnel did. On a range from lowest to highest paid, women ranked in the middle. Moreover, as in combat, men did most of the dangerous work in industry.[23]

It is perhaps worth emphasizing that although many men lost only time during the war and did not risk their lives, 27 percent (3,375,000) did, and many "jobs" were shockingly dangerous. Until the end of 1943, Army air raids over Germany routinely lost 10 to 20 percent of their planes and crews. On the famous Schweinfurt raids (casualties, 20 percent), the German countryside was illuminated for hundreds of miles by fallen and burning Flying Fortresses. So if the issue is pay equity, we must remember that one of the most conspicuously gendered aspects of the payroll question was the disparity between the earnings that men collected from the military services versus the income women received in homefront war work. Moreover, the issue of gendered pay is also clouded by men's ability to do more and heavier work. Women often commented that they could not perform certain heavy lifting jobs, and management kept them out of these. In addition, as welder Effie Walling noted, men could weld twice as fast as women. She thought women welded as well in a qualitative sense, but that due to men's ability to withstand greater heat, they could turn it up and weld much faster. Charlcia Neuman spoke frankly of her work at Vega: "The experience was interesting, but I couldn't have kept it up forever. It was too hard."[24]

Another aspect of male-female relations is the postwar jobs issue. According to a Women's Bureau and New York State Department of Labor study at the end of the war, 75 percent of female defense workers wanted to keep their jobs or get similar ones instead of returning to home or to women's traditional wage-labor. However, that apparently was not the case for many women, who wanted to return to the home. Susan Laughlin, counselor at Lockheed and Vega, with great experience dealing with women during the war and herself an advocate of women working outside the home, said that most women expected to quit when the Japanese did. "They didn't expect anything else," said Laughlin, "it was an understood fact." Women often noted that the kind of defense work that they embraced during the war was not suited to them because it was too heavy, hot, fatiguing, or dangerous. Effie Walling spoke for most of these women when she said, "I don't know how the women are today, but boy I'll tell you[,] a man's job they can have. I don't want them." She quit voluntarily and was not fired. In short, women had their own version of the "for the duration syndrome." Their excursion into the workforce was a temporary expedient to aid the war effort. Many never went that far, as "thousands [of women] rejected factory work as physically hard, dirty, and dull."[25]

The issue of postwar job loss was never gendered to the extent that some historians have argued. Most people, whether men or women, lost their defense jobs after August 14, 1945, and often well before, because the war was over or winding down. Industries simply disappeared. Shipbuilding in the Bay Area fell from nearly 300,000 workers to only a few thousand. Aircraft declined less, but still precipitously, from some 280,000 to 76,000. Most defense jobs would not reappear until the era of the Korean War. It has often been said that after the war women lost jobs for which they had more seniority than men, but the case of California cities does not support that claim. For example, by December 1, 1942, a full six months before women entered aircraft manufacturing in force, the industry already employed 113,000. That is almost twice the number of postwar jobs, so few women had a seniority advantage.[26]

Many did not have skills advantages either. Because of the war, shipbuilders adopted near mass-production techniques and trained women as semi-skilled workers. With peace, the industry reverted to its prewar concentration on constructing and repairing few but unique ships, which required more complex skills, instead of mass-producing identical ones. Unemployed skilled males from the defunct Kaiser and Marinship yards got on at the repair yards such as Bethlehem and Moore, but semi-skilled women did not. Not many semi-skilled veterans did either. For example, Moore had one thousand postwar jobs, but twenty-four thousand veterans had passed through their yards before being drafted.[27]

The jobs issue is perhaps the one where the unrealism of many historians of the war is most evident. As Effie Walling pointed out, many women did not think it was fair for them to take the jobs of men who were fighting the Nazis or the Japanese fascists. As Walling put it "[The] boys were coming home. They needed their jobs. I felt I had done my job and I wasn't needed. To me it was time for me to come home and I did happily." Moreover, keeping women on in industries that did transfer from war to peace, like some aircraft and much automobile manufacturing, would have ignored the political realities of the time. Men would certainly have resented learning that someone else had taken their places while they were risking their lives or wasting away at a desk job in Washington. Returning veterans would not have accepted this situation, and the political fallout from it would have been impressive.

The veterans themselves became a political bloc even without the goad of job displacement, and they certainly would have become even more stridently vocal had massive dislocation occurred. GI politicians took over several American city governments after the war ended, displacing some well-entrenched political machines. American congresses, state legislatures, and city councils have a long history of being generous to veterans, and this case would have been no different. One of the largest buildings in Washington today is the Pensions Building, constructed to house the administration of veterans' pensions after the Civil War. There were even more veterans of World War II, some 12.5 million, mostly men. California alone had 700,000 men in uniform, some 10 percent of its prewar population. No politician in his right mind was going to alienate such a political bloc. Moreover, each soldier, sailor, marine, or airman had a mother and father, who also would not have fancied veterans' displacement. And finally, to pose an even more disturbing specter, we must remember the near-contemporary examples of soldier militancy in Nazi Germany and Communist Russia. Disaffected soldiers played a key role in bringing these two totalitarian and genocidal regimes to power. It would have been suicidally ill-advised for the American government to train 12.5 million men to kill and then bring them home to be told that women now had their jobs. Soldiers and sailors actually rioted when their return from Europe was delayed by shipping shortages. Imagine how well they would have tolerated the news that they were being displaced by the 4.5 million (75 percent of 6 million) women who worked in industry during the war.

Finally, Walling and many other women were intensely proud of their enhanced self-esteem and their contributions. Women were very pleased at doing a job, even if they then left the workforce. Historians such as Gloria Ricci Lothrop and Joan M. Jensen, who emphasize the present as a mental watershed in self-respect, may well be correct. However, their grandmothers were also extremely proud of their defense efforts, a fact that historians often diminish. As Maureen Honey points out, those wooing women to the war effort specifically appealed to blue-collar women on grounds of patriotism. To them, war was not an entitlement. These women wanted to win and to limit the time that their men were away, in danger in some foreign land. Whatever their mix of motives, patriotism was almost invariably one of them.[28]

Although the literature often ignores housewives, their experience overlapped that of working females. As Kimberly Hall shows, San Diego, known as the "Port of Navy Wives," illustrates the process. Counterintuitively, the war made women both more independent and more able to work in groups. Rationing and wartime conditions curtailed everything from canning to clothing to recreation. Women responded by trading their rationing stamps, swapping vegetables, cooking and laundering communally, sharing diapers, and pooling babysitting. Since downtown was off-limits to respectable women, they created their own recreations—a community picnic at the beach, "buffets and potlucks" at someone's home. And rationing also promoted international travel because goods that were scarce at home were available across the border. Women could go to Tijuana to get a bacon-and-eggs breakfast, meat, vegetables, and shoes and could sometimes get into trouble trying to smuggle 150 pair of stockings into the United States on the same pair of legs. Everyone learned to improvise around shortages, to find transportation, to get to the store from the isolated housing projects, to clean and launder without appliances, to garden, to cook with then-exotic vegetables such as zucchini and squash, and to schmooze that all important person, the grocer. In the Port of Navy Wives, they also learned to accept "stoically" the cold fact of death. "The woman was viewed as a role model who should remain unafraid," noted Kimberly Hall. "Her emotions and needs were to be subordinate to those around her."[29]

The gender and discrimination approach also overshadows the salient feature of women's work in the war effort, their contribution. D'Ann Campbell pointed out this contribution long ago, but somehow that issue has not become the most important one for historians of women at war. Perhaps the most important contribution that women made was to provide the necessary labor force to win the struggle. Some 5 million to 6 million women entered the workforce during the Second World War. Thus they made up approximately one-third of the numbers necessary to offset the draft and then provide the extra 5 million persons to create the ultimate total of workers that won the war at home. They had lots of help from seniors, underage males, and others, but still the female contribution was extraordinary. Both German and Japanese rulers disliked putting women in the workforce and did so only reluctantly. Of course, this cultural attitude on the part of both rulers and ruled helped them lose the war.[30]

Some historians have de-emphasized the patriotic motive for women's entering the workforce and have emphasized instead the importance of the money or excitement or other personal reasons. Money certainly counted for a lot with women coming out of the Great Depression, and some also did desire the personal fulfillment, excitement, adventure, or experience, but the patriotic motive was overriding. Whatever the diversity of their motives, they usually shared the motive of patriotism. We should take them at their word. And, thanks to some very good oral history programs, we do have their word on the issue. For example, Phyllis Burns went to work for the San Diego Post Office in part because the income tax, newly imposed on most working families, created financial difficulties for her family. "We really needed money," she admitted. But as she put it, "The radio was on always, and every 15-minute commercial break was of how they needed people to come and work in the war plants." She continued, "I got the job at the post office because I just couldn't bear hearing them talk about the need that there was." Evelyn Harper Briggs taught school in San Diego during the day and then worked four more hours at the filter center and the radar center that replaced it, *without pay*. At times of crisis, such as when military intelligence temporarily lost track of the Japanese fleets bearing for Midway and Alaska and feared they were heading for California, she worked the next shift as well. Briggs, whose husband was a fire warden and whose family station wagon was littered with splints and first aid kits, also drove the station wagon 220 miles to Arizona and back each weekend to help teach pilots to fly. To say that she worked in the war effort would be to indulge in understatement. Lots of other women echoed these sentiments.[31] In short, whether they were Chicanas working in Midwestern war work or other women laboring in aircraft and shipbuilding, women repeatedly stated their own war aims. They wanted to do something productive in this national emergency, get the war over, and get their men home.[32]

None of this is to say that the impact-and-discrimination school is totally mistaken. The equal pay issue was a valid one if the work was indeed equal, and the argument for keeping stores open longer into the evening so that women could shop after work and not have to take a day off is equally valid. However, some West Coast cities did try to keep stores open longer, but that practice flew in the face of the necessity for dimouts in the early portion of the war. Nonetheless, as William O'Neill has noted, the government did not make full use of the womanpower available to the war effort. For example, if more day-care facilities had existed, more women would have entered the workforce. Thus day care was an unmistakable military issue, and providing sufficient facilities would not have compromised some other part of the war effort or stored up political dynamite for the postwar period. Moreover, the provision of day care could have been accommodated easily without using scarce building materials for new structures or finding new spaces in a crowded city on which to place them. There were hundreds of churches and synagogues in the cities with already existing educational and play facilities that could have easily converted to day care. They would have been happy to help in this manner.[33]

But the sheer number of women war workers tells only a part of this important story. We can better understand their contributions by recognizing the astonishing variety of jobs that they performed as well. By concentrating on wage-earning females, women's historians have overlooked the fact that all work, paid or unpaid, in strictly defense or in non-defense industries, was vital to the war effort. The faux distinction between war work and non-war work illustrates the point. For example, restaurant employment was not considered defense work, but airplane manufacturing was. Yet without the one, the other could not continue. Especially during wartime, Fortress California was jammed with single men and women, working hard, playing hard, boarding where they could, and eating out much of the time. Even families that had a room often did not have cooking facilities. *San Diego Union* reporter John Held recalled that downtown was choked each evening with persons standing in line to eat. It was clogged much of the rest of the day as well, and for the same reason. If these war workers could not find places and morsels to eat, they could not continue building B-24 bombers and Catalina flying boats at Consolidated Aircraft. Almost every job outside the defense industry contributed to keeping the products of the defense industries pouring out of these plants in such profusion. Thus the distinction between war and non-war work was usually irrelevant.

The same was true of the distinction between paid and unpaid work. Women volunteers who drove ambulances, jeeps, or generals' staff cars made a vital contribution as well. Historians have complained that these volunteer women should have been paid, just as factory workers were. But if soldiers made great pay and career sacrifices, it was appropriate that civilians did too. And women were intensely proud of voluntarily sacrificing in their own ways. Moreover, if volunteer women had been paid at the prime rate of aircraft workers, this extra financial burden would have resulted in a greater national debt that their families would have had to pay off in later years in the form of taxes. One way or another, the citizenry would have to pay for the war. There was even something egalitarian about volunteer work. Most volunteers were more affluent people who could afford to donate their time, and most women who labored in factories were less affluent ones who could not afford it. Thus, looking at the war from the point of view of women's contribution to it rather than solely at their windfalls from it creates a much fuller understanding of their roles in World War II.

The work of women in transportation, defense and non-defense, paid and unpaid, illustrates the point. One of the earliest labor shortages developed in the transit industry. To cope with the loss of manpower to the draft or to higher-paying war work, companies eventually had to hire women. Leaders such as William McRobbie, president of the San Francisco Municipal Carmen's Union, screamed bloody murder, and management expressed some equally decided ideas, but these seemed to be a cover for their real agendas. For example, Samuel Kahn, president of the Market Street Railway Company, could accept women conductors, "but it is not prudent to use women to operate either street cars or motor coaches," he argued in his bid to get permission to operate one-man cars. Milton Maxwell, "labor union member of the Civil Service Commission," barked, "Once you get them on the cars, you'll never get rid of them." This opposition was based both on bias and on the workers' desire to retain the large overtime earnings that the labor shortage allowed them. Gradually this opposition began to yield. The San Francisco press commenced agitating for women conductors in April 1942, by which point San Diego already had them. The argument behind the agitation was simple. National defense required that the transit systems carry more people rather than fewer, and there simply were not enough men to meet these increased schedules.[34]

First, the San Francisco Civil Service Commission had to consent to schedule examinations for women, and then the State of California had to relax its restrictions against women working after 11:00 P.M. and other regulations. The Civil Service Commission first opposed women and then retreated on May 14, 1942, and the other opposition followed suit. Some parts of the exam had to be changed, especially the strength and agility requirements. For example, the reigning rules required a person to climb a ladder carrying a 140-pound bag of sand. The *Chronicle* wondered wryly what that requirement might have to do with the duties of a streetcar or bus conductor (tickets and hand-punches weighed considerably less). Very little, it would seem, and the requirement became a casualty of the war. Reporter Betty Turner explained, tongue in cheek, one of the first experiments: "Motorman Edward Charlton managed to get the B car (Geary Street) through on time—the front end, that is. The rear end [where Turner served as conductorette], was 10 minutes late all along the line." The conductorettes (the contemporary term) apparently "learned" eventually how to keep the rear platforms on the same schedule as the front end, because by early August women began to trickle onto the rear Market Street Railway trolley platforms (twenty-five), and the Municipal Railway was set to follow. By January 1943, so was the Los Angeles Railway. These gave women a breakthrough and helped meet a defense emergency, since the inflexibility of housing prevented many people from walking to their war jobs.[35]

Women served transportation in other ways as well. Again San Diego seemed ahead of its rival towns. Before the month of January 1942 was out, the San Diego Cab Company was forced, by the drain on manpower, to resort to womanpower. Six weeks after the fires of Pearl Harbor were doused, on January 23, 1942, five "cabbyettes," as they were promptly dubbed, began "darting through traffic," and five more came on the next day. None of the customers fainted dead away or resisted, and the tips were good. Their supervisor said that they took the work more seriously, were "more courteous," and drove more safely than men. Others drove for free, including 210 young San Francisco women, who worked for the Red Cross Motor Corps and logged thirty thousand miles a month. Many others chauffeured. Obviously officers could have driven themselves, without injury either to their dignity or to the war effort, but armies everywhere require drivers. Women thus freed soldiers for more soldierly work. And it should be recalled that female driving was far from universal in 1941 and still hotly debated, as the continuing stereotype attests. Another group made and then delivered lunches, coffee, hot chocolate, and sandwiches all over the city as members of the Red Cross "mobile canteens," explained their leader Mrs. Tadini Bacigalupi, the supervisor of the Red Cross Canteen at 625 Sutter in San Francisco. The food and drink went to "State Guardsmen on duty, to Army and Navy stations, the interceptor Command Workers and similar active service groups," sentries, and "men on watch for the safety of San Francisco." These women not only brought the men food and coffee in the dead of night, but also drove them to and from their sentry stations "and aircraft listening posts" at what Zilfa Estcourt called the "strategic points along the city's ramparts." Mrs. George Cameron, like Mrs. Bacigalupi a San Francisco aristocrat, supervised the entire motor corps. Still others, especially from the Sunset District, trained to serve as ambulance drivers in case of enemy attack and the need for evacuation. As usual, they got their training in obstetrics, radio, map reading, and mechanics at a local school, Mission High.[36]

Another group of women transported even more important cargoes. Since the coastal cities were the first stop in the United States for those wounded in the Pacific Islands, they became centers to doctor men as well as ships. As one of its many services, the drivers of WADCA, the Women's Ambulance and Defense Corps of America, picked up the injured at the clearing stations and drove them to hospitals such as the Veterans Administration facility in the San Fernando Valley of Los Angeles. Later, the women taxied the healed men back to their units. And, for good measure, the Los Angeles outfit also provided twenty-four-hour emergency ambulance service for Fort MacArthur and Santa Ana Air Force Base. As refugees poured in from Pacific outposts overrun by the Imperial Japanese, women succored them as well. Both the Red Cross and the American Women's Volunteer Service met the refugees with food, coffee, transportation, and advice in getting settled in the cities or getting to their next destination.[37]

Other women facilitated the travel of the many persons at the pulsating, bewildering, impersonal, crowded, enormous railroad depots, such as Union Station in Los Angeles. The war doubled the number of anxious people passing through, hunting husbands, looking for sons, transferring to a train bound for Oregon. Women at the Travelers Aid stations struggled to sort them all out. An Army wife had been told to rent lodgings at Paso Robles, where her husband was being transferred. Travelers Aid hurriedly called Paso Robles and found that none existed.

Better stay put! A young bride from Georgia was riding the rails to reach her husband in Tacoma, unaware that he had since been transferred to California. A frantic telegram from her sister to Travelers Aid in Los Angeles arrived in time for them to find the woman on the train and put her up in a room, and then they "went to the Army to locate her husband." Then came a group of hearing-impaired children from a state school, trailed by a woman "with eight young children," then a "traveler suffering from epilepsy," followed by a mentally ill person. To the south, a young Australian woman appeared in San Diego searching for the wounded American soldier she had come to marry, only to find he had been mended and shipped off to Africa. Travelers Aid hunted up the soldier's mother in the East and dispatched the Aussie bride-to-be there to wait. The next problem might be soldiers who "had lost their transportation, wives and children of soldiers who have got stranded here and doting parents who have set out to visit sons in the armed forces." Then there were the runaway boys and girls. Then, then, then . . . Union Station never lacked for young wives, with younger children, anxiously checking the train schedules and debarkation platforms to meet military husbands coming through, sometimes for only an hour in between trains.[38]

Because of the greatly expanded populations flowing into town and the wounded streaming across the docks, the war vastly increased the need for medical services. The manpower shortage also produced a medical "famine," and women helped meet this emergency and in turn began to profit from it. Since the draft had taken so many doctors into military service, civilian therapeutic institutions were left shorthanded. So were schools, which also had fewer medical students training for the future than they normally would have. The long-range solution to this problem was to begin educating more female doctors, and "for the duration" the practice of limiting women medical students was slightly modified. However, the payoff of that reform would not become available until the students finished a multi-year training program. A more short-term solution was also needed. One way to compensate was to upgrade nurses' work and give them more assistants. Thus many of the routine procedures, such as taking temperature or blood pressure, that doctors had normally done were now performed by nurses. All over the country, the war radically upgraded the status of nurses. By mid-1943, nurses' aides already staffed forty military hospitals in the Los Angeles area alone.[39]

Future United States Treasurer Elizabeth Rudel Gatov remembered the rewards for women in this work and the contribution that they made. She volunteered two days a week at Hamilton Air Force Base in

Marin County, where even that well-run facility was swamped with the wounded.

> The conditions [in the hospital] were sometimes perfectly awful. The men were laying [*sic*] on litters in the corridors, and so forth, because the authorities hadn't been able to get patients out fast enough to make room for others coming in.

She reminisced too about how desperately the military men needed things that they had missed: "They wanted to drink just *quarts* of milk, *gallons* of milkshakes, [and eat] *tons* of ice cream," she mused. "This seemed to be what they all wanted." That and to talk of home, no matter how modest a place that might be. The aides listened endlessly to talk about "home," shared the wounded men's "ecstatic" relief at having escaped death, scrounged up the ice cream, brought the presents from relatives, and sent the letters to their loved ones.

> Some of the men had family problems, and then another branch of the Red Cross, if we notified them, would come in and pick that up, to see what could be done, or get information if they couldn't reach their wife on the telephone, and wondered what happened to her.

This experience, of course, reemphasizes the vital importance of the female drivers who delivered these men to the hospital and then rushed them to the airplanes, waiting to fly them, "within a week, to a general hospital near their home." With breathtaking understatement, Gatov modestly recalled: "So I felt that I was doing worthwhile work." Dr. J. C. Geiger, San Francisco director of the Department of Public Health, gave a similar estimate of these volunteers, who sometimes worked twelve hours a day: "Those women are the most important asset we have."[40]

A further wartime errand of mercy was just being considered at the same time. Although the Imperial Japanese did not observe the Geneva Convention in the treatment of prisoners, the Germans did. That made it possible for Americans to mitigate the rigors of confinement in European prison camps. This was done in part by sending letters and in part by dispatching packages of food, clothing, and other necessary articles through the Red Cross. In mid-1943, the Los Angeles chapter of the Red Cross visited a volunteer Red Cross food-packaging group in New York City and was apparently considering the establishment of one of its own.[41]

The war also greatly increased Red Cross activities, for example by tenfold in metropolitan Los Angeles County alone. Some forty-five thousand of the recruits in that city were volunteers, many of them women.

They did all kinds of jobs, taking blood from one hundred thousand donors, mending hospital linens, making uniforms and gowns, and serving as nurses' aides in the hospitals. They also stocked all of the Red Cross first-aid stations in churches and schools across the cities. Women of the WADCA—three thousand (enough to free up a regiment of men) in Los Angeles alone—not only drove vehicles to deliver these supplies, but largely manufactured them as well. This was one job where being an older woman was not a handicap, and they produced articles galore: sheets, pillowcases, bandages, surgical towels, rest pillows, bed slippers, stretchers, thousands of gauze bandages, and even three thousand gas masks. In fact, these women created a whole cottage industry of their own. They organized in their own clubs and churches and, like the garment workers of an earlier generation, labored in their homes. However, the communal rather than family nature of the work made it more like a throwback to the frontier or rural tradition of the quilting bee. As the casualties mounted in the Pacific War, the Red Cross chapters multiplied to meet the need. Sometimes they were organized by religion or ethnicity. A San Francisco Filipino Red Cross unit appeared almost at the beginning of the war. In Los Angeles, a Jewish Red Cross unit of 471 volunteers put in 53,006 hours to turn out six hundred thousand items, from bandages to officers' insignia for the Army, Navy, and Cedars of Lebanon Hospital.[42]

The dynamics of this cottage industry can be glimpsed through the activities of one Southland unit. So many women volunteered to help out at the Glendale Red Cross headquarters that the work had to be "subcontracted" out to smaller organizations. Thus the women of Rancho San Rafael formed their own branch and ultimately sent their products back to the Glendale mother chapter. Like so many other voluntary achievements in the Good War, this one began with a donation. Dr. and Mrs. A. J. Scholl offered the group the use of their three-room guest house, and the subcontractors moved in and set up shop. To finance the purchase of their manufacturing materials, the women organized a barn dance, and when that money ran out, they arranged a golf exhibition. The great female golfer Babe Didrikson Zaharias was the featured professional, along with celebrities Bob Hope and Joe Caldwell. Nor were the products that emanated from these workshops of trivial importance. For example, one emergency order from the San Pedro Navy Dispensary was for three hundred "first aid bags for men in the merchant marine to carry in the gun turrets." As *Times* correspondent Christy Fox explained, "The group made and paid for these bags—and delivered them in quick order." It is worth reemphasizing that the merchant marine suffered among the highest casualties in the war, so the first-aid bags were

frontline contributions. So was most of their other work. In one stretch
of thirty-two working days, the women of Rancho San Rafael manufactured 23,786 surgical dressings. They also collected, "reconditioned,"
and sent clothes to "Navy families, the Needlework Guild of America,
and the Children's Home Society." Fittingly enough, the women became
a social group, meeting at the workshop to have tea and review "the
activities of their first year."

To cite just one other example, a Santa Monica chapter also began in
a donated structure, this time a residence. They turned the garage into "a
workshop to repair furniture, lamps, radios and many things donated to
furnish day rooms for soldiers on duty in the Santa Monica Bay district."
In the home itself, they produced "surgical dressings, pajamas, surgical
coats, and refugee clothes," to help meet "the huge quota for bandages
and garments needed by the armed forces Medical Corps."[43]

So prevalent was this kind of female volunteer work that, nationwide,
it caused a most curious sort of de-industrialization. At war's beginning, the government estimated that it would require 40 million bandage
dressings annually. Private industrialists threw up their hands, averring
that they could meet only 10 percent of this staggering demand. Instead,
women sat down to the task, and by war's end they were producing not
40 million but one billion dressings per year nationwide. Foster Rhea
Dulles noted that

> a curious spectacle was presented of factories equipped to do the job by
> machinery standing idle while millions of women made dressings by hand.
> The explanation was the shortage of manpower. Here was something that
> volunteer workers could do, of vital importance, and thereby release po-
> tential factory employees for other production.

Still others nurtured in different ways. The American Women's Volunteer Service maintained a chorus of singers who entertained at bond
rallies, hospitals, and military camps. The service also established the
only courses dedicated to the "psychological rehabilitation of the blind."
The volunteers, sometimes sightless persons themselves, were "trained
to assist the new war blinded to adjust themselves to living though the
light for them has failed," explained Zilfa Estcourt. One of the most
outstanding efforts began when six women noticed that the wounded
and psychically maimed in Bay Area hospitals responded well to music.
So the six created the "Tune Timers," which toured the hospitals, in-
volving the hurt servicemen in music. Sometimes the hospital piano was
out of tune or the bottom of the metal wastepaper basket had to do for
percussion, but one way or another, the women got the boys involved,
much to their psychological benefit. They did so for five full years up to

1947. The women insisted upon anonymity to their historian, but to his credit, he engaged in enough editorial skullduggery so that the names of Helen Shutes, Genevieve Wood, Mary Jacobus, Eleanor Price, Dorothy Pearson Chapmen, and Leila Thompson would be remembered.[44]

The experience of these women bears on several important World War II interpretive questions. Many books and articles have emphasized the role of the war in benefiting big business. Numerous accounts of the so-called military-industrial complex begin with the bulking up of business during the war. By the same token, analysts have stressed the role of commercial subcontractors during the conflict. Both interpretations are correct, but the voluntary work of women calls for a further emphasis on the importance of voluntarism in the war and on the reversion to the primitive, or to the renaissance of earlier home manufacturing practices, rather than the march toward the future. These volunteer organizations were usually affiliated with some governmental agency. Even the Red Cross was affiliated with the Office of Civilian Defense, but it was nonetheless a voluntary agency. As the aircraft manufacturing subcontracting map of Los Angeles reveals, commercial subcontracting was a vital part of the war (see p. 11, this volume). But so was the voluntary subcontracting of hundreds of thousands of women working in a home, a church, a school, a Santa Monica garage, or a Glendale guest house. Finally, the emphasis on the state requires modification. Obviously, war greatly increased the range of the state, but it was crucially assisted by the immense range of voluntary organizations that it could depend upon. The war, together with the Depression, did bring about the birth of the modern American state—and the rebirth of the vigorous American tradition of voluntarism as well.[45]

Also, women did other work that helped preserve both capitalism and democracy. Although these beachheads were not always maintained after the war, a lot of them were established during it. One very strategic one was in the stock market. These barriers fell earlier than those in shipbuilding and aircraft. By April 1941, women such as Ann Hadzes and Ramona Cargill worked both the big board and the floor of the San Francisco Stock Exchange. The Spring Street markets in Los Angeles made the same transition. Before the war, women held 50 percent of the positions, but gendered ones. By early 1943, they held 80 percent of the jobs, and not just the gendered ones. "Heretofore a man's sanctum," said the *Chronicle*, "the bars have been let down to the fair sex because of the exigencies of war." Bars came down in the movies as well. Mrs. Alice Evans Field, of the Will Hays Office, noted that "a new field for women in the executive branches of the motion picture industry is being

Even starlets contributed to the war effort, here promoting rubber collection.
Courtesy Huntington Library.

opened as a result of the war." Heretofore, "motion pictures have used
the talents of women chiefly as actresses and writers. But now they are
successfully holding positions as film directors, supervising editors, and
stylists."[46]

The Hollywood story was typical of the numerous breaches women
made in the walls of traditionally male bastions. However, discrimination
in strictly women's work also began to recede. For example, the "employment of women in clerical jobs, at one time restricted to those below the
age of 30," noted the *Chronicle*, "now has expanded to such an extent that
many women between 50 and 55 are now getting jobs in private industry."
Illogically, age discrimination continued for women over 55.[47]

And just as the stock market, movies, and offices were crucial to
the good health of capitalism, political parties, juries, grand juries, in-

vestigative panels, rationing, draft boards, journalism, and independent investigations were vital to maintaining democracy. The same manpower crisis that hit the regular work scene also struck the irregular ones. Government had to go on, despite war, and womanpower helped it do so. By August 1942, "Women are doing the major part of jurors' work in the superior courts of San Diego county [sic] and in the municipal courts as fewer men have been available in recent months," explained the *Union*. At the time, half the states barred women from jury duty, which made them ineligible for federal jury duty in such states. In a famous case, the Hollywood matinee idol Errol Flynn was charged with sexually molesting two underage women, one of them aboard his yacht in Santa Catalina harbor. Whether this hurt his case, as the prosecution hoped, or helped it, as a commentator familiar with the actor's box office attraction suggested, Flynn took his chances before a jury composed of nine women and three men.[48]

Party and press were likewise bailed out by women during the conflict, and for the exact same reasons. Scholars have discussed the threat of censorship during the war but have largely overlooked the fact that just keeping the newspapers going was a major achievement. As a "veteran reporter looked about the City Room [of the *LA Times*] on this Christmas [1942] morning of a war year," he found that the war had torn through the newspaper offices like one of the Pacific hurricanes that the absent male reporters would soon encounter firsthand. In every department of the *Times*—sports, marine reporting, the morgue [library], city desk, messengers, office boys—the males were in service. The paper lost two hundred staff to the Second Great War, and in their places sat young women doing their "part in the job of keeping the nation going while our men are in the armed forces."[49]

As Jacqueline Braitman has observed, women also made advances in the party structures during the war. Riding on the impetus of the California 50–50 plan, which allocated party jobs below that of county chairman on an equal gender basis, and the exigencies of the war, women began to become much more prominent in the party organizations. For example, Republican women helped elect Governor Earl Warren, and Democratic women aided Representatives Chet Holifield and Helen Gahagan Douglas to power. They also attended party conventions at all levels. Though this was not a revolutionary breakthrough, women steadily advanced during the war. And since so many men were gone and there were so many problems with absentee voting, female influence at elections was potentially greater too. Thus women helped keep party structures that undergirded democracy alive during a worldwide war over the very existence of democracy.[50]

Others pondered equally momentous issues. The United States government very shrewdly drew volunteers into two of its most sensitive operations, rationing and the draft. Few matters are really life-and-death ones, but the draft was one of them. Draft boards had to make excruciating judgments to determine whether men had disqualifying health problems, whether they were needed in Los Angeles agriculture more than in Guadalcanal combat, and whether their contributions to Bay Area shipbuilding outweighed those of New Guinea road building. Through World War II, draft boards were all male, but women could serve as clerks and "associate members to advisory boards."[51]

Rationing, where women served directly, was not so immediately life-and-death, but still very important to both the health and morale of the civilian population. Food, clothing, and gasoline were common necessities that touched every one, every day. As in the case of the draft, anything but an evenhanded administration of rationing would have been destructive of civilian morale, not to mention the long-term health of American democracy. It was demanding labor, as Mildred Finley Wohlford of Escondido recalled. As a member of the rationing board, "I went in four or five days a week [in the mornings]. That takes a lot out of a housewife with kids and all," especially one who was pregnant, as Wohlford was. Just as the draft board had to make tough decisions, so did the rationing board. Women would have heard about any unfairness because it was their neighbors and friends to whom they were administering the laws. As Wohlford explained it, she "met everybody in town," especially the "restaurant people, who were determined to get more sugar than they should have for desserts and all that," but "you couldn't give them more stamps without cutting somebody else off who had a right to them."[52]

The Office of Price Administration was closely related to the rationing and the draft and was equally involved with fair play. For example, "200 men and women were hired, mostly women, to receive the multitudes at counters, answer 25 telephones, and file, file, file" for the Los Angeles OPA office at 1016 South Broadway. Here trooped the sightless, hearing impaired, elderly, and foreign to petition for a rent increase to augment their pitiful incomes or to oust an "obnoxious, destructive" tenant. Said tenant might be just behind the plaintiff in the same line, poised to petition the same authorities to end the "outrageous, gouging" behavior of her or his landlady or landlord. The volunteers filled out forms for the sightless, translated for the non–English speakers, and listened to the pitiful stories of all and sundry. It was a terrible job, and unlike the modern joke about the person who has it made, someone did *not* have to do it. Women just did this chore to help the war effort. In doing so, women such as Mrs. Sidney Scott, "prominent in the Ebell Club," learned about the soft underbelly of the realty market, not to mention the underside of the war effort in L.A. and other California bastions.[53]

And just as women helped impose the government's rationing, draft, and OPA systems, they also served as watchdogs for those programs. The Truman Senate Committee is famous for trying at the national level to ensure fairness and prevent corruption. On the local level, the League of Women Voters performed the same essential services. For example, the Wilshire–Beverly Hills League, in early 1943, set out to "study the theory and mechanics of food rationing." They found illegal hoarding in L.A. and unworkable rules from Washington that encouraged it. Modern commentators sometimes find fault with the genteel studies of the League, but this one played hardball, especially in ferreting out offenders. League official Mrs. Rollin Brown noted that it was no use trying to hide because "knowledge of these stores in garages and basements becomes pretty generally known to servants, to children, [and] to men who come to the house on one service or another." And when it did, woe to the local offenders. Besides ferreting out the malefactors, the League also developed support for rationing. As correspondent Bess M. Wilson explained:

> The building of public opinion is one of the big jobs dependent upon women of the United States for its [rationing] success. Housewives will not be casual about food shortages nor food rationing. They will go to nutrition classes and learn how to cook what is in the market and how to make their families like it. They will carry this gospel to their neighbors as well as to members of their own household.

Others enforced informally by spurning the black market and shunning the people who patronized it.[54]

The League of Women Voters investigated many of the other outstanding problems of the war. These included emergency war housing, collective bargaining, day care, "prenatal and maternity clinics, community sewage systems, medical care, health and job insurance, veterans facilities, and quality control of county and state hospitals." They also investigated the role of women in civil defense and the Land Laws that barred Japanese from ownership, supporting the first and opposing the second.[55]

Just as women took care of others, they had to find new ways to take care of themselves. Two groups to do so were the Women of Wake Island and the Sponsors of the Heroes of the Philippines. Both were composed of women whose sons or husbands had been captured or were unaccounted for in the Wake Island and Philippine fighting at the outset of the war. By early 1943, the Heroes of the Philippines were still trying to locate their loved ones. They reached out to other women across the country in the same situation to share information about prisoner location, photographs, addresses, and government policy. The 120 Women of Wake Island were more of an all-purpose mutual-support group. They not only shared information, but got jobs for each other, helped find shelter for one of their number burned out of her house, and paid the "mortgage on the home of a seventy-three-year-old whose son was killed at Wake Island."[56]

Many urban Californians made this ultimate contribution to the war effort, and some made even greater ones. A short story in the *Los Angeles Times* tersely announced the maximum sacrifice of one woman: "Mrs. James Buchanan Austin, who lost her husband in the First World War, learned yesterday that she had lost her son in the second." Flight Sergeant Frederick Carleton Austin, of Pomona College and Los Angeles High School, who volunteered for the Royal Canadian Air Force in 1940, was declared "missing and presumed dead overseas" in January 1943.[57]

Women's reminiscences uniformly note the novelty, excitement, and upheaval of the period. Yet when the war was over, most of them went back to their customary jobs in the home or to traditional jobs in the workforce. William Chafe has written that World War II was a catalyst for change in women's history, and that theory seems appropriate. Women were by no means equal even by 1972, when he wrote his book, but the war did help to build a foundation from which those women who wanted to could advance toward greater equality. Despite the magnitude of the war upheaval, no social revolution occurred. The female labor force receded to its prewar proportion, and the volunteer activities faded as the defense emergency paled.[58]

It is obvious that women contributed in many more capacities than as "Rosie the Riveter." Moreover, in doing these other tasks, women took on responsibilities much more important than those of blue-collar wage earners. This advantage was due to the fact that they discovered more about how the "system" worked, and indeed they worked it themselves. The traditional emphasis on the World War II lives of factory women has been useful and revealing. Yet the story of middle-class women may well be the more revealing one. Those who drove generals learned of the structure of military bureaucracies; those who fronted for the OPA began to comprehend the workings of the real estate market and other economic markets; those in draft and rationing work comprehended the often painful choices of public policy, not to mention something of human nature; those who tended the wounded learned compassion and medical skills; those who rolled bandages understood how to organize, raise funds, manufacture, and publicize; and those who watch-dogged the system of rationing learned about every phase of urban existence. Women who tended the stock market and the city desk at the newspapers probably found out more about how their society worked than any of the others. As women's historians have noted, those who labored at mass production learned skills that would not be very useful after the war.[59]

The usual estimates of women workers in World War II count only those who went into paid work or into the workforce. This number does not begin to portray the full contribution of women to the war effort and the stimulus of the war effort to women. A huge portion of the female contribution was made in the unpaid, but nonetheless vital, sector of volunteer work. Generals had to be driven to office and meeting; but more important, wounded men had to be ferried to the San Fernando Veterans facility; bandages had to be made for the merchant marine gun turrets; blood, collected; the sick, nursed; meals, delivered to sentries; babies, sat; and soldiers' wives, located. And someone had to make the tough calls on the draft and rationing. Alma Whitaker, women's correspondent for the *Times,* understood what these experiences meant. "Women are going to be a major problem when peace comes. Masculinity, in both dictatorships and democracies," she warned, "is finding it psychologically necessary to flatter us into realizing how surprisingly competent we can be in countless realms hitherto regarded as beyond our scope."[60]

The impact-and-discrimination school is often prone to judge 1940s conditions by 1980s and 1990s standards. As D'Ann Campbell reminds us, we cannot evaluate the actions and culture of one era by the actions and culture of another. Historians of women in World War II charge that the government did not pass enough legislation to aid women, complain about job bias in pay and promotions, criticize war supporters for making different appeals to blue-collar and white-collar women, attack men for being patriarchal, object to the assumption that women should have been supersensitive to the needs of returning servicemen, pound management and labor for preferring male to female workers, and criticize the war effort for not producing enough positive change for women.[61] All these arguments apply standards of the 1980s and 1990s to the history of the 1940s. The point of the war in 1941 was not to elevate the status of women. The point of the war was to destroy three totalitarian societies and contain another. That was not such an ignoble goal and achievement even if a women's revolution did not accompany the struggle.[62]

Most women's historians of the World War II experience are agreed that the war did not create a revolutionary transformation of women's social position. D'Ann Campbell has written that the war accelerated certain fundamental trends favorable to women: recovery from depression, urbanization, and more equal distribution of incomes. This is quite true, but the war had an even more fundamental and usually overlooked impact on women. The most important impact of the war was to preserve the democratic and capitalistic thrust of a society that had been moving toward equality since well before the war and has moved even more rapidly toward that condition after it. And that is the fundamental reason that historians should emphasize the contributions of women to the war effort in addition to telling the story of their progress toward equality. The war gave women progress toward their Double V. The impact of the war was hardly equalitarian, although it did begin to remove some barriers.[63] Women made modest progress toward equality, and they greatly helped destroy predator governments that were a preeminent threat to the idea of equality—defined by gender, race, class, or any other way. By emphasizing gender and discrimination, women's historians have concentrated on the lesser story instead of the greater one. The war was a public occasion to which women contributed magnificently.

5. The Universal Double V
War and Ethnocultural Accommodation

The Japanese are showing themselves our equals in arms and machinery, if that is what counts. The Chinese have for ages been at least our equals in the cultivation of human personality, if that is what counts. Their half of the human race has its rights, too, the first of which is respect for its racial dignity.

—"White 'Superiority' Gone Forever," Editorial, *San Francisco Chronicle,* March 20, 1942[1]

World War II moved Americans toward this ethnocultural accommodation. The varied peoples of California cities lived in close proximity during the war, rode the same streetcars and buses, worked together in factories, and competed for jobs, space, and recognition. How did war affect these realms of space, profession, pay, and power? Charles Wollenberg argued the disruption/revolution hypothesis as forcefully as anyone when he said that "like the Gold Rush a century earlier, World War II was a watershed in Bay Area history, ushering in revolutionary changes that dramatically affected the region's subsequent development."[2]

Japanese Americans experienced a revolutionary dislocation of their lives, but nothing that dramatic happened to any other group. In fact, those groups for whom we have stories experienced modest progress. African Americans, who wanted to support the war effort but wanted to use it to win something in return, devised the political slogan of the Double V: fighting fascism abroad but also combating discrimination at home. However, though it is not widely recognized, each cultural or other organized group of any kind had its own version of the Double V. All wanted to win the war but also to preserve or enhance their place in society. With the exception of the Japanese, few ethnocultural groups experienced radical change. Each made modest gains from the war while making major contributions to its success.

The tragedy of the Japanese Americans is epitomized by the commencement exercises at the University of California at Berkeley in the spring of 1942. The press reported that President Robert Gordon Sproul observed that the "graduating student who had achieved the highest scholastic standing," Harvey Akio Itano, a twenty-one-year-old premedical student from Sacramento, could not receive the honor in person. "The winner of the university medal cannot be here today because his country has called him elsewhere," Sproul euphemistically explained; Itano had been "evacuated April 22 to a resettlement center." "It's tough to be an American imbued with the ideals of democracy and to be looked upon as a potential enemy," Itano poignantly told friends upon his departure.

His predicament captured exactly the sad drama of one of California's and America's best adapted minority groups. Since their arrival in the United States in the late nineteenth century, Japanese Americans had succeeded very well. They had moved up economically from day laborers to proprietors of farming, nursery, and fishing enterprises. They were industrious, smart businessmen, strongly familial, and educational strivers (as Itano's case indicates), who caused their communities very few welfare, criminal, or other problems. Yet they soon became the target of nationalist opinion.

The attack on Pearl Harbor stunned mainland American Japanese as much as it did other groups, and they did not immediately become the target of anti–Japanese American sentiments. However, the papers did portray international events in pictures, cartoons, and language that could easily have rubbed off onto the Japanese Americans who were themselves not directly attacked. A *San Diego Union* editorial argued on December 29, 1941, that "we must completely obliterate Japan as a nation entitled to the respect of decent peoples. After that we must maintain guardianship because they can't be permitted to govern themselves." Simultaneously, the newspapers carried many stories about the FBI and local law enforcement raids, which netted the most dangerous Asian or Caucasian aliens. All the while, the press and radio incessantly shouted the word "Jap" from the headlines and radio airwaves.

Still, in this earlier period, the media also carried numerous stories friendly to Japanese Americans. For example, the *San Diego Union* ran a piece on the Japanese American Citizens League stating that the principal "pro-American" Japanese American group "unequivocally condemn[s] Japan for this unprecedented breach of good faith." Japanese residents of suburban Chula Vista strongly criticized "the treacherous infamy of Japan's attack upon the United States." "We do not hesitate to repudiate and condemn our ancestral country when Japan deliberately attacks us and American blood was shed." Deeds followed words: mothers volunteered their sons for military service; picture brides rolled bandages; and fishermen willingly gave up their livelihoods to reassure the Navy about maritime espionage and offered their boat radios, critical skills, and other equipment to the Navy.

Governor Olson welcomed this Japanese American participation in the war effort but urged them to "avoid rousing friction and animosity and hysteria in those with whom you come in contact." When Eleanor Roosevelt came to town and counseled toleration of Japanese Americans, the *Union* ran the story. Unfortunately, the First Lady made the prediction that Americans might have to defend themselves on their own shores. Such a military eventuality was rather implausible, but Roosevelt's statement was apt to make the Japanese Americans more suspect. The first overtly anti-Japanese tone sneaked into the *Union* in the last week of December. The San Diego County agricultural commission warned housewives to wash vegetables thoroughly because of the rumor that Japanese farmers had poisoned them. To the north, the *San Francisco Chronicle* went far beyond the *Union* in condemning such nonsense. In an article entitled "Persecution of Innocents Won't Win the War," the editor explained that "the witch smellers" are "trying to be busy amongst us. Letters come to the *Chronicle*—some of them, to our amazement, from persons who should . . . know better—proposing various sorts of witless persecution of Japanese, Germans, and Italians in our population." However, in the beginning, the paper did not stand out, for the media in general remained friendly or neutral to the Japanese through December.

Even the *Los Angeles Times,* later a diehard advocate of relocation, stayed neutral. The paper remained editorially quiescent on the Japanese question, and then after about two weeks produced an editorial that was neutral in tone. From there on, the paper slipped toward a pro-relocation stance. The Hearst papers, the Los Angeles and San Francisco *Examiners,* remained editorially quiet on the subject right up to the relocation and then became a sturdy defender of that policy. As Morton Grodzins has explained, the general newspaper restraint lasted about one month.

However, almost before the fires of Pearl Harbor had cooled, some papers called for expulsion. The first editorial demand for exclusion came from the *Independent* of San Luis Obispo only five days after Pearl

Harbor; it took about one month for general editorial opinion to shift. Letters to the editor soon dropped their friendly tone. Although some continued to support fair play for all aliens, most turned against the Japanese. News stories carried a much less positive picture from the start, portraying the Japanese Americans as the target of FBI raids, picturing them turning in their cameras, binoculars, and small arms, and showing the general retreat of American forces in the Pacific.

Outside the newspaper world, opposition to the Japanese Americans accelerated. Eventually very powerful pressure groups, including the California State Grange, the California State Federation of Labor, the Los Angeles Chamber of Commerce, the American Legion, and the Native Sons of the Golden West, joined the attack against them. In addition to these pressure groups and the press, a number of radio commentators and politicians joined the hue and cry.

Although Mayor Fletcher Bowron minimized his role after the war, in 1941–42 he vigorously led and forcefully defended the relocation movement. In most respects Bowron was an excellent mayor, but he took a very stern line with the Japanese. Much of Bowron's "information" about the issue came from his "spy" among the Japanese. For example, the operative, Alfred Cohn, reported on January 21, 1942, that the Japanese newspapers ought to be suppressed because they were the principal means of communication and information among "alien Japanese." Two of the three papers had been pro-Axis before the war, Cohn informed his boss. He further claimed that the nineteen Shinto temples in the Los Angeles area were assembly points for aliens and that "many . . . Shinto Priests are known agents of the Imperial Government." Predictably, Cohn urged the elimination of Japanese Americans from Fish Harbor on Terminal Island, where the Navy maintained numerous activities. He complained that "much political pressure is being brought to bear, especially the fish canning companies, to keep several thousand Japanese now living there in the fishing business."[3]

Cohn thought that all of these people, alien and citizen alike, should be removed and that the authorities should direct their attention to winning the complete loyalty of the half of the Nisei population that was partially loyal. "As to the propaganda campaign," Cohn reported, "we are now collecting as many letters as possible written by interned Japanese to their families" which express the "amazement" of the detainees at the good treatment they are receiving. "I believe that publication of these letters would serve a very valuable purpose," at home and abroad, Cohn observed. Later, the secret agent went so far as to incite these unfortunate people to inform on each other, using threats to force them to do so.

Many other Californians favored resettlement of the Japanese Americans. Pressure groups inspired many of the demands that congressmen received, and newspapers chose the letters to the editors that they wanted to print. Whatever the exact number, enough people favored exclusion to create political pressure sufficient to banish the Japanese.

The major metropolitan onslaught took shape about six weeks after the war began. Till then comment on the Japanese Americans had been mostly favorable, and the opposition remained muted. In fact, favorable opinion so predominated in the first few weeks after Pearl Harbor that their friends were caught completely off guard by the anti-Japanese backlash.

Relocation demands arose from complex motives. Most historians have stressed racial intolerance; others have noted the political gain to be made by catering to it; others still have focused on the economic motive of eliminating Japanese business competition, and most have emphasized the pretext of military security. Analysts have also stressed the unusually complicated interplay of pressure group advocates, Japanese military success in Asia, politicians, federal bureaucrats, military personnel, and the Japanese Americans themselves. This interaction caused the government to make its decision in the midst of utmost haste and confusion. For example, Lieutenant General John L. De Witt, the commanding general on the West Coast, vacillated between removal and non-removal right up to the end. In the meantime, he and his staff operated in an atmosphere that kept out most hard information but let in bias, fear, rumors, lies, half-truths, politicos' nonsense, and outrageous predictions.

There were lots of these. Some charged that the Japanese were largely dual citizens whose main allegiance lay with the Emperor: The Japanese supposedly belonged to secret societies that stood ready to strike at key defense installations when the Emperor gave the word. Others thought that they sent signals from shore to Japanese vessels off the coast, flew Japanese flags from their fishing boats when offshore, poisoned the vegetables destined for urban markets (admittedly a dubious marketing strategy), or were storing munitions for a rising to be coordinated with a Japanese invasion. Even the prestigious and usually reasonable Town Hall discussion and policy group feared a carrier-based attack on the shore-hugging Southern California aircraft plants. Yet others believed that the Japanese Americans spied on U.S. defense activities from their fishing boats and even located their homes, farms, nurseries, and fishing businesses to facilitate espionage. Hostile orators pictured the Japanese Americans as an unassimilable group, gobbling up the land and breeding indiscriminately, hoping someday to outnumber California whites. (With a population of perhaps 120,000 out of 7,000,000, they certainly had their work cut out for them.)[4]

Although the press remained editorially friendly or neutral for six weeks, it also circulated many of these charges even during the period of benevolence, which came to an abrupt end in mid-January. Most of these charges were never substantiated, but unfortunately, perhaps the most damaging allegation did stand up: some Japanese Americans in Hawaii did indeed aid the attack on Pearl Harbor. A Japanese spy had carefully observed the Navy for months and knew that on weekends most of the U.S. fleet in that area was tied up in port. A few Hawaiian Japanese Americans aided his efforts. That is why the Sunday assault paid such large dividends. However, these were individual acts and not those of the Hawaiian Japanese American population as a whole, and, in any case, had no bearing on the loyalty of the California Japanese Americans. Even the military commandant of Hawaii, Delos Emmons, recognized that the spies had acted as individuals. He did not condemn the group and also refused to relocate the 150,000 Japanese Americans from Hawaii, a much more sensitive place militarily.[5]

No comparable act of espionage was ever pinned on the mainland Japanese. And reliable information was already available to confound the insinuations about dual citizenship (a common phenomenon affecting some three million Americans, of which the Japanese were a tiny minority), ship-to-shore communication, the sinister nature of Japanese organizations, Shinto religion, Nisei loyalty, and even their ability or inclination to win a breeding derby. Nor did they ever pose a military threat to the cities of the West. Both the FBI and Commander K. D. Ringle, "naval intelligence officer of the eleventh naval district (San Diego and Los Angeles), categorically denied the necessity of mass evacuation." Ringle favored investigating sabotage and espionage on an individual basis.[6]

In fact, the government had already done so. The Justice Department had begun systematically investigating potentially dangerous aliens a year and a half before the war. Pearl Harbor found them fully prepared to select out the potentially dangerous aliens from the remainder. Beginning on December 7, the department incarcerated the enemy aliens they believed to be dangerous. These actions contributed to the security of the West Coast, which both the FBI and the security officer of the Eleventh Naval District recognized. This roundup continued into the first months of 1942.[7]

Ironically, as the West Coast cities became more secure, the political furor created the exact reverse impression. Since nothing had happened, said the anti-Japanese lobby, it proved that the Japanese Americans were a well-disciplined group, lying in wait to coordinate an uprising with Japan's air attack or invasion of California. Even usually sensible men like Attorney General Earl Warren and Mayor Fletcher Bowron accepted this notion. It was a no-win situation for the Japanese Americans. The more innocent the Japanese were, the more suspect they became. On February 19, 1942, President Franklin Roosevelt signed Executive Order 9066. The order allowed the military to relocate Japanese American aliens *and* citizens. They were first taken to assembly centers and then sent to eight relocation centers in the West and two in Arkansas. Two of these centers were in California, at Manzanar in the Owens Valley and at Tule Lake in northeastern California.[8]

Several factors facilitated the campaign of misinformation. The Japanese Americans were not yet well integrated politically or economically. In neither of these realms did they have enough power or influence to protect themselves. In fact, their economic success created an animosity among their competitors, who wanted to inherit the Japanese share of the produce, nursery, and fishing markets. The Los Angeles Chamber of Commerce, the American Legion, the Native Sons and Daughters of the Golden West, the California Joint Immigration Committee, the labor unions, the various growers' groups, the competing and antagonistic ethnic groups, and especially the newspapers and politicians like Warren, Olson, Bowron, Angelo Rossi, and the California congressional delegation took up the cry against them. The anti-Japanese lobby usually justified its attacks on grounds of "stern military necessity," but obviously there was more to it.[9]

Resistance to relocation came mostly from religious groups, the American Civil Liberties Union, and the Northern California Committee on Fair Play for Citizens and Aliens of Japanese Ancestry, led by University of California Vice President and Provost Monroe Deutsch. Some CIO spokesmen and a few San Francisco politicians opposed relocation, as did owners of suburban land farmed by Japanese and the canning factory operators. But no pro-Japanese alignment existed that had the influence of their enemies. The Japanese also lacked newspaper support. The government suppressed many of the Japanese Americans' own newspapers, but these had limited influence outside the Japanese community anyway. The defection of the mainstream media from their cause was especially damaging because it constantly circulated defamatory misinformation about them.

Neither could the Nisei and Issei count on the open support of any important California or national public figure. The United States attorney general, Francis Biddle, fought tooth and nail behind the scenes to

An apple provides scant comfort for a
Japanese American child en route to a relocation camp.
Courtesy Library of Congress, Prints & Photographs Division, FSA-OWI Collection.

prevent the detention, but he did not have any major political allies in the Golden State and few in the national government.[10] Most importantly, President Franklin D. Roosevelt failed to protect the Japanese. Not only did he overrule Biddle in his fight against the War Department, which wanted ever sterner measures toward the Japanese, but Roosevelt *agreed* with the harsher actions, including mass evacuation of citizens and aliens alike. At one point, Roosevelt even approved a proposal to remove 20,000 Japanese Americans from Hawaii.[11]

The Hawaiian military command successfully opposed such a move as unnecessary to the defense of the islands. Had 150,000 people been deported to the mainland, another 150,000 people would eventually have had to be imported to replace them in the labor force, wasting priceless shipping space in both directions, as well as the materials to build fresh mainland camps. Had Roosevelt stood up publicly for the Nisei and Issei instead of working behind the scenes against them, had he defended the very good record of his own Justice Department, had he ordered his more excitable generals such as De Witt to calm down, or had he read the record of Japanese loyalty or consulted with the military authorities in Hawaii, who were faced with the same situation yet took different action, the tragedy of relocation might have been avoided.[12]

It is of little consequence whether one singles out the excitable rumor-mongering of General De Witt, the explosive impact of the Roberts Report, the publicly aired opinions of Secretary Knox, the famous article of Walter Lippmann accepting the less-is-more guilt theory, or the contribution to the notion of collective responsibility offered by Hearst columnist Damon Runyon, radio commentator John Hughes, or some other individual. The general situation was overwhelmingly against the Japanese Americans, and they had few resources to change the situation.

As historians have made clear, the principal major causes of the tragedy—ingrained bias, the ever-faltering American military position in the Far East, economic cupidity, and political ambition—combined to create an impossible situation. My interpretation differs from these opinions in only one respect. Although the anti-Japanese forces often spoke of race in their arguments and although one cannot doubt the presence of large-scale bias in the state, the racial interpretation of Californian behavior is not persuasive. When people spoke of the "Japanese race," they usually were talking about *nationality;* there was no Japanese *race.* The Japanese were and are a nationality within the larger group of Asians. Moreover, the supposed "racial" animosity against the Japanese did not rub off onto other Asians—Chinese, Koreans, and Filipinos. In fact, at the same time that Californians stigmatized the Imperial Japanese, they romanticized the Chinese and Filipinos fighting against them. For example, in the early months of the war, the anti-Japanese Los Angeles Chamber of Commerce launched a campaign to supply each Philippine soldier with a gruesome bolo knife with which to disembowel the supposedly subhuman Japanese invaders. Moreover, many anti-Japanese events did not involve whites. Nationalism was just as efficient at provoking hostility. Of the thirty-eight bona fide anti-Japanese incidents of violence between Pearl Harbor and relocation, including seven murders, the Filipinos accounted for eighteen, nearly one-half. Spokesmen for the Chinese community actually supported Japanese relocation, and so did Mayor Rossi of San Francisco, whose own Italian American group was itself a target for war-inspired discrimination. The Sino-Korean Peoples League went further, criticizing the government for not taking even more comprehensive relocation measures than it did.[13]

Some have argued that the selection for relocation of Japanese Americans, and not of Germans and Italians, demonstrates the racial basis of the policy. However, practical matters were more important. The Italians and Germans were much more numerous, at close to 300,000 each in the first and second generations alone. In California, Italians were the largest European-derived foreign stock group. If one adds the third and more remote generations to these figures, it would have produced a number too large to relocate unless the zeal of relocation advocates had equaled that of Hitler. In that case, a maniac wasted needed materials, transportation, and personnel to eliminate one segment of the population. The Americans were neither that biased nor that foolish. Stephen Fox has given the definitive opinion about the importance of racism in this sorry episode. As Fox points out, the Hawaiian Japanese Americans were not relocated, though they were of the same origins as the California Japanese Americans and some, at least, had indulged in espionage. Moreover, General De Witt actually wanted to relocate California German American and Italian American aliens, despite their race. The job was simply too big and the effect, too disastrous to contemplate. As Fox argues, if racism was important, it was the racism that was used to ban completely Japanese immigration to the United States in the 1920s. That act prevented them from building up a population large enough to defend themselves in World War II.[14]

The Germans and Italians had not only done so, they were better assimilated into the state's population and had more political and economic power. In San Francisco alone, applying the *citizen and alien formula* to Italian Americans would have meant the incarceration of Mayor Angelo Rossi; two members of the board of supervisors, including the much-respected Alfred Roncovieri; A. P. Giannini, one of the real builders of the West and a sometime partner of defense shipbuilder Edgar Kaiser and Hollywood moviemakers; the owners of the Del Monte Corporation; leading vintners, including those at Gallo and Italian Swiss Colony; civil defense block captains; many of the fishermen and market gardeners; all of the city scavengers; and Joe, Dom, and Vince DiMaggio, just to mention a few! By the same token, two German Americans sat on the board of supervisors; many excelled in the economic life of the city and, in the case of the Spreckels family, in the development of San Diego as well; Henry Schmidt held a high position in the powerful longshoremen's union, and so forth. Many of the Germans in the cities were also Jewish, and refugees at that, which added another complication to the evacuation of enemy *aliens,* much less citizens.[15]

The Japanese differed in one other important respect. The German and Italian governments had no fleets capable of operating offshore, and therefore even hysterics could not very well suspect their related American groups of collaborating with attacking forces. Although the formidable Japanese navy largely neglected the California theater, they did sink at least one tanker off the California coast, in full view of spectators on shore. That incident made the threat of submarine or carrier hit-and-run attack at least plausible.[16]

No serious military observer believed in the possibility of invasion, but an attack on the many ports, dams, aqueducts, pumping stations, power lines, bridges, railways, factories, or civilian housing sites was by no means out of the question, especially if American defenses were as badly organized as some historians have made them out to be. Nor was consequential sabotage an impossibility in Southern or Northern California. The 1928 bursting of the San Francis Dam in the Santa Clara Valley, with its attendant death toll of hundreds, was still fresh in California minds, and sabotage was one of the leading theories to explain that disaster.[17]

In the long run, the war may have shamed mainstream American society into accepting the Japanese, but that was the only possible bright spot in that sad episode. The war's impact on Chinese Americans, Mexican Americans, Italian Americans, and African Americans was more positive: they found new vistas opened up to them. The demand for total mobilization and labor markedly improved the job prospects and status of each group.

Since Chinese and Japanese Americans were Asians, their comparative fates bear on the question of racism in the story of World War II. Despite their race, Chinese Americans did not share the fate of Japanese Americans. Judy Yung argues that the mainstream changed its attitudes overnight, as did Chinese Americans, who now considered themselves American. October 1942 saw Mayor Bowron actually apologizing to the Chinese consul for Pacific Coast cities' prewar export of scrap iron and steel, destined to become munitions, to Japan. As Ronald Takaki points out, Filipinos, Koreans, and Asian Indians also benefited from this change of attitudes. Instead of being outcasts, they were being courted.[18]

Fortunately, we now have histories, especially those by K. Scott Wong, Judy Young, and Xiaojian Zhao, that cover San Francisco Chinatown, the principal California settlement, so its much-neglected war story can be told. World War II caught the Chinese between two cultures. By the 1930s, an American-born generation had finally emerged. More Americanized than their parents, they had adopted American dress, speech, music, and sports, but had not been accepted by the mainstream. They were aware of their rich Chinese heritage, but they could not go "home" because of war, revolution, and poverty in China. They could not go there, yet could not get in here.

World War II helped resolve this classic immigrant dilemma. Since Japan had attacked both China and the United States, affirming their opposition to Japan allowed Chinese Americans to embrace both their new and old countries. In addition, Chinese Americans competed with Japanese Americans for business space within the historic confines of Chinatown, a situation that added another impetus to their rivalry. Unlike most ethnic groups, Chinese Americans already had considerable experience in homefront efforts, in fact, ten years' worth, ever since the Japanese invasion of Manchuria in 1931. From then until the United States entered the war, the Chinese perfected their political techniques in their own War of Resistance.

These activities were diverse. They included fund raising through the Chinese War Relief Association. Judy Yung explains that war relief also allowed Chinese American women "into the inner sanctums of the Chinese Six Companies to participate in CWRA deliberations as equals for the first time." Indeed, Chinese American newspapers linked female participation in the war effort with the movement to gain equality. Sometimes the protests took the form of boycotts and demonstrations against Japanese American shops on the south end of Grant Avenue. There were also pro-Chinese theater plays and fashion shows. Rice bowl parties produced both money and publicity. Featuring parades, fashion shows, street theater, dancing, and western and Chinese music, the rice bowl party of 1938 drew two hundred thousand people to Chinatown and raised fifty-five thousand dollars in one day. Similar parties in 1940 and 1941 nearly doubled this figure. From 1938 on, Chinese women and others picketed ships loading scrap iron bound for Japan. The 1938 protest ultimately drew five thousand Bay Area Chinese Americans and the support of the longshoremen, who honored the picket line. Red Cross women sent aid to Chinese soldiers and held receptions for visiting Chinese heroes and heroines.[19]

When Japan attacked Pearl Harbor, Chinatown was already brimming with homefront activities, and it was simple to merge the defense of America into these War of Resistance networks. The community continued to buy bonds, raise money, and send supplies and bandages, and they turned the silk boycott into a campaign to conserve silk for the American war effort. Women expanded their unprecedented beachheads outside the home. Unlike black women, Chinese American women faced no discrimination from the Red Cross, USO, YMCA, and American Women's Volunteer Services.[20]

One of the oddest homefront efforts was made by Dr. Margaret Chung. In 1931, she befriended some American airmen who were "hungry and broke." Thereafter, they went to see her when they were in town, and they urged others to do so. The visitors increased and began calling her Mom Chung. Margaret explained that she was not married, which would make them illegitimate. The airmen decided to make a virtue of necessity and agreed to call themselves the Fair-Haired Bastards Club. This benevolent treatment caused "bastardy" to multiply wonderfully—to 1,500! Mom Chung wrote them, gave them gifts, and brought them to her home on their visits. On one such occasion, 175 flying illegitimates threatened to swamp her Chinatown home. Subsequently, she created groups for submariners and for Kiwis, "a women's auxiliary."[21]

Since the building of the railroads, most urban Chinese Americans had not been allowed into good jobs outside those in the restaurants, grocery stores, laundries, and curio shops of Chinatown. They now rapidly escaped into non-segregated work. These included "shipyards, aircraft factories, offices, and other white collar professions." By May 1942, "Bay Area defense establishments began to advertise jobs in local Chinese newspapers." Henry Kaiser himself urged the Chinese to join the defense workforce, and Moore Shipbuilding hired Chinese-speaking instructors for their welding school and ran buses from Chinatown to their Oakland yards. The government operated similar schools. "Minorities" were seldom promoted to supervisory positions and "were often assigned to segregated work units, such as the all-Chinese electrical crews," although a *Chronicle* reporter explained that this was a way to minimize friction between Chinese and some still biased co-workers. Yet not only were these jobs in formerly forbidden territory, they paid a lot better. A member of one family recalled that "everyone worked fewer hours and made more money." The segregated job market also boomed. Given the huge mass of service and defense personnel, Chinatown restaurants and bars flourished. According to one cocktail waitress, she earned as much as fifty to sixty dollars nightly in tips.[22]

Because of problems ranging from lack of transportation to traditional Chinese views on women's role in the home, not as many women, especially married women, sought defense jobs as did men, but women entered the workforce in unprecedented numbers. One historian estimates that five thousand Bay Area Chinese Americans worked in defense jobs, including between five hundred and six hundred women. Sam Lee, a contemporary Chinese American working for the United States Employment Service, put the figure higher still. He estimated a total of seven thousand out of a Chinese American population of twenty thousand to twenty-two thousand, a small number of all Bay Area defense workers, but about one-third of the Chinese American work force in 1940.[23]

So despite the barriers of transportation and traditional views, Chinese American women entered the defense workforce. Surprisingly, Chinese women usually found their defense jobs less onerous than the laundry, garment, and other work they had previously done. The widowed Ah Yoke Gee cooked food for her six grown children and "on weekends, shopped, washed, and cleaned," while remaining faithful to her swing-shift defense job! Mannie Lee worked at a Kaiser shipyard, as did her husband and her three daughters and daughters-in-law, while her two sons and son-in-law were in the Army. As in the case of the "Fighting Sullivans," it could unquestionably be said that this family made the maximum war effort.

Though Chinese women made substantial advances, in general Chinese men made the greater breakthroughs, especially in the professions. They also moved out of the grocery stores and garment shops into better manual-labor jobs. However, Chinese women gained important work mobility as well. Their gains included moving up within the Chinatown economy, where they also faced discrimination, as well as moving into that of the mainstream. Judy Yung has argued that both Chinese men and women made and held onto larger gains than did African Americans during the forties.[24]

Other advances came in social sectors. Chinese Americans met and mingled with many other unfamiliar Chinese. And they met non-Chinese as well. "For the first time among the Chinese," said Lim P. Lee, secretary of the Chinese YMCA, "there is an inter-racial contact and for the first time too, the average American has learned to know and highly regard his Chinese co-workers." One female shipyard worker agreed: "There was such a terrific mixture [of people] and everyone got along well. They were there to do a certain job." And while doing it, they were introduced to the social mainstream as well as the economic one.[25]

The military services provided another opportunity to secure "a new position in American society." Most Chinese American men served in the Army and Army Air Force, in part because the Navy restricted Chinese Americans to steward jobs until early 1942. Unlike blacks and Japanese Americans, most Chinese men were in integrated units. Aside from the 1,200 in the Flying Tigers in Asia and one other unit, Chinese Americans served with Caucasians. So did most Chinese American servicewomen and nurses. Women experienced some discrimination, but overall found the service "rewarding." For Chinese men, the military meant a merit system, from which they benefited. They had an opportunity both to prove their manhood and to protect their country. In turn, they began to share some of its benefits. Attainment of citizenship was one. One amusing incident occurred when eighteen Bay Area men training in Florida could not satisfy citizenship requirements. To keep them, the Army flew them to Canada, entered them legally, and thus qualified them for citizenship.[26]

That was just the beginning. Service also gave veterans the GI Bill of Rights and VA loans, which helped finance postwar education and homes. Some learned new trades; some made the military a career; and all shared the intangibles of pride and access. A uniform also meant admittance anywhere in California, a solid benefit. The politics of the era likewise benefited Chinese Americans. In 1943, Congress repealed the Chinese Exclusion Act, allowing a tiny number of people to enter the country legally and eliminating a burden of racial censure. The 1947 amendment of the War Brides Act of 1945 permitted the entry of six thousand Chinese war brides and their six hundred babies, crucially aiding the family.[27]

The dividends were both material and spiritual. For the first time, Chinese Americans began to enter the American mainstream and to experience group pride in their participation in something national rather than communal. Even prejudice seemed to budge a bit.[28] Their historians describe their entry into the mainstream as gradual, but also insist that the war represented a turning point. The war did not touch such fundamental discriminations as the housing covenants that locked most Chinese into specific ghetto neighborhoods and the sometimes awful housing conditions in the Chinatowns. For example, Chinatown Los Angeles had such bad housing that it was targeted for nearly complete elimination to make way for a new civic center. In addition, the replacement of reform housing with war housing forced San Francisco to postpone a badly needed housing project in Chinatown.[29]

So this new status was not perfect, but it laid the foundations for more impressive advances later on, and it was certainly a far cry from the anti-Chinese agitation and riots of the nineteenth century. "Through the hindsight of historical inquiry, it is now evident that the war left Chinese Americans at the threshold of social mobility and increased assimilation," argues K. Scott Wong, "but in the years immediately following the war, Chinese Americans were simply happy to emerge from the shadows of exclusion."[30]

Like the Chinese, the generation of Mexican Americans born in the United States led their advance. And like the Chinese Americans, the goal was "integration of Mexican Americans into the mainstream." Finally, since Mexicans were, in large measure, peoples of color (to employ the historiographical terminology of the last thirty years), their experience bears on the question of California racism. Like the Chinese Americans, Mexican Americans made modest gains.[31]

These gains did not come without a struggle, especially in Los Angeles, where the largest concentration of Mexican Americans resided. They also seemed to derive more from politics, from the activities of the "Mexican American Generation." According to Mario T. Garcia, the Coordinating Council for Latin American Youth (CCLAY), led by Manuel Ruiz Jr., was central to this work. The group counseled *pachucos,* organized youth sports, fought educational segregation, and reached across lines of culture and power to the leaders of Los Angeles. Mexican Americans were educationally segregated because of residence and were excluded from many schools because they supposedly posed a health threat and because of the language barrier as well as on grounds of race. Section number 8003 of the California Educational Code allowed school districts to establish separate schools for Native Americans, Japanese, Chinese, and Mongolians (Asians), and since many Mexican Americans were of Indian heritage, they were segregated on this pretext. Manuel Ruiz protested that "segregation prevents assimilation" and also contravened the Good Neighbor Policy. These activists gained some important, if somewhat incongruous, allies in Mayor Bowron, State Senator Jack B. Tenney of Los Angeles County, and Assemblyman William H. Rosenthal of the 40th Assembly District. In 1945, the assembly repealed section 8003, but the senate refused to go along. In that same year, Mexican American activists successfully lobbied the El Monte School System to repeal segregation there. The next year, a federal court ruled in *Mendez et al. v. Westminster School District of Orange County et al.* that segregation contravened the equal protection clause of the Fourteenth Amendment, and in 1947 the legislature repealed section 8003. Garcia explained that this victory "did not eliminate de facto segregation nor did it eradicate inferior education," but it laid the foundation for later progress.[32]

This ethnic group work was supplemented by local organizations. In San Dimas, a citrus community in eastern Los Angeles County, the intercultural approach appeared even before the Zoot Suit Riots scared other towns into it. San Dimas in 1942 may have been the community in which the "Americans All" program first appeared. In any case, Mexican and largely southern and southwestern non-Mexicans organized a community center, day care for cannery plant mothers, Spanish- and English-language classes in the schools, and anti-bias workshops for both groups. The community "gradually eliminated" school segregation completely by the 1943–44 school year, even before the El Monte District and the California Supreme Court did so.[33]

Economic gains reduced discrimination, too. Like others, Mexican Americans benefited from the war labor shortage. The CCLAY urged state and national leaders to allow both Mexican Americans and Mexican nationals jobs in defense work. Partly because of this campaign, President Roosevelt "redefined policy" in the summer of 1942 so as to allow the employment of foreign labor. The Council also successfully urged the establishment of the Pan American Trade School in East Los Angeles. Although it trained people only in vocational skills, "still the school aided in creating opportunities in skilled trades: jobs, for the most part, previously unavailable to this population." Mexicans seemed to progress on the union front, too. For example, in late 1942 the CIO claimed that of the one hundred thousand CIO members in Southern California, fifteen thousand were Mexicans.[34]

If anything, Mexican Americans made more employment progress in San Diego. In a sophisticated study of San Diego, Eric M. Mosier has shown that Mexican Americans made significant, though not revolutionary, advances. Mexican American men profited from military service, advanced within their vocations, got into new vocations, and found a home in the union movement. They dominated the Cannery Workers Union, won a few offices in other labor organizations, and got membership in many. Women did not fare as well.[35]

Politics complemented economics. The CCLAY fought bias. Although ambivalent about the Indian part of their heritage, the Council insisted that it was racist to label Mexicans as peoples of color, fearing that discrimination would certainly ensue. They also protested what they perceived as anti-Mexican attitudes in the press during the Sleepy Lagoon Case of 1942 and the Zoot Suit Riots of 1943. Ruiz demanded that FDR "moderate the attitudes of the local press," which "openly approved of these riots." In electoral politics, the Council unsuccessfully backed candidates Eduardo Quevedo and Fred Rubio in races for assembly districts 40 and 51 and backed Quevedo again in 1945 for city council. Both races were firsts for the group. "Let it be heard, for the first time in an election, the courageous voice of the Mexican Colony," read an advertisement. "If you do not have the right to vote, advise those that do have it to support Eduardo Quevedo for councilman for the ninth district of Los Angeles. It's an obligation towards our race." Of course, Mexicans were not a race, but usage indicates the tendency to confuse race with nationality. In fact, Manuel Ruiz strenuously insisted that Chicanos were a white ethnic group, which hoped to be integrated and assimilated while retaining some Mexican cultural traits. Thus, according to Mario T. Garcia, Ruiz missed an opportunity to unite with African Americans to oppose racial grievances.[36]

It has been argued that the war proved decisive in creating a "new political activity and consciousness in the Chicano population throughout the Southwest." Albert Camarillo believes that the explanation is more complex. Their childhoods, their activist family backgrounds, prewar involvement in politics, and alienation from the Catholic Church, together with the war, made them postwar activists. Mexican Americans in San Diego eschewed "traditional methods," political parties, and *mutualistas* to pursue their political goals, but they relied on unions to advocate Hispanic civil rights. Although they did not make electoral gains, they did achieve political experience and protected their interests through their membership in the San Diego labor movement.[37]

Italian Americans shared a different fate. They experienced censure like the Japanese but also greater economic progress than the other groups. The largest European group, three hundred thousand first- and second-generation Italians and fifty-two thousand aliens resided in the Golden State. They ranged from wage earners in Del Monte to the owners of the canneries, the Bank of America, and Gallo. Scholars have debated how many Italians were pro-fascist. Gary Mormino explains that fascism failed to win Italian youth but appealed to many of their parents. However, many non-Italians, ranging from liberal to conservative, also found reason to praise Mussolini. It seems realistic to agree with Mormino and Stephen Fox that most Italian Americans were not fascists, but many admired Benito Mussolini. That persuasion grew out of their affection for Italy, heightened by Il Duce's success in creating an image of competence at home and success abroad. Mussolini exploited this sympathy through Italian schools, radio and newspaper propaganda, and by encouraging Italo American trips to Italy. However, when war with Italy began, the fascist illusion quickly vanished.[38]

Before it did, fearing the fascist connection, Washington rounded up Italian, German, and Japanese Americans thought to be dangerous. Secluded temporarily in places such as the Santa Ana Jail, the Camarillo State Hospital, a camp in Tujunga in southern California, and a Silver Avenue detention center in San Francisco, most California Italians were soon freed. By mid-June 1942, nationally the government had interned 1,521 Italians (sometimes the wrong ones), including 25 Californians, in a camp at Missoula, Montana. Simultaneously, they classified noncitizen Italians, Germans, and Japanese as "enemy aliens." This status stigmatized individuals and groups. These aliens were not enemies; they

were hard-working, permanent residents. General John De Witt, head
of the Western Defense Command (WDC), wanted to intern *all* enemy aliens of whatever descent. Attorney John Molinari explained that
struggles between pro- and anti-fascists abetted this anxiety, as people
denounced political opponents. So did pressure from groups as diverse
as the California congressional delegation, Native Sons of the Golden
West, the L.A. Council of Women's Clubs, the American Legion, and the
L.A. Young Democrats. Cooler heads prevailed, due to the impact that
a huge, alienated Italian and German American population would have
had on morale and war production. Interning one million aliens was not
feasible for a nation straining for manpower and materiel. Thus Italian
Americans avoided the extreme treatment meted out by Great Britain,
Canada, and Australia.[39]

Still, Washington often restricted "enemy aliens" in unfortunate
ways. Fishermen could not fish; others could not work in high-paying
defense jobs or in civil service; and many could not live at home or be
out after curfew. Rose Trovato was barred from a restricted zone, though
her son had died at Pearl Harbor. Father Zavatarro could visit San Francisco for funerals, marriages, and services, but had to live in Oakland.
Joe DiMaggio's father was banned from his "son's restaurant." Raids on
Terminal Island, searches, and seizures of property alarmed Italians.[40]

On Columbus Day, 1942, the Administration finally revoked the
"enemy alien" status. The rapid collapse of American fascism mitigated
that concern. Moreover, FDR was prompted by the importance of the
Italian vote, by the Italians' not having the same authoritarian image
as the Germans and Japanese, and by the Italian Americans' having
already stolen their way into the hearts of the American people. As
Gary Mormino notes, there were simply too many prominent Italians:
Frank Capra, the DiMaggios, A. P. Giannini, Fiorello LaGuardia, and
many more. In 1941, baseball *was* the national game, and Italians won
Most Valuable Player in the American (DiMaggio) and National (Dolph
Camilli, San Francisco) leagues and the batting title of the latter (Ernie
Lombardi, Oakland).[41]

Professor Mormino explains that the enemy alien issue, heartbreak-
ing as it was, has overshadowed the transcendent subject of Italian
American social change. Because of their fund raising, their roles in
community organizations, and their disproportionate numbers of servicemen, Italian Americans gained acceptance. Like the Chinese, they
also moved toward the mainstream. The uprooting of young Italians
and the circulation of military personnel through San Francisco and
Los Angeles led to many marriages outside the group. Community war

work brought the "former[ly] isolated Italian Americans into more frequent contacts with others." As it had for many, the war opened better
jobs to Italians. The military added another common experience, as
did volunteer work among the elite. For example, Dr. Mariana Bertoia
chaired the San Francisco Federation of Women's Clubs, and Dr. A. H.
Giannini headed the USO Board of Los Angeles. The demise of fascism
added another nudge into the mainstream.[42]

The war even eroded the near monopoly of the San Francisco Scavengers Protective Association. A highly prized blue-collar elite, most
scavengers descended from inhabitants of the Genoan village of Lorsica.
Since the military took so many men, the group had to be opened up,
first to other Italians and then to Hispanics. The war rapidly urbanized
agricultural Italians, who found it difficult to compete with growing
agribusiness. Defense wages forced these Italians to join a diverse town
crucible.[43]

The conflict unceremoniously dislodged long-term resident Italian
youths from neighborhoods while newcomers flooded in. In 1940, communities such as Eureka, Arcata, and Monterey were monolithic. Twenty-
five percent of San Francisco's Italians lived in North Beach in 1940 but
only 10 percent in 1970. Obviously, the decentralization of the community was well underway before 1940, but it was still substantial beyond
that point. After the war, suburbanization drained veterans and others
from the neighborhoods of North Beach, Lake Temescal in Oakland, East
Oakland, San Lorenzo, Hayward, and San Pablo, and institutions such
as fascist Fugazi Hall, World War I veterans organizations, Italian newspapers, and, temporarily, Italian language classes closed. When fascism
died, the question of dual loyalties perished with it. Unlike the Chinese,
the Italians had to choose, and they chose the United States.[44]

The war apparently changed the Italian communities more than it
did those of the Mexicans and Chinese. Intellectual Max Ascoli explains
that the war destroyed "the segregation of the Italian communities in
America." Mormino concurs that it "dramatically altered the contours
of Italian American California." The conflict moved California's Italian
Americans closer to the mainstream, and like the Chinese, they gained
wealth, acceptance, and status.[45]

To a lesser degree, African Americans did, too. Historians have criticized black leaders for being too timid and only marginally successful.
However, Albert Broussard argues that black leaders in San Francisco
played their hand shrewdly, courageously, and realistically. They knew
that they could not attain full equality at that moment. Yet they realized
that the war presented an unparalleled occasion for present gains and the

foundation for future ones. They also understood that while demanding democracy at home, they must uphold it abroad. Here as elsewhere in the United States, the strategy of the Double V prevailed, and it succeeded to a modest degree.[46]

Broussard has written that "the era of the Second World War was a period of rapid economic progress for black San Franciscans," and Keith Collins echoes that judgment for Los Angeles. Broussard argues that "the wartime emergency created an unprecedented demand along the entire Pacific Coast for laborers, and the San Francisco Bay Area was the focal point for large-scale black migration." Los Angeles claimed even more. Although not confined to a ghetto economy, as were many Chinese and Japanese Americans, blacks had been restricted by custom to low-paying custodial or heavy labor jobs. By 1943, they had broken out of these into several other industries, including aircraft, construction, iron and steel, San Francisco transit, government, and shipbuilding. Charles Wollenberg estimates that their employment in San Francisco "region's shipyards" rose from "less than three percent in 1942 to seven percent in the following year to more than ten percent" by 1945. This figure was far above the percentage of African Americans in the area. They advanced up to skilled workers on a large scale. African Americans were aided by a number of Bay Area allies, especially the CIO, the San Francisco Labor Council, the Fair Employment Practices Commission (FEPC), and other federal agencies. Harry Lees Kingman ("a white Bay Area liberal" who chaired the local FEPC), the *Daily People's World,* the *San Francisco Chronicle,* and the Public Utilities Commission were especially supportive. Commission manager Thomas Cahill began training African American streetcar motormen in December 1941, long before the labor shortage gave him the leverage to buck the resisting Carmen's Union.[47]

Los Angeles had an even more extreme labor shortage. From mid-1942 onward, the bars to black employment fell, especially in the shipyards and aircraft plants. By late 1944, African Americans made up 14.7 and 11.0 percent of the workers at the California Shipbuilding Corporation and Consolidated Steel yards respectively even though they were only 6.5 percent of the area population. By contrast, Collins points out that on the Gulf Coast, blacks were 33 percent of the population but only 14 percent of the shipbuilders. James Wilburn and Collins found that in California aircraft the percentages ranged from 3.2 to 7.2 percent depending on the firm, the latter figure in excess of the black percentage of the workforce. When the aircraft industry started hiring African Americans, most worked at assembly line positions rather than the custodial jobs in which they first entered other industries. In all, blacks claimed 27,000 to 30,000 Los Angeles area defense jobs by war's end.

Alonzo Smith found striking African American gains in transit, rising to 5.5 percent of motormen and platform jobs by 1945, jobs which they kept after the war.[48]

However, not every business was that accommodating. For example, in San Francisco, FEPC failed to get a "single hospital to change its policy" against employing black physicians and succeeded in getting them to hire blacks as menials only after "some initial resistance." Therefore, black breakthroughs came mostly in government, aircraft, and shipbuilding. Black women made even fewer advances from their heavily domestic employment. Many white workers refused to work with blacks, and unions and management used this opposition, plus their own bias, to limit African American employment. Even when either gender got upgraded work, they seldom got supervisory positions except in all-black units.

Los Angeles workers also suffered from residential problems. Largely limited in residence to the Watts–South Central area, they were remote from much of the aircraft and all of the shipbuilding activity because of a horizontal urban morphology, which spread defense jobs all over the metropolitan area. Collins reports that employers usually assigned blacks to the graveyard shift, and since taxis, buses, and trolleys ran infrequently at that time, transportation to the scattered defense plants was an ordeal. By contrast, African Americans in Hunters Point and the East Bay lived close to Navy and other shipyards.[49]

Bay Area African Americans mounted their greatest efforts against the Boilermakers Union. That union controlled 70 percent of the Bay Area shipyard jobs and refused to allow African Americans union equality. The yards had to hire black workers in order to meet war demands, but the union put blacks into auxiliary unions, whose members could not vote or bargain collectively, while other minorities joined the parent union. This prompted Marinship worker and NAACP head Joseph James and a Bay Area civil rights coalition to retain the law firm of Anderson and Resner. In *James v. Marinship,* the California Supreme Court ruled the auxiliaries illegal and mandated full equality for blacks. In theory, all benefited from the victory of Joseph James. It forced the Boilermakers to grant equality; yet it did not protect the bulk of black workers from massive postwar layoffs. But despite these layoffs, "this fight was a basic turning point in labor relations for Afro-Americans in ending segregated unions and second-class membership."[50]

In the East Bay, African Americans faced the same situation as Marinship workers before the court decision. They got jobs, but often in segregated gangs, and they were placed in auxiliary unions. In contrast to the Marinship group, which was allied with the NAACP, the East Bay

Shipyard Committee Against Discrimination, led by Ray Thompson, a Tuskegee graduate, "grew out of the local Communist party network." Their court battles were either "stalled or defeated." Unions such as the CIO, machinists, and longshoremen "championed the rights of newcomers in the East Bay" but could not persuade the Boilermakers. Southland blacks also protested, refusing to pay dues to the Boilermakers, for which three hundred were fired. Other Bay Area unions such as the Teamsters did not discriminate within their membership; they simply excluded blacks. The L.A. transit unions did not exclude, but they kept blacks at the bottom of the job hierarchy.[51]

Not all unions followed these policies. The International Longshoremen's and Warehousemen's Union was one-third black, and some seven hundred African Americans eventually broke into the San Francisco transit field. However, even that union could not guarantee advancement because promotion depended on seniority. Charles Johnson found that the Bay Area Marine Cooks and Stewards, the United Packing House and Allied Workers, the United Transport Workers, and the United Electrical Workers unions had "sizeable Negro membership." Also, "many AFL" unions on the West Coast did not have discriminatory clauses in their charters and accepted blacks as members. Some Bay Area attitudes changed, too. As Katherine Archibald points out, most whites were biased against African Americans, but to varying degrees. California historians have stressed whites' opposition to black job gains, but as she explains, white attitudes spanned the spectrum. Many whites, even those who intensely hated African Americans, accepted the blacks' right to work.[52]

The International Association of Machinists in L.A. eliminated its anti-black clauses and helped integrate the rubber and aircraft industries. In fact, despite initial bias, the aircraft industry, with an enlightened management and its competing CIO and AFL unions, compiled a much more egalitarian record than the boilermaker-shipbuilder team. As in the Bay Area shipyards, however, blacks found themselves in auxiliaries when other minorities could join the full-status union. However, these men did not undermine the war effort by striking. Instead, legal action, led by Walter Williams and backed by the NAACP and shipyard workers, who "prided themselves on their patriotism," forced acceptance of African American demands. Postwar layoffs hurt, but blacks still retained 1,680 California shipyard jobs.

Aircraft management, starting with Lockheed, hired blacks early, bused "thousands" to the plants to overcome the residential isolation of African Americans, and even decentralized the subassembly phase of their operations so that they would be close to black residential areas. Lockheed's efforts were like the initial phase of affirmative action. The company pledged itself to make "a special effort" to hire more blacks, and they did. Both the CIO United Autoworkers and the AFL Machinists cooperated, accepting union members on an equal basis rather than in auxiliaries. And when the Los Angeles Transit Union continued to oppose black streetcar operators, they heard from the Catholic auxiliary bishop of Los Angeles. The press minimized the fervor of his testimony before the FEPC, but His Excellency, the Most Reverend Joseph T. McCucken, D.D., insisted upon a second article restoring the passion. He reminded readers that African Americans had compiled "an enviable record for efficiency and honesty" as Pullman porters and suggested strongly that employment bias added to the dangerous level of racial tension.[53]

The worst conditions prevailed on Suisun Bay. Pressed to export munitions rapidly, the Navy's Port Chicago facility suffered a fatal explosion on July 17, 1944, killing 328 persons, 202 of them black. The Navy called the blast an accident, but Peter Vogel believes that "the evidence . . . strongly indicate[s] that a nuclear fission device was intentionally detonated at Port Chicago." Humanitarian considerations aside, it seems implausible that the government would destroy its principal ammunition-loading depot on the Coast at precisely the moment that the Pacific Theater opened its final act. Still, the explosion and the outrageous mutiny trial of fifty blacks who refused to work under unsafe conditions led to the desegregation of the Navy.[54]

Blacks made gains in other kinds of employment, too. It is a cliché of urban studies that economic specialization depends on the concentration or urbanization of a large number of people. The war migration, and even crowding, created a critical mass that led to the proliferation of African American businesses. "The influx of black migrants into established black neighborhoods did, in fact, help consolidate an emerging black middle class," Marilynn Johnson writes. "Black landlords, merchants, and businesspeople—primarily old-timers—prospered amid the boomtown atmosphere of the East Bay." San Francisco, Los Angeles, and other cities experienced the same growth. Many of these businesses were night spots in places such as West Oakland and Central Avenue, as musicians and artists catered to the tastes of the growing African American clientele. At the same time, they began to make inroads into the all-white part of the entertainment market. Count Basie and Duke Ellington regularly played to white audiences, and "Blackout Vaudeville" allowed groups such as "Tip, Tap and Toe, the dynamic colored dancers" to perform for white patrons. One San Diego black firm, believed to be the first in the nation, even broke into the defense industry by creating a parachute factory.[55]

California cities were not marred by incidents like the hate strikes in Mobile or the racial upheaval in Philadelphia, where federal troops took over the striking transit system. Historians have usually emphasized the opposition to blacks in wartime work; yet growing acceptance, however grudging, was the more important trend. And, as Collins, Josh Sides, and Wilburn note, African Americans retained many wartime gains after 1945 despite lopsided unemployment. The gains were not always minimal. African Americans' 1,680 jobs represented 9.2 percent of all the shipyard employment in the state, a much greater proportion than the black percentage of the population. Still, peace brought layoffs of last-hired and deskilled blacks. As Broussard and William Chafe agree, the war did not create job equality; it laid the bases for it.[56]

Housing rapidly became an even more important issue as African Americans swamped the housing market, causing tension between whites and blacks and between established black residents and migrants. Blacks doubled their numbers in Watts. Despite inheriting 6,000 dwellings from the relocated Japanese, the black housing deficit in Los Angeles County grew to 11,193 out of a total deficit of 58,000 by April 1945. This meant that African Americans endured 19.3 percent of the housing shortage but were only 6.5 percent of the population. They were approximately 6 percent of the war workforce and got 6 percent of the public housing, but the private market was less open to them. In spite of their moving into some of the housing of the relocated Japanese Americans and the building of 5,000 units at Hunters Point, San Francisco blacks never caught up. In addition, Fillmore District housing deteriorated with wartime crowding. Doubling up and subletting flourished. As in Los Angeles and the East Bay, long-time African American landlords dominated this practice of carving up housing spaces and then charging high rent to live in them. Investigator Charles Johnson called it a "mild form of racketeering." San Francisco had built five city housing projects by 1943, but blacks benefited only from Westside Courts, opened on a segregated basis.[57]

Albert Broussard notes that San Francisco realty interests won out over housing reform, but war did, too. Reform housing gave way to war housing, and materials shortages further limited city housing projects to five of eleven.[58] Covenants and realtor practices also restricted blacks' private housing choices, causing higher rents for less space. So despite liberal backing and protest, the war heightened housing exclusion and racial tension and laid the groundwork for postwar segregation, although the Fillmore District housed many more whites than blacks. Unlike other areas, the mixed housing of this neighborhood did not turn into a ghetto *during* the war, but that trend was clearly underway.[59]

White "neighborhood groups, merchant associations, improvement clubs," and builders demanded further segregation even before the guns fell silent. The Hyman brothers, who had purchased Laurel Hill Cemetery for subdivision, requested the Real Estate Board to lead a movement for restrictive covenants. They failed, but the Central Council of Civic Clubs and others successfully urged adoption of covenants in several other neighborhoods. Housing deterioration also targeted African American areas for postwar urban renewal. Even before 1945, government, business, and liberal reformers designated run-down districts for replacement. That meant black removal, and such evictions actually began, despite the housing shortage. No Detroit-style race/housing riot erupted, but that was about the only housing gain blacks registered.[60]

Much the same outcome occurred in the East Bay and at Marin City. Oakland's and Richmond's prewar worker integration had largely vanished by 1945. Public housing was segregated by building, by area, or by project. And whether located in Richmond, Berkeley, Albany, or Oakland, public dwellings were often cheaply constructed, temporary war housing, located in areas of flooding, cold winds, industrial and railroad noise, and atmospheric pollution. Since the familiar residential exclusion prevailed, blacks had the usual limited choice of private lodgings and thus a greater need for public ones. East Bay officials allocated them anywhere from 10 to 20 percent of the housing, but it still was not enough, even in Richmond, where public housing sheltered 78 percent of the black population. There was always a tension between the goals of adequate housing and integrated housing. If housing officials allocated more than 10 or 20 percent of the housing to blacks, whites would protest or leave. African Americans undoubtedly preferred more housing over integration. Historians stress that "wartime housing programs" laid the foundations for future ghettos. That is true, but public policy and the large-scale black postwar migration did, too.[61]

Historians disagree about wartime urban life. Gretchen Lemke-Santangelo finds that East Bay blacks did find housing—first temporary, then public, and finally owner-occupied. Public housing was communal and therefore friendly to women who needed to network, share day care, mount social activities, and gather information. Moreover, public housing was vastly superior to homes the migrants had fled from, and, surprisingly, blacks owned homes at a higher rate than whites. Unlike other cities, Oakland's African American areas were 85 percent black by war's end, but these communities were "remarkably successful." Despite militant protest, Richmond was segregated, but not successful. In 1945, both faced urban renewal.[62]

Los Angeles city's public housing was integrated, though black public housing was located in African American areas and based on quotas. That in the county remained unintegrated. Moreover, as in the Bay Area, private residential segregation was the rule. Restrictive covenants largely excluded blacks from the San Gabriel and San Fernando valleys by 1941, and wartime construction occurred outside black areas. So when the government exiled the Japanese from their adjacent Central Avenue neighborhood, African Americans had little choice but to pile into it. Overnight, "Little Tokyo" became "Bronzeville." By 1943, the black population of the city had doubled, while their housing remained limited.[63]

Then, to add insult to injury, at the height of the wartime housing crunch, the Supreme Court declared relocation unconstitutional, and Japanese Americans returned to claim their homes. As in San Francisco and the East Bay, deteriorating housing doomed black areas to postwar renewal, and, as Keith Collins notes, the restricted market allowed black apartment owners in the Watts–South Central area to "take advantage of the situation by restructuring apartment buildings into smaller units to . . . increase renters and profits." But as in San Francisco, black areas remained partially integrated. For example, Watts had a one-third white population at war's end. The migration boom crested in 1943–44; yet despite this decline, nearly as many blacks arrived after the peak as during it: 53,000 to 65,000. War alone did not make ghettos. The conflict may have laid the foundation for the ghetto, but postwar migration consolidated it.[64]

African Americans in all cities suffered considerably from this discrimination. They lost privacy by doubling up; their female children often left home for live-in maid jobs; the market forced black buyers or renters to pay more for less space, fire insurance, repairs, and hard-to-secure credit. These conditions caused housing decay, which provided white apartment owners a pretext not to rent to blacks. Buildings did not meet code requirements, but the inspectors did not enforce repairs. Both old and new construction was flimsy and conducive to fire, and it often was near the railroads. Location made many of the defense sites relatively inaccessible to potential workers.[65]

Albert Broussard, Marilynn Johnson, Shirley Moore, and Katherine Archibald believe that Bay Area blacks gained more in the realm of leadership. As the latter put it, "On the whole, however, the appeals by Negroes [for equality] and their frequent victories unquestionably gave

them status as a people in the eyes of their white companions in toil."
Charles Wollenberg notes, "During the 1940s these men and women won
battles that established important legal principles." The war migration
greatly augmented the black elite also. These new leaders were younger,
college-educated, southern, activist, and dedicated to working with white
liberals. Their goals did not differ from those of the established cadres
except in the "urgency" they brought to the task. With the exception of
Joseph James, businessmen led. This vanguard sparked an explosion. The
NAACP was energized, and newspapers, a branch of the Urban League,
and interracial and civil rights groups were founded. The Church for the
Fellowship of All Peoples opened; in the words of its pastor, Howard
Thurman, it was the first "fully integrated" church in the United States.
Men, especially ministers, dominated the leadership, but women, chiefly
ministers' wives, played large roles.[66]

From 1940 to 1943, "dissension" neutralized the NAACP, so new
organizations filled in. One was the Bay Area Council Against Discrimination, or BACAD, which was not just San Francisco–based. It
sprang up, agitated, and faded after mid-1944 due to apathy and lack of
money. The San Francisco Council on Civic Unity succeeded it, added
a few gains, and merged after the war into the California Council for
Civic Unity, which also floundered. Run by whites, with ample foundation support, these organizations succeeded no better than those run by
blacks. Even several years after the war, African Americans could not
get into Bay Area medical schools; they visited hospitals on a segregated
basis, remained outside many unions, did not have a seat on the board
of supervisors, suffered high levels of postwar unemployment, and generally remained in a subordinate position. However, the additions to
leadership, the leverage of the war, and the greater urgency of the new
leadership did bring many immediate gains. Generally, the war brought
defense jobs, though it did not break down many of the barriers that
carried over into peacetime. In addition, blacks made important contacts
with elite whites. Broussard held that the Bay Area was far ahead of any
California or eastern metropolis in interracial cooperation. But mostly
they laid foundations.[67]

The East Bay did, too. One long-time observer explained, "The
southern migrants had pointed out that the Bay Area was not as liberal
as many had believed." Despite residents' initial resentment against the
newcomers, East Bay black politicians welcomed them and began to
combat discrimination. African Americans also began to address broader
community issues in alliance with liberal whites. A number of important
future leaders emerged during the war, including C. L. Dellums of the

Sleeping Car Porters and the East Bay NAACP, Byron Rumford, and Matt Crawford. After 1945, they formed part of a coalition of businessmen, communists, CIO and AFL unionists, and religious leaders that briefly challenged the entrenched politicians of the East Bay. Interestingly enough, East Bay Draft Board No. 73 "was the only board in the country" with black members, half the number. Their work planted the seeds of "civil rights activities that would blossom in the postwar era."[68]

In Los Angeles, the flowers had already bloomed. The activities of Southland blacks refute the argument that African American leaders became quiescent after the threat of African American collective violence appeared in 1943. They remained anything but quiescent. For the first time, blacks ran successfully in local races, electing Mrs. Eva Allen to the city school board for one term. Leon Washington led the 1939 primary for city council in his district, only to lose in the runoff to a white liberal. Politicians created alliances that spanned the gap between old settlers and new, NAACP and unions. Union men successfully combated discrimination in several key unions; African Americans made up a disproportionate number of workers in the defense industries, and they campaigned successfully for transit jobs. Blacks also assumed important positions in the local bureaucratic oversight committees—the city housing authority and the crucial airport committee. Several African American newspapers, including one run by Charlotta Bass, an increasingly important leader, flourished, prospered, and attacked segregation. Blacks politicized the issue of police brutality and demanded black teachers in African American schools.[69]

As blacks flooded into Bronzeville, businessmen organized their own chamber of commerce with the typical Southern California growth ethos. Reformers believed that the influx into the Central Avenue–Watts area created slums and blight, but the Bronzeville Chamber of Commerce thought the migration produced markets and clout. They added to it by networking across racial lines to "patriotic white workers" who supported black job rights. By the end of the war, Mayor Bowron was appointing blacks to important positions. John Anson Ford, the dominating figure on the Los Angeles County Board of Supervisors, helped African Americans stretch across town to Hollywood liberals to mingle with the stars, learn to reach them, and set the stage for the Southside-Westside alliance that would pay rich rewards in the 1970s. Black leaders obviously were not intimidated by the threat of mass violence.[70]

The bars of discrimination fell in San Francisco and Los Angeles restaurants, stores, and hotels. The victory came from both a tight labor market and militant protest. The Los Angeles Negro Victory Committee, which was led by Reverend Clayton Russell of the Independent Church and spearheaded much of the change, illustrates the point. They got the United States Employment Service (USES) to list blacks for jobs, "persuaded" the school board to establish training centers convenient to African American neighborhoods, and faced down transit union discrimination. The Committee shrewdly wooed white support, united churches, the NAACP, the Urban League, and other leaders, and indulged in something close to modern militant tactics. Often called a march, their intimidation of the USES was closer to a stand-in. African Americans appeared at the USES offices in force, lined up around the block, and created an incident. The Service quickly relented and listed blacks for jobs. The Committee shrewdly insisted on the patriotic significance of their actions. For example, they got white support against the transit company by pointing out that it hurt the war effort to allow three hundred cars to remain idle for lack of operators when blacks wanted to operate the cars to win the war. Whites who needed transit to get to work sided with the blacks. Lawrence de Graaf ably summed up the impact of war: it "represented significant steps" toward ending discrimination but still left plenty to combat.[71]

The Los Angeles Negro Victory Committee provides both a good story and a good guide. As de Graaf notes, black experience is much more than just discrimination. Historians of African Americans' Second Great War experience have concentrated almost exclusively on bias and resistance, but the Double V insisted on winning both the war and the peace. This was much more representative of what actually happened. By concentrating only on the bias part of the V, historians have made it seem that African Americans were indifferent to the most important event of the twentieth century. Specialists in black history have not told the story of African Americans' support for the war effort, so the generalist cannot create a larger story for which the specialists have not provided the pieces. Still, at least one major general contribution of African Americans and others stands out. United States mobilization depended on mass production. It took four years to train a skilled ship worker, and business did not have that kind of time. They either had to organize unskilled workers into mass-production forces or produce many fewer goods. So African Americans, women, Italian Americans, Southwesterners, Chinese Americans and all the others helped the country do what it had to do in order to win. The miracles of victory depended fully as much on the deskilled workers who staffed the production lines as upon the skilled engineers and businessmen who organized them.

Southwesterners, like blacks, were drawn to the Golden State by the acute labor shortage. Less well known to history than the Dust Bowl migrants, the 1940s émigrés were twice as numerous. James Gregory counted 621,000 migrants from Oklahoma, Arkansas, Texas, and Missouri alone during the 1940s. Thousands of others fled the San Joaquin Valley and other California agricultural areas and, like blacks, followed the jobs and their relatives to the cities.[72]

There they hired on at the shipyards and aircraft plants at undreamed-of wages. Like blacks, they invaded the war effort en masse. Nineteen percent of the thirty-four thousand workers at Calship on Terminal Island in Los Angeles were Southwesterners, as were 29 percent of the ninety thousand workers at the Kaiser Richmond yards. Aircraft and housing witnessed the same incursion. Just as blacks, Italians, Chinese Americans, and Mexicans concentrated in such neighborhoods as the Fillmore, Hunters Point, Watts–South Central, North Beach, Chinatown, and East Los Angeles, the Southwesterners congregated in Bell Gardens, Santa Monica, Culver City, El Segundo, Torrance, North Long Beach, and Hawthorne in Southern California. They also massed in Vallejo, Brisbane, Bayview, and "most important, in Richmond" in the Bay Area. Depending on the place, they constituted 25 to 30 percent of the migrants to such cities. As they were for others, accommodations were scarce, overcrowded, and nasty, and the Southwesterners coped in about the same way: "With affordable housing all but impossible to find," notes Gregory, "people imposed on relatives, crammed into undersized apartments, or made do in trailer parks."[73]

Unlike housing, bias was never in short supply. As Gregory and Archibald explain, the word *Okie* had a very negative 1940s connotation. Their white skins deflected some of the bigotry suffered by other ethnic groups, but it was still plentiful and brutal. Southwesterners were seen as lazy, transient, ignorant, stupid, unable to deal with machinery, unwilling to learn, dirty, violent, and greedy, just as blacks were. Cruel jokes circulated about them. Someone labeled a shipyard urinal an "Okie Drinking Fountain" and placed a cup close by. Supposedly these "farmers" did not value unions or, contradictorily, they understood them only too well and would steal the unions from their "rightful owners." As with African Americans, it was admitted that some Southwesterners were agreeable, but the group was not. Like blacks, these migrants did not suffer in silence. To the belligerent worker, the Southwesterners offered their fists, and to the exclusive, stigmatizing "native sons," these white migrants matched slur for slur. One ditty ran:

> The miners came in forty-nine,
> The whores in fifty-one,
> And when they bunked together
> They begot the native son.

Unlike other groups, the Southwesterners seemed to have no organized ethnocultural defense organizations. Perhaps that is because they needed none. Archibald discovered that the promotion ceiling did not apply to Southwesterners as it did to blacks and women. And bias did not deny them full-fledged rather than auxiliary union membership. In one Steamfitters Union election, the old guard went down to defeat despite their Okie-baiting, perhaps confirming the unionist fear that the newcomers could "take over."[74]

Nonetheless, as with the other minority groups, the war encouraged growing acceptance in Southern California of these white migrants, for which "the press deserves much of the credit." Gregory and Archibald find that the Bay Area was less congenial, and Marilynn Johnson stresses undiminished resentment throughout. And, of course, war brought prosperity. James Gregory calls the war a turning point in the history of this cultural group. He emphasizes that increases in earnings raised metropolitan Southwesterners up to lower-middle-class status by 1950. However, their occupational status changed hardly at all.[75]

The Southwesterners were only one element in an extremely diverse urban mixture that observers considered dangerous. Yet Kevin Leonard suggests that people worked effectively to prevent violence. He discovered that relations between African Americans, Mexican Americans, and Japanese Americans were relatively benign. Tension rose in 1943 after the Detroit riot, but instead of convulsions, interracial committees dedicated to bettering relations erupted over the California landscape. They wrestled with housing, police-community relations, continuing prejudice, postwar unemployment, the return of the Japanese Americans, and the Port Chicago munitions disaster. Police retraining and education programs were begun. The San Francisco Board of Supervisors resolved resoundingly against bias of any kind; Mayor Bowron spoke repeatedly in the same vein, and so did the newspapers. Leonard's thesis can be extended to the rest of the spectrum as well. Given the novelty, frustrations, and "social disunity" of war, relatively little cultural violence took place.[76]

Not that Urban California was a paradise of ethnocultural relations. Oakland witnessed the Twelfth Street Riot in May 1944, when "some 5,000 black swing fans were turned away from a sold-out Cab Calloway dance, [and] the restless crowd began smashing" property. After the ball, violence spread to streetcar conflicts between blacks and white sailors, a conflict that resulted in one dead and four wounded. Although not a race riot, it "had racial implications." Katherine Archibald also witnessed interracial fights at Moore Dry Dock. Even after the war, the Richmond city manager feared the outbreak of a race riot in that war-torn home-front city. In Los Angeles, whites violently resisted black entry into their neighborhoods; crosses burned on the lawns of the newcomers, and fights occurred on the streetcars. Keith Collins notes that in May 1944, a crowd of one hundred black teenagers "mobbed a trolley and beat several white passengers." The Ku Klux Klan even experienced a renaissance. When a Japanese Buddhist priest returned from the relocation camps and tried to evict seventy-five blacks living in his temple, anti-Japanese violence followed "in an effort to discourage their return to Los Angeles." City health officials, the NAACP, and others warned of the potential for additional disorder, and sometimes it occurred.[77]

However, from specialist historians' accounts, one would think that the war effort was a rough-and-tumble affair everywhere. Mauricio Mazon believes that "the Zoot Suit menace pales when compared with the violence taking place between civilians and servicemen throughout Southern California." Marilynn Johnson writes that "conflicts between civilian and military personnel were a major source of violence and disorder" in the East Bay and that "aggravated assaults" there doubled between 1942 and 1948. James Gregory holds that fighting was an integral part of Southwesterner culture. Finally, Keith Collins has unearthed numerous examples of African American intramural violence as well. The interracial conflicts were not disproportionately more important than the others. Charles Johnson, a meticulous observer, minimized racial turbulence. Regarding San Francisco public housing, he wrote, "Most officials interviewed on this point say that there is no greater difficulty between Negro and white families occupying these projects than is normally found between families of the same racial background occupying a given housing development."[78]

The Zoot Suit Riots of June 3 to 13, 1943, are California's most famous wartime upheaval. More than any other single event, they have come to characterize wartime California's ethnocultural relations. Neither scholars nor contemporary Navy officials have established exactly how these riots commenced. The disorder got its name from the wonderfully peculiar clothing worn by Mexican American and some African American youngsters. The broad-brimmed hats, pegged pants, elongated watch chains, and slicked-down hair became the Zooters' trademark to themselves and to outsiders. They were called pachucos and their girlfriends, pachuquitas. Psychohistorians believe that pachuco jargon and uniforms had great cultural and psychological significance. In any case, their wearers had a number of collisions with sailors who frequented their neighborhoods in search of good times and pachuquita dates.

According to some accounts, this singular interest in the pachuquitas resulted in several beatings of sailors, which was more excitement than these mariners had bargained for. So they swore vengeance, organized at Chavez Ravine armory, and returned in strength, reinforced by other servicemen in search of Zoot Suits.[79]

They found them, and there quickly followed several nights of "fury" against persons Hispanic and their habiliments, which various observers have turned into a cause célèbre. The sailors and valiant but badly outnumbered pachucos rocked, socked, and rolled for several days. The Navy finally declared Downtown and East Los Angeles off limits, and one thousand city police, plus military police and shore patrols, enforced the order, quelling the riots. Lots of bruises but no deaths, no serious injury, and little property damage grew out of the rocking and socking, reemphasizing the minimal importance of the riot to the history of either defense, ethnocultural relations, California, or American collective violence—and perhaps even less to urban history. Sailors, not a civilian population ostensibly warped by all kinds of psychological frustrations, precipitated the riot.

Despite supposedly "seething" tensions, California cities proved that Leonard's thesis of surprisingly irenic relations among blacks, Mexicans, and Japanese Americans applies equally to the broader ethnic and race story. Mauricio Mazon stresses the psychology of symbolic annihilation and even symbolic castration in his account of what even he calls "pseudoriots"; yet neither castration nor annihilation occurred. In the lynchings of the Jim Crow Era, the lynchers did not similarly restrain themselves. If California urbanites were caught in the "massive psychic and physical upheaval" of war, "beset by the uncertainties and pressures of war," and if "wartime society" required a scapegoat or an object for psychological displacement, the need must have been very modest indeed.[80]

Ironically, the "Zoot Suit paradigm," often used to exaggerate the gravity of World War II collective violence, suggests the reverse. If anything, this and the Twelfth Street Riot establish that California cities survived the war with little serious cultural violence. By contrast, the Detroit Riot of 1943 killed thirty-four, and even the 1943 Harlem riot claimed six lives.[81]

In fact, the riot and conflict has overshadowed the more important trend toward acceptance. People began to know and accept each other. Several observers in the Committee for Interracial Progress even maintained that the returning Japanese Americans had a "fine reception . . . throughout Southern California." Gary Mormino and Scott Wong have called this "mainstreaming." Ethnicity and pluralism certainly endured on a large scale, but the war nationalized Californians just the same. Nelson Lichtenstein has argued that the war mainstreamed the white working class by raising and equalizing wages, by disciplining working men through large organizations (unions, business), by the cosmopolitan experience of the Army and Navy, and by the embrace of racism. As we have seen, racism in California unions waned instead of waxed, but Lichtenstein's other contributing factors fit the state's experience. Many other influences melded people. Italian Americans abandoned fascism, made economic gains, intermarried, traveled, and often left North Beach. Chinese Americans earned more money and entered new fields, gained acceptance, and benefited from the Army and the GI Bill. Chinese women, for the first time, began to work for wages in businesses outside the home, as did Mexican women. Black men made gains in aircraft, transit, government, and longshoring, and women established beachheads outside domestic employment. Mexicans had similar experiences. Large numbers took out citizenship papers. Historians' heavy concentration on race has often obscured the fact that great prejudice existed against and between white ethnics. The war helped end it.[82]

And everyone experienced the war as they had hardly any other American adventure. Millions shared the condition of migration and mobility; millions felt the standardization of war; thousands worked in civil defense; nearly everyone participated, one way or another. The departure from familiar neighborhoods of North Beach or a small Texas town brought together people from all over. One woman was amazed to meet Texans, whom she apparently previously had thought came from the nether side of Mars. Helen Knox of the Interracial Progress Committee noted an impacted Long Beach school where students came "from all sections of the country and . . . a great variety of social backgrounds and cultures."[83] And each group was introduced to members of its own group that they would never have met save for the war. For them, the war was an introduction to each other.[84] Even segregation began to give ground—a school here, a swimming pool there.[85] Training classes for policemen were sponsored by the state, and teacher training sessions popped up at Stanford and UCLA.[86] All these happenings edged people closer to the mainstream. So did the exhortations of press and governments against bias and division.[87] Even the most distinctive cultural traits began to blend. Mexicans, Southwesterners, whites, and blacks each brought a musical tradition to California cities. Once there, their rural music was influenced by the city and by each other. They held huge barn dances at Venice Pier, staged concerts at the Palladium, strummed and drummed in their ethnic ghettos, visited and listened to each other, hearkened to their radios, learned, and changed. Whether Bob Wills, Nat Cole, or a Mexican band, they had access to one another. These groups may have been very skeptical of each other, but when they went dancing, despite not knowing it, they found themselves swinging to an amalgamated music. That is because they were becoming an amalgamated society.

So far, historians, with a few exceptions, have concentrated on the individual group experience in the war. They ask similar questions: what did each group gain, how did they coexist, and were they accepted by others? For obvious reasons, these are valid questions. Many observers of this war have emphasized the omnipresence of conflict. I doubt that many contemporaries ever thought that the United States was one big, happy, gladiatorial mass; yet historians have long written of such conflicts, and more recent social historians have filled in this picture. Still, neither group has concentrated on the degree to which these outbursts hindered war production.[88] In their eagerness to chronicle groups, historians have overlooked the greater significance of ethnicity. That is, how did ethno-cultural relations affect the war effort? The answer to that question is not much. Some of the labor disturbances endangered defense production, but California's social conflicts had a minimal effect.

Katherine Archibald, in her classic study, describes the Moore Dry Dock yards as a boiling cauldron of tensions. Men resented women, whites disdained blacks, old-settler African Americans resented new-comers, most whites looked down on Southwesterners and hated blacks, and exclusive Californians and native-born Californians disliked new-comers.[89] The result was "social disunity." Mauricio Mazon, in his provocative study of the psychohistory of the riots, perceives similar tensions among civilians, servicemen, whites, blacks, pachucos, and older Mexicans.[90] Others insist on racism and sexism. Yet why would such "seething" cities and workplaces produce so few major disturbances? Archibald insists that southern whites talked incessantly of lynching, yet they hanged no one.[91] The press, contemporary observers, and modern historians have waxed eloquently about the Zoot Suit Riots, yet these were closer to farcical than to fatal.

The irrelevance of "social disunity" to the war effort is evident in defense output. Despite the supposed mutual rancor of shipyard workers, they managed to achieve one production record after another. On one occasion, a Kaiser Richmond yard produced the Liberty ship *Robert E. Peary* in *four* days, fifteen hours, and twenty-nine minutes. The average was seventeen days![92] It is hard to imagine how any set of workers could build and launch an entire ship in less than five days, even if brotherly love had prevailed to a heavenly degree. The aircraft industry registered equally remarkable records.

With the exception of the Japanese, each group advanced modestly toward the V at home and contributed magnificently to the V abroad. Realistically, the war yielded enough gains to keep the upthrusting minorities from revolting against the defense effort, and the mobilization effort asked little enough to keep the defenders of the status quo from disruptive reaction. It was a sophisticated compromise.

6. War and the Sources of Urban Racial and National Diversity

Japanese relocation from California cities has left us with a rather chauvinistic image of the state. Yet both Northern and Southern California had long been the destination of migrating Americans, Latin Americans, Asians, and Europeans in addition to Californians from the countryside and Canadians from the Northwest. When the Imperial Japanese bombed Pearl Harbor, California cities were among the most diverse in the United States. Some Eastern and Midwestern cities held more European-derived diversity, but none combined the rich mixture of European, Latin American, Asian, and many strands of American culture to be found in the cities of the Golden Land. As historians have recently come to note, California cities are the new Ellis Islands of the nation, but this observation is made mostly with regard to the foreign born. In fact, California cities have long been the destination for both immigrants and other Americans.[1]

Historians of the West and California have ignored much of this wartime diversity. To the extent that they have considered ethnocultural subjects, they have concentrated upon the disruptions in the lives of Japanese Americans. To a lesser extent, they have discussed Mexican Americans and African Americans. The story of these three groups is crucial to an understanding of the war, but it is only a part of the story. The history of the others is just as important and perhaps more so, since unlike the Japanese, Mexicans, and blacks, the others made up the vast majority of the population.[2] This narrative cannot make up for all of this neglect because there is still an insufficient monographic literature to draw upon. However, one can at least begin: this chapter documents the astonishing and continuing variety of California cities.

Western history customarily measures diversity by race and ethnicity, thus overlooking the multiplicity of peoples born within the country. Western historians consider Indians, Hispanics, and blacks to be bona fide cultural groups and lump everyone else into the enigmatic omnibus category of "Anglo." Unless we assume that there was no significant difference between the Protestant Northwest and the Catholic Northeast, the prosperous Midwest and the deprived Southeast, Yankees and Okies, Cajuns and Mormons, Jews and Gentiles, Arkies and Anglicans, we must admit that the Hispanic-Indian-black-Anglo measure of diversity is neither a precise nor an inclusive indicator.[3] In 1940, there were great dissimilarities between peoples of American regions, which must be considered in any tenable investigation of ethnocultural change.[4]

Their narrative begins with an improbable, and possibly counterintuitive, statement: Los Angeles and Southern California were very cosmopolitan, more so than many other American urban regions and more so than San Francisco and the Bay Area. In 1940, two principal groups formed the bulk of the populations of the three major cities in Northern California. The vast majority were American-born whites, with those from the West census region making up 69.32 percent of the population in San Francisco, 64.21 percent in Oakland, and 67.2 percent in Sacramento. Using the smaller Pacific census division rather than the larger West census region, the area they came from narrows further still. In San Francisco, 64.34 percent hailed from the Pacific census division, while in Oakland and Sacramento, 58.22 percent and 60.15 percent did. These cities were predominantly Caucasian, western—and largely Pacific Coast—places.

Foreign-born whites or their children, known to the census as "foreign stock," made up the second major group. This segment of the population, of course, overlapped the western and Pacific categories, since many of the ethnic populations were native born in the West of foreign parents.

The Southland also housed large numbers of foreign stock, but Los Angeles, Long Beach, and San Diego drew from a much broader "native-born" base. The census employed this term to denote people born in the United States of American parents. Los Angeles gained only 38.94 percent of its native-born population from the West and only 31.09 percent from the Pacific Coast. In Long Beach, the percentages were 34.2 percent and 26.13 percent, and in San Diego, 37.17 percent and 31.04 percent respectively. These Southland cities drew from a much more heterogeneous American native-white population, which added considerably to their diversity. (See Appendix, Table 6.1.)*

---

*For the convenience of readers who want full statistical details, the tables for this chapter have been gathered in the Appendix.

None of the Southland urban centers drew more than 31.09 percent of its residents from a single census division, and all had much more balance than their Northern California competitors. Long Beach, which endured taunts for being the principal seaport of Iowa—a denigration of the supposed insularity of that part of its populace—was more diverse than any of the northern California big cities, as were San Diego and Los Angeles. San Francisco drew nearly two-thirds of its people from the Pacific Coast. Despite its reputation for diversity, San Francisco was the more insular city in terms of native-born whites.

Like other native-born residents, Southern California African Americans were markedly more diverse than those in Northern California. Not much of the population of Urban California was black in 1940; most African Americans were concentrated in Southern California, and their origins were different from those of native-born whites. (See Appendix, Table 6.2.) The overall black population was far less diverse than the white, and in Northern California the overwhelming majority of blacks, just under 90 percent in the case of San Francisco and Sacramento, hailed from only two places, the Pacific division and the West South Central division.

In reference to the white ethnic dimension of the arsenals of democracy the year before the war engulfed them, the census provides a breakdown for only two California cities, but since the largest foreign-born colonies resided in Los Angeles and San Francisco, it is of some value. (See Appendix, Tables 6.3 and 6.4.) The two great California cities contained the lowest proportions of peoples in the top five groups of any of the eighteen ethnic cities listed in the census. They were more diverse because the leading groups made up much less of their populations. (See Appendix, Table 6.5.) California cities did not lead in the percentage of foreign white stock as a percent of the population, but they did lead the cities listed in the census in demographic diversity. Neither San Francisco nor Los Angeles had an overwhelmingly dominant group like the Germans of Milwaukee or St. Louis, the Italians of Providence or Newark, or even the Swedes of Minneapolis. At 17.8 percent, the Italians of San Francisco comprised the largest single percentage group of California ethnics, but as a percent of the city's total population, it was the smallest leading category among the cities listed except for Pittsburgh, Cleveland, and Los Angeles. So the white ethnic mélange of California's cities was striking, and unlike with the native born, Northern and Southern California did not diverge. San Francisco and Los Angeles ranked one and two.

Each of those cities also contained a major Asian population. Sizable colonies of what the census called "other races"—Chinese, Japanese,

Filipinos, and Indians—lived in San Francisco, Los Angeles, Oakland, Sacramento, and, to a lesser extent, San Diego. These figures must be taken with a grain of salt because these minorities seem to have been undercounted. However, enough appeared in the census to reinforce the image of complexity. (See Appendix, Table 6.6.) None of these groups made up a large percentage of Urban California or a large number of people. Still, they totaled nearly 75,000, and San Francisco and Los Angeles each contained more of these "other races" than either Vallejo or Richmond had total residents before the war began.

The American West, especially Los Angeles, has often been derided as a parochial place, but that charge is not accurate in an ethnocultural sense. Los Angeles contained remarkable cultural variety. Besides great native-born and European-derived ethnic diversity, Los Angeles had the largest Mexican and black communities in the state.

Like their manufacturing and service economies, California cities' ethnocultural makeup was already mature before the war began. The war changed this urbane world only marginally. The conflict produced perceptible population gains for blacks and lesser ones for Mexican Americans, but it did not significantly alter the general cosmopolitan character of the cities. It did not markedly rearrange the internal shares of the ethnocultural market held by various groups, except in Oakland; it did not radically modify the percentage held by any single group or set of groups; and it did not transform the long-range ethnic, native-born, or other racial population trends.

Blacks and Mexican Americans registered the greatest population gains during the conflict. The black population of Los Angeles city shot up from 63,774 in 1940 to 171,209 in 1950. In San Francisco, the figures rose from 4,846 to 43,502; in Oakland, from 8,462 to 47,562; and in San Diego, from 4,143 to 18,364. These figures were healthy percentage increases, and in Los Angeles, Oakland, and San Francisco, ample absolute ones. Even so, only in Oakland did blacks reach 10 percent of the city population. (See Appendix, Table 6.7.)

Ultimately black populations would grow, and in the case of Oakland they would reach a majority. Even so, the overall thrust of this trend in World War II did not significantly modify the general population diversity of California cities. Each already possessed a well-established African American colony before the war. Moreover, the large wartime migration did not fundamentally alter the black population's long-term relationship to the remainder of the cities' populations. Most of the growth in African American areas of Urban California would occur only after the war (as did some of the 1940s increase), and even with these new additions, the cities remained overwhelmingly non-black.

The impact of World War II is often called a "Second Gold Rush." In the first one, some fifteen thousand Hispanics (the figure varies) were swamped by several hundred thousand non-Hispanics in a few years. Nothing comparable occurred during World War II, even in Oakland. African Americans did not gain a majority, much less an overwhelming preponderance.

By 1980, California cities still ranked way down the list in black population. (See Appendix, Table 6.8.) Just as surely, war did not instigate a major trend that markedly changed the African American share of urban populations. If one puts the 1940s black population into a metropolitan context, black growth was even more marginal. We should not focus upon the black gains of the wartime period because they did not set the stage for future large-scale growth. We should concentrate on the question of why, despite the wealth of opportunity in the state and its relatively milder racial climate, the African American population of California metropolitan areas remained modest, at or below the black percentage of the national population and below many other less benign metropolitan areas.

Hispanic gains were less striking, but of more long-term significance. Spanish settlements had long been established in California, and the war in no way created them or even made them significant. They were already substantial. However, assessing their numbers is complicated by the fact that since 1920 the census has employed four different measures to count Hispanics: Mexican, mother tongue, Spanish surname, and Spanish origin.[5] The census records some 94,423 Mexicans in 1930 in Los Angeles alone, a figure that declined to 92,680 in 1940, perhaps due to the Depression and the repatriation pressures on Hispanics. So at best, the war accelerated a trend of very long standing and one that would continue and grow long after the war ceased.

In fact, in Los Angeles city and the state as a whole, the Mexican American percentage actually fell, and in San Francisco it gained less than one point. Although the 1940 census does not record Mexican American figures for Long Beach or San Diego, the war could not have had much of a quickening influence because the postwar percentage in each was still so small, less than one percent in the case of Long Beach. Nor did the Mexican American group necessarily grow faster than the general community of the principal cities. In Los Angeles, the war decade produced a 31 percent rise in the general populace and only a 24.7 percent advance in the Mexican American sector. In San Francisco, the Mexican American advance outpaced that of the city by 48.4 percent to 22.2 percent. Despite that striking increase, the group's numbers remained under 2 percent of the whole population.

There is always the possibility of a census undercount of a people who have had a long history of underground immigration. However, even if the census had missed one out of every three Mexican Americans, the picture would not be significantly different. In Los Angeles, the addition of the uncounted Mexican Americans to the 1940 and 1950 totals would have increased their share of the total population from 6.16 percent to 9.24 percent in 1940 and from 5.86 percent to 8.79 percent in 1950—in either case, a modest change. California as a whole in 1950 was only 4.54 percent Mexican. (See Appendix, Table 6.9.)

Eventually, the Mexican American contingent would vastly increase, but as in manufacturing, the postwar census periods would register more striking absolute gains than the years of the Second Great War. In the 1940s, the Mexican American population gained by 126,582, or 35.71 percent; in the 1950s it jumped by 214,629, 44.62 percent, a greater absolute and percentage increase.[6] Again, as in manufacturing, earlier decades had also shown more striking growth. The census provides figures for foreign-born Mexicans only back to 1920. In the 1920s, the Mexican born leaped from 86,610 to 199,169, a 130 percent increase. This figure does not compare exactly to later figures on general nativity, which take in both foreign born and native born of foreign parents. However, it is enough to make the point that the decade of the 1920s registered striking Mexican immigration to California, or to put it more accurately, a large percentage increase of the Mexican population, especially when compared to figures for the 1940s. And the absolute increase of the foreign born in the 1920s is only slightly less than the increase of both foreign born and native born of foreign parentage in the 1940s. In this decade, the Mexican foreign born increased by only 20.84 percent, a much slower advance of the foreign-born population than that of the 1920s. So the war decade did not match the 1950s, and although we do not have figures for the 1920s for first- and second-generation Mexicans, the war decade probably did not equal the 1920s either.[7] No demographic revolution comparable to the Gold Rush had occurred *even by 1980*. (See Appendix, Table 6.10.)

The war had a similar effect on the remainder of the ethnocultural base. By pouring more native-born Americans into Urban California, the war watered down and diversified the first- and second-generation immigrant component, but did not markedly reduce the ethnocultural variety of 1940. The figures also indicate that dumping all of this astonishing cultural diversity into an "Anglo" category is going to miss a lot.

Though often overlooked, immigration from abroad, especially Europe, made up one of the most important population trends in the state.

Although the drift to the West from other countries was overshadowed by the migration of the native born to California cities, it was nonetheless very significant. Including Mexicans, immigration accounted for an increase of some 618,588 persons. That is just over 20 percent of the rise in California's population in the 1940s. Even without Mexican immigration, the total is over 492,006, highlighting the fact that immigration from countries in Europe and North America dwarfed that from Mexico. Europe alone accounted for nearly three times as many immigrants as did Mexico. (See Appendix, Table 6.11.) Nor did the war markedly affect the white-ethnic makeup of Urban California.

Although the census figures are somewhat sketchy, it is clear that in San Francisco the overall foreign stock percentage of the population declined from at least 1900 through 1950, although it rose again in 1960. In Los Angeles, the decline began in 1930 and continued through 1960. In both cities, the percentage of decline in the 1940s was similar to that in the previous decade; in Los Angeles it was smaller and in San Francisco, larger but virtually identical. Thus the war did not significantly affect the long-range trends of the first- and second-generation European immigrant stock population. For the state as a whole, the decline was even more consistent, running from 1900 to 1960. (See Appendix, Table 6.12.) For most of that period, the absolute numbers of foreign stock increased while their proportion of the total state population decreased. Once again, the war decade saw a decline in the percentage of first- and second-generation immigrants, but the percentage dropped more in the 1930s. The 1920s drop exceeded the 1940s in an absolute sense, but the greatest absolute change occurred in the 1950s. The changes in white ethnic numbers, which includes Mexican Americans, were long-range trends in which the Second World War decade did not stand out in either absolute or percentage terms. (See Appendix, Table 6.13.)

It did not markedly affect the diversity within these groups either. As we have seen earlier, California cities were quite diverse ethnically, more so than any of the others for which the census provided figures in 1940. In 1950, the census supplied statistics for five California cities rather than two, and this time all five of the Golden State cities were more diverse than the other American cities from the 1940 census. San Francisco and Los Angeles became slightly more diverse than in 1940, 51.93 and 54.11 percent respectively, nothing close to a revolutionary change. (See Appendix, Table 6.14.) (This does not mean that California cities were more diverse than any in the country, but merely more diverse than those for which the census bureau supplied figures in both 1940 and 1950.) The city figures reflect the broader case of the state as well. (See

Appendix, Table 6.15.) As early as 1930, Mexican Americans were the most numerous minority group in California, and the Second World War did not alter that demographic fact. Nor did the war do much to transform the proportions claimed by the leading five ethnic groups. Mexican Americans gained a bit, German Americans lost a bit, Italians climbed slightly, the British inched downward, and so forth. Seven East European countries—the USSR, Poland, Lithuania, Czechoslovakia, Hungary, Rumania, and Yugoslavia—registered absolute gains of 160,483, an average of 76.44 percent. East Europeans gained markedly, but not enough to upset the existing ethnocultural hierarchy. No single group gained or lost as much as two percentage points of the total ethnocultural market. (See Appendix, Table 6.16.)

Although national, western, and California historians have not paid much heed to the larger ethnocultural picture in the nation, region, or state in the Second World War, this matter needs to be stressed. Immigration history has been one of the most important constants in American history, and, as we have seen, California was over half foreign stock in 1900. Yet World War II affected this major component of American and western history only very slightly.

War affected the non-white population just as marginally. The census carries the category of "other" or (statistically) "minor" races, which included African Americans, Japanese, Filipinos, Chinese, and Indians. Unfortunately, the census did not pick up African Americans until 1920 and collected Filipino statistics too erratically to include in tabular form. (See Appendix, Table 6.17.)

With the exception of blacks, the war's influence on non-white population numbers was negligible. None reached majority status or anything close to it, nor would they by the end of the century. The conflict affected Indians' numbers least. The state's population of that group, which was mostly rural, grew slightly in the 1940s, but not as much as it had in the 1920s. Although Indian historians believe that the war led Native Americans to migrate to cities, not many resided in California cities in 1950.[8] As with many other population phenomena in California, this urbanization had been going on for some time, at least since 1910. In that year, 5.07 percent of California's Indians lived in cities for which the census provides information. In 1920, the figure rose to 11.79 percent, in 1930 to 14.03 percent, in 1940 to 21.94 percent, and in 1950 to 25.53 percent. The hungry 1930s urbanized a larger proportion of Native Americans than the fighting 1940s. However, at 5,094 people in 1950, they were one of the smallest urban groups, exactly .005 percent of California's

8,539,420 urbanites at mid-century. The figures for individual cities are so small as to hardly register a percentage.

The war had more influence on the Chinese and Japanese populations, both of which were highly urbanized. Japanese numbers, doubtless due to the tragedy of relocation, declined somewhat, while the Chinese group climbed. In both cases, however, the movement represented prewar trends. In most cities, Japanese population had fallen since 1930 as Chinese numbers rose, but neither experienced major change. As K. Scott Wong has shown, the Chinese population of San Francisco grew by 39.53 percent, but the numbers were very small and did not represent a very large percentage of the total population.[9] The war's *demographic influence* on Indians, Japanese, and Chinese was not very important. It did not initiate any great growth or decline; it did not inaugurate the trend toward urbanization nor unduly accelerate it.[10]

Blacks made the most appreciable population gains among nonwhites, increasing their numbers in the Golden State from 124,306 in 1940 to 462,172 in 1950, an advance of 337,866 people and 271.08 percent. This was the largest absolute or percentage gain for any racial or national group. However, this trend was a movement of long standing. At least since 1910, African Americans had moved to California, almost all of them to cities. In the 1920s, the black population more than doubled, a gain of 109.08 percent. However, this impressive advance was dwarfed by that of the Second World War. By 1950, blacks were the second largest minority group in the state and had experienced a much larger advance during the 1940s than did the leading Mexican American segment of the population. Blacks, therefore, are the principal evidence for the argument that the war wrought unprecedented change. Even so, large-scale African American growth was limited to a few cities—such as Oakland, Los Angeles, and San Francisco—and, in any case, their gains did not boost black totals to a large fraction of state or city populations. As with Mexicans, the state's black population remained under 5 percent. Oakland, at 12.42 percent, was the only city in double figures. The impact of the war on this group was not on a Gold Rush scale.[11]

Most Californians did not fall into any of the categories discussed so far. They were mostly white, native born, non-Hispanic, and inmigrant. Where did these people come from and how did the war affect them? This group overlapped that part of the foreign stock that was native born of one or two foreign parents. Nevertheless, the entire white foreign stock population, together with the non-whites, did not comprise one-half of the population. Although historians have written more about minorities,[12] the majority is a more accurate test of the transformation hypothesis and is an indispensable subject with which to fill out the history of the war.[13]

The story begins with impressive numbers. One and three-quarter million people migrated to the Golden State during the turbulent forties, mostly to cities. Unfortunately, the census does not consistently provide net migration gains for the years 1910–1960 by cities. However, it does supply such figures for states and census divisions. These show that the Pacific division gained greatly from 1890 to 1960. Since some 84.41 percent of the net migrants to the Pacific division moved to California, that division provides a solid estimate of California's gains. (See Appendix, Table 6.18.)

The census provides comparable historical statistics for California, as opposed to the Pacific division, but only those from 1910 to 1970. (See Appendix, Table 6.19.) The 1940s registered the largest absolute net gains, 1,776,832 people through interstate migration, but the difference between that decade and that of the Korean War is only 73,361, or less than 5 percent. It is quite possible that the absolute gains of the preceding decades created more of an upheaval because the earlier cities had fewer people with whom to dilute the newcomers. Moreover, the percentage increase of the 1940s was outstripped by the 1880s, the 1900s, and the 1920s, thus providing ample precedent for the percentage changes of the Second Great War. Predictably, California figures of the 1920s outshone the 1940s in percentage terms, 96.38 percent to 56.48 percent for the war. The 1890s and the 1910s also outpaced the 1940s in percentage terms. Perhaps the most astonishing figure for this entire era is the 32.24 percent gain of the Depression years. In a state which grew that markedly during a bitter depression, few demographic facts will seem startling.

Interstate migration also implied diversification, in the sense of watering down the Golden State's population with outsiders, and this trend was equally long standing. (See Appendix, Table 6.20.) The outsiders outnumbered the insiders throughout this era. The numbers of those born in-state fell in the 1920s and then rose slightly again by 1960. The war did not substantially alter this pattern of outside dominance, since the difference between in- and out-of-state residents remained at about the same level throughout the epoch. Nearly half of Californians in 1960 were from other states, and residents born in the Golden State had not achieved the 40 percent mark by 1960. So the diversification of California was long standing and not markedly affected by the war. As usual, the 1920s percentage outstripped the 1940s, and the 1950s represented the first real drop in the proportion of out-of-staters. The number of those born abroad fell steadily from 1920 in modest stages every decade, including the 1940s.

That change, in turn, made the Golden State markedly cosmopolitan. In 1960, only three states and the District of Columbia had lower proportions of residents born in the state. Nevada led with 26.2 percent, followed by D.C. at 35.3 percent, Arizona at 35.5 percent, Florida at 36 percent, and California at 39.9 percent. Especially compared to northeastern and southern states, where the percentage of residents born in-state ranged from 86.4 percent in the case of Mississippi to 80.6 percent for Pennsylvania to 77.6 percent for Maine, California seemed very unprovincial. Even the East North Central states averaged close to 70 percent born in-state.[14] Kevin Starr has written eloquently of the cultural cosmopolitanism of California in the twentieth century, and the statistics bear him out.[15]

Neither the origins of California's population nor the proportion of outsiders to native Californians varied markedly. We have seen that in 1940, a majority of the population in Northern California cities were born in the West and a majority of those in Southern California cities had been born elsewhere. Between 1940 and 1960, the two populations tended to converge. In 1940, 69.33 percent of San Francisco's population was born in the West, a figure which fell only to 62.24 percent for the combined San Francisco–Oakland metropolitan area in 1960. In Sacramento, the 1940 figure stood at 67.20 percent, and the Sacramento metropolitan area was 60.41 percent in 1960. In Southern California, the Los Angeles figure climbed from 38.94 percent in the city in 1940 to 46.31 percent for the metropolitan area in 1960. The San Diego population rose from 37.17 percent in 1940 to 42.09 percent in 1960. The census gave only metropolitan statistics for 1960, so these must be compared with those for strictly urban places in 1940, with Long Beach and Oakland subsumed under their respective metropolitan areas. However, this slightly changed configuration does not invalidate either the comparison or the conclusion that the twenty years after 1940 saw gradual rather than profound change in the origins of the native-born population. And the divisional sources of native-born peoples did not vary much either.

The Second World War did usher in some dramatic population changes, especially for African Americans. That population jumped greatly, and the percentages of several other groups, especially the Chinese and Japanese, were substantially affected. However, even with its marked wartime increase, the black population did not become a very large segment of Urban California. In none of the metropolitan areas did it constitute 10 percent of the population by 1950, and this proportion must be contrasted to eastern cities in both 1940 and 1950, where the dominance of one ethnic group ranged from 20 to 38 percent. The African Americans of Golden State cities did not come close to matching the Irish of Boston at 25.27 percent, the Poles of Buffalo at 28.8 percent, the Swedes of Minneapolis at 24.97 percent, or even the Poles of Cleveland at 14.3 percent, much less the Italians of Rochester at 35 percent, the Italians of Providence at 36.44 percent, or the Germans of Milwaukee, who towered over the rest of that city's population at 38.72 percent. Compared to these ethnocultural concentrations, those of the Golden State cities were minor. Blacks may have created large colonies in a single part of a metropolitan area, as in Oakland, but even those absolute gains do not equal Gold Rush percentages or absolute changes. The biggest minority gainer did not then or later transform the population of Urban California.

Moreover, Mexican Americans, the state's largest minority before and after the conflict, experienced only modest absolute growth in the decade and actually declined as a proportion of California's total population. Otherwise, the sources of Urban California's ethnocultural diversity remained remarkably stable, given the upheaval of the war. It still drew its residents from about the same foreign and domestic sources, and these sources contributed about the same proportions to the population that they traditionally had. By singling out the Japanese, black, and Mexican American experiences and leaving out the remainder, historians have overlooked the majority of the state's people. If viewed in isolation, the fate of blacks was striking and that of Mexican Americans, at least noticeable. However, when put into the context of the larger wartime story, what befell these groups hardly stands out.

Diversity has been the focus of modern California and New Western historians. Other historians have also debated the impact of World War II on diversity (cultural pluralism). Gary Mormino found that the war pulled Italian Americans into the mainstream, and Nelson Lichtenstein held that the conflict drew the smaller ethnocultural groups together into the larger whole of the working class. On the other hand, Philip Gleason discovered that "cultural pluralism in all its ambiguities and complexities is the crucial legacy of World War II in respect to American identity."[16] It is not entirely certain which is correct, nor should we underestimate the possibility that the war was both things at once. We need more research, but in terms of population recruitment, one can document that California cities were extraordinarily diverse before the war and remained that way. Continuity prevailed.

Nor can many of these people realistically be called "Anglos." They represented the diversity still prevalent in the United States in the 1940s plus that which previous immigrants had imported from Europe. Ex-Soviets (62,000) met Southerners; Rumanians got to know Scots; Lithuanians became acquainted with Canadians; Italians bumped into Southwesterners; Mexicans were introduced to Midwesterners; and Yankees encountered African Americans. The state was a very cosmopolitan place. If we insist that the degree of change in California cities be measured by set standards, then the 1940s did not create a revolutionary new system of ethnocultural groupings. The alterations did not equal the demographic upheavals triggered by the Gold Rush; they were not unprecedented, measured by previous California experience; and they were usually not greater than those of succeeding decades.

This is especially true of population growth, as the census makes clear. To gauge the transformative effect of the Second Great War, one ideally should look at both percentage growth and absolute growth. World War II certainly accelerated growth rates. However, it should be remembered that California's population grew vigorously even during the Great Depression. The population increased by some 21 percent, which would be a striking change for almost any other American state. Therefore, in trying to assess the demographic importance of the 1940s, it is useful to place that decade into the stream of history that includes the two preceding and two succeeding decades. Doing so indicates that more cities and urban counties experienced record percentage increases in the twenties than in the forties. These included most of the important places: Los Angeles, Los Angeles County, Alhambra, Berkeley, Beverly Hills, Glendale, Long Beach, Inglewood, Monterey, Monterey County, Oakland, Palo Alto, National City, Oceanside, Pasadena, Redwood City, Sacramento, San Bernardino, San Bernardino County, San Diego, San Francisco, San Mateo, Santa Barbara, Santa Barbara County, Santa Monica, and Ventura. Among the state's bigger towns and major cities of the 1970s, only Burbank, Alameda, Fresno, Stockton, and Richmond set records in the 1940s. Thus the war accelerated rates over Depression increases and *partially* restored the robust ones of earlier years. Much of our misreading of the 1940s stems from discussing that decade out of its historical context. The forties' percentages were not unprecedented, much less revolutionary or cataclysmic.[17]

The *absolute* increases did not set records either. Historians argue correctly that the war had a more dramatic effect on suburbs than on center cities.[18] Nonetheless, even suburban increases were usually well within the experience of urban areas. For example, Los Angeles County, a good index of suburbanization, gained 1,366,000 residents during the forties but added almost as many, 1,272,000, during the twenties, starting from a much smaller population base. One could hardly argue that the disparity between the two figures represents the difference between ordinary change and revolutionary upheaval. Clearly, the Golden State was accustomed to radical population growth. Its experience in World War II was not all that different from its own past.

It was also not that different from its future—that is, the Korean War and Cold War decades. In our haste to pay homage to World War II, the population impact of the Korean and Cold War eras has often been undervalued. Of the major metropolitan counties in the state, four made their largest absolute gains in the 1940s and ten, during the era of Eisenhower. These latter counties were Los Angeles, Marin, Monterey, Napa, Riverside, Sacramento, San Bernardino, San Diego, San Mateo, and Santa Clara, or in other words, most of the great growth centers of the post–World War II era. For example, what happened to Orange County in the 1960s is much closer to an explosion and much more impressive than any of the absolute increases of the 1940s. In one decade, the 1960s, Orange County grew by 706,000, more than the World War II *total* of Alameda, Contra Costa, San Francisco, Solano, and Sonoma counties put together![19] Los Angeles County's population gain in that period was more than twice as great as the population of *all* the counties that set records in World War II. Finally, both Los Angeles city and Long Beach grew more in the 1920s and 1950s, and even war-wracked San Diego expanded more in the fifties.[20]

Several counties did experience their greatest absolute growth in the war decade. These were not scattered at random about the state, but rather confined to two locales: the San Joaquin Valley and the central, eastern, and northern Bay Area.[21] So the boom of the forties was mostly suburban and exurban. In San Francisco, which lost people in the next several decades, the war temporarily reversed the stagnant depression rates of the city but did not alter the long-term course of its demographic history. Except for Marin and Napa counties and Sacramento city, the pacesetters of the 1950s were in the southern Bay Area and Southern California.[22]

One of the key assumptions of the transformation hypothesis is based on the fact that the government lavished money on the West.[23] Supposedly, dollars produced unprecedented growth. However, at this point in our research into World War II and urban society, the relationship of defense spending to population growth is not at all clear. The government spent more in absolute, and nearly as much in per capita, sums in the North Central states as in the West; yet that money did not produce the same supposedly transformative growth in that part of the Midwest. Elsewhere in the United States, war-induced expenditures did not automatically drive a proportionate population increase. In several areas of heavy defense outlays, population growth was modest, stagnant, or even negative. The greatest growth in population occurred in places that already had a positive population growth curve in the Great Depression, not simply in those gorged on the spoils of war.[24]

The World War II era produced significant growth, but if put into context and considered from both a qualitative and a quantitative standpoint, it is not so exceptional as we have believed. The growth was neither unprecedented, comparable to the Gold Rush, nor revolutionary.

7. Urban Economies in a Statist War

The war ended the Depression in undulating waves of economic history. Contracts came to certain shipbuilding and aircraft cities like a stone cast into a pond, and prosperity rippled out through other businesses and neighborhoods.

Although California received more than its per capita share of war contracts, this feast was not equally distributed. In general, Los Angeles enjoyed a more balanced diet, but San Diego consumed the per capita lion's share. By September 1942, L.A. had obtained 64 percent of all California aircraft contracts, but also 28 percent of shipbuilding awards. By contrast, San Francisco–Oakland garnered 65 percent of shipbuilding agreements but no aircraft ones. San Diego gained 35 percent of aircraft contracts but negligible shipbuilding. Even with other industrial and nonindustrial purchases added in, San Francisco–Oakland still lagged behind West Coast competitors. San Diego led at that stage with awards of $5,100 per capita, followed by Seattle at $2,770, Vallejo at $2,500, Bremerton at $2,180, Portland and Los Angeles at $1,140, and finally San Francisco–Oakland at $980.[1]

Fortunately, defense production escalated through stages. First came the outbreak of war in Europe, then the U.S. defense buildup, Lend Lease, formal entry, peak production in 1943–44, the invasion of Europe, the Pacific buildup, victory in Europe, V-J Day, and finally demobilization. These stages gave Californians time to adjust to the inevitable.[2]

Ruggedly free enterprise cities also needed time to accustom themselves to "some arbitrary interference with individual decisions." Everywhere the government's visible hand regulated, stimulated, suppressed, manipulated, tinkered, readjusted, coaxed, and cajoled. Ere long, a large percentage of urban employers and employees worked for the government. This adaptation began in March 1941 with "allocation and priority orders" on aluminum. In August, the authorities required "acceptance by producers of defense orders ahead of others" and limited auto and light truck production. Restraints on other durable goods followed. The government controlled in order to curb inflation and in September imposed "control over installment credit." In January 1942, Washington imposed new excise taxes to cut consumption, rationed tires, and banned auto sales to civilians.[3]

The history of the impact of war is usually recounted in terms of growth. A year into the conflict the Twelfth Federal Reserve District *Monthly Review* found more ambiguity in the new "war economy":

> To some it means long hours of work in industries at excellent rates of pay; to others it means the necessity of changing occupations; to still others it means the serious impairment of established business enterprises; to others it means the building up of thriving new business enterprises engaged in war work.[4]

Industrial activity picked up markedly in response to the outbreak of war in Europe in late 1939. Month after month, the pundits strove for ever more flamboyant superlatives to capture the rapid rise of aircraft and ship building. By January 1941 the defense progress of the Pacific Slope had already "shifted from the stage of contract negotiation and the like to that of actual output of armament and equipment and the construction of facilities." The added stimulus of Lend Lease by May 1941 had ironed out seasonal economic swings by providing heavy demand year round. By October 1941, the two glamour industries were poised to overtake lumber and food processing, the traditional manufacturing leaders. Two months later aircraft builders became the largest manufacturers in Los Angeles County, at 113,000 workers, up from 13,000 in January 1939. Almost overnight, one industry gobbled up 40 percent of wage earners. In 1939, food processing had led at 11 percent! To the south, San Diego airframe workers soared to 33,000, representing two-thirds of its workers. Eventually employment climbed to 244,000 in both cities. In 1940–41 the government awarded almost all defense contracts in these two cities to the aircraft industry. Just before Japanese planes tore Pearl Harbor asunder, San Diego produced almost one-third more planes than Seattle, the future industry leader. Pundits now feared aeronautics would turn cities into metropolitan-military monocultures.[5]

Aircraft illustrated the greater statist role. This was not a regulatory partnership where one party commanded wisely and the other modified graciously, as was the case of Samuel Insull's relationship with Chicago and Illinois government in the Progressive Era. World War II government was the industry's partner, planner, financier, and sole market. War is the ultimate hazardous business, and aircraft manufacturing had been precarious enough all along. During hostilities the government removed the risk from this business. For the benefit of any surviving "Merchants of Death" theorists, it could be added that statism partially purged something else as well.

> The Federal Government has participated directly in financing part of the expansion of plant and facilities while advance payments and contract deposits by customers [government] have provided firms with a substantial proportion of their working capital requirements . . . capital stock issues and bank loans have played only a relatively minor role.[6]

Stockholders and markets now meant less. Firms could buy federally financed plants or return them "to the Government upon the termination of hostilities." They did some of each. The Defense War Plant Corporation subsidiary of the Reconstruction Finance Corporation poured nearly half a billion dollars into Los Angeles plant expansion and new construction alone. The "use of cost-plus contracts, under which the customer is billed for costs as they are incurred" further lightened the financial load. Then the government purchased everything that the companies turned out. It was a sweet deal, but, as in banking, the ratio of profits to sales declined as volume rose. This issue was a very complex one, in which profits had to be judged in a very broad context of incentives, such as rapid amortization and sale of government plants, sufficient to first mobilize the industry and then tide it over reconversion into peacetime use.[7]

"Essentially, the period through 1941" was one of "preparing for . . . later enlarged production." This groundwork soon paid off when 1942–43 brought the highest growth. Thereafter, airframe employment rose modestly through July 1943, then sagged. Nonetheless, increases in productivity offset these losses and made 1943 and 1944 record years. "Despite a nearly continuous decline in employment since mid-1943, . . . aircraft factories are . . . adequately staffed at the present time," noted an observer, "although shortages . . . in highly skilled and heavy production classifications, remain in several plants."[8]

Productivity increases took many forms. Most of the increase took place in plant expansion, but many new plants appeared as well. Some conversion, including most of the former auto plants (the L.A. Ford plant became Lockheed), provided further space. The Aircraft War Production Council (invented in California and later copied by eastern firms) made up of all West Coast firms, shared everything from blueprints to parts to production. Led by Consolidated, whose system was "headquartered" in Santa Ana, and Lockheed, which established "a large feeder plant in Maywood," companies established feeder plants to supply everything from subassemblies to upholstery. A B-17 Committee coordinated Lockheed, Vega, and Douglas production of that Boeing workhorse. Perhaps the oddest institution was the Coronado plant that sorted and recycled "rivets swept from plant floors." North American had decentralized into leased buildings in Pasadena and Los Angeles, putting its purchasing department in the Hollywood Race Track. Subcontractors were still more important and useful. Consolidated had 100, Lockheed had 2,000, and Northrop had 1,200. At one point, 2,700 Los Angeles parts manufacturers employed eighty thousand persons to produce 50–60 percent of parts needed locally.[9]

Since military experience necessitated constant changes, modification centers arose to provide them. Created in order to avoid interruptions on the production line and further burden to the assembly plants, these centers provided a congenial role for the maintenance shops of the airlines companies. Usually "adjacent to the assembly plants," some were spread out to Daggett (Douglas), Chula Vista (Rohr), and even crowded San Francisco, where Matson Navigation, of all firms, ran one. The McCone-Bechtel construction company even operated one center in Birmingham, Alabama. Mechanization, standardization, and deskilling added to the picture, although airframe assembly never reached the mass-production level of the auto industry.[10]

All this more than doubled productivity. Still, as Arthur Verge has said, the contribution went well beyond mere numbers to the splendid wartime record of planes like the Lockheed P-38 fighter-bomber, the North American P-51 fighter, the legendary Douglas C-47 (DC-3) "Gooney Bird" transport, the Consolidated B-24 bomber, and the PBY Catalina flying boat, the workhorse of Navy patrol.[11]

Employment peaked at 244,000 in 1943, when Lockheed employed 90,000, North American 28,000, and Northrop 10,500. Members of the Aircraft Parts Manufacturers Association of Los Angeles employed another 75,000 to 80,000. Production crested in the first quarter of 1944. After V-J Day the Air Force canceled contracts rapidly, and employment plunged nearly three-fifths by late 1945. In the Twelfth Federal Reserve District aircraft industry, of which California represented 90 percent, employment fell from 200,000 on V-E Day to 150,000 on V-J Day to 76,000 one month later. Factories in Santa Monica, Inglewood, San Diego, Burbank, Long Beach, and Hawthorne suffered extensive layoffs.[12]

Much of the literature on the economy of the war emphasizes the windfalls to big business. American big business certainly benefited from the conflict, but California aircraft manufacturing was not a big business when the worldwide military conflagration began. As late as 1939, the net current assets of the entire West Coast industry did not total $30 million, about one-fifth of what it would be in 1945. When the war began, Douglas, the West Coast leader, employed only 7,589 men. Additionally, plane production was a skilled business that only a few firms had the technical and financial competence to undertake.[13]

Even a highly advanced industrial operation like Ford Motors had great difficulty entering the airframe industry. Indeed, Henry Kaiser, a storied western industrialist with an enviable track record in ventures in which he had no previous experience, failed to break into the business. At the outset of the war American planes were often markedly inferior, especially compared with the deadly Japanese Mitsubishi Zero. One can only imagine the situation if aircraft contracts had been doled out to greenhorns unfamiliar with either aviation or aerodynamics.[14]

Although the war greatly enlarged Lockheed-Vega, North American, Douglas, Consolidated-Vultee, and some smaller firms such as Menasco, Rohr, and Ryan Aeronautical, it also benefited a host of humble subcontractors. By mid-1942, analysts noted that "manufacturers of machinery, including oil well equipment, are turning in increasing numbers to the fabrication of aircraft parts or ordnance." Assuredly, some of the jobbers like Ford were giants, but many were not. An industrial map of the Los Angeles area shows literally thousands of subcontractors (see p. 11). They produced between 30 and 38 percent of the 900 million pounds fabricated by the thirty-three major aircraft companies in 1944, "the peak year." Small business employed sixty-one thousand to produce what it was qualified to fabricate, that is, parts.[15]

Although these are much more complicated benefits than is often assumed, corporations probably did get windfalls from the war. In any case, these corporate windfalls were also urban ones. When the airframe industry markedly expanded its plants as a result of the war, it also augmented the employment opportunities and tax bases of Long Beach, Hawthorne, Santa Monica, San Diego, Burbank, Inglewood, Maywood, and others. Southern California gained 167,000 new dwellings that enhanced the war effort; these helped buffer the postwar housing crisis that war left in its wake. The war and reconversion battered cities, and Washington did little to alleviate the pounding. It is not outrageous that the war left a residue of jobs and taxes as indemnity.[16]

Shipbuilding diverged in an even more dramatic and idiosyncratic manner. The war turned this small industry into a giant, and peace cut it down to a pygmy. The sector netted a few thousand jobs, but unlike autos or aircraft, except in the Navy yards shipbuilding did not have a bright postwar future. Once again, the Golden State was exceptional.

Private shipyards concentrated mostly on merchant ships, the famous Liberty ships, and the faster and therefore safer Victory ships, plus tankers, oilers, and transports. Until "Black May" 1943, Nazi submarines nearly shut off the flow of supplies across the North Atlantic to the hard-pressed British and Russians. As British Admiral Max Horton threw ever more deadly techniques and technologies at the subs, American shipbuilders launched progressively more ships from the ways. Overwhelmed by both targets and techniques, the subs eventually withdrew, and the Allied pipeline poured men and materiel into Europe. California yards contributed immensely to this outcome. The Bay Area alone received $3.9 billion in merchant and Navy contracts, one-third more than any other U.S. area.[17]

Shipbuilding commenced slower than aircraft manufacturing. The Maritime Commission "revived slightly" the industry in 1939, but "huge contracts during the last half of 1940" brought the enormous expansion of existing plants and the construction of new ones. As in aircraft, the government paid for the plant or reimbursed the firm and offered an option to buy after the war. Nearly all of the facilities from the "brief period" of prosperity in World War I were "dismantled," so most of the 1940s plants were constructed anew. Analysts claimed that "the most marked [defense] expansion in 1942 was in shipbuilding."[18]

As in aircraft, efficiency mounted rapidly. In early 1942 it required 130 days to construct a ship; by the end of the same year, some yards turned them out in 41 days. Some took even less time. However, that burst of efficiency lasted only through 1942. In 1943, shipbuilding output per man-hour increased somewhat, while airframe production continued to expand sharply.[19]

Various factors encouraged greater efficiency. One was the urgent necessity to counteract the submarine. Another was existing shipyards' limited capacity to expand their plants radically. This incapacity allowed builders to lay out new yards altogether, according to a plan, "in contrast to almost all the old yards that began in a small way and gradually grew, like Topsy." Moreover, the paucity of skilled labor required a renaissance of World War I mass-production techniques. These included the use of small ready-made parts and the prefabrication of whole forepeaks, keel sections, and bulkheads for the hull and massive superstructure parts. More important was "the general replacement of riveting by welding." One Marinship manager called welding the "most important" "single device to win the war," especially the "specialization of welding." He was in a position to know. Marinship employed three thousand welders, one-third women, who melted one million pounds of welding rod per month onto five tankers. The firm also employed radiography, both gamma rays and X-rays, to check the viability of the crucial welds.[20]

"Heavy duty cranes" working in tandem could lift 75-ton boilers, whole engines, and even 96–ton deck houses into place.[21] Most important was the "use of labor," learned from the auto industry: infinitely special-izing simple tasks, which required minimal time to train workers and therefore allowed their rapid recruitment. Not the least rationalization of labor grew out of generous suspensions of union rules by the metal trades, such as the boilermakers. These concessions allowed the extensive deskilling that specialization demanded. Much skilled labor remained, but these improvements allowed widespread, but not complete, applica-tion of mass-production techniques. That, in turn, "made possible a striking reduction in the average time . . . in ship construction." The replacement of the bow shot off the devastated Pearl Harbor destroyer *Shaw* was perhaps the most spectacular use of this heavy machinery and prefabrication. In addition, "by having numerous subcontractors we increased our resources of manpower and equipment," explained Kenneth Bechtel. Dispersing production around the major assembly sites also lessened congestion and resulting inefficiencies. Fabrication at cities with adequate housing reduced commuting and absenteeism. Quality remained high despite the haste to construct.[22]

Output increased sharply in 1943, but largely because of augmented labor rather than efficiency. Thereafter, high labor turnover undermined "attempts to increase efficiency at most" yards. A changing emphasis ac-tually lowered output. Assembling larger, longer-range, complex vessels and converting others, such as the Victory ships to transports, required more man-hours per ship. This shift reduced the number of boats manu-factured by July 1944, but tonnage remained robust. Construction of vessels such as tugs, lifeboats, and wooden barges was not included in this record, though it added to the total.[23]

Total ships, tonnage, and jobs peaked in mid-1943. The situation held together fairly well till war's end. Then the Maritime Commission and the Navy Department canceled contracts wholesale. By the end of 1945 most uncanceled ship contracts and repair work had also run out. Shipbuilding employed 282,000 at its peak, but these jobs vanished after

V-J Day. Mare Island employment fell from 40,000 to 12,000, and that yard was one of the lucky ones. Others, such as Marinship, Richmond 2, 3, and 4, and Todd-California, simply expired.[24]

Overall, the West Coast gained one-half of Maritime Commission contracts and many Navy contracts, and California received the lion's share. The patriarch of public yards was the storied Mare Island Naval Shipyard at Vallejo. In addition, the government opened plants at Hunters Point and Treasure Island in San Francisco, at San Pedro–Wilmington in Los Angeles, and at the destroyer base in San Diego. Navy yards mostly constructed smaller fighting ships—destroyers, escort ships, and submarines—but eventually graduated to "fairly large craft," like baby aircraft carriers. Maritime yards fabricated quite a few military craft too. In terms of value, American Navy yards, public and private, built more than Maritime Commission yards.[25]

The latter included Marinship in Sausalito, Los Angeles Shipbuilding and Dry Dock Corporation and California Shipbuilding (Calship) in Wilmington–San Pedro, Bethlehem in San Pedro, and Todd-California (Richmond Number 1) and Richmond Number 2, 3, and 4 in Richmond. Moore Drydock in Oakland, Bethlehem Steel and Western Pipe and Steel in San Francisco, Bethlehem Steel in Alameda, and Consolidated Steel in Long Beach and Wilmington rounded out the lot. The famous "Six Companies" originated much of the private shipbuilding. None boasted much, if any, seasoning in the trade. However, experienced manufacturers were so overloaded with Navy contracts that the Maritime Commission had to turn to these western road, irrigation, dam, tunnel, and bridge builders and hope for the best. And that is pretty much what they got. Shipbuilders produced miracles fully equal to those of airframe fabricators.[26]

Despite Henry Kaiser's precocious record, most of the major private shipbuilding was a "joint venture" of the Six Companies. The Bechtel firm ran Marinship by itself, but other Maritime Commission yards featured extensive interlocking operation. As before, the Six Companies worked jointly, even though one of them took chief responsibility for management, as in the Kaiser yards. Marinship borrowed personnel and fabricated steel for its initial vessel, the *William Richardson,* from its half-sister, Calship. Joshua Hendy, the engine-building firm, was jointly owned by Bechtel, Kaiser, and four others.[27]

Ordinarily these yards constructed Liberty, Victory, or other cargo ships, together with some naval vessels and combat auxiliaries, "including tankers, refrigerator ships, landing craft, frigates, escort aircraft carriers, and attack transports." Because of the steel shortage, Barrett and Hilp of Marin and Concrete Ship Constructors of National City built transport and maintenance barges, refrigerator ships, tankers, and floating warehouses of Rocklite concrete. Up to 1944 the non-Navy yards constructed merchant vessels while the Navy yards built Navy vessels, like the *Tang,* the pan-destructive killer sub from Mare Island that wrecked nearly one hundred thousand tons of Japanese shipping before succumbing to a freak accident. However, as kamikaze violence mounted, both kinds of yards shifted toward more repair.[28]

Although ship construction grabbed the headlines, repair was also vitally important, both to win the war and to protect the future of the industry. As the yards launched ever more ships, ever more required fixing. Unlike the construction yards that worked on a schedule, the re-pairmen coped with vessels that came in at random. Instead of identical vessels, they mended ships of different sizes, power plants, functions, and hulls—wood, steel, or cement. Rather than assigning an eight-hour schedule, the yards often rousted repairmen out of bed in the middle of the night to work twenty straight hours. Workers had to be highly skilled and experienced. Los Angeles Shipbuilding, San Francisco General Engineering and Dry Dock, Moore, and Bethlehem San Francisco were major repair yards, the latter two alone fixing over 4,500 ships. Unique building and repair were the future of the industry, so these yards were well positioned to make the transition to peace. By 1945, Bay Area yards handled one hundred repair jobs at any given time.[29]

The war plants were staggering in size. Marinship employed twenty-two thousand; Richmond and Todd-California, another hundred thousand; Calship in Los Angeles worked forty thousand to fifty-five thousand (the L.A. yards totaled ninety thousand); and between yard workers and subcontractors, Mare Island employed one hundred thousand. If laid end to end, Mare Island LCTs (landing craft, tank) would have stretched six miles, and the piping in the seventy-eight Marinship tankers would have reached nearly to Denver! Marinship lighted at night looked for all the world like a whole city.[30]

As in aircraft, these builders were "practically the agents of the Government." Depending on what they produced, either the Maritime Commission, the Defense War Plant Corporation, or the Navy supplied "plant and materials to the shipbuilders." As in aircraft, this partnership removed most of the risk and much of the profit from the venture. Ship-building profits were questioned after the war, just as with aircraft, but despite some congressional skepticism, they do not seem excessive. In any case, as Gerald Nash has argued, profit was less important than proper incentives to build masses of ships. The incentives were sufficient.[31]

B-25 bombers being assembled in one of California's giant airplane manufacturing plants.
Courtesy Library of Congress, Prints & Photographs Division, FSA-OWI Collection.

Shipbuilding encouraged the growth of the largest number of ancillary industries. "Until the outbreak of the war, the heavy metals and metal working industries were relatively undeveloped" in California. The conflict created a demand that swamped eastern manufacturers, and the overloaded railroads could not deliver. A similar problem was caused by the temporary "cessation of intercoastal shipping via the Panama Canal." Coast metal working expanded from fifty thousand to one hundred thousand jobs to remedy this deficit.[32]

More than in any other region, coast shipbuilding was mostly a matter of assembly. This mass-production practice facilitated extensive subcontracting. By mid-1943 the government had let 380 contracts of fifty thousand dollars or over to district firms, and the shipyards had placed "a substantial volume of subcontracts." Most were "prefabrication and carpentry work," done by local firms. Kenneth K. Bechtel's Marinship Corporation placed ninety-four subcontracts as well as four primes. Even the legendary Mare Island, which did not subcontract before the war, now did so on a large scale. The subcontracted and farmed-out work of the Vallejo yard employed some 29,549 persons. The "operation of the Fresno war industry pool was a typical example of the way small business and Mare Island got together to further the war effort." Migration to defense centers and the resultant numerous home vacancies hit the Raisin Capital hard. To cope, twenty-eight firms pooled their resources into the Central California War Industries and won defense contracts. Similar alliances arose in Stockton, Sacramento, San Francisco, San Leandro, Salinas, Martinez, San Mateo, Sutter Creek, and San Rafael. The prefabrication of LCTs in Denver and their assembly at Mare Island was perhaps the most flamboyant example of subbing and farming out.[33]

Of the Marinship subcontractors, only a few, such as Bethlehem, General Electric, Jones and Laughlin, and Babcock and Wilcox, were large firms. Even Moore Drydock was hardly known outside the Bay Area. Most subs were virtually unknown names, such as Ace Roofing, Langlais Marine Equipment, H. F. Lauritzen, Marconi Plastering, Monihan Stauffacher, Leo J. Meyerberg Inc., Harry Parsons Inc., Sausalito Hardware and Plumbing, and Shanahan Brothers. The company hired more giants as principal vendors, but twenty of the twenty-four vendors were hardly monopoly capitalists. The war created several disposable shipbuilding giants like Marinship; it also sustained a host of firms like Ace Roofing.[34]

Such companies were superbly adept at changing to war production. Before the war, Fraser and Johnson of San Francisco fabricated gas heating equipment. In early 1942 its plant "completely converted" to war work—ventilation ducts, ammunition magazines, refrigerator floor gratings, radio operating desks, ammo shell racks, and galley equipment for various vessels. The Korktone Company of Los Angeles left producing granulated cork insulation for civilians and began supplying it to L.A., Richmond, and, ultimately, eastern shipbuilders. L. A. Young Spring and Wire Corporation of Oakland moved from bed and auto springs to debarkation nets, ship berths, lumber slings, cargo nets, and mosquito nets. Perhaps the prize should go to the Food Machinery Corporation of Riverside, which leapt from "peach defuzzers" to amphibious tanks.[35]

Foundries and forges spurted under the same stimulus. These enterprises were formerly restricted to a small market primarily of railroads, auto manufacturers, dams, and irrigation districts. These companies now found themselves bombarded with calls for stern "frames, rudder stocks, propeller tubes and struts, [and] anchors." Forty district firms promptly poured $25 million into maritime products, and the Defense War Plant Corporation built the largest foundry west of the Mississippi at Pittsburg, in the Bay Area, where what had been the biggest western foundry was already located.[36]

Steam and diesel marine engine firms graduated too, from fishing boat and tugboat engines to motors for "mine sweepers, landing vessels, tugs, sub chasers, and patrol boats . . . as well as for auxiliary engines and generator units for larger vessels," and land transport firms grew and multiplied. The Joshua Hendy plant produced one-third of all "Liberty ship reciprocating engines" during the war and ultimately graduated to large marine turbine engines for C-3 and Victory freighters. Hendy employed 60 persons before the war and 11,500 during it.[37]

Steel followed engines. The war first pumped up to capacity the small industry, largely devoted to melting scrap into steel, and then demanded more. Henry Kaiser had long hoped to diversify the "industrial base" of the West by adding a local steel industry. Kaiser soon found that it was hard to get steel for his shipyards because eastern mills favored their old shipbuilding customers nearby. As Mark Foster put it, Kaiser was "at the end of the line." Moreover, western fabricators needed more steel than eastern firms could produce or transcontinental railroads could haul. Therefore, Kaiser and other Westerners immediately lobbied Washington to underwrite facilities on the Pacific Slope. Fortunately, President Roosevelt already favored the idea on military grounds.[38]

First Kaiser had to do battle with the steel companies. Eventually, the government agreed to allow U.S. Steel to open a plant at Geneva, Utah, and to allow Kaiser to start up at Fontana, California. Part of the rationale was that "for strategic reasons it would be desirable to make the West Coast substantially independent of eastern mills." Legend has it that Kaiser herded the authorization papers from one Washington office to another as the papers were sequentially signed. Eventually, he borrowed "over $100 million." Fontana produced its first steel plate in August 1943, and Geneva did so only in March 1944. Fontana got the most publicity, but other producers expanded too. Southern California output grew by 250 percent; Northern California, 33 percent; and everyone grew in both "furnaces and finishing facilities." Peace cut into the industry, but its descent in 1945 was only from 2,380,000 to 2,315,000 tons in the Twelfth District, largely due to the closure of Geneva. So California output held up well.[39]

After the war, "Kaiser Steel became the dominant integrated steel facility in the West," notes Mark Foster. Nonetheless, California steelmasters never produced more than a negligible proportion of U.S. output. By 1956 the West consumed "40 percent more steel than local plant capacities." The dream of steel independence died long before Japanese competition shuttered the Fontana plant in the 1980s.[40]

Despite that shortcoming, city manufacturing reconverted well. In

April 1946 industrial production stood at 50 percent higher than in 1940, and it grew to 100 percent by the 1947 Census of Manufactures, largely in California's traditional industries. Disappointingly, shipbuilding and steel netted but a few thousand extra jobs, and aircraft, only some 53,000. A sixteen-year depression- and war-induced construction deficit, the marked increase of population, and, until inflation cut into them, wartime savings all afforded larger markets for traditional industries. Food processing, printing and publishing, construction, paper products, and so forth conferred more industrial independence than steel.[41]

One of the little-noticed ramifications of the conflict was the urbanization of industry, as opposed to people. As war industry dominated progressively more of the California martial economy, ever more extractive industries closed. One observer noted:

> As in 1942, there was a continuous shift in emphasis from widely scattered industries based essentially on the exploitation of natural resources to heavier industries concentrated in a few areas. Concurrently, the once dominant extractive industries, located in outlying areas suffered losses in production and employment, while the out-movement of workers from rural and less highly industrial areas to the war industries gave rise to localized labor crises.

Thus war also brought about an industrial and demographic reorganization toward California cities.[42]

In contrast, banking witnessed "increased demands for credit by virtually all private borrowers." As early as June 1941, analysts found that "a considerable proportion of the increase in these loans over the past year is traceable to . . . defense." That included shipbuilding facilities built or contracted for by mid-1941. In late 1941, consumer loans from banks and other lending companies reached an all-time high. However, as plant capacity filled, consumer goods disappeared, and as government lending and restrictions waxed, private lending waned. By early 1944, it was at a record low because income increased more than twice as fast as consumption. There were fewer goods to buy; when they were available, flush consumers needed fewer loans to buy them. Meanwhile, deposits accumulated as prosperous businesses and well-paid war workers ploughed their cash into demand deposits.[43]

Slowly, consumer lending recovered. From February 1944 on, the resurgence of the demand for used cars, or clunker trade, revived lending. Simultaneously, government adaptive-use programs to combat the housing shortage by converting buildings to multiple residence encouraged repair and modernization loans. With peace, production caught up with incomes and government controls gradually ended. Then banks aggressively pursued consumer loans and prices rose, resulting in more lending. By the end of 1946, consumer installment credit neared its prewar high.[44]

So, until the used car–used housing renaissance of 1944, the banks bulged with savings but had nowhere to put them. Fortunately, Washington intervened. As the *Monthly Review* explained, a bank ordinarily can lend capital to individuals, lend it to governments, or let it lie idle in reserves. Since private borrowers no longer needed many loans, the banks channeled lending toward the war effort. That act in turn led to an ambiguous outcome because "the assumption of risk by private lenders . . . practically ceased." Banking influence fell too. "The influence exercised by the banking system and other financial institutions upon enterprise through the conditions and terms upon which credit is made available is at a minimum," observed a spokesman.[45]

"Federal finances continued in 1945 to be the predominant factor in monetary and banking developments" and remained so into early 1946. "At the year's end [1945], Government securities constituted 75 percent of all loans and investments of member banks, compared with 37 percent in 1941." In the interim, federal cash flowed into the banks. Member banks in 1945 held $10.406 billion in government securities compared to $1.738 billion in 1941. Profit margins "declined markedly" as the government role ascended, but the huge volume assured ample earnings.[46]

Construction began a striking upswing in May 1940, spurred by orders for Army camps and barracks and Navy housing. Simultaneously, building firms fabricated both bases and defense plants. The outbreak of war initially intensified this role, as realtors and builders scrambled to house in-migrant workers, especially around defense plants and other war establishments. Los Angeles alone added "167,857 dwelling units," 75,000 new and 92,857 conversions, between 1940 and 1944. Eventually, the conflict throttled residential construction and intensified defense and defense-housing building. By 1942 monthly residential construction had fallen to $7 million from $27 million–$30 million a year earlier. Hostilities also squelched nonurban construction projects that benefited contractors and urban hinterlands. Thus in October, Washington halted work on Davis and Keswick dams and slowed that on Shasta and Grand Coulee dams. Still, as private contracts disappeared, the federal building boom made 1942 a banner year for construction, cement, and lumber.[47]

That trend peaked in August 1942, and thereafter building declined sharply until near the end of the war. Building experienced a "sharp upswing in the second half of 1945 following the . . . relaxation . . . of wartime controls," and residential construction soared by 80 percent. By early 1946 construction was revived, mostly by civilian patronage.[48]

Not all businesses prospered equally. Supposedly nonessential industries often fared badly. The traditional industries of California did not increase output as fast as the war's glamour industries. Therefore, as the war wound down, these businesses found themselves with maintenance "delayed," new equipment "deferred," and inventories "reduced."

The war boomed retail too, initially "in localities in which the principal and rapidly expanding district defense industries—aircraft and shipbuilding—are located, or in which heavy defense construction and training of troops" occurred. In 1941, San Diego sales were 40 percent higher than a year earlier.[49]

Although the conflict eventually created extensive prosperity, its advent also caused widespread concern. Historians have noted the fear of postwar unemployment, but contemporaries also dreaded joblessness *prewar.* Both employers and workers feared that expanding defense priorities would deny them materials. This concern proved groundless for two reasons. The first was "the comparative unimportance of vulnerable [California] industrial activities"—perhaps no more than 3 percent of total factory output. Luckily, those vulnerable businesses were located in areas where the government was spending heavily for defense anyway. For example, in early 1942 automobile, rubber, motion picture, auto sales, metal consuming, and retail firms laid off personnel, but defense industries quickly gobbled them up. In addition, many consumer goods industries, such as automobile and tire manufacturing (reinvigorated June 1, 1942, after temporary layoffs to retool for war); fruit, fish, and vegetable canning; petroleum production and refining; and motion pictures had a bright future in the war effort. California did not manufacture refrigerators, silk, aluminum ware, washing machines, or metal furniture, and so was spared layoffs in these impacted fields. Thus the specter of unemployed men, idle plants, and depressed areas did not materialize.[50]

A sustained labor shortage emerged instead, which endured through 1944.[51] The shortage was both qualitative and quantitative. As early as August 1941 aircraft and shipbuilding created jobs faster than the labor for them emerged. Social groups such as women and blacks supplied urgently needed labor, but many other sources were important too. As the draft stole more men from the labor market, industries sought alternatives.[52]

Employers tried education and technology first. Aircraft plants began "training-within-industry" some time before August 1941, and both federal and local government soon joined the effort. The government also dispersed plants, such as Marinship in Marin County, to make maximum use of the surrounding labor supplies. To accommodate women and boost productivity, companies replaced much riveting with welding, overhead welding with down-hand welding, and muscle power with power hoists. Then they turned to new groups. The unemployed were suddenly in great demand, and in-migrants poured into California, 323,000 between May 1940 and May 1942 alone. Seniors came out of retirement and young men came out of school to man the factories. Some students worked half days, while others dropped out and worked full time. Special summer programs got students through school in three years, leaving them one year of factory work before the draft. Workers shifted from restaurants and gold and silver mining into war work. Schoolgirls harvested fruit and put together airplane subassemblies. Housewives picked tomatoes, casual workers left the skid rows, domestic servants departed the kitchens, and disabled veterans built airplanes. "During the war Douglas hired twelve thousand of the latter most of whom performed very well." Gordon Wagenet remembered that the labor market was so tight that the U.S. Forest Service could find no other workers than derelicts from Sacramento's skid row.[53]

Although opposition to women workers is stressed in the literature, employers eagerly and early sought women replacements. They even instituted "Victory" or "split" shifts to allow women to work a half day if they could not labor a full one. The aircraft buildup came a year earlier than the shipbuilding one, and airframe employers quickly increased their female labor force from 5,000 "at the beginning of 1942" to 80,000 a year later. Private shipbuilders substituted women from mid-1942 onward, although Atlantic and Pacific "government yards... had been using women in industrial occupations on a fairly large scale much earlier." By the end of 1943, California female factory workers had risen from 60,000 to 249,000, nearly all in the durable goods industries. According to one estimate, by 1943, 40 percent of aircraft workers were female. In November 1943 the acute shortage forced the War Manpower Commission (WMC) not only to favor the hiring of women, but to *mandate* it. The WMC ordered that "no employer of 50 or more persons may hire ... more *men* than 90 percent of the maximum number of men on his payroll in October." In the Kaiser yards in Richmond, women reached 20–23 percent by 1944. As Sheila Lichtman points out, "Most shipyard women were not new to the labor force."[54]

Employers, especially San Francisco Bay shipbuilders, also quickly hired racial minorities, including Chinese, but mostly blacks. By November 1944, minorities made up 13 percent of shipbuilders, far in excess of their percentage of the Bay Area populace or the workforce elsewhere. Despite much larger black populations in other places, the deficit was two to one over Gulf yards and almost three to one over Atlantic ones, another case of western exceptionalism. African Americans also formed from 4.5 percent (Douglas) to 7.2 percent (North American) of airframe employees, "most on assembly work rather than custodial jobs."[55]

By September 1943, "women constitute[d] the only significant remaining local source of labor."[56] So employers turned to less significant ones. Prisons supplied some as San Quentin manufactured textiles for the war. When food processing seasonally slowed, employees switched to defense for the winter, and in February 1943, a presidential executive order created a wartime stretchout by lengthening the "work week" to forty-eight hours. Lockheed pioneered in hiring the blind, using seeing-eye dogs to "guide their masters to their work benches."[57]

Washington tried shifting war contracts out of local "acute shortage" areas, only to find that other defense centers had scarcities just as distressing. Subcontracting work to less impacted areas succeeded better, but that tactic freed up only limited numbers. Finally, in 1943 the government began raiding shipbuilding and other firms for underutilized workers. Still, in September 1943, the government listed "Los Angeles, San Francisco Bay, San Diego, Stockton, and Eureka as acute shortage areas"; Bakersfield, Brawley–El Centro, Fresno, Modesto, Sacramento, San Bernardino–Riverside, San José, Santa Ana, Santa Barbara, and Ventura-Oxnard as "near shortage areas"; and all the rest of California as "future shortage" areas. The future arrived the next year, when all these other areas also qualified.[58]

Trends in manufacturing employment explain the shortages. Although the war industrialized many previously unindustrialized areas, it did not break the metropolitan dominance of that realm; in fact, it temporarily increased it. Before and after the war some 77 percent of factory wage payments went to the San Francisco and Los Angeles metropolitan areas. In 1943, 83 percent did.

Because of countervailing forces, the struggle for labor was implacably dialectical. Companies hoarded workers for fear of being short-handed. As production peaked in 1943–44, workers, calculating their peacetime interests, began trickling back home. Others had second thoughts about leaving home in the first place, so late in the war, interstate migration slowed considerably. Simultaneously, the government heightened these doubts by raising the subject of reconversion. High-schoolers dropped in for the summer and then out for the fall. And the draft remorselessly took its toll. So did huge rates of turnover, especially among women. Not all employers met women's family needs, so their absenteeism also grew. Then early in 1944, just as selective service hit the bottom of the draft barrel, employers hit the bottom of the willing housewife pool. Wives shunned defense jobs for fear they could not do the work or failed to realize the need, and "thousands more rejected factory work as physically hard, dirty, and dull." Thus began the late war drive for conscription.[59]

Obviously, relocation hurt the Nisei and Issei most, but it also hindered employment efforts. Only weeks after their removal, the local economies "keenly felt" the absence of these industrious and thrifty small-business families. Since few labored in factories, their absence was not "keenly" missed there, but customers lost "Japanese operated service industries," domestics, and fishermen, especially around Los Angeles. Since these enterprises paid less well and their employees worked longer hours, the businesses left shorthanded were precisely those businesses that found it difficult to compete for employees with the high-wage defense plants. Japanese Americans resided mostly in and about cities and produced chiefly for the local urban markets rather than for "export" to the rest of the U.S., as the citrus and movie industries did. Cities depended on them for about one-third of their food. Thus relocation was not only unconstitutional and pernicious to the Japanese, it also hurt defense efforts.[60]

To recoup, in mid-1944 employers imported fifty thousand Mexican men to perform heavy labor for which women were unsuited. Even German prisoners of war were not safe from the insatiable maw of full employment. By this time, the manpower crisis had changed from quantitative to qualitative. General employment actually declined, while skilled labor remained in short supply well beyond the end of the conflict.[61]

Urban California's peculiar economic structure protected it from conversion layoffs at the war's beginning, but it seemed that its singular wartime industrialization, based largely on aircraft and shipbuilding, would heighten its suffering at the end. Reconversion to a peacetime economy, the return of hundreds of thousands of servicemen to the job market, heavy "immigration of servicemen" especially to the Southland, and strikes did cause idleness, but it was both mild and odd.

Most of the layoffs occurred in the durable goods industries, especially steel, aircraft, and shipbuilding, notably among women. From March 1945 to March 1946, durable goods dropped from 560,000 to 210,000 workers. At the peak, women were 40 percent, or one hundred thousand, of aircraft workers; 20 percent, or fifty thousand, of the shipbuilders;

and 33 percent, or thirty thousand, of steelworkers. In March 1946 their numbers stood at ten thousand, six thousand, and ten thousand. Nondurable goods production could not absorb those idled.[62]

Strikes in San Francisco Bay shipbuilding, steel, canneries, and railroads, and in California generally, reduced either jobs or the materials to do them with. Grain shipped to aid Europe denied California workers the opportunity to mill it. But persistent shortages of skilled labor still handicapped "the increase of production in many lines."[63]

The incongruous yet coexisting unemployment and labor shortage continued into the summer of 1946. At war's end, the state found itself with a large out-of-state workforce, trained to build planes and ships, but with few of these to build. Housing exacerbated the problem. One observer considered it improbable that "surplus labor in San Diego will seek jobs in the Los Angeles area so long as [its] existing housing shortage" continued.

Almost everyone had to sacrifice something in the war, and one thing sacrificed was training in skilled occupations. These included "machine tool operators, building and construction mechanics, and a wide range of engineering and specialized industrial occupations, as well as the more skilled clerical employments, such as stenographers, bookkeepers, salespeople, and the like." War prosperity did not teach people to fancy the uninviting wages and working conditions "in laundries, foundries, domestic service, logging, agriculture, railroad track maintenance, and the lower grades of clerical and sales work." The war also did not train many younger veterans for anything but war. Thus as employers increasingly raised the standards of skill for new hires, young veterans became "more difficult to place." Women and the many war-effort high school dropouts had been especially prominent in industries that had deliberately deskilled their work forces in order to indulge in mass production or to accommodate less experienced workers. In terms of know-how, most women were not necessarily different from unskilled returning servicemen. Unfortunately, color bias added another "unusually difficult" problem.[64]

Through 1946, wartime complications, strikes, materials shortages, railway car scarcity, price controls, and so forth continued to create economic bottlenecks and therefore unemployment. Some critics also blamed the liberal handout of unemployment benefits, but these do not seem to have been important. Craftsmen could pick their vocations, and everyone else could choose between a less skilled position or unemployment until they found a suitable job or the benefits ran out. During the defense buildup, analysts and boosters had hailed the "industrial diversification" brought by the war, especially by aircraft and shipbuilding.

However, with modest exceptions, that is exactly what these industries had not caused.[65]

It remains to answer the question that has been at the heart of the discussion of the war in California and of much of the war-and-society literature. Writers have contended that the war had a revolutionary impact, that it was comparable to a second Gold Rush, that it was unprecedented, and that it transformed California from a colony of the East to the "pacesetter" for the remainder of the country. Careful scholars of war and society make these arguments, but they do not convince because American California was always a place of extraordinary change. It is not easy to experience the unprecedented when it is so often the norm.[66]

Since that term *revolutionary* is used for everything imaginable and since it is not measurable, it need not detain us. The Gold Rush argument is also easy to deal with. Although it is an impressionistic view conceived by a San Francisco newspaperman, historians have widely accepted it. Unquestionably, the war did usher in large changes. Yet the real Gold Rush transformed California's economy from a narrow, sleepy, contented one with few European-derived people and with restricted overseas markets to a hyper-capitalistic, energetic, conflict-ridden one with worldwide markets and several hundreds of thousands of European-derived people. This change occurred in just a few years. Transformation did not happen in 1941 because California was already an advanced economy, a highly advanced one.[67]

Is the pacesetting argument better founded? Not in 1945. In manufacturing, for example, Los Angeles set the pace only in 1977, not in 1945. Among major metropolises, Los Angeles advanced from seventh place in 1939 to fifth place in 1945, while San Francisco remained stuck in thirteenth place. In absolute job terms, L.A. gained 108 percent and San Francisco jumped 62 percent, but neither gained ground on the leaders. The so-called colonials actually lost ground. New York *created* more jobs during this Census of Manufactures period than *Los Angeles had total at the end*. Chicago almost did. Within the state, Los Angeles's lead over San Francisco–Oakland grew from 71,654 jobs in 1939 to 195,131 in 1947. So war accelerated the major industrial reorganization underway since 1920 within California, but it did not alter San Francisco's long-term relative decline. The Bay Area also lost ground in absolute terms to eleven of the twelve American metropolitan areas that had been ahead of it in 1939, including Los Angeles. The reason was simple; other cities' industries were growing too, and faster.[68]

It should be added that as one of the leading manufacturing states and one of the top agricultural states, California was hardly a colony, despite what politicians like Robert Kenny urged. In addition, the state produced all the movies and many of the airplanes of the country and possessed a wide range of industries, including apparel, food processing, furniture, petroleum machinery manufacturing, printing and publishing, metalworking, and others. No state is ever completely independent, but California's economy was already diversified and quite sophisticated before World War II began.[69]

Still, how significant was this change in the context of California history? The largest percentage increase of manufacturing jobs occurred between 1909 and 1919, and the biggest absolute gain happened from 1947 to 1954. During the Progressive–World War I era, jobs grew by 107 percent; in World War II they advanced by 86 percent. In the Korean era the absolute number of jobs jumped by 388,913; during World War II, they rose by 306,774. The percentage change of World War II was not unprecedented, and the absolute gain was unprecedented only until the next census.

Much of the misunderstanding of the war's effect stems from the fact that many of its economic benefits, though spectacular, were ephemeral. Aircraft employed 21,327 in 1939, 244,000 in 1943, and 65,551 in 1947. Since the census did not list aircraft in San Diego, the real postwar figure is probably 75,000. That number represents a steep decline from 1943, but is a net gain of 53,673 and a percentage gain of 251.2 percent over the 1939 figure. Still, the industry in 1947 was about 31 percent of its wartime peak. Shipbuilding suffered a radically worse fate. The 1939 census recorded 4,458 employees. War elevated the total to 280,000, and peace lowered it to 18,289 in 1947 and 8,254 in 1958, fewer than 3 percent of the wartime peak. Six times more people worked in food processing in 1947 than in shipbuilding.

Steel netted a few jobs, but did little to alter the metallurgical balance of power between East and West. At 11,205 positions in 1947, California steel had 2 percent of the American total of 545,725. By 1958 the figure had edged upward to 15,605, about 3 percent. Electronics did not become important enough to make the census until that of 1954, and aluminum also proved negligible. The war pumped up California motor trucking, supposedly a means of overcoming railroad rate discrimination and thereby achieving transportation independence, but those gains too proved ephemeral. At their peak in 1945, the Pacific Coast states had 24.2 percent of American motor trucking; by 1965 they retained 8.6 percent. Neither aircraft, shipbuilding, steel, electronics, aluminum, nor trucking brought economic independence.[70]

The lowly, traditional, prosaic industries created most of the new industrial jobs from 1939 to 1947. These provided 255,000 of the 324,000 new jobs that the 1947 census revealed. Food processing at 120,000 jobs, not aircraft, was the leading manufacturing employer, having grown by one-third during the war. Almost every Standard Industrial category advanced a robust though not spectacular percentage.

Perhaps the gains were qualitative rather than quantitative. The airframe and shipbuilding industries' adoption and partial adoption of mass-production techniques would emphasize qualitative change. Of course, the shipbuilding gains were ephemeral because the shipbuilding industry largely was. Scholars have also argued that the "most important wartime contribution" of the aircraft industry "was the newfound role of research and development." Research did take place in the aircraft industry, but much was what the aircraft industry called development research, improving the product as it went along. That, of course, is what the airplane companies had been doing since at least the Douglas DC series, 1, 2, 3, 4. The use of the Cal Tech wind tunnel for testing by all of the airframe industry represented prewar basic research as well.[71]

That basic research did not suddenly explode during the midst of war production can be seen from a couple of points. First, the aircraft industry pretty much fought the war with models that had been conceived well before or just before the war. The famous B-17, manufactured by several Southern California firms on license from Boeing, is not the least of them. To mention the main craft of the other majors, the equally famous Douglas DC-3 (C-47), Lockheed P-38, Consolidated Catalina PBY flying boat and Liberator B-24 bomber, and North American P-51 fighter-bomber all were prewar planes or concepts. John Northrop had already experimented with both the flying wing and jet (gas turbine) engines before the flames engulfed the world. The jet plane was partially developed during the war, but by Bell Labs and General Electric, rather than by a California firm. The Cal Tech whizzes had by 1941 worked out the rocketry that led to the founding of Aerojet General, narrowly avoiding blowing themselves and the CALCIT Laboratory in Pasadena to smithereens in the process. For the record, the B-29 had progressed through ten prewar developmental stages from 1938 to the XB-29 in 1940. Gliders and helicopters are other aeronautical forms often associated with the war, but gliders had originated one thousand years earlier, and although helicopters had appeared in the 1920s, they were not developed in time for this conflict.[72]

Examining the issue of research illuminates the problem of doing business with the government. The National Advisory Committee for Aeronautics (NACA) had responsibility for basic research, yet after the war several airframe executives bemoaned its dereliction. Ward W.

Beman, chief of aeronautical research at Lockheed, told the Truman Committee in 1945 that NACA was fully five years behind in aeronautical research and ignorant of industry needs. Lockheed encountered the problem of compressibility in the P-38, and NACA failed to complete that research by war's end. As Beman put it, "In other words, we have been doing development research as distinguished from basic research, which in the field of aerodynamics would have to do with these phenomena such as compressibility, for example, which has retarded the progress of the whole [aviation] world." NACA and the Army held up Lockheed for two full years.[73]

Most California industry was not research and development oriented to begin with. At least, we do not have studies that show that industries with the vast majority of jobs at war's end, such as food processing, printing and publishing, lumber manufacturing, machine tools, and so forth, were driven into research by the war.

The war also affected labor. Strikes dipped in the Roosevelt Recession, then ascended from 1939 to a record high of 384 in 1941. The global conflict put this local activity on hold, reducing disputes by three-quarters by the end of 1944. Actual days missed fell even more than stoppages, making the war years less prone to industrial interruptions than any other year after 1933. This quiescent pattern diverged radically from the national one, where many strikes occurred in both 1943 and 1944. In 1945, the California numbers climbed to 246, and they remained close to that level until 1950. At their postwar peak in 1946, stoppages idled 258,200 people (more than twice the number in 1941), totaled three times the lost hours, and included a general strike in Oakland. Historians have held that the war and "the rightward drift of politics in the 1940s" would "demobilize union membership and limit organizational and political activities for more than a generation." But if postwar workers had been any *more mobilized,* their picket lines would have reached the Farallones.[74]

Many stoppages did occur before American entry, especially those of the Bay Area machinists and the Los Angeles aircraft workers in 1941. The machinists won their strike.[75] The aircraft workers both won and lost. After 1941, rank and file support for the war was very high. Moreover, San Francisco radical unions led by Harry Bridges, whom Robert Cherny has shown to have been a member of the Communist Party, and moderate ones led by centrists such as Jack Shelley and John O'Connell both supported the war, although for quite different reasons. So did the influential Catholic Church, which since the thirties had encouraged unions to follow a middle course between laissez-faire capitalism and Bridges's Stalinist communism.[76]

Union membership mounted with the crescendo of the guns. State publications do not list the number of members prior to the outbreak, but the number of unions hints at wartime membership advance. State locals grew from 1,222 in 1939 to 1,243 in 1942 to 1,870 in 1945. In that year, 946,639 persons belonged. If membership reflected the same percentages, it is possible to estimate membership in 1939 at 629,236 persons. Thus, war provided a 317,403, or 50 percent, gain. By 1950 the total had increased to 1,354,500, an additional jump of 407,861 members, or 44 percent. By 1955 the union advance reached 3,430 locals with 1,618,500 members, a much less impressive gain of 20 percent. Without figures for pre-1939 membership, one cannot decide if the advances of the war period were unprecedented, but the percentage increase was only slightly higher than in the succeeding five-year period. Absolute gains were less.[77]

Individual unions sometimes exploded. At Lockheed, reputedly one of the most enlightened airframe employers, International Association of Machinists (IAM) Local 727 shot up to 45,000 members, the largest local in the nation. The unions of the Metal Trades Department of the AFL, especially the Boilermakers, enhanced their numbers greatly. Lockheed, North American, Consolidated, and Vega recognized unions before Pearl Harbor. After hard campaigning, Douglas shops began to yield in 1943, and the Santa Monica flagship plant fell to the IAM in 1944. Only Northrop remained unorganized.[78]

Earnings ascended with membership. In 1939 manufacturing employees earned $27.80 a week. This sum nearly doubled by 1944 to a peak of $55.21, then fell the next two years to $53.53 and $51.29 before rising again to $65.39 by decade's end. So war wages greatly outpaced the 1945–50 rise. Manufacturing employees toiled four to five hours longer to earn these wages. From September 1939 to the end of the fighting, the cost of living in San Francisco and Los Angeles rose by thirty-two points above the 1935–39 index of 100. So, real wages in 1945 stood at $37.55, a gain of 38 percent. Hourly wages rose from 70 cents to $1.00.[79]

Unions vociferously disputed these calculations. Unions protested that the Bureau of Labor Statistics' method of calculating the cost of living ignored some items, such as the rising cost of restaurant meals necessary to so many wartime workers, the multiplication of shoddy items, the black market, and the disappearance of low-priced goods. The *Wall Street Journal*'s Standard and Poor's service as well as recent scholarship agree that the cost of living grew more than the government admitted, and eventually the Bureau acknowledged as much.[80]

World War II is often thought to have given California and the West a boost toward a Sunbelt tomorrow, but per capita income suggests the reverse. From 1929 through 1940, California hovered between 37 and 40 percent above the national average. The war initiated a drastic decline from 40 percent above in 1940 to 27 percent in 1945 and 25 percent in 1950. Californians earned more during the war, but other Americans made more still. In this realm, war *discouraged* exceptionalism.[81]

Industrial accidents soared as California per capita income plummeted. Fatal injuries reached an all-time high in 1926 of 748, and nonfatal injuries achieved an early peak of 98,192 in 1929. Thereafter both declined until 1933 and then rose through 1937, dipped during the recession, and crested again in 1943–44, together with output. Nonfatal injuries outpaced fatal ones, however, and the latter, despite advances during the conflict, did not regain the peak of the twenties. The effect was ambiguous since nonfatal injuries per capita rose while fatal ones fell.[82] War work broke more toes, but fewer heads. (See Appendix, Table 7.1.)

The war also eroded San Francisco–Oakland's union dominance. Before the conflict, the sister cities led in membership, but by war's end metropolitan Los Angeles pulled almost even, 265,036 to 252,396. In 1945–46, 28 percent of union members lived in the Bay Area and 27 percent, in metropolitan Los Angeles, or together, 55 percent of the state total. Los Angeles surged ahead by 1950, 494,200 to 424,800, so the postwar period, not the war, displaced the Bay Area.[83]

The war triggered wage problems that were both complex and insoluble. Pay scales derived from different demand for products, unlike skills, distinct levels of managerial generosity, varying labor power, diverse points on the economic cycles—in short, from a long history of worker-management interaction. Different jobs, such as aircraft and shipbuilding, paid unequal scales, sometimes in plants adjacent to each other, as in Los Angeles. Within a factory a vast hierarchy of pay existed, frequently for performing identical jobs.

Ordinarily, working people had three ways to cope. Wages could be accepted as inevitable or considered reversible by either the individual action of relocating or the collective action of bargaining or the strike. However, the war vastly complicated each remedy. The no-strike pledge that labor leaders gave was complicated by the slowness of the War Labor Board decisions. A second complication was the great number of inexperienced workers recruited and the hiring of new workers. A third was the heavily insistent concept of equal sacrifice, and a fourth was an extremely tight labor market that allowed workers to change jobs without sacrifice. These wrinkles in effect minimized collective bargaining and the strike, made passivity unthinkable, and thus made relocation the only viable option. Labor turnover plagued the war effort throughout.[84]

Union officials must have been terminally frustrated by the pressures of World War II. Management strove to achieve peak productivity, sometimes at the expense of what unions considered worker rights. The war added infinite restrictions on union activity and a War Labor Board to enforce them. Labor disputes swamped the board, which was years behind in resolving them. Resentment against the no-strike pledge and other wartime frustrations simmered beneath the surface. Then at the bottom of the industrial structure, militant members demanded protection, wage increases, stabilizations, and job reclassifications, or they would leave the union. Minorities and women demanded equality, on threat of going to court. Government and management demanded acceptance *of* management initiatives, and members demanded protection *from* them. Surprisingly, unlike in other areas, California unions and management somehow resolved their differences with few wildcat, quickie, or hate strikes.[85]

Although the usual picture of California unions at war is a negative one, that perspective should not dominate the picture. Unions in California normally struck to gain better wages during times of prosperity, when their bargaining power was highest. They not only gave up that weapon, but they suspended their work rules, put up with shoddy goods, accepted rising work injuries, watched much of their wage increases eroded by inflation, and took it on the chin from the California Supreme Court and African American militants like Joseph James. It is true that unions did not meet the expectations of blacks and women. Still, they sacrificed a lot and balanced competing pressures well enough to win the war, which was the larger issue.[86]

It is beyond the scope of this study to discuss the postwar period, but one point can be made: despite widespread anxiety about reconversion, "a large consumer influx, extensive industrial expansion, large-scale building operations, and a continuation of large-scale aircraft construction made possible a satisfactory conversion to a postwar economy."[87]

8. Government I
Managing the City in a Madcap World

Nothing demonstrates the complexity of World War II's impact better than the fate of city government. Most historians writing about the war, including myself, have assumed more of a monolithic impact than actually occurred. The war pulled government in several directions at once. Most importantly, the conflict forced a temporary cessation of normal government expansion by denying it personnel and materials. For more than a century, cities had provided an increasing range of services. War quelled this expansion. Simultaneously, it added its own agenda. Cities had to use their school, fire, police, and recreation services for federal purposes. Since cities could not add normal new functions, the conflict forced them to use their funds to pay off their debts rather than incur new ones to add services and buildings. The war also added another layer of governmental interaction, already building rapidly since the New Deal—that of intergovernmental relations. Local officials found themselves interacting with the top of the federal system more and the middle (the state), less. As usual, Mayor Fletcher Bowron perfectly captured this burgeoning contact with the nation state:

> In aid of the war effort we have built new streets and improved old ones. We have extended our sewage facilities until our sewers are now overloaded to the danger point. The increased population has added to our police, fire, and health problems and has taxed various other functions of municipal government. We are doing these things for the Federal Government, cheerfully and gladly, without compensation. Our police protect military highways, [and] convoy military units through our streets. Army units are camped in almost every city park. The members of the armed forces use our playground and recreation centers. We supply water and electricity, buildings, [and] office space. At our municipally owned harbor the navy has practically taken possession.[1]

The prosaic matter of fire pumps illustrates this important shift in focus. In mid-1943, the government disclosed that it would increase the number of American urban fire wardens from 342,000 to a Fire Guard Corps of 1,500,000. In addition, the government announced that it would shortly distribute fifty thousand stirrup pumps to San Francisco to help extinguish fires that might be started by Imperial Japanese incendiary bombs. These would be allocated six to the block, with ten thousand in reserve for "fire squads." James M. Landis, the national director of civil defense, explained that the Fire Guards had worked well in Great Britain.[2]

Probably so, but San Francisco no longer needed the pumps nor the fire guards a full year after the battles of Midway and the Coral Sea had blunted the thrust of Japanese expansion. The Japanese Navy no longer had the capacity to raid, much less support an invasion of, the American mainland. Too, San Francisco already had a full civilian defense fire-watch system in place plus the regular fire department, and it could ill afford to devote the extra personnel necessary to quadruple its civil defense firefighting force at a time when employers were practically shanghaiing workers to find enough labor for the strapped defense factories. Every city needed personnel and equipment—police radios, sewer pumps, and autos—much more than thousands of new wardens and stirrup pumps that would probably never be used.

Other intergovernmental relations were less frustrating but just as relentless. Almost every urban government action, from traffic to health, suddenly acquired a federal dimension. When workers flocked to the defense citadels, they created a need for housing. Who should build it, the federal government or private enterprise, and where? In Los Angeles City or Los Angeles County? In Sausalito or Marin County? Regardless of how these questions were answered, most neighborhoods answered, "Not in my backyard!" When these decisions were sorted out, the question of race intervened. Should blacks, who desperately needed lodgings, be allowed into housing projects against the wishes of white tenants? When the shore patrol volunteered to help with policing duties, the cities had to make certain that this wartime incursion into urban policing would not reduce the peacetime role of the city cops. When the government took over harbors, the cities strove to ensure that wartime changes would not endanger future commercial expansion. And when the government gobbled up increasing amounts of land, the cities fought to guarantee some form of compensation for their shrinking tax bases. All these matters required a negotiation—between city and national government, between city and county, between county and state, and sometimes between all four.

Obviously, the federal government came into the lives of city officials on an unprecedented scale, but local connections also multiplied. For example, the war encouraged municipalities to cooperate on matters of police, civil defense, and fire.[3] Los Angeles County was already a maze of intergovernmental relations, with two major governments and many minor ones. So was the Bay Area. The East Bay Municipal Utilities District (EBMUD) brought several cities together to acquire water, and San Francisco sold its water to several communities on the peninsula. The war did not originate the trend, but it certainly augmented it.

Several historians have expressed the conviction that the Second World War provided the nation state with the capacity to manage large affairs such as national economies and perennial defense crises. However, from the urban perspective, the government's actions often seemed callous, incomprehensible, and incompetent. Several historians, including Marilynn S. Johnson and Arnold Hirsch, have pointed out the counterproductive actions of the nation state in creating racial segregation during World War II. We need more investigations of wartime federal-urban relations before we can state definitively whether the actions of the nation state were muddling or masterful. Still, the news from the Western Front, to use Johnson's very apt phrase, is not encouraging.[4]

The financial news is particularly discouraging. The global conflict simultaneously decentralized urban tax bases, preempted alternative sources of revenue, co-opted building materials, and imposed significant new burdens on the already strapped urban areas. The war caused marked short-term effects, but the long-term ones were even worse, particularly the rapid acceleration of metropolitan tax base decentralization. The 1940 census documented that some American cities, such as San Francisco, had stopped growing, and some had even declined. This news brought the first birth pangs of the modern urban crisis. By 1990, cities such as St. Louis had experienced truly cataclysmic change, as half or more of their people deserted, moving to what Kenneth Jackson has called the suburban Crabgrass Frontier. This process had gone so far by the 1990s that the crabgrass now grows in center cities, enough to recreate absolute open space and even a return to kitchen gardening.[5]

Nothing like this occurred in the 1940s, but the foundations were laid. But since cities also grew—some places doubled and even tripled in population—the full destructive impact of the war was not immediately felt. In the short run, war stanched center-city population decline, but by greatly adding to the viability of suburbia, the war markedly aided the decentralization of the metropolis. War industries that located outside the city continued to attract people long after the shooting stopped.

If the long-term consequences did not immediately unfold, the short-term ones appeared soon enough. The fighting reduced the construction industry, upon which cities depended heavily for revenue through the property tax and construction licenses. Of course, new aircraft, rubber, cement, and shipbuilding facilities went up pell-mell, but unfortunately these establishments largely grew up outside the jurisdictions of the biggest cities. San Francisco possessed only forty-four square miles of mostly covered land and therefore had few eligible building sites. Los Angeles contained many times that land mass, but most of its war industries were already in its suburbs or began to locate there anyway, in part to avoid paying city taxes. San Diego did better in the competition for factories, but it also lost several to its suburban rivals. At the same time, the government owned many war plants, such as the massive Hunters Point and Mare Island naval and other shipyards, which made them not subject to taxation. Yet many of the war workers commuted to work in the suburbs from homes in the central cities. So workers demanded services in their home jurisdiction, but the martial employers who generated these demands did not pay taxes in the jurisdictions where their employees lived.

Center cities suffered much of this injury, but suburbs did not escape unscathed. Government-owned plants did not pay taxes in suburbs either. Thus, suburbs often gained the population, but not the tax base to provide it with services. Sometimes both lost. At least half of the twenty thousand employees of the Marinship yards in Sausalito commuted from San Francisco, and most of the rest lived in a government housing project called Marin City. Neither San Francisco nor Sausalito could tax the yard or the Marin City housing project, while each had to respond to the increased demands for services. Thus the war often generated a tax base in one jurisdiction and service demands in another, and in other cases it generated service demands in both without creating a tax base in either. The war struck Richmond and San Diego, the shock cities of World War II, especially hard. Richmond ballooned from 23,642 to 99,545 and San Diego, from 203,341 to 340,000—321.1 and 64.4 percent increases respectively—while simultaneously restricting the tax base necessary to supply these large numbers of new residents with services.

At the same time, the federal and state governments soaked up alternative revenues. The state sales tax diverted revenues from the hard-pressed cities to the state governments. The Second World War brought most Americans into the income tax system for the first time, so these federal taxes increased the competition for tax moneys. These extra-urban taxes made tax increases all the more unpopular just when the martial metropolises needed them most. To add insult to injury, the national government also took much property, in addition to factories, off the urban tax ledgers by occupying real estate or buildings formerly on the tax rolls. Sometimes they forgot to say please and thank you, as when they "seized" a portion of East Anaheim Road in Long Beach for "a new Navy Hospital." The Navy and Maritime Commission condemned over two hundred acres in National City in mid-1942 without procedures or payment, according to the mayor, practically at gunpoint.[6]

By late 1943, Washington owned or occupied "approximately eighteen percent of the real property in San Francisco" (the federal government owned 42 percent of the state of California) and by war's end possessed 40 percent of the much larger county of San Diego. So the national government not only squelched the expansion of the cities' tax bases, but also actually cut into them. In San Francisco alone this cost $1.625 million in lost revenues.

Other cities, especially Vallejo, suffered from a different version of this problem. There, not only did the Navy take up a lot of physical urban space, preempting other activities that might have paid taxes, but the Navy yard also drew a huge number of employees into the city and its environs, for which Vallejo would have to provide at least some services. In this case, neither the city *nor* its suburbs gained compensating tax revenues in the form of private factories that could be added to the tax rolls. Huge public housing complexes, also off the tax base, clobbered the city again. Richmond had the same experience. And while the tax base stagnated, the physical infrastructure declined. With city governments unable to repair the infrastructure because of materials shortages, rationing, employee shortfalls, or financial problems, it crumbled away for nearly four years. For example, federal vehicles, which markedly increased the traffic over the streets and bridges of Urban California, rode free over expensive structures like the Golden Gate Bridge, which other riders paid to use.

Neither city nor suburb gained from the intensification of environmental degeneration. Perhaps Los Angeles was hardest hit. From the mission era, the Los Angeles Basin had been known as the "Valley of Smokes," so the impact of World War II would hardly have surprised the Indians who so named it. Although the automobile is usually convicted of this crime, it is not entirely guilty. Artificial rubber increased the smog greatly. In order to compensate for the loss of rubber sources in Southeast Asia, the government stimulated the synthetic rubber industry in this country. The butadiene plant in the Los Angeles area helped reduce the rubber shortage, but it also repaid the city with a rich mixture of pollutants, which stained both city and suburb. Not every war city produced butadiene, but all generated sludge in greatly increased quantities. War industrialization swelled the residues to be disposed of and changed the abominable brew qualitatively by adding new chemicals and other substances. The increased flow and more complex nature of waste forced cities to run their plants at capacity, which deprived them of any overload capability. Beyond that point, cities either had to invest in larger capacity or simply empty the sludge into the rivers and bays. Since the government would not grant priorities for materials to build, dumping prevailed, and water pollution increased dramatically. San Francisco and San Diego had plants that could handle a portion of their waste, but they dumped the remainder; Los Angeles, Sacramento, and Oakland dumped it all.[7]

The Los Angeles story is illustrative. That city faced a sewer crisis even before the war got fully underway. Its fifty-five-mile-long sewer outfall, which stretched from the San Fernando Valley to El Segundo, was so badly overloaded that during storms the "tremendous pressures blow off manhole covers and geysers of sewage spurt upward," complained the *Times*. "For the last seven miles, the ground shakes and the cracked sewer lid rumbles." The war worsened these conditions, while denying materials to build new treatment plants to alleviate them. Beautiful Santa Monica Bay became seriously polluted by waste, and Los Angeles ended the conflict with a sewage capacity both seriously inadequate and gravely run down. That city and others throughout the state faced large postwar bills to repair and expand these facilities.[8]

And as the sludge roared and groaned its excruciating way to Santa Monica Bay, ground shaking and geysers spouting, the aquifers subsided. The war demanded huge amounts of petroleum to drive General George Patton's tanks and Admiral Chester Nimitz's carriers and service fleets. Hence Southern California oil companies pumped with a vengeance, depleting the water table and at the same time encouraging "salt water infiltration" in the face of the retreating underground pool.

The prospects above ground were not much better. The war demand drove the companies to request permission to drill within the city of Los Angeles. The mayor refused to retard the war effort, but mindful of the unsightly derricks, pipes, and waste produced by oil extraction, he agreed only to short-term drilling, to be ended immediately on the return of peace.

Though not caused by the war effort, noise pollution was counterproductive to it. "Many people did not realize the amount of unnecessary noise and racket in Los Angeles until the intensive industrial development required many thousands of war workers to sleep during the daytime," Mayor Bowron explained.[9]

The built environment declined less clangorously, but just as significantly. Cities that had physical structures to accommodate one population found themselves suddenly asked to provide for many more. For example, the relocation of the Japanese Americans opened up lodgings. These were snapped up by worker migrants, especially African Americans with scant housing choice, who quickly overloaded these structures. Predictably, by war's end the formerly Japanese American areas of the Fillmore District in San Francisco and the Central Avenue neighborhood of Los Angeles were run down, making them targets for the new and ultimately mysterious "science" of urban redevelopment. Of course, that strategy would remove even more property from the tax rolls—and for a whole lot longer than contemporaries realized.

The nation state also constructed war housing, sometimes large amounts of it. These temporaries helped provide accommodations, but at a price. They co-opted valuable space that cities could not tax. Planners and boosters wanted these areas for permanent homes, which would both enhance the tax base and provide the amenities to keep the middle class in town. In shock cities the problem could be immense. The federal government built most of the thirty thousand new housing units that sprouted in Richmond between 1940 and 1945, which meant that close to half the housing stock was off the tax base in a city whose population and service demands had quadrupled. Hunters Point in San Francisco, Chabot Terrace in Vallejo, Cabrillo Homes in Long Beach, and Linda Vista in San Diego created similar problems. Hence cities everywhere agreed with the Vallejo master plan that temporary housing "is perhaps one of the most serious threats to the legitimate [post-war] growth and expansion of the community."[10]

And although the government eventually imposed price, wage, and rent control, it did not do so before significant inflation occurred. Thus cities saw the buying power of their revenues from their narrow real estate tax bases eroded by inflation before the controls hardened.

Harbors were just as important to cities' dreams of growth, and cities lost both control of their harbors and all or a large part of their harbor revenues. The Navy Department simply took over and operated much of the waterfront. This action damaged San Francisco least because the State of California owned and managed its port, but Oakland, San Diego, Long Beach, and Los Angeles owned their harbors and lost greatly to military preemption.

War claimed personnel as well. Excessive pay increases and overtime pushed up wages in war industries. And real inflation, however much denied, cut into municipal salaries at the same time that these tempting opportunities surfaced in outside businesses. This phenomenon coincided with the draft to create a severe labor shortage for many employers, including government. The maritime business was so hard hit that they found it difficult to keep arriving sailors from jumping ship. Old timers likened it to the Gold Rush, when the lure of money emanated from the Mother Lode rather than from Marinship or Moore Dry Dock. Thus defense plants put an irresistible upward pressure on government salaries. In San Francisco, for example, Mayor Roger Lapham signed a salary standardization ordinance in 1944 that for the first time allowed a forty-hour week to municipal employees, provided excellent retirement and other benefits, and set city wage standards by those prevailing in other local industries. This development marked a historic landmark in a controversy over salary standardization that had alternately scorched and sputtered in the city for over a decade. Los Angeles, too, granted wage concessions. As in so many other areas, war broke a longstanding civic stalemate to the benefit of employees, if not the city. And city employees, like their industrial counterparts, worked a lot of overtime.

Between the lure of glory on the battlefield and glorious wages in the factories, cities could not effectively compete. In April 1943, the Los Angeles police force had 460 vacancies (18.4 percent) in an already inadequate force of 2,500, and 232 openings (12.9 percent) in the 1,800-man fire department. Moreover, as Bowron correctly explained, these fewer city workers were called on to do more, not less, because of the war emergency. The same was true of teachers, auditors, laborers, assessors, and other city employees. Some of the same suburban factories that were jeopardizing the mayor's tax base were situated close to the Los Angeles city limits, where they could depend on the understaffed firefighters to help them if a cigarette butt lighted a pile of shavings or a welder's torch lit up the whole place. A diminished work force inevitably led to the stretchout. In 1943, Mayor Rossi advised all departments to look for ways of carrying on the work of employees lost to the draft rather than immediately requesting replacements. Los Angeles and Long Beach officials criticized the government for refusing deferments to firemen, policemen, and key aides, and in 1944 they joined with other cities and Governor Earl Warren to pressure Washington. However, San Francisco actually created its own no-nonsense agency to facilitate the transfer of employees into defense work or military service.[11]

It has been argued that World War II marked a watershed in American political culture, both because it brought an acceptance of big government and because it greatly expanded city planning. As the numbers will show, neither proposition tests out. Government did not grow at the local level as it did in Washington. Government programs were not expanded across the board, simply because cities did not have the personnel to run them and did not have the priorities to build structures to house them. At the local level, neither the political culture nor the extent of programming changed much at all, and to the extent that the latter did, the change was transient, linked to the war.[12]

Under these circumstances, city tax rates and expenditures edged up, but only gingerly. The government of Los Angeles was not a consolidated city and county administration like San Francisco's, so it had two major urban governments, the city and the county. Los Angeles *County* did not raise its tax rates at all for six straight war-torn years; San Francisco, which had one of the lowest tax rates of any large American city, kept it that way by advancing its taxes per $100 of assessed valuation from $4.295 in 1940–41 to $4.69 in 1944–45. Oakland's tax burden actually declined slightly, from $5.20 to $5.09. San Diego and Los Angeles *city* raised their rates somewhat higher, to $5.45 and $5.26 respectively, but none of these reached the $6.40 average of the ten largest American cities. Moreover, San Francisco employed a lower assessment ratio than these other cities.[13]

Overall spending tells the same minimalist story. In the last year of peace, fiscal year 1940–41, Los Angeles County spent $89,996,540. The 1945–46 budget, the first postwar one, *requested* only $95,301,274. That represented an increase of under $1 million per year, or just under one percent. Considerable inflation reduced even these unpretentious figures. The large increases in the county's budget came after the war. By the 1948–49 budget, county manager Wayne Allen was asking for $192,537,850, over twice the figure in the last war year.[14]

The figures for the city governments tell the same tale, especially when compared to the huge increases in federal spending and debt. (See Appendix, Table 8.1.) The full impact of war on government appeared in the 1942–43 budgets. War did not expand urban government; it squelched it. Everywhere, cities cut spending, sometimes below the 1942 figure. This development is not hard to explain. Cities did not have the personnel to run extensive programs, they did not have priorities to secure building materials, and they did not even have enough gasoline and rubber to run their equipment full time. Like George Patton in 1944, the government simply turned off the gas. In 1942–43, Los Angeles, the biggest California city, spent a grand total of 1.8 percent *less* than in 1942. In 1943–44, the figure got back into the black by 6.1 percent, and in 1944–45 it rose 11.5 percent. The latter figure was much higher than in other cities. While these unimpressive numbers were unfolding, inflation undermined the buying power of these tax dollars at the same time that in-migration expanded the demands upon them.

San Francisco had a much worse bookkeeping experience—a 24.0 percent decline in 1942–43, a 1.5 percent rise in 1943–44, and a 6.6 percent comeback in 1944–45. To further show the impact of migration, by late 1943 San Francisco's population had increased by 8.4 percent, while its expenditures declined by 24 percent. Thus, the city was spending quite a bit less per capita on its citizens in 1942–43 than the $67.21 it spent in 1941–42. Oakland's spending rose 0.2 percent in 1942–43, an increase that climbed to 5.8 percent in 1943–44 and ascended to 8.3 percent in 1944–45. Of course, population here and in Los Angeles rose considerably during the same time. As the table indicates, other cities had about the same experience: modest increases in 1942–43, modest to marked decline in 1943–44, and modest to marked recovery the next year. The pattern is quite clear.[15]

Revenues were slightly more robust. San Francisco's rose 4.0 percent in 1943–44 and 3.6 percent in 1944–45. Revenues in Los Angeles and Oakland went up slightly more. Nor was there much of a change in the composition of the revenue. At the federal level, the big change came in 1943, when new tax laws incorporated most of the remaining untaxed people into the income tax system. No such change occurred at the local level. The property tax continued to be the workhorse of the system, accounting for roughly 70 percent of revenues in San Francisco, 71–74 percent in Oakland, and 58 percent in Los Angeles.

The central government did not help the cities much. According to a recent account of federal-city relations during the war, the mayors concentrated on civil defense and postwar planning. The former allocated some moneys to cities, but the latter brought little. Despite congressional hearings and much discussion, the federal government appropriated only about $17 million to the task of postwar planning. In addition, the government designated funds under the Lanham Act for defense housing, but of course those houses actually hurt the cities' tax bases. By 1944–45, federal payments in lieu of taxes had entered the city budgets, but in very unimpressive amounts. For example, in San Francisco in that year federal payments totaled only 0.7 percent. This figure was mostly for housing and did not involve payments for impacted schools and hospitals, commandeered real estate, or preempted harbor fees. Even San Diego, which its historian Abraham Shragge aptly calls a "Federal City," received no more than 6 percent of its budget from its federal sponsors.[16] As late as 1954, the figure was even more negligible.[17]

Although the cities labored under heavy burdens, state officials basked in unprecedented prosperity. Because it was a state with heavy in-migration, California reaped a huge windfall from its three-cent sales tax, paid by its growing population earning greatly increased wages and salaries. By mid-war, this surplus had risen to $285 million. In late 1943, a bill to divide the windfall was bottled up in legislative committee, and the state did not share with cities until after the war. Instead of granting some relief, the state actually cut the sales tax, despite the plight of the hard-pressed arsenals of democracy. The state would not even help fund the fight against venereal disease. There was little recognition at either the federal or state level that cities were bearing a huge share of the war's burdens and needed help in carrying them.[18]

Parsimonious though it was, state aid continued to be the principal source of outside help, and it did rise during the conflict. San Francisco got the most generous share. That city received some 17 percent of its budget from Sacramento in 1942, a figure that rose to over 21 percent in 1945. Surprising as it may seem, state contributions were a much larger part of San Francisco's budget than were national contributions to the budget of the "Federal City" of San Diego. In Los Angeles, state grants advanced slightly, from 7.5 percent in 1943 to 8 percent in 1945.

To place all of this continuity in perspective, one must remember that the contemporary federal budget grew markedly; despite war bonds and higher taxes, the federal government ran up a staggering debt. The deficit skyrocketed from $40,439,532,000 at the beginning of the European phase of the Second Great War in 1939 to $258,682,187,000 in 1945. Despite some criticism of the unwillingness to tax Americans heavily, there was much to be said for passing along some of the debt to the soldiers' children and grandchildren, who would benefit from the sacrifices made by the 1940s generation. Fortunately, modern cities did not have to go into debt, too, as Civil War cities were forced to do. Instead, World War II cities paid down their debts, for the very good reason that there was not much else to spend their moneys on.[19]

Terrence McDonald has noted that the debate over "bringing the state back in" has not generally looked at the bottom of the federal pyramid. City government has been largely ignored in this debate, especially the effect the Second World War had on it. Yet until World War II, civil expenditures in the United States were primarily state and local rather than federal. World War II, more than the Depression, changed that relationship; therefore its impact on local government needs to be investigated in detail. In California, the federal-city relationship was not really very much of a partnership. The federal government imposed many of the costs of war upon the local level and refused to compensate urban entities for their expenses. It also terminated programs that might have helped the beleaguered cities. Since the phrases "new federalism" and "federal-urban partnership" occur so frequently in the literature, it seems important to define exactly what kind of arrangement it was. If this was a partnership, it was undoubtedly an ironic one in which the cities were clearly the junior partners.[20]

The operation of government bears out this claim. California cities in 1941 already suffered from transportation problems. Autos choked downtown streets at rush hour, and mass transit had long been struggling. Although historians have been loath to admit the connection between war and human progress, there undoubtedly often is one. The global conflict kept alive a balanced transportation system by forcing patronage of mass transit and reviving the San Francisco Bay ferries; it brought a merger of competing companies; it led to the universal transfer; it forced the idea of freeways to the fore to cope with the auto; it stimulated the use of car pools; it somewhat slowed the advance of the auto; it required the staggering of downtown working hours; it led transit to charge economic fares; it encouraged transit to adopt the merit principle by mandating the hiring of women and minorities; and, in general, it exercised sound influence on this crucial urban enterprise.

Each city was an arsenal. As Supervisor Schmidt put it on the Monday after Pearl Harbor, San Francisco "is not only a city from a military standpoint, it is a fortress!" By the outbreak, the Bay Area had become the great decentralized military base that interwar boosters had labeled "the American Singapore" in what then seemed like one of their more fanciful flights of imagination. Los Angeles was a similarly decentralized base, and San Diego was something of a centralized one. Military fixtures bristled from every part of the urban landscapes. These presented a transportation problem in case of possible evacuation, and they also created a vast extra daily burden of military traffic shuttling men and goods between the various points.

City fathers repeatedly warned that the traffic and transportation problems must be solved to avoid hampering the war effort, keeping defense production at a high level. As usual, contemporaries understood the dependence of the frontlines on the well-being of the urban areas in the rear. The *Chronicle* explained in early 1942:

The armed forces of any nation depend on the civilian population behind
the lines and upon smooth industrial and social operation, America is very
largely dependent on its metropolitan areas. These cannot be thrown into
disruption. The morale of their people cannot be upset without upsetting
the whole structure. Certainly the Government is not going to allow this
or any other metropolitan area to be upset unreasonably, and it is mischie-
vous to upset morale by trying to spread panic.[21]

The war placed an immense strain on this supposedly "obsolete trac-
tion service" in all California cities because they suffered from unique
disadvantages. Unlike some parts of the urban system, Golden State cities
experienced extraordinary population growth. San Francisco jumped
from 634,000 to 800,000 during the conflict; San Diego, from 200,000
to 340,000; Vallejo, from 40,000 to 90,000; and Richmond, California,
the true shock city of this war, from 23,000 to 100,000–110,000. City
transit had to cope with these increased numbers, and California cities
also depended disproportionately on the auto, whose gasoline and rubber
tires the government had begun to ration. Los Angeles, the quintessential
automobile city, in particular chafed under this regime.

The war promptly brought staggering overloads to, and as in other
cities stimulated a revival of, mass transit. San Diego's trolley patronage jumped from 46 million in 1941 to 129 million a mere two years
later, after a 50 percent increase in the previous two years. The Golden
Gate Bridge, which handled only auto traffic, experienced its best year
in 1942, despite rationing. Each city succeeded in carrying these added
burdens, but not without varying degrees of difficulty. If the opening and
closing hours of businesses, factories, naval bases, schools, and other
institutions could be staggered away from the nine-to-five routine that
normally governed working hours, the increasing number of residents,
shipyard workers, schoolchildren, and servicemen would not all demand
transportation at the same moment. San Diego buses and trolleys, for
example, would not run empty for most of the day and be stuffed at nine
and five. Although this seemed like a relatively painless and rational partial solution, it took a long time for it to be adopted. Everyone seemed to
be enthusiastic about the solution in December 1941, but nearly twelve
months after the bombing of Pearl Harbor, San Francisco was just com-
mencing to spread out its hours.[22]

However, in Fortress California, automobile traffic did not immediately drop. In early 1942, transportation surveys that questioned how the
defense force got to work showed a continued overwhelming dependence
on the auto. In Los Angeles, the preference ran at the rate of 92 percent,
and of those who got to work in this manner, each car averaged fewer

Waiting for the bus in wartime San Diego.
Courtesy San Diego Historical Society, Photo Collection.

than two riders. In the Bay Area, 80 percent of the Richmond shipyard workers rode to work in autos. San Francisco finally banned parking on some downtown streets, a matter of great controversy in all cities up to that time. One-way streets began to be adopted more frequently, together with left-turn prohibitions on major arteries. The wartime rationing of materials, men, and money choked off the actual construction of freeways but nonetheless heightened the popularity of the idea. Even in tightly packed San Francisco, freeways seemed like the way to overcome the "traffic blockade" (gridlock) of downtown and to save that district from the competition of outlying center-city neighborhoods or suburbs. As a part of the freeway idea, traffic and transit rationalization flourished.[23]

So did the idea of ride sharing, or carpooling, especially to sites where transit did not go. San Franciscans commuted to the East Bay, to Berkeley and Oakland and the Richmond shipyards. Angelenos drove to the Consolidated aircraft factories in San Diego, and Orange County folk migrated daily to the Lockheed works in the San Fernando Valley. Urban development had gone much too far to allow for the massed populations to commute comfortably between well-defined concentration points. Newspapers, governments, civil defense, and employer spokesmen continually urged the car pool upon these errant Americans, but the latter seemed to have decided to use their cars until gas and tire rationing left them with bald tires and without gas quotas. However, as the war wore on, carpooling did increase substantially. The vice president of Ryan Aeronautical estimated in late 1943 that "share the ride" programs were working properly and that a majority of Ryan workers were utilizing "private automobiles to the maximum extent possible by carrying capacity loads." The solutions were never brilliant, but they were good enough to maintain defense production at a high level.[24]

The vested interests of mass transit proved just as obstreperous as the automobile preference. The war created an immediate labor shortage, and unions promptly moved to take advantage of it. East Bay workers walked off an evening rush hour in 1942 to force a wage increase, and San Francisco workers did not lag behind in asserting their own interests. Although it was generally assumed that San Francisco transit employees deserved their raise, it took a strike threat and an appeal to the War Labor Board to get it. Their stand against women and African Americans involved both prejudice and profit. In addition to the usual bias against these two groups, streetcar workers saw them as a threat to their own wartime wage bonanza. San Francisco transit was short over 80 men as late as mid-1943, and Los Angeles, 600 of 2,500 in December 1943, so the remaining operatives would reap considerable overtime income. At first, the San Francisco Civil Service Commission sided with the conductors, engineers, and trackmen, but it eventually reversed itself. Both women and African Americans entered this previously segregated segment of the workforce.

Women did so relatively early. By late 1943, the public line employed 62 and the private line, 120, but by that time, the transit lines were having trouble recruiting more women because of the higher wages paid elsewhere. The breakthrough on the Municipal Railway seems to have been the key to the general lowering of bars to female city employment. "All departments must eventually be adjusted to the use of women in positions for which men have been used heretofore," said the Civil Service Commission, "and for which men are not now available." The *Chronicle* editorialized that "it has taken a major war to open the eyes of the people to a great many facts of life. San Francisco's transit problem is one of them."[25]

In some cases, it actually took more. For years the city had limped along with inadequate transit caused by a dual system. By 1941, the public Municipal and the private Market Street railways each transported about one-half of the city's riders. The Muni regularly prospered. It had better equipment, it maintained the five-cent fare to its opponent's seven-cent one, and it opened the western districts of the city to development. It had less rolling stock than the Market Street line, but regularly ran loaded to the limit due to its lower fare. The Market Street Company had obsolete equipment, refused to mend the streets when it replaced trolleys with buses, charged a higher tariff, continuously meddled in city politics, let its rolling stock run down, and carried fewer passengers than it could have. Together, the two lines clogged Market Street, the city's great ceremonial and business artery, with four tracks, did not provide a universal transfer, and duplicated some lines. The Market Street Company failed to operate fifty of its cars because of its abundant unpopularity. They also rendered such bad service as to jeopardize both the war effort and the future of the city.

Just as San Francisco strove to keep its tax rates below those of Los Angeles, Oakland, San Diego, and other California cities because it did not want to lose residents to them, it resented its own lumbering transit. Chamber of Commerce spokesmen argued that one could get home to Oakland faster than to the outlying districts of San Francisco. For years, city builders had proclaimed the virtues of transit merger to eliminate the inconvenience to riders and the drag on San Francisco's fortunes. A merger of several private companies in 1921 had created the Market Street Railway, and since that moment, the city government and boosters had been trying to buy them out. However, the city's voters repeatedly rejected bond issues to purchase the private company. In the meantime, the automobile steadily cut into the revenues of the ailing private line, and both it and the Municipal Railway had to put on more buses to compete with individual transportation. The Market Street Railway steadily declined in service, value, and customer satisfaction but continued to make a profit due to the great wartime demand for transit. However, poor transit hurt the war effort and theoretically jeopardized thousands in case of an evacuation.[26]

The Market Street Railway's franchises expired in 1956. Perhaps the voters hoped to force the company to abandon operations at this point without expense to the city. But as usual, the voters thumbed their noses at the idea of merger at the November 3rd election by a margin of six thousand ballots.

Meanwhile, gasoline rationing, which California had heretofore avoided because of its oil-producing status, finally went into effect on December 1, 1942, and more people took to the trolleys, buses, and cable cars. The Municipal Railway soon prospered, with each new year setting a record for ridership and revenues. Suddenly, the city had the money to maintain its tracks in excellent state, to buy new buses (if the Feds granted priorities), to put on new lines, to give its employees a deserved pay hike, to maintain the five-cent fare, and to buy out the Market Street Railway as well. So profitable had transit temporarily become that the California Railroad Commission forced the Market Street Railway to reduce fares to six cents.

By 1943, the circumstances for merger seemed ideal. The war demanded greater efficiency, Samuel Kahn favored the sale, and the city could purchase the firm from current revenues without a bond issue. So the city tried again on April 29, 1943, to convince its voters to purchase the Market Street firm, this time for $7.95 million. By a staggering majority of 88,418 to 53,619, the voters rejected the plan and left "the City that knows how" looking like it didn't. In October 1943, the Office of Defense Transportation suggested a plan of merger, but both the Municipal Railway and "interested civic bodies" rejected this plan as likely to complicate the city's transit woes further. In the meantime, the federal government held up approval of the sale of new buses to the Municipal Railway until the city solved its transportation dilemma. Finally in early 1944, the voters relented, and San Francisco acquired the derelict private firm for $7.5 million.[27]

The electors had driven a hard bargain. In the thirties, the company had wanted $12.5 million for its properties. However, Samuel Kahn and the eastern investors whom he represented drove a hard bargain, too, since his company was behind some $2 million in paving repairs and handed over to the city a lot of very bad equipment. Still, in the long run, the merger seems valid. The city needed to acquire control over all of its transit to establish the standard fare, universal transfers, city transportation planning, equal working conditions, and uniform safety regulations and to eliminate duplicating lines, remove the four-track bottleneck on Market Street proper, repave the streets where the government took up the trolley tracks, and shift from trolleys to buses. Without the war, this solution might have been further delayed. After all, San Francisco had suffered along with inefficient transit since 1921, and, as the *Chronicle* resignedly put it in 1942, "a little more inconvenience will only be more of the same." This historic shift in its transportation policy represented an important windfall to the community. Almost unnoticed was the elimination of the world's first cable car line, which came when the Market Street Company removed the line to put on buses.

The Los Angeles area experienced a different outcome. There, mass and rapid transit had long been in decline also. In 1940 the Los Angeles Railway (LARY) planned to save itself by substituting buses for trolleys, but war prevented implementation of this plan. The war brought more riders but enhanced the system's capital decline. As Alonzo Smith has shown, "By the beginning of 1944, only 493 of 800 streetcars, and only 212 buses out of 256 were in operation" on the LARY. This led to repeated breakdowns, fractured commuting schedules, lessened service, and steaming customers. LARY did not even operate between 12:00 A.M. and 8:00 A.M. In addition, the labor shortage necessitated longer hours on the platforms. In May 1944, this overload led AFL Local 277 of the Amalgamated Association of Street Electric Railway and Motor Coach Employees, supported by the Communist Party, to strike both Los Angeles and Long Beach, thereby further alienating 1,000,000 daily commuters in the former and 115,000 in the latter.[28]

Then, as Scott Bottles has shown, "in late 1944, the Huntington Estate sold the railway lines to American City Lines," a subsidiary of National City Lines (NCL). By that time, buses were half as costly to buy and cheaper to operate than trolleys. So NCL sought to implement the abandoned 1940 plan, which substituted buses for trolleys. That led to investment of fresh capital and the progressive modernization of the system. This trend was stopped after the war by the government, which declared that General Motors, which supplied NCL with equipment, had a captive market. Thus the war only temporarily halted the long-term decline of LARY, which eventually collapsed into the hands of the city of Los Angeles. Unlike in San Francisco, the war did not restore transit; it further crippled it.[29]

The region's rapid transit suffered a similar fate. The Pacific Electric (PE) was already abandoning lines before the war started, but it got a reprieve from the increased ridership during the war. However, the PE could not operate at maximum efficiency because of a manpower shortage that womanpower could not alleviate. Using women in transit was controversial at first, but was soon accepted. The problem for the war effort was that women found that they could earn more at the shipyards and aircraft plants. So by November 1943, the PE was running hundreds fewer cars daily because it had too few platform and maintenance people. Unfortunately, the War Labor Board would grant neither deferments nor pay increases to match the wages of the glamour industries. Long Beach was in the same fix. This led to the ironic situation of companies' gaining riders but failing to operate efficiently because of the lack of spare parts, operators, or mechanics. After the conflict, the PE continued to decline, eventually falling under control of the state Metropolitan Transit Authority in 1961.

The government took a direct hand in solving the transportation problems of both Los Angeles and Oakland. In the former, the Maritime Commission built a "shipyard railway" to get workers to the yards. They constructed a similar sixteen-mile line from Moore Dry Dock in Oakland to the Kaiser yards in Richmond, using derelict rolling stock from the Third Avenue elevated line in New York City. None of this eliminated the traffic congestion in either city.[30]

Curiously enough, San Diego was the exception to most of these experiences. San Diego received lots of buses, new streetcars, carbarns, power stations, garages, trackage, maintenance machinery, tools, and Navy buses. Unlike San Francisco and Los Angeles, for some reason San Diego did not run out of women willing to work in transit, so they faced only a tight labor situation, not an impossible one. That allowed them to operate all of their equipment instead of letting some sit idle, as the Market Street Railway, the LARY, and the PE did. Furthermore, the Navy helped the city obtain new equipment. They aided with priorities, and when the government did not grant these, the Navy got the buses themselves and turned them over to the civilian agencies to operate. Vice president and general manager S. E. Mason of the San Diego Electric Railway Company estimated that in the two years ending in November 1943, the system saw a fivefold increase in ridership. The city had a few bottlenecks, especially equipment shortages, but for the most part San Diego was the golden boy of California urban transit. Abraham Shragge, who has called San Diego a "Federal City," hardly mentions Second World War transit in his excellent dissertation, but the *transit evidence* would fully support his claim.[31]

Why San Diego got favored treatment when the other cities were begging for labor, equipment, priorities, and materials is not certain. As usual, San Diego officials bent over backward to cooperate with the Navy and government programs. For example, in the Congested Areas hearings, Congressman George Bates of Massachusetts repeatedly attempted to get the San Diego Electric Railway manager to criticize the Office of Defense Transportation for certain matters, and the manager steadfastly refused. It is clear from the testimony of San Diego officials that they knew how to work with the government, and it paid off. As general manager Mason pointed out, "I want to say that the O. D. T. has gone out of its way for us. I have called on O. D. T. and they have diverted busses [sic] to this city from other cities."[32]

The large numbers of transit riders are important to bear in mind because so many historians have stated that 85 percent or more of war workers drove their own cars to the job. We still need definitive studies of wartime transportation, but the 85 percent figure conveys a misleading impression. That figure derives from a study done in April 1942, seven months before gasoline rationing went into effect. A year and a half later, the number riding transit had increased dramatically. For example, in 1943 in Long Beach 24 million people annually rode the Lang Bus Lines in just eleven months. That figure represented an increase of 89.6 percent in just two years. Still others rode the PE cars to the Terminal Island shipyards. The manager of the San Diego Electric Railway said 40 percent of the workers at the huge Consolidated aircraft factory rode his railway, and additional people took it to Rohr, Ryan, and other factories. In San Diego, where 85 percent of the transit riders were defense related, the metropolitan-wide San Diego Electric Company saw a rise of 500 percent ridership. The other cities witnessed the same phenomenon. In the East Bay, so many war workers patronized the Key Route and other transit that it was nearly overwhelmed. Even the lowly Martinez Ferry could transport two thousand persons and fifty autos every hour to the Benicia Arsenal and Mare Island Naval Shipyard at Vallejo. Obviously, a lot of people rode their own cars to work. Nonetheless, busted, poorly maintained, parts-starved, and shorthanded as it was, transit carried a very large number to work.[33]

On other fronts, however, the war brought progress to a halt. Street lighting was one of them. For one thing, essential war industries, from shipbuilding to public-school training programs, required extra energy, and the war imposed new burdens on the L.A. Bureau of Light and Power. Rationing denied construction materials, and the dimout forced the lights to be lowered over most of the streets and eliminated entirely in a few. Even after the lifting of the dimout on November 1, 1943, 871 San Francisco lights remained out.[34]

Like public housing, police, health, and other affairs, ports became a subject of intergovernmental relations and urban rivalry as well. Los Angeles believed that the military services seriously underutilized the joint port of Los Angeles and Long Beach. By using public port facilities already built by the cities, the port could handle 1,000,000 tons per day instead of the 250,000 it currently did. Los Angeles officials opposed the building of more facilities at the Navy Supply Depot and Army Transport Service in Oakland to handle the proposed Pacific Theater buildup and demanded that the military use city harbor facilities already in place. They wanted the Army to build railroad holding yards into the port area to increase its ability to handle the load, and the Army was going to do so. Los Angeles also used the emergency to try to get the federal authorities to construct a tunnel from San Pedro to Terminal Island. Since 14,000 persons and 1,350 cars and trucks daily had to use the ferry to get to "T" Island each day, L.A. officials were certain that a tunnel, costing some $4 million, would greatly ease the flow of people and goods and therefore aid the war effort. Since the tunnel would take too long to build, and since it was an intercity tunnel, it did not have much appeal to the government. And, of course, Long Beach was equally convinced that a tunnel ought to connect *it* to the *other end* of Terminal Island. For equally compelling "national defense" reasons, a tunnel would facilitate the traffic from Long Beach, which now crossed a two-lane lift bridge and a temporary structure. After all, some 80,000 defense workers came that way to their job every day.[35]

War also kept the police shorthanded a good bit of the time. Because the military struggle thrust upon them numerous new duties, many of which were military or quasi-military, the police and fire departments were even more indispensable. That role did not shield them from the draft nor from competition with the well-paid defense industries. Los Angeles alone suffered from a 10 percent vacancy rate in April 1943. San Francisco's normal 1,322-man force declined to 1143 by early 1944, over 14 percent. By September 1942, Berkeley had experienced a 52 percent turnover in its police ranks. The police forces were particularly short of experienced men; it took approximately six months to train a rookie policeman, and even then he would remain a greenhorn for several years to come. In addition, some police work necessitated further highly specialized training. By contrast, aircraft manufacturers simplified tasks so as to require little training.[36] The departments argued that trained people were crucial to the war effort, but, as the Oakland chief of police noted in the fall of 1942, the Navy had taken his best detective for patrol boat duty and put one of his radio operators in office work. Others, needed by the FBI in its vastly augmented identification work, found themselves doing non-related jobs in a military uniform instead. One especially troubling impact of the war was that due to military regulations, servicemen could not testify in civil cases. So if a sailor witnessed a holdup, solicitation, or beating of a civilian, he could not be used as a witness in the case. Since so many cases where "uniforms" were implicated involved statutory rape, this restriction was particularly onerous for law enforcement.[37]

By mid-1943, the government had decided to grant deferments to policemen in certain categories, but departments continued to be understaffed. The military police and shore patrol supplemented the regulars but often were too few in numbers. And the shore patrol had to share police headquarters and use the city jails to house their enlisted transgressors.

Congested areas brought new duties. For example, the chief of the California Highway Patrol considered "travel-transportation as an adjunct of production, in fact an extension of the assembly line." And to keep the assembly line going, the police had to enforce the thirty-five-mile-per-hour government speed limit, set to conserve rubber. They had to impose dimout and blackout regulations, deal with the resulting numerous auto accidents, cope with greatly increased drunken driving, train and supervise an army of civil defense volunteers, supervise police auxiliaries who were used largely in traffic control, and guard military convoys.

Without the police, the consequences could be downright comical. In the evening after Pearl Harbor, a military convoy got completely lost for hours in the blacked-out city of Los Angeles. On another occasion a driver hauling military equipment became stuck for half a day under a low clearance underpass. The hapless man was extricated by an acetylene torch, only to become stuck for the rest of the day on a narrow bridge down the road.[38]

War also vastly enhanced the need for identification. Aided by the California Division of Criminal Identification and Investigation, the police had to identify and investigate a variety of things: civil defense workers (well over 100,000 in Los Angeles alone); firearms, which flooded cities in response to citizen anxiety and military necessity; potential saboteurs; larger problems with stolen property stemming from population increases; and a constant flood of public employees, caused by the high turnover rates. Wartime communications increased the same burdens. The government drafted police forces' skilled radio operators, refused the departments new equipment, and simultaneously loaded police down with new demands for communication. The police responded by sharing the expertise of the remaining officers, spare parts, radios, and information on how to cope with war.

Not least of the problems was overcrowding in the jails. The Richmond slammer was an extreme case; there a jail built for eight miscreants was sometimes stuffed with sixty. And the police had to provide jails for the shore patrol and military police as well. The services usually prosecuted their own but had no facilities to hold them until trial.[39]

The manpower shortage led inexorably to the use of auxiliaries. San Francisco, for example, began with 4,500 volunteers, which it narrowed down to 2,500 through training and examination. The police department then began a crash course at twenty public schools for two hours at night, five nights a week, to train the survivors. In addition, police officers had to examine every recruit, secure a physical, and fingerprint the men. Moreover, the explosion of defense production in the cities required armed plant guards, and in San Francisco alone, these new training responsibilities ran "into the thousands." Although the police

department trained the volunteers in police procedure, in the law of ar-
rest, and in the "handling and the use and care of firearms, including the
pistol, rifle, shot gun, and the Thompson sub-machine gun" (!), most of
the auxiliaries directed traffic in the downtown area and stood ready to
help with emergency traffic duties in case of an air raid or evacuation.
Others formed motorcycle and mounted units in the outlying areas of
the city, and still others enforced dimouts and policed the beach on Sun-
days, "all football games in Kezar Stadium," and parades. In addition, a
250-man detail worked "the opera season" (a highly unlikely place for
disorder unless the soprano was egregiously miscast), the prize fights, and
functions at the auditorium. Eventually, however, the wartime increase in
crime and the decline in regular police manpower forced the auxiliaries
into crime prevention work as well. San Francisco Police Chief Charles
Dullea thought that his department was "unique" in using the auxiliaries
in actual police duties.[40]

Police departments recruited many of the men from the American
Legion and the Veterans of Foreign Wars, but also hired workingmen.
Each wore a uniform of a "trench cap, zipper jacket, arm band, star,
whistle, and long baton." The Los Angeles department employed its
auxiliaries in traffic duties similar to San Francisco's. These men were
organized by geographic district in "the city and Los Angeles," so that,
in case of emergency, they could walk to their assembly points, thereby
not clogging traffic, and they were trained to mobilize in fifteen to twenty
minutes of the sounding of an alert.[41]

The war also added the burden of controlling so-called aliens. Although this was a federal government activity, much of the actual work
fell on the shoulders of the men in blue, especially in Los Angeles. When
the federal authorities began their initial arrests of dangerous Japanese,
Germans, and Italians, the police helped detain 2,035 Japanese aliens.
After the federal authorities banned Japanese possession of "flashlights,
radios, firearms of every description, cameras, etc., . . . having no other
place of concentration for this property, it devolved upon the police to
receive and store it issuing receipts therefore." When it appeared that
Japanese Americans might be in danger from collective violence, the
police cordoned off and protected their residential areas. And when the
government decided on relocation, the police had to provide "escorts,
traffic officers and guards at the various points of concentration within
the city, prior to the sorrowful trip to the reception bases."[42]

Although less true of San Francisco than the Southland, the Pacific
War also increased urban crime problems. Migration created a larger
criminal population; working parents left children unattended, with the

consequent multiplication of juvenile delinquency and gangs; the vast numbers of military personnel caused a proportionate opportunity for the world's oldest profession; dimouts and blackouts set up ideal conditions for burglary, theft, robbery, and automobile accidents; a diminished police force reduced its deterrent capacity; and "crowded accommodations," docks, and depots maximized the opportunities for pilferage. Hefty wages, rationing, and servicemen's boredom raised the incidence of gambling. Meanwhile, the growth of racial and ethnic groups created the usual crucible for group friction. Thrown into an equally diverse and transient soldiery, this mix could become mildly explosive.[43]

However, despite a lot of hand wringing by the public authorities and media about collective disorder, crime, and juvenile delinquency, none rose alarmingly. Crime increased sporadically everywhere except in a few cities like Alameda. For the year ending on December 31, 1942, San Francisco crimes against property decreased, while offenses against persons rose. By 1945, the murder rate went up again, along with automobile theft, assaults, sex offenses (other than rape), petty theft, and weapons carrying. However, in the same year rape, robbery, burglary, and grand theft declined. As of late 1942, San Diego and Los Angeles reported a decline in the general rate of crime, but an increase in juvenile delinquency, an advance shared with the City by the Bay. In Southern California, juvenile delinquency took the form of gang activity, especially among Mexican Americans. Both the non-Hispanic Los Angeles chief of police and the Hispanic American county sheriff, Eugene Biscailuz, along with many leaders of the Hispanic and non-Hispanic communities, viewed this activity with alarm. These gangs would become the famous, and to scholars, Byronic, pachuco gangs that ultimately fought the Zoot Suit Riots. However, juvenile offenders multiplied everywhere, though usually clad in less splendidly imaginative garb.[44]

Many of the offenders wore bobby sox. Juvenile delinquency, gambling, prostitution, and crimes against servicemen especially perplexed Californians. Servicemen were special targets of criminals because they often arrived in the Golden State with considerable back wages and were headed to the Pacific Theater. A robust last fling at the urban vices seemed to be a good way to spend a man's last dime on what might be his last opportunity. As the war wore down, juvenile delinquency became so prevalent that downtown Los Angeles was something of a haven for crimes against servicemen and a target for greater police efforts.[45]

The war-induced gaming renaissance created other problems. *San Francisco Chronicle* columnist Richard Donovan depicted "the thousand unseen miniatures that are the thriving backrooms of this town." During a typical evening in such a place, "a big party of live ones comes in—a writer, a band leader, two newspaper men and an automobile dealer. They are heroic figures, like gods of Olympus, and they are out to humble this joint." Had he added sailors and soldiers to his slumming party, he would have captured the reality of all the martial cities. Los Angeles banned card rooms and other forms of gambling, but they flourished nonetheless. Fearing nonenforcement, prolific social problems attendant to an underground business, and political and police corruption, the San Diego city council chose regulation of the traditional card houses over suppression. In 1944, the Port of the Palms ordained "that only Draw poker—as defined by Hoyle—may be played" in licensed card rooms. It banned minors, limited stakes, prohibited outlandish advertisement that might tempt the unwary, limited ownership to one card room, and decreed that tables must be visible from the street. This ordinance survived for approximately two months before the chief of police, the city manager, and Christian ministers secured the passage of another ordinance suppressing card, dice, and other money gambling except in social clubs. By now, the gamblers had banded together into the San Diego Cardroom Owners Association. Through petition and legal action they stymied the threat of government action and left the police with the original ordinance to enforce.[46]

Prostitution proved even more intractable than games of chance. Although the services demanded that prostitution be suppressed and city law enforcement and health authorities agreed, the prostitutes continued to add their contribution to the gross urban product. Nor was it an inconsequential one. In San Francisco, Oakland, Los Angeles, and San Diego, the police succeeded in closing houses of prostitution, which were considered the greatest source of disease because of the larger number of sexual contacts of their working women, but the call girls, bar flies, drink pushers, and other less vulnerable practitioners continued to ride the same wave of prosperity that other working people in Urban California did. In contrast to Hawaii, where tolerated prostitution operated openly, in California prostitution operated discreetly. Also unlike in Hawaii, a very large percentage of women were nonprofessionals. The trade was usually pursued by young women, eighteen to twenty-two years of age, and most often patronized by servicemen. Nearly 40 percent of San Diego women were nonresidents, a vast increase, and many were "runaway girls." Beth Bailey and David Farber considered San Francisco "the capital of American vice," but at least the servicemen/customers were not lined up halfway down the block as they were in Honolulu.

Still, according to Bailey and Farber, San Francisco served as the center of this traffic and even the center of the "export trade" that shuttled prostitutes to and from Hawaii.[47] Police Chief Charles Dullea denied this charge and believed that he had suppressed the professional trade, but he did admit to problems. These stemmed from the alarming increase of venereal disease.

With forty thousand to fifty thousand sailors turned loose on the town every weekend, San Diego also made a major contribution to the vice trade. Vice was tolerated in San Diego until the war broke out. Unaccountably, and in contrast to their policy in Hawaii, the military shut down the segregated prostitution district in San Diego one day after Pearl Harbor. However, this attack did not inflict a comparable defeat on the courtesans. They simply regrouped, took to the streets, and counter-attacked as individuals rather than from segregated fortresses. In any case, they had little choice since the nightclubs hired women with badges to keep prostitutes out of the bars. The Navy's decision to demand that San Diego eliminate the segregated district was ultimately ineffective. At first, the Navy allowed sailors to go south of the border to Tijuana, then banned such trips, only to permit them again. Sailors could simply change into civilian clothes and cross to Mexico to patronize the houses of prostitution there. In 1943, the Navy rescinded the ban, so the sailors did not have to travel incognito. The Army never had a ban, so their dress code did not change. In effect, by banning the segregated district in San Diego, the Navy simply shifted part of the trade south of the border without materially hampering it.[48]

Although the city closed down the red light district, no one knew if the professional prostitutes had not simply gone out into the radically underpoliced county territory to work. Armstead Carter of the San Diego "Committee to Control Venereal Disease" was certain that they had suppressed the trade in San Diego, but admitted that the business was not ended. It had merely taken a different form. With the connivance of taxi drivers, hotel clerks, bartenders, and others, the prostitutes simply went to work in other venues. And of course, the regulars were greatly reinforced by the novices, which made repression even more difficult. Between that problem, the taxis and clerks, the county, and the border, it was not likely that sexual commerce diminished by very much. The policy of suppression merely meant that vice would be a more clandestine or multicultural experience for all.[49]

Since prostitution was considered a crime, the police were stuck with dealing with it. They seemed none too pleased with this assignment, nor quite certain how to handle it. Arrested women spent 60 to 180 days in jail and underwent treatment if they were diseased. They performed sewing needed in prison operations while incarcerated. In addition, the Big Sisters League provided them cloth to "use in making doll clothes," so they could while away their time in the slammer in isolation from the other female prisoners. Rehabilitation was seldom attempted, and after their sentences they were sent home. The Sisters planned to establish a home and pursue rehabilitation, but they had not done so by the end of 1943. San Francisco believed itself unique in the United States because it used psychiatrists and doctors to rehabilitate the women both psychologically and physically, but that treatment did not stem the trade.[50]

Of all the crimes that the war imposed on beleaguered Fortress California, none bothered its citizens more than juvenile delinquency and prostitution—in abbreviated contemporary terms, JD and VD. Urban dwellers feared both, in large part because they seemed, and often were, linked together as problems of youth. The former was the path that young women trod toward the world's oldest profession and young men followed as their customers. "Experts" perceived an alarming advance in youthful misconduct. They cited a host of reasons for the problems, but youth watchers universally believed that broken homes caused most of the increase in juvenile delinquency. As San Francisco district attorney Edmund "Pat" Brown informed Mayor Lapham, 32,000 marriages occurred in Los Angeles in 1943, but also 28,000 divorces, close to a modern average. San Franciscans married 13,033 times and divorced only 7,639, a lower rate, but a disturbingly high one for the time.

Some offenders came from stable homes, but many had two parents working in the plants. In such cases, adults turned these "eight hour orphans," or "house key orphans," loose on the theaters, where they sat all day, or let them skip school or gave them the key to the house to come and go as they pleased. Other youth came by the thousands to work in the war industries and lived on their own, often from the age of sixteen, seventeen, or eighteen until inducted into the services. Even when their parents were at home, some children were truant, louse-infected, or abused. The martial cities offered numerous temptations to these unsupervised youngsters. Theaters attracted youth abusers; some, although not most, taverns served liquor to under-aged customers. Pornographers plied their trade amongst the unsuspecting innocents. Though public dance halls and the fantastically popular roller rinks generally enforced good conduct, children had to travel to and from these places by themselves, vulnerable to all of the city's wiles. Some of the latter wore servicemen's uniforms. These lonely, probably scared young men pursued and tempted the locals.[51]

In the homes of Filipino and Hispanic immigrants, a generational revolt added to the non-supervision and disorientation of juveniles. These young people, in turn, formed gangs, like those in East Los Angeles or the industrial district at Eighth and Howard in the San Francisco Mission District. They became both the victims of the problem and predators on other youth. The experts said that war relaxed everyone's morals, making both youthful indiscretions and adult indifference more likely.[52]

There was more for them to be indifferent toward. In Los Angeles, for example, juvenile arrests more than doubled, from 4,174 to 9,457, between 1941 and 1946. Auto theft, burglary, and robbery dipped in 1942, but juvenile arrests rose sharply in 1943 and steadily in every other year. In 1943, about 1,800 such crimes, about 5 per day, occurred in San Francisco in a population of 180,000 under the age of eighteen. That would be one juvenile offense per 1,000 potential offenders, 100 for every 100,000 population. In Los Angeles, the ratio reached a higher level per thousand. In Los Angeles the figure was 25 crimes per day out of an under-eighteen population of 390,000. In 1944, some 60 percent of the youth arrests were youngsters from broken homes. The other social conditions seem not to have made much difference, despite the massive prevalence of transiency, non-supervision during the day, roller rinks, roadhouses, roving sailors, and all of the other supposed enhanced pathologies of a big city. At these rates, one crime would have been committed in L.A. each day for every 15,600 juveniles and in San Francisco, one for every 36,000. Clearly, society was not coming apart at the seams, however alarming the percentage increase and JD crime rates may have been.[53]

Nonetheless, the defenders of youth redoubled their efforts to stamp out the "plague." Most of the major cities passed curfew laws, San Francisco, San Diego, Los Angeles, and Vallejo among them. San Diego passed a law that forbade youngsters under seventeen from being on the streets after ten o'clock unless accompanied by an adult or on some legitimate mission. Even then, they could not gather or loiter. San Diego bars hired extra hands to prevent liquor's being served to minors. The police had to enforce this law and also ensure that pinball machines paid out free games instead of money. In this case, both cops and Christians opposed youth gambling.[54]

San Francisco had a variety of people looking at its juveniles. The League of Women Voters surveyed the youth of the city. The district attorney strove to prevent youthful transgressions. He established the Seekers Club, a group of reformers among the inmates of the youth facility, to educate offenders in that jail. Bartenders, movie house operators, and roller rink owners all pledged not to allow misconduct in their establishments. The police established a special youth division housed in the old North End station at Scott and Greenwich to deal with all juvenile problems. They employed "modern" methods to get to pre-delinquent cases, including a Big Brother and Big Sister program to provide role models to youth. And the city established the San Francisco Coordinating Council, composed of the mayor, superintendent of schools, district attorney, and others to coordinate all of the city's youth efforts. Edmund Brown even proposed turning the Civic Auditorium and other public buildings into dormitories to keep the homeless off the streets at night. Newspapers ran editorials and news stories about the problem, and churches redoubled their youth outreach programs.[55]

The government did assist the police departments by creating shore patrols and putting military police in all the urban areas. In San Diego alone, the Navy brought the shore patrol up to 292 officers by 1943, a number that probably equaled the entire city police force. These measures did not fully compensate the police for the added strain of supervising an enormously increased civilian population, but they at least eased it somewhat.[56]

However, neither police nor shore patrol coped with the most explosive of these conflict-related situations. War-induced riots are well known in American history: Civil War draft riots; Confederate women's food riots; World War I riots for jobs, turf, and power; World War II upheavals over recreation space and bias; and Viet Nam collisions over everything imaginable. The worst Second World War upheaval in California was the only "peace riot" that I am aware of. At 4:15 P.M. on August 14, 1945, the government flashed word of the Japanese surrender, and a spontaneous celebration erupted on Market Street. However, that did not satisfy the sailors, who returned the day after the Japanese threw in the towel for a three-day San Francisco victory celebration that turned into a melee, killing eleven and injuring one thousand. A crowd of ten thousand sailors and bobby-soxers stormed onto Market Street, smashing windows, ripping off barber poles, attacking trolleys, trashing cars, throwing missiles, looting clothing and jewelry stores, and snarling traffic. Some of the sailors also stripped and assaulted women. Although the crowd theories of Gustave Le Bon are often criticized by historians, this outburst would seem to fit them perfectly. The outbreak was senseless, indiscriminate, brutal, and amoral. The attack seemed almost to be against the city, an anti-urban riot, for older residents were attacked physically, and every species of property, public and private, was assaulted. Police and shore patrolmen failed to contain the upheaval, and Admiral C. H. Wright, commandant of the Twelfth Naval District, had to slap a 4:00 P.M. curfew on one hundred thousand sailors to prevent further turmoil. Obviously this riot was infinitely worse than the Zoot Suit Riots of 1943.[57]

9. Government II
Mission Improbable

Even more than the police, the firemen held the fate of the metropolises in their hands. As in the case of the police, the draft and higher-paying war work took men from firefighting, and the government refused priorities. The firefighters also suffered their significant manpower losses while taking on added responsibilities—war greatly increased cities' vulnerability to fire.

In San Francisco alone, the volunteer firemen, designed to supplement the regulars in case a successful incendiary attack overwhelmed the regulars, numbered 3,884, of which 1,406 were active. These auxiliaries did not take part in normal fire prevention activities, so they did not reduce the demands that war made upon the firemen. Sometimes they were not even immediately available because they were working in the war plants and shipyards. Because the military drafted the younger men, the fire departments were often left with older ones, who could not cope with the heavy exertions of a serious fire.

War priorities prevented the acquisition of new equipment, and overcrowding vastly heightened the chances that the departments would need it. In residential neighborhoods people lived in rickety buildings with inadequate heating arrangements, cooked in their rooms, smoked in bed, and in general multiplied the hazards. Industrial expansion added as many or more, as did a congested waterfront choked with "immense quantities of inflammable and explosive war materials." Mayor Roger Lapham of San Francisco described all of Fortress California when he observed that these "many circumstances . . . make our city . . . one of the most hazardous spots, from the fire protection standpoint, in the nation." Alameda and Oakland were especially vulnerable. Numerous shipbuilding and Navy operations required the storage of hundreds of thousands of barrels of gasoline in places where the fire department could not douse them in case they ignited. The fire chief there believed that an oil fire in Alameda would quickly spread via the estuary and engulf Oakland as well. In addition, the department lacked the water pressure to put out a fire and could not get priorities to build larger mains.[1]

Long Beach was in especially dire straits because it had lost so many fire stations in the 1933 earthquake and had not had the money to rebuild because of the Depression. The war struck them hard. A differential gear that cost $360 in 1938 now cost $820, and the "War Production Board was reluctant to grant a priority on these parts as they classified it as a truck part and not a fire apparatus." Through 1943, the government refused to protect firemen from the draft and repeatedly refused to grant priorities to replace engines, hoses, tall ladders (for taller buildings), and firehouses, which had also been neglected because of the quake and Depression. The city alarm center was in a hotel for lack of a suitable structure, and the firemen were forced to forgo days off and go to an overtime basis because of the lack of personnel.[2]

Miraculously, large fires happened infrequently, and none of the cities suffered from the kind of general conflagration that swept San Francisco in 1906 after the earthquake or even the large fires in nineteenth-century cities. However, one major blaze illustrated what the consequences of such neglect could be. In 1944, an arsonist put the torch to the New Amsterdam Hotel in San Francisco, resulting in the loss of twenty-two lives. The worst fire in Golden State cities occurred in 1944 at Port Chicago in the North Bay area when a munitions ship exploded. Despite their manifest disadvantages of overwork, enhanced responsibility, and shortages of equipment, the city firefighters suffered no tragedy comparable to this disaster.[3]

The war brought temporary relief to the eternal Hetch Hetchy power controversy, but no solution. Since the 1920s San Francisco had tried to pass bond referenda to allow it to build distribution lines for the power produced by its Hetch Hetchy water system. The Defense War Plant Corporation built an aluminum plant at Riverbank and agreed to purchase the Hetch Hetchy power. The federal government allowed the city to continue distributing its power through Pacific Gas and Electric (PG&E) until the plant opened its doors. As Lawrence Kinnaird notes, "The Pacific Gas and Electric Company, for a consideration, permitted the city to use its lines for all municipal purposes and the remainder of the power was sold directly to the Kaiser Aluminum Corporation and the Permanente Cement Company who were ultimate consumers." However, the public power advocates did win something in the compromise. PG&E

got the lion's share of the market, but the city government gained the right to supply itself with electricity and to sell some to others as well. Yet in August 1944, when the Defense War Plant Corporation shut down the aluminum factory, it left San Francisco in the lurch again. Another stay of execution allowed the city finally to find a compromise solution that would please Washington. So in the case of public power, by providing a market that allowed the city to put off the ultimate resolution of its problem, the war delayed rather than facilitated a solution.

In the field of housing, the government helped to cope with the problems that it created. San Francisco established a housing authority in 1938 to provide homes for those who could not afford them. However, there and elsewhere, war changed the housing mission overnight to one of supplying homes for the surging in-migrant workers. The war also improved the cash flow of the housing authorities. These usually counted on a government subsidy to balance rents that their largely deprived tenants could not afford and to amortize housing properties. Instead, high wages allowed the system to operate in the black.[4]

Largely allocated to cities under the Lanham Act, the housing units lodged impressive numbers. In crowded San Francisco alone, 27,000 people lived in dormitories and single-family dwellings. Although that total represented more people than the number that lived in all of Richmond in 1940, it did not come close to sheltering the thousands that poured into San Francisco. Estimates of San Francisco's wartime population growth ran from 170,000 to 220,000, so public housing sheltered from 12 to 16 percent of the invading hordes. The East and North Bay urban areas fared somewhat better. By early 1945, the government had programmed or built thousands of units, especially in the Richmond and Vallejo areas, adjacent to the enormous government and private shipyards. Vallejo, which by North Bay standards grew a modest 125 percent, had acquired 35,000 public housing residents by 1945. Put another way, the city had almost as many public housing dwellers in 1945 as it had total people (40,000) in 1940. Richmond, which exploded from 23,000 to 100–110,000, had nearly twice as many people in public housing in 1943 (41,000) as it had total people in 1940. By mid-1943, this shock city of the war had built 12,650 public housing units and had another 12,000 under construction or allocated, which ultimately would hold 70,000 persons.

In 1943, these figures made Vallejo and Richmond not only favored places in the Bay Area, but also very unusual communities. Even today, American cities average only about one percent of their population in public housing, and even a European country, such as Britain, averages only about 29 percent. Yet in Richmond and Vallejo, the percentage was close to 40 and 50 percent respectively. Much was made of the terrible impact of the Second World War on these Bay Area suburbs, but the impact was much more adverse in San Francisco. There, public dwellings sheltered only a small portion of the wartime invasion. Trans-Bay Alameda County experienced more modest population growth, from 513,000 to 630,000, but this rise still created housing problems. By mid-1943, the population of the island city of Alameda had jumped from 36,000 to 47,000. With seven shipyards and the Alameda Naval Air Station, the city expected a population between 65,000 and 70,000 when the war boom peaked in 1944. In anticipation of this explosion, by the spring of 1943 the federal government had already constructed 5,496 units, which probably housed 18,900. In Oakland the figure was a more modest 3,122 family units and 1,200 single dormitory rooms, which would house approximately 11,900 residents. In the San Diego area, by April 1943 the government had constructed another 15,000 dwellings, designed to shelter 50,000 persons, but San Diego grew by over 100,000 people.[5]

Los Angeles, ever the individual city, and its home county diverged from the pattern. There, private housing dominated the quest for shelter. The government planned most of the public housing authorized or constructed in the area up to April 1943, either in the black neighborhood of Watts–South Central or in the war-congested harbor area. The government programmed 3,250 family units for black areas and another 3,000 dwellings elsewhere. Few were completed by spring of 1943, and not many more were projected. On the other hand, from the spring of 1943 to mid-1944 the government authorized 18,000 private homes.[6]

Exactly why "Los Angeles, the Magic City and County," evaded the government ban on private construction is not entirely clear, but several contributing factors played a role. In the first place, Los Angeles County possessed a much larger labor force than the other metropolitan areas. Therefore, its labor supply went farther toward stocking the war industries without resort to in-migration than in the other cities. At the same time, it possessed a larger housing stock to shoehorn the in-migrants into when they did come. That supply was abetted by both the good fortune of the area's prewar housing boom and the extreme misfortune of Japanese relocation. The latter "freed up" dwellings formerly occupied by sixty thousand Nissei, Issei, and Kibei, a much larger number of dwellings than were left behind in any other city due to this tragedy. In addition, metropolitan Los Angeles profited from the chief housing boom in the nation just prior to Pearl Harbor. Therefore, L.A. had sixty-eight

(a, b). Instant housing for defense, 1942.
Courtesy Huntington Library.

thousand empty dwellings at the onset of the war, enough to shelter over two hundred thousand persons.

Finally, the aircraft industries in Los Angeles turned to female labor relatively early to overcome the manpower shortage, and that, too, eliminated the need for so much in-migration. It is possible that political considerations abetted the outcome, too. Despite all of its federal contracts, Los Angeles still maintained a militantly free-enterprise stand on matters economic, and public housing struck its leaders, such as those in the chamber of commerce, as anathema. When asked by the Izac Committee why the government built so little public housing there, the administrator did not give a satisfactory reply. In any case, Los Angeles County ended up as odd in one extreme as Vallejo and Richmond were in the other. Small numbers of private dwellings were built in each of the metropolitan regions, but, with the exception of Los Angeles city and county, public housing dominated new construction.[7]

To the south, public housing served both war workers and naval personnel and their dependents. With the exception of San Diego, local authorities managed the public units, but the government owned them. The National Housing Authority owned most; the Navy, many in San Diego; and the Maritime Commission, a few. The war squelched reform housing by giving preference to defense workers, especially in-migrant, and it also eliminated construction of permanent public housing. Most of the housing was temporary, "for the duration only." A postwar housing shortage delayed the demise of the temporaries, but all the cities looked forward to their removal, even strapped Vallejo and Richmond.[8]

Washington unwittingly contributed to the housing crunch by controlling rents while allowing wages and maintenance costs to rise. Depending on the city in question, Washington fixed rents as of a certain date. Those who charged too much at the point of alignment could go on charging exorbitant rates, while those who charged too little had to suffer in comparison. The very nature of the war, with its transiency, anonymity, heavy use, lack of material for repairs, stretchout of building inspectors, and doubling up, guaranteed maximum wear and tear on rental properties. So landlords' costs rose, their property deteriorated, and their tenants' wages went up, but the owners' income from rental property stayed the same.

Government rent policy was diametrically opposite to that in defense contracting. Defense contracts were usually let on a flexible, sometimes cost-plus, basis. This allowed contractors to renegotiate contracts or to cope with inflation by charging for the *actual* cost, plus a fixed profit of 6 or so percent. Rent control denied landlords the same inflation-proof pricing. Complaints were so numerous that officials could not process claims rapidly enough to provide equity for those in need of it. The centering of authority in Washington increased delay. Despite numerous protests, the government had not corrected the situation by war's end. The policy did not punish the super-rich or the munitions makers, but rather harmed people of modest means, many of whom were elderly.[9]

In San Diego, for example, landlords typically possessed a small number of units. Many landlords responded to controls by keeping their properties off the market, thereby diminishing the government's efforts to staff the factories. Others rented to smaller numbers of people, families of two instead of four, because the Office of Price Administration (OPA) would not allow enough extra rent for the added dwellers. In either case, the practice diminished the available shelter. OPA controls also meant that houses that were for sale were kept unoccupied while awaiting a buyer because of the difficulty of getting a renter out. In addition, controls dictated that property owners found it more advantageous to sell rather than rent, and thus potential renters were often forced to buy in order to get any kind of housing.

The mischief of this policy was manifested in 1943 Los Angeles, which had "a surplus of housing for 170,000 people" at the very time that Washington was authorizing men, materials, and money to build 13,000 units to relieve the supposed housing shortage in that area. The Apartment House Association of that city estimated that for an additional charge of $1.00 to $2.50 per person, or something close to a 10 percent increase, these 170,000 people could be accommodated without further building. Of course, the government anticipated tearing down the 13,000 temporaries three or four years after they opened. And national elites expected to replace broad swaths of the housing, invariably of the poor, that their policies had helped to blight.[10]

Weekend housing for servicemen was an additional problem. Servicemen who wanted to see the sights of the cities came ashore in staggering numbers. By mid-war, some forty thousand to fifty thousand servicemen came into San Diego on weekend or overnight liberty. These men so desperately wanted to get away from the atmosphere of the ships that many would rather sleep outside in the city parks than go back to the ships for the night. Serviceman Gordon Wagenet remembered thousands sleeping in Balboa Park.

The federal government did rectify the cities' longstanding grievance that building public housing and other structures on city land unfairly depleted the tax base. After more than three years of negotiations, Washington finally agreed to pay a lump sum to impacted local governments in lieu of taxes. Both city and county governments benefited, and Los Angeles County authorities believed that this arrangement was the first of its kind in the United States.[11]

The shortage remained acute because the government authorized only enough public and private housing to scrape by and hoarded building materials, personnel, and capital for the defense effort. Therefore, one wonders how the martial metropolises *did* house their greatly expanded populations. Part of the need for an excess of workers over residents was met by busing and commuting. In Vallejo alone, the bus companies brought in fourteen thousand daily, a large percentage of the work force. Towns as distant as Napa, Sonoma, Santa Rosa, Healdsburg, Woodland, Sacramento, and Calistoga helped to solve the Bay Area's shelter deficit with their own housing and workforces.[12]

Metropolitan housing reserves contributed much more. Urbanists have long understood that cities are a vast reservoir of latent resources. Everything, from automobiles to junk yards to spare rooms, is disproportionately concentrated in them. During World War II, the government needed these spares, especially lodgings. In some cases, the war did not even fully utilize the excess capacity. For example, the advertisements for vacancies far outran the single persons looking for shelter. The government built a few dormitory lodgings, but private citizens rented out basements, spare rooms, attics, and garages to those in need. San Francisco created dormitories for servicemen in the Ferry Building and Commerce High School gymnasium and built special dormitories for weekending servicemen, especially the Hamilton Square and Civic Center dormitories. As many as 160 servicemen were accommodated on weekends at the Laguna Honda Home for the elderly indigent, and shipyard workers occupied all of the city's smaller hotels. These latter two resources housed 143,487 people over a period of sixteen months. Private groups like the Catholic Church sheltered another 263,150 over nine months in 1944 in gymnasiums, auditoriums, meeting rooms, and so forth. San Francisco went so far as to ban all conventions coming to the city for 1944 and 1945 and urged tourists to stay away in order to free up the hotel rooms for servicemen.[13]

The latent housing resources of the cities were no penny-ante game. Since new construction could not shelter the many thousands of in-migrants and servicemen who needed it, local householders had to make up the deficit. Much of this effort went unrecorded statistically, as unsung individuals simply let a room, took in a boarder, or converted a basement. Yet some idea of its magnitude can be found from the activities of the War Housing Centers, established to place servicemen and defense workers in private homes. In San Diego, from 1941 to 1943, some 40,000 people found housing through this agency alone. In April 1943 the entire San Diego metropolitan district contained only 425,000 people. This figure does not include the many who found homes through newspaper ads or by beating the pavements. Eugene Weston, the regional representative of the National Housing Agency, the umbrella federal agency that managed all government housing policy, captured the magnitude of the San Diego contribution:

> The real significance of this wartime accomplishment is not appreciated until one considers that it has been done without the use of critical materials or additional labor, and has been brought about with a saving of time and with a minimum of dislocation of the normal life and habits of the community. The patriotic response of the people of San Diego in making their homes available to war guests is a credit to the character of the community, as well as a direct contribution to the war effort. I would like to add my personal opinion that, without this response and the early development of this voluntary type of housing service, it is unlikely that so critical a war area could have avoided the necessity for commandeering homes and "billeting" workers, as has been the experience in England.

The city manager of Oakland claimed that 30 percent of the workers in Richmond lived in Oakland, where not much public housing had been built. He also believed that 20 percent of all Bay Area shipyard workers lived in that city. As much could have been said of San Francisco, Los Angeles, and the rest of the urban arsenals as well.[14]

Ultimately, crowding and improvisation had to supplement more conventional means. People living in public housing sublet a part of their space to others. Families doubled up. People occupied trailers, converted business buildings to residences, and utilized every extra space. Japantown in San Francisco and Los Angeles housed large numbers—sixty thousand in the latter. In the shock cities such as Richmond and Vallejo, men slept in autos, in tents pitched in open lots, and on back porches. And in San Diego, where forty thousand to fifty thousand servicemen descended on the city every weekend, many slept outside in parks and on streets. One way or another the communities did house their war workers and military personnel.[15]

That those people suffered discomforts goes without saying. However, as urban leaders constantly reminded their followers, the war demanded sacrifices of everyone, and those undergone by the men tenting in Richmond or slumbering on a back porch in Vallejo amounted to very little compared to the discomforts of the soldiers and marines sleeping in fetid foxholes on Guadalcanal. As the production experts pointed out, a really critical shortage of housing could have disrupted production, either forcing the manufacture to be done somewhere else that did not enjoy the economic advantages of the martial metropolises or simply reducing the flow of arms to the Pacific and European theaters. That production did not decline or shift was due to the ability of cities to find enough vacant lots, back porches, hotel rooms, Catholic-school gyms, spare rooms, and abandoned bakeries in which to house the vital workers. Had California cities been small or nonexistent, as in the American South, the war effort would have been much more uncomfortable and less successful. That would have been the ultimate failure, next to which some housing discomfort is not very significant.[16]

The latent resources of war appeared more strikingly still in the field of recreation. The servicemen and defense workers indulged in mindless spectating, gambling, drinking, and whoring aplenty, but the overall story is much more complex, humdrum, laudable, and public. Scholars within the last thirty years have begun to recognize the importance of the play, recreation, and sporting instincts in American civilization, and the experience of the Second World War should add measurably to this understanding. Play brought all kinds of people together to recreate and cooperate. If World War II generated the most significant revival of the idea of community after the Progressive Era, and perhaps in the twentieth century, the field of recreation revealed this new spirit strikingly.[17]

It did so vividly in city parks and playgrounds. The military drew on these latent resources incessantly. The unending housing shortage, which built to a crescendo as the Pacific war did, had to be met in part with open-air "accommodations." Hard on the heels of Pearl Harbor, tent colonies blossomed in Griffith Park in Los Angeles, Balboa Park in San Diego, Aquatic Park in San Francisco, and Houston, Crocker Amazon, Potrero Hill, Father Crowley, Julius Kahn, Columbia Square, and other playgrounds and spaces in the same city. In San Francisco alone, the military took over "sixteen parcels of park property," and in San Diego they preempted the entire magnificent Balboa Park, the pride of the city.[18]

Similar initial impacts of the war reduced the ability of all to play. The government co-opted other recreational assets, such as Mission Beach in San Diego. This loss greatly crowded the remaining beaches in the city and a part of Terminal Island in Long Beach. San Francisco also devoted some of the open space in the Civic Center to military dormitories, and other servicemen were actually stationed at the Cow Palace. Horse racing, football games such as the East-West game, and any other activities, except night baseball, that generated crowds of more than five thousand soon followed the Rose Bowl into eclipse. Some colleges actually canceled their sports programs for lack of manpower. Tourism and bus sightseeing fell prey to the excitement of the time, the rationing of rubber, or both. Night playground or sports activities often ran afoul of the dimout regulations until they were lifted in 1943. Sports fishing could take place from only a few government-authorized ports, six in all of Southern California. Vacation escape from the cities became another victim of gasoline and rubber rationing, which reduced both Sunday trips and summer holidays. Rationing did not initially force war workers to stop commuting in their cars, but it did greatly reduce their use for recreation. There were even more subtle dampers on fun. Bartenders swore to curb idle gossip in the taverns, and some people moved to eliminate enemy music (Beethoven, Bach, Wagner) from the air waves. And many restaurants shut down because of food shortages. Even the famed Ciro's nightclub in Los Angeles closed its doors, ostensibly because the tourists stayed away in droves.[19]

Between the curtailment of auto traffic and the forbidding prospect of riding the overloaded streetcars and buses, war forced a renaissance of pedestrianism. More often, people now walked to shop, eat, and play, and this redoubled their interest in both their parks and their neighborhoods. At the same moment, literally millions of service personnel and defense employees descended upon the arsenal cities in desperate need of getting off their military post, escaping the tension and clamor of the keyed-up factories, or relieving the anxiety of the filter command. Sailors, marines, soldiers, and other servicemen were so urgently anxious to find off-post recreation that they would go to almost any length to find city recreations, including staying out all night. Too, the decline of parenting left many more children in need of supervised recreation. In short, just as the war had somewhat reduced the population's ability to play, it had also greatly increased their need for this outlet.[20]

As the war wore on and nerves calmed down, recreation made a startling comeback. As it did, the latent resources of the cities reasserted themselves. Of course, many of the recreational resources were not so latent. The commercial pleasures of even battered Vallejo, Richmond, and San Diego were impressive, and those of Los Angeles and San Francisco, magnificent; thus the emphasis by historians and contemporary leaders on gambling, drinking, dancing, and whoring. Drinking continued to be heavy and people still ate out, often braving long lines and hurry-up signs on the tables caused by the decline in the number of restaurants. They celebrated New Year's Day in the traditional manner, as Herb Caen's columns indicate. The movies enjoyed an unprecedented prosperity. Penny, nickel, and dime arcades, where one could see anything from naughty movies to "art" photos of young women or fire rifles at Japanese targets, did a land-office business. Victory and morale parades supplemented these more tawdry entertainments. The Pacific Coast Baseball League continued to draw its thousands; the legitimate private theaters, many fewer.[21]

However, the consuming need for recreation in an anxious world drew millions into the public parks, museums, playgrounds, gymnasiums, and dance halls of the cities. These served the recreators well. Therefore, in the parks and playgrounds, thousands of anonymous urban dwellers met each other and a host of transient, lonely military men and women as well.

Not all of the *villes de guerre* could accommodate these lonely, recreation-starved invaders. Long Beach, for example, could not provide as much recreation as the services or the city's own residents required. The earthquake of 1933 devastated all twelve schools and their gymnasiums, which left Long Beach with only one temporary wooden structure for its own school, recreation department, and military recreation activities. Others could draw on more impressive resources, but even the relatively well-endowed city of San Diego still found the demands beyond its ability to meet. San Diego suffered a huge recreation loss when the Navy took over all of Balboa Park, the principal park of that city, and its three museums. There and elsewhere the services ran extensive recreation programs. Los Angeles and San Francisco could draw on more imposing resources. Critics often accused San Francisco of being confused and hapless during the war, but it provided a vast range of play resources.[22]

As the mayor's annual report laconically observed, the San Francisco parks department had seen "a phenomenal increase in attendance" during 1944. So had the recreation department, the Opera House (the only municipally owned one in the United States), the Veterans Museum, and the civic clubs. The recreation department supplied activities for each of the city's new war housing projects and operated 151 playground and schoolyard programs. By early 1945, the department ran eight "Teen-age Centers" for 4,000 youngsters. The Junior Museum of the department conducted a series of classes in geography, map making, astronomy, and airplane building to prepare kids for the "Air Age" of tomorrow. The recreation department also held an annual festival, Midsummer Music, in Sigmund Stern Grove and a Christmas pageant in the Opera House; taught thousands of civilians and servicemen swimming skills and the arts of self-preservation in the water; supervised a weaving center; operated a photography center for servicemen; ran sports leagues for both men and women; and opened, in cooperation with the department of public health, the first day-care center in the city. In the face of food, gas, and tire rationing, the city ran Camp Mather in the mountains, where 17,288 youngsters got away from the city in 1943 alone. Another 145,000 attended the music festivals in Stern Grove, a record number. Some 30,000 children worked in victory gardens at the Junior Museum, playgrounds, and parks.[23]

The Park Commission ran its own victory garden program of four hundred plots successfully enough to evade some of the food rationing. "The Park Department established its own vegetable garden in Golden Gate Park and provided the Park restaurants and the San Francisco Zoological Gardens with this commodity." The Conservatory flower gardens alone pulled in 156,000 visitors: "most conspicuous among the visitors are the many servicemen." The Conservatory featured seven flower shows plus many other displays including those of the 3,500 orchids that bloomed there annually. Public Kezar Stadium continued to be the "center of football competition in San Francisco and the Bay Area," as high school, Coast Guard, Army, Navy, and professional teams competed there. The annual report expected "revenue from rental and concessions in the stadium" to rise by 25 percent in 1945. In addition, Kezar Basketball Pavilion hosted a full lineup of teams; the Golden Gate tennis center operated full tilt; the zoo displayed its animals and seal show to "very large" crowds; the Golden Gate Park Stadium hosted polo; the Fleishhacker swimming pool drew thousands; and two of the three golf courses enjoyed "heavy patronage." "Undoubtedly one of the most popular units administered by the Park Department is the Coit Memorial Tower on Telegraph Hill," the annual report stated. The overlook of the harbor and Bay Area kept the tower elevators humming, with civilians who paid and servicemen who rode free. Overall, the department concluded that "our parks are frequented much more than formerly by the people of San Francisco and the many visitors to our city."[24]

The art museums, opera, theaters, aquarium, and other city facilities carried their own share of the added burden. The Art Commission provided concerts by the San Francisco Symphony Orchestra, one of the finest in the country, which entertained the public at very reasonable prices and the servicemen, free. In 1944, the municipal band devoted sixty-three concerts to the military, playing everywhere from Letterman and Fort Miles hospitals to Treasure Island to the Stage Door Canteen. Despite the absence of a bus route to the Palace of the Legion of Honor, it attracted 45,000 visitors in 1944, an increase of 18 percent. Ironically, this monument to the California dead in the Great War attracted many fewer patrons than the more centrally placed de Young Museum in Golden Gate Park, which drew 526,000 in ten months. The Renoir exhibition alone pulled in 25,000. The museums presented their own collections as well as war effort material.

These activities give at least a flavor of the public recreational offerings, but a closer look at a weekly schedule will give it body. The recreation department sponsored the FBI softball tournament at Rossi Playground; it ran softball leagues for all Twelfth Naval District personnel daily in the playgrounds; it made the Crocker Amazon Field available to English sailors, who "use the area for cricket, rugby, and soccer"; it lent the 4th Air Force the Father Crowley Playground, where 450 men "trained" for basketball daily; and it supplied the Aptos Gymnasium to the 140th Signal Corps, the Francisco gym to the Coast Guard and the Livermore Naval Air Station, the James Lick gyms to the 4th Air Force, and the Marina gym to the Port Directors League and the Twelfth Naval District. In addition, the department ran numerous leagues in basketball, baseball, softball, volleyball, and tennis and kept all the gyms open from seven to ten o'clock every evening. It also operated a center for servicemen on Market Street; it allowed them to sit in with the community singing and orchestral programs, and it nearly danced their feet off. Young hostesses regularly marched off to Treasure Island, the Crystal Palace Ballroom at Lombard and Taylor, and anywhere else they were needed. The Crystal Palace alone held two invitational dances per week for Army personnel and Coast Guardsmen. Sometimes the department supplied 90 to 350 young hostesses for this activity, in what must have been the hardest-swinging war in American history.[25]

Other cities provided similar public recreation. Long Beach had its own Music Week, and its recreation commission sponsored Women's Symphony Orchestra and Long Beach A Cappella Singers performances during it. Its beaches were used by servicemen and war workers from all over the area and even from all over the U.S. On major holidays, the shrunken Terminal Island Beach accommodated 150,000. In addition, the city provided softball diamonds for Douglas workers and military personnel after the dimout regulations were lifted in 1943. In Long Beach, as in Los Angeles, the government, up to mid-1943, refused priorities to build recreation units, and they would not plan public housing in relation to existing recreation facilities or supply such facilities in their projects. To help fulfill the need, the city moved to secure more beach property and to create a yacht harbor. In Berkeley, the university lent the Navy its swimming pool, as did YMCAs in the area.[26]

These efforts do not include those proferred by private clubs, churches and synagogues, or individuals. For example, it had long been custom-

ary in San Francisco and San Diego for residents to invite soldiers and
sailors into their homes for special holidays like Thanksgiving and
Christmas.[27]

The importance of big cities to this aspect of the homefront can be
seen in the plight of the smaller ones. Richmond was swamped with defense workers. This crowding necessitated a two-shift system of schools,
and therefore children in the first shift could not use the playgrounds after
school. Here, too, large amounts of property were taken off the tax rolls
by the shipyards, and the State of California, although benefiting from
the sales tax, refused to divvy up with hard-pressed cities like Richmond.
That state largesse made national legislators unwilling to assume the cost
of Richmond's problems when California would not help out. Martinez,
Port Chicago, Vallejo, and Pittsburg were equally overwhelmed.[28]

Despite these problems, the war produced an extraordinary revival
of recreation and community. Civilians and servicemen worked, played,
danced, and planned together. Civilians interacted in their own cities.
People of all kinds walked to and from the parks and within them, and
everyone used the community facilities more often. The conflict integrated civilians and servicemen into a wartime community.

The public schools felt the same integrative impulse. From the beginning, they played a large role in the war. Just as servicemen and civilians
came together in the parks, playgrounds, gymnasiums, and dance halls,
they did so in the schools as well. As we have seen, the educational system
had a major role in civil defense. It hosted endless classes on this subject
and conducted air raid drills. When the necessities of life became scarce,
the schools helped to allocate those that existed and to gather those that
were in short supply. Community was reinforced when schools distributed the ration cards for food, forcing every home in the neighborhood
into contact with the schools, whether they had ever had that experience
or not. At the same time, schools served as the partial fund-raisers for
the war, selling war bonds and stamps weekly. And when the war effort
required old newspapers and scrap metal, the schools served as the orga-
nizers of these drives to exploit still another set of latent urban resources.
In a reversal of the classic principle of beating swords into plowshares, the
school children collected literally millions of tons of metal and paper for
conversion into martial material. Since much of the victory garden effort
centered on school lawns, playing fields, and open space, they added the
production of food to its distribution.[29]

They played a leading role in creating and accommodating the workforce, too. With the outbreak of war, the military producers needed not
just more hands to do the work, but skilled ones. Shipfitters and aircraft

Young "soldiers" buying war stamp corsages.
Courtesy Huntington Library.

workers needed training, even after their jobs were broken down into
very simple tasks. San Francisco educators trained 53,000 people in defense jobs from January 1941, when they began their defense programs,
to January 1944; Oakland added 45,000 in about the same period. San
Diego was another pioneer in this activity, providing vocational training
for defense from March 1941 on. By March 1942, the Port of the Palms
system had already trained 10,000 people, including 1,161 women, for
war work. By the outbreak of war, its vocational school in Balboa Park
had another 2,500 students in training, including 1,200 women. The
plant worked twenty-four hours a day (as did Oakland's), six days a
week and was considering working seven.

In addition to training these outsiders for war work, the schools also
trained school children for the same tasks in order to increase the workforce. Many youngsters went to school for four hours in the morning,
then worked for four hours in the factories. By early 1944, six thousand
San Francisco young people contributed in this manner, sometimes by
doing direct defense production and sometimes by freeing retail, finance,

VJ Day celebration.
Courtesy San Diego Historical Society, Photo Collection.

restaurant, or other nonessential employees for more important defense employment. To contribute to the workforce further, the schools initiated a summer school program designed to get their students through their degree in three years instead of four, thus allowing them to graduate at age seventeen so that they could put in a year in war work or college before being drafted into the armed forces. In San Francisco alone, some three thousand attended summer school in 1943, and Long Beach began the twelve-month school year in 1943. Finally, the schools tried to recruit labor for the chronically short rural workforce. They did not succeed so well in this effort, but despite criticism from such a loyalist as Jack Shelley that the schools were holding up the war effort, they seem to have contributed much to the in-town labor force.[30]

Schools helped the in-migrant laborers too, especially women. Not only did they train people for the shipyards and aircraft plants, they facilitated the movement of women into the factories. In San Francisco alone, the city provided five new schools to care for the children of crowded Hunters Point, next to the shipyards, and by early 1945 the city had opened twenty-three day-care centers to care for children who were not yet school age.[31]

Newspaper headlines on VJ Day.
Courtesy San Diego Historical Society, Photo Collection.

The schools also created bandages, Christmas cards, entertainment programs, and even morale for the war effort, as each department strove to find ways to contribute. For example, courses designed to make students "air minded" suddenly became popular. Some critics would have added compulsory military training, thus making the educational system the producer of soldiers as well as defense workers. However, the schools did not adopt this suggestion, although the traditional ROTC courses continued to be offered. In June 1942, San Francisco alone enrolled two thousand young men in this program.[32]

All this effort caused educational expenditures to rise modestly. In San Francisco the increase came to about 7 percent and in Los Angeles, to some 18 percent. Federal aid to education helped to hold down the increase. Although bills to provide national aid to education had been introduced into the Congress from 1937 on, they had not been accepted by that body. However, the war emergency brought some federal expenditures for schools. These subsidized day-care nurseries for working mothers, and they helped defray the costs of training war workers. Washington also helped to offset the expense of creating new schools by payments to the localities in lieu of taxes, thus partially and tardily nullifying the loss of part of the tax base caused by government occupation of city land or use of it by tax-exempt factories of the War Plant Corporation.[33]

Whether all of this activity amounted to a militarization of the public schools is uncertain. Geoffrey Perrett, in his history of the war years, concludes that the schools were indeed militarized, going so far as to argue that academic freedom was seriously compromised. The evidence on these points from Urban California is fragmentary. The schools certainly did shoulder much of the military burden of the war, but to picture them as "spartan" hives of "discipline," hastily replacing their modestly "progressive" curricula with something conservative, seems implausible. Americans have never been overly disciplined, and they were not so during this war either. They drove their cars to work; they drank and gambled; they migrated all over the country in search of work; and they conducted strikes, all in the teeth of government and military regulations and pronouncements to the contrary.[34]

San Francisco did experience one controversy over academic freedom, but it illustrates the difficulty of forcing teachers to do what they were determined not to do as much as it illustrates a general threat to academic freedom. This controversy erupted over the social studies textbook authored by Harold Rugg of Columbia University Teachers' College. The book had been used for some twenty years in the seventh through ninth grades before coming under this attack by the American Legion, the Sons and Daughters of the Golden West, the Pacific Advertising Association, the Public Welfare Council, superintendent of schools Major James P. Nourse, and the editor of the *Chronicle*. Nourse actually ordered his social studies teachers to select a new text, and they promptly refused. Grayson Kefauver, the dean of the University of California School of Education, backed the teachers, as did Jack Shelley, head of the Labor Council and future mayor, the Classroom Teachers Association, the American Federation of Teachers, the Municipal Employees Association, the director of the Presidio Open Air School, Henry C. Fenn, some *Chronicle* columnists, and, ultimately, the League of Women Voters, led by none other than Mrs. Paul Eliel, wife of the former head of the supposedly benighted Industrial Association![35]

Whether the offending text was a subversive document or simply a New Deal interpretation of history was hotly debated. It was probably more of the latter than the former, and some of its interpretations were accurate. The book informed its readers that George Washington drank wine and loved fashion, that the fathers of the Constitution pursued economic goals as well as patriotic ones in framing that document, that most Americans were ignorant of socialism, and that laissez-faire was not a perfect economic philosophy, especially from the perspective of the year 1933. However, it clearly erred (it had not been updated) in claiming that one-quarter of the working people of the country were unemployed, in implying that Russian planning had brought into balance the needs of consumers and producers, and in stating that with "the increase of social-ism and communism, government is becoming much more representative of the many." That may have been true of West European socialism, but it was directly contrary to facts about the Soviet Union. In short, as in many controversies, the subject of this one was debatable.[36]

That was not necessarily the way the matter was treated. The Rugg proponents, for example, called the attempt a witch hunt, a book burn-ing, a Nazi-Fascist purge, an assault on academic freedom, and so forth, generally treating the matter as non-debatable. The principal from the Marina Junior High School argued that only experts with proper train-ing could select textbooks and that public pressure groups should be excluded from the process. Apparently forgetting that the superintendent of schools had recommended replacing the book, others echoed his posi-tion. The letters to the editor of the *Chronicle* overwhelmingly favored Rugg. For his part, Superintendent Nourse argued that "social studies must teach what is right with America rather than what is wrong." The school board did not accept this logic, and by a four to two vote refused to ban the book. Instead, they turned to an expert panel of educators composed of the heads of Stanford, UCLA, Mills College, the University of San Francisco, Santa Clara, and the Dominican College.[37]

Regardless of the outcome of the Rugg controversy, it seems that forcing the history of public education in World War II into a "liberal versus conservative" mold misses the larger point of the experience. Some parts of the experience support either side of this perennial ideo-logical stalemate. For example, the war brought into being such liberal dreams as federal aid to education, day-care facilities for some working mothers, admittance of women to school industrial training programs, neighborhood interaction, and a general revival of community. If military imperatives simultaneously dominated a part of the school experience, that is hardly surprising during a war.

More importantly, in education, as in other realms, the war could draw heavily upon both the manifest and the latent resources of the cities. Whether scraps of paper from their attics; the rusting metal from their junkyards or backyards; the vastly underemployed female potential of their kitchens; the underutilized capacity of their schoolrooms, parks, playgrounds, and lawns; the welding of their vocational shops; or the excess capacity of their infrastructures, the cities provided important sinews of war. They trained literally hundreds of thousands of people to build ships and planes, and they provided thousands of people to build them or freed others to do so. And war, in its turn, helped to kindle and fan the flames of urban community.

It was fortunate that cities possessed these resources because the federal government often refused to pick up the tab for the problems of war. These hit San Diego, "The Federal City," in Abraham Shragge's words, especially hard. Far from throwing money at the city, the government actually doled it out like a nineteenth-century shopkeeper. Not only did the Navy and other services occupy much otherwise taxable real estate, the government refused to give payments in lieu of taxes and generally squeezed the Port of the Palms' education system like an orange. It actually took back a payment of $300,000 in lieu of taxes; it helped build one school for 600 children, only to flood the plant with 1,500 defense-related students; it did not put play facilities into the schools it built in the Linda Vista housing project; and it located the Azure Vista housing project on Point Loma, not close to transit lines or within walking distance of a school. At the Linda Vista school, the government refused to construct facilities for either vocational education (in the midst of a war!) or physical education. Three of the five schools the government did build were sited on landfill, and two others teetered on hillsides unsuitable for their presence. The hillside schools did not fall off into the bay, but lots of their fill dirt did wash into it. Both the hillside and landfill sites were dusty in dry weather and marshy in wet.[38]

Getting help led school officials into an even bigger quagmire. This one was of intergovernmental relations. Money was sometimes available under the Lanham Act, and requests or approvals had to be directed to or wrung from the Public Works Administration, the War Production Board, the Public Buildings Administration, the Federal Works Agency, the U.S. Office of Education, or the Navy, and, of course, the federal housing officials. The drafting of male teachers led into the same intergovernmental tangle. Just as the war had depleted city government personnel, it drafted teachers. By mid-1943, Long Beach had suffered enough from this problem that the Superintendent of Schools, Will French, demanded that "instructions from the National Selective Service Office should be issued to local boards requiring them to leave in school service the men now there as essential to the maintenance of necessary civilian life activities."[39]

Schools both lost and gained students, depending on their ages. The migrant worker impact, for example, inundated the Oakland schools with an extra four thousand children from kindergarten through elementary school age, just from the eight housing projects and two trailer camps, a 20 percent addition. At the other end of the spectrum, the system lost three thousand high schoolers, or 20 percent. According to Assistant Superintendent Dr. H. R. Stolz, the latter left for defense jobs. Another 50 percent of students aged sixteen to eighteen worked one-half day in the factories. Still, somehow Oakland coped with this turmoil largely without federal help.[40]

Hapless Richmond had both more problems and more federal sympathy. With a quadrupled population, Richmond inherited more war problems per capita than almost any other city. The city had to double-shift its students, and even then pupil ratios per teacher shot up to sixty because of the shortage of instructors. Under these conditions truancy was high. Superintendent Walter T. Helm testified to the Izac Committee that federal officials had "been most cooperative." That was fortuitous, for there certainly were a lot of them to cooperate with. Richmond's requests had to stagger through the same intergovernmental morass as San Diego's, with the Maritime Commission thrown in, and they took a circuitous route to Washington indeed. As the superintendent explained, "The difficulty lies in the fact that the applications go from Richmond to San Francisco, from San Francisco to Los Angeles, from Los Angeles to Salt Lake City, and then to Washington, D.C." And of course, that was only the beginning, since the requests then had to fan out to the seven or eight agencies for decisions by several levels of officials in each. In all likelihood there would also be several interagency transactions in Washington as well. Yet the government could move fast when it wanted to. Moneys for the school defense training programs got to cities quickly despite the bureaucratic stop-offs. Officials wondered why regular education, school recreation, and other funds took so long in coming. And in Richmond, a problem faced by all California public schools was made much worse by rapid population increases. The state allotted school moneys based on enrollment figures from the beginning of the school year. Cities growing by leaps and bounds were automatically penalized by this mechanism.[41]

The war also jeopardized the health of these cities, although not equally. Vallejo, Richmond, San Diego, and Los Angeles had the roughest time. San Francisco and Oakland endured much less, but all cities suffered some. Migrants from other parts of the United States and servicemen returning from the Pacific front brought their diseases with them. Since so many men returned infected by malaria—two hundred cases had appeared in San Diego County by 1943—mosquito eradication became a pressing need. San Francisco experienced the import of bubonic plague from both the countryside and Hawaii. With increased air travel, the exchange of viruses, bacteria, and infected malarial patients happened more rapidly, and heavy shipping helped to circulate the world's rats. Civilian migrants also brought their diseases; VD, especially from the southwest, and tuberculosis were not the least of them. Similarly, many migrants hailed from underdeveloped parts of the country where health practices were poorly understood and health problems abounded. Many of these migrants had never been vaccinated against smallpox or diphtheria. By mid-1942, measles, mumps, whooping cough, chickenpox, and other communicable diseases had risen alarmingly—three-, four-, and twenty-fold in San Diego alone. Epidemic meningitis appeared in both San Francisco and San Diego, and sixty cases of infantile paralysis were diagnosed in Los Angeles. There were over ten thousand cases of measles in San Diego County by 1942, up from some three thousand in 1940. The rate of TB was high among blacks and Mexicans in Los Angeles.

Moreover, the war greatly stimulated the merchant marine injuries of Fortress California. Given the increased number of ill, maimed, or wounded merchantmen, usually cared for in government marine hospitals, and the heavy casualties of that group of workmen (four times as high as combat), California ports found themselves caring for many that the government should have taken responsibility for.[42]

Wartime conditions combined to worsen these troubles. The closing of food processing plants and restaurants (15 percent in San Diego and many in San Francisco) made eating a problem, so people filled up on whatever food they could, healthful or not. Even when open, restaurants had limited food supplies, and servicemen who ate in restaurants diminished the stock for defense workers and civilians. When the food ran out, the restaurant simply closed for the day. Stores might have alleviated the problem but, due to their hours, defense workers often found the shelves largely picked clean by the time they escaped the plant. And even when they got to the store in time to shop, the variety of foods, especially fresh fruits and vegetables, was in short supply. Dr. Alfred Dick, the medical director for Consolidated, estimated that "several thousand" San Diego factory workers got only one good meal a day, the one at the plant cafeteria. All this scarcity definitely contributed to absenteeism. Sanitation was equally compromised because of the stretchout of restaurant and bakery workers, who worked long hours and could no longer thoroughly clean up. The draft and lack of deferments decimated the ranks of scavengers. Only by working a fourteen-hour day could they maintain normal trash-pickup services. Labor shortages and the black market made it more difficult to inspect food products. And pollution added to the mix. Los Angeles lost ten miles of beach to sewage pollution, and La Mesa suffered seriously as well. Vallejo chucked its greatly increased sewage directly into the river where the Navy was launching ship after ship amid great fanfare.[43]

Adequate water supplies were just as big a problem. San Diego teetered on the brink of a water crisis from mid-war onward. The Navy believed new supplies were imperative, but the city could not build until after the war. Crowded housing, shipyards, schools, churches, hospitals, amusement facilities, public gathering places, and streetcars maximized the spread of communicable disease, as Dr. Alex Lesem, San Diego County director of health, Dr. J. C. Geiger, director of the San Francisco Department of Public Health, and Dr. Frank Stewart, city health officer of Long Beach, attested.[44]

Venereal disease added to the health burdens. Geiger estimated that 25 to 35 percent of venereal infections originated in the crowded bars. The Navy had its own VD control programs, which provided both treatment and prophylactics. Like so many other war operations, this one quickly developed into an exercise in intergovernmental relations. Oakland, for example, operated a VD clinic at 282 8th Avenue, with the civilians working by day and the Navy men by night. The health department treated infected women. The assistant health officer reported that girls' promiscuity was the principal source of female infection (ignoring the men's role in spreading VD) and that once treated, they went right back to the behavior that got them infected in the first place. San Francisco operated more than a dozen prophylactic and VD clinics. Although officials from several cities minimized the spread of this disease, the newly created prophylactic and treatment clinics would seem to belie their optimism. Los Angeles, however, minced no words. Their infection rate climbed by 60 percent between 1942 and 1943; 20 to 25 percent of the arrested prostitutes had VD, and many sexually active young women and girls were infected as well. When Los Angeles opened its VD clinic on Central Avenue in 1941, it treated 250 patients a month. By late 1943, the monthly number had climbed to 8,000. The state's unwillingness to fund measures to combat these problems significantly was especially galling.[45]

Civilians had only declining personnel and overcrowded facilities to cope with these problems. The Navy actually took over some hospitals, and in emergencies, the Army sent patients to civilian hospitals. Because of the drafting of doctors and male orderlies, the loss of nurses, and the rise in case loads, medicine was hit with the same personnel shortages that other institutions were. Doctors came out of retirement and nurses volunteered, but there were never enough. Alameda had twelve doctors for forty-five thousand residents. In San Diego, the loss of doctors and dentists ran to fully 50 percent. There and in Long Beach and Los Angeles, the hospitals were so critically short of beds that they had to create priorities for treatment, postponing some procedures. For example, elective surgery for a rickety but not yet risky appendix had to wait while emergency procedures were finished. And even persons needing hospitalization had to be sent home to allow still more extreme cases in. Sometimes the emergencies also had to wait. In 1943, San Diego County Hospital had filled all of its tuberculosis beds and had to refuse admittance of forty-three active cases of this highly communicable disease.

However, a part of the medical crush was precipitated by the good fortunes of war. Wage earners could afford treatment that they could not before. As Representative Ed Izac, surely an expert on wartime problems, put it of the prewar population: "People were not using hospitals in those days so much because they didn't have any money to get sick on." Ironically, the war created a greater civilian population and growing per capita civilian use just at the moment the cities lost doctors, nurses, and aides.[46]

It should be obvious by this point that the Second World War did not have a tonic effect on California city government. It delayed the capital expenditures of cities; it forced them to alter their priorities to cope with recreation needs, VD, JD, schooling, and health; it disrupted their planning operations; it pumped up but ultimately wore down their transit; it created housing blight; it further subjected them to federal government dominance; and in general it derailed the movement toward ever more city services. The effect of the war on cities in no way approximated its effect on the major war industries, which made money and developed new technologies. Cities were derailed, but in the final analysis, their activities were simply postponed rather than disrupted, or they were directed anew toward some fresh goal.

Conclusion
The Bad City in the Good War:
Transformation or Heroic Interlude?

Cities and war have coexisted from time immemorial. In the last two centuries of western civilization, the connection between war and urbanism has been especially close. The 1940s' images of war and urbanism are especially vivid: Flying Fortresses or B-29s over urban targets; wreckage and destroyed buildings; children playing in the rubble; refugees fleeing the carnage; soldiers fighting house to house; tanks slogging down the streets; factory yards jammed with martial materials; tanks, planes, and jeeps rolling off assembly lines; civilians standing in lines for scarce products; civil defense workers pounding their beats.

And the realities match the images. Urban areas have become the arsenals of both democracy and autocracy. In an age of industrialism, cities have provided most of the material sinews of warfare. Workers in Boston, New York, Baltimore, Philadelphia, Norfolk, Wilmington (North Carolina), Mobile, and Houston turned out all manner of ships. Those in Baltimore supplied planes; in Detroit, they fabricated planes, tanks, trucks, and jeeps; on Long Island, they manufactured planes; and in practically every city, they provided parts. In Memphis, St. Louis, and Chicago, they built airplanes, and in Denver they turned out landing craft. Many Midwesterners contributed parts for military vehicles. Workers in Seattle supplied planes and ships, and Portlanders added more. Even in tiny Sycamore, Illinois, they constructed landing craft. The Bay Area sent military and other ships to the seven seas, rolled tanks out of its factories, and fabricated ammunition at the Benicia Arsenal. Firms manufactured planes at a dozen Southern California locales, put together ships at Los Angeles and Long Beach, and turned out parts at a thousand Southland mom-and-pop machine shops.

One of the principal reasons that the Allies won the war was that the Axis could not attack these urban arsenals of democracy. Unlike those of all the other principal parties to the war, American cities were a sheltered, protected haven of prodigious military productivity. There the sinews of war could be mass-produced without hindrance, free from the threat of attack. Much of the difference in the outcome of the war was the difference between the two sides' military access to their enemies' cities.

Moreover, cities have been increasingly important to military strategy. In the American Civil War, the most deadly one that the United States has ever fought, cities were especially important. Obviously, both sides sought to destroy enemy armies in the field, and battles were fought at nonurban places like Chickamauga, Gettysburg, Shiloh, Spotsylvania Court House, Cold Harbor, the Wilderness, Bull Run, Bentonville, and Lookout Mountain. However, the opposing armies fought many of their most important conflicts over genuine urban entities. The Union and Confederate armies in the East struggled perennially to capture or neutralize their enemies' capitals, Richmond and Washington. A Confederate army actually camped on the outskirts of Washington in 1864, and the Union armies fought the Peninsular and Wilderness campaigns to capture Richmond. Union forces finished the struggle by pinning down the army of Robert E. Lee in a struggle of attrition around Richmond and Petersburg. Strategic battles at Vicksburg, Nashville, Chattanooga, Atlanta, and others illustrate the point. And even when the armies contested the ground in the countryside away from town, their point in doing so was to gain access to a city. Union forces fought battles like the two Bull Runs, Chancellorsville, and Fredericksburg in order to get to Richmond. And getting to Richmond allowed Union armies to force the Confederates to defend their capital rather than fight and maneuver in the open, as Lee preferred.

In World War I, Americans helped their European allies to fight other armies rather than conquer cities, but World War II put cities back into the strategic limelight. Even before American entry into the struggle, the Nazis and Communists vied for control of Leningrad, Moscow, Kharkov, and eventually—fatally for the Germans—Stalingrad. And in the West, the Nazi Blitz of London and other British cities and the British and American countercampaign against German cities provided the main military focus before the invasion of Normandy. After the Allied invasion, cities continued to attract their attention. Successively, Allied strategy was dominated by the capture of Caen, the Brittany ports, the port of Antwerp, and finally the Rhine city of Arnhem, which they thought crucial to victory. By the same token, the fortress city of Metz held up George Patton's attack on the German West Wall and lengthened the war by some time. And when the Allied armies broke into Germany, the Russians headed for Berlin, whose fall ended the war. (The Allies have been criticized ever since, wrongly in my opinion, for not doing so.) Campaigns were fought outside cities as well, in North Africa, Italy, France, and Germany, but urban targets continued to draw huge armies to them.

In the Far East, more often than not the Allies fought away from cities, either in the small islands or in large ones such as New Guinea and the Philippines. Still, the Philippine campaign featured a major struggle for Manila, and the American bombing of the Japanese home islands leveled one Japanese city after another, even as the fighting raged in the islands campaigns. The atomic blasts at Hiroshima and Nagasaki brought the campaign to a crescendo and the war to a close. Nonurban fighting was more durable in the East, but urban fighting was more decisive.

It is obvious that war and cities marched together through the grisly conflict of World War II. Equally evident, neither American, California, urban, nor western historians have taken much notice of this alliance. Gerald Nash and Carl Abbott put war on the agenda of western historians some thirty years ago, but not many have followed their lead. That is especially true of urban historians. For the last thirty years they have gravitated increasingly toward the issues of race, class, and gender and a focus on ever more narrow topics. When war and cities appear, they are treated as a backdrop to the main show, which is something else. These subjects are both legitimate and timely, yet cities are the principal habitation for the majority of the American population, and World War II was the most important event in a tumultuous century. It cannot be in the interest of historical truth or of urban, California, or western history to be indifferent to the connection between cities and war. This book has highlighted the momentous nexus between them.

To the American participants the connection seemed to be a universal experience of upheaval, estrangement, and progress. Between the 16 million who were drafted and the 15 million who moved to work in war industry, the war rendered nearly one quarter of the population mobile. It is doubtful if anyone in the entire country was untouched by the conflict. Every family had a brother, uncle, daughter, cousin, or husband in either war work or the military. Many others had people in civil defense or other volunteer work. To the participants, the war seemed like an unprecedented disruption. Everything appeared to be in flux. On the most fundamental level, population change was omnipresent. People from all over the United States flooded into California cities and jammed them well beyond capacity. Okies from the San Joaquin Valley crowded into the shipyard towns. Midwesterners journeyed to Oakland and mingled with African Americans fleeing the Southwest. Native-born Californians thronged to their own metropolises to meet the others in steel mills, shipyards, aircraft factories, canning plants, and mom-and-pop defense subcontractors. Women flocked into men's work as men poured into the services. Texans met Northerners in every line of work. Hispanics added another spice to the stew, and servicemen from all over seasoned the blend vastly more. German prisoners of war provided the ultimate flavoring.

Once in Urban California, nearly everyone moved ceaselessly, which urbanists call "churning." Residents continually churned about within the cities as better housing or jobs opened up. They left one job for another, abandoned that for something else, and quit again for greener pastures still. Millions played a game of musical chairs for housing. Many a couple began in a room rented by a family (sometimes doubled up), graduated to a two-room apartment with a bath down the hall, moved up to a two-bedroom public housing unit, bought a house and moved to the suburbs, sold the dwelling and moved back to Arkansas, all in the space of a couple of years. In cities, people never ceased moving for long.

Or they moved between them. All seemed to be transient and un-stable. Women quit jobs too heavy for them and moved away to lighter ones. Military wives and sweethearts came to see their men off and then left to live with their parents. Husbands came to town to scout the areas, returned to bring their families, moved from city to city, and finally returned to familiar hearths. Soldiers came and sailors went as they answered duty's call, returned hurt or were discharged, settled in or left for home. The fact of mobility was well-nigh universal.

Wherever they went, they found themselves estranged. Much that was familiar remained, but enough novelty appeared to surprise, wound, and intimidate. Old residents resented the intrusions of newcomers, even as they profited from the larger market for goods and services, union membership, votes, and rentals that the migrants provided. And the new residents resented the old settlers in turn, even as they came to depend on them for housing, legal services, political leadership, groceries, and so forth. Men went to work in the shipyards only to find women welding, burning, creating patterns, and drafting. Women appeared on the street-car platforms, sat on juries, wrote for newspapers, and watchdogged the war effort. Races met, mingled, settled in grudgingly or willingly, or skedaddled. No one knew quite what to make of this mix; yet all seemed to agree that it was upsetting, different, and fascinating.

At the same time the upheaval was exhilarating. Witness after witness testified to "having fun," enjoying themselves, being excited, feeling challenged, finding fulfillment, doing something for their loved ones and their country. The upheaval brought a new start for individuals.

Given all of this change, it was natural for historians to think that the experience of the war was unprecedented, a massive shift of Gold Rush proportions, or transformative. How could it be otherwise, they reasoned. Industrial growth, population migrations, increasing diversity, the transplantation of cultures, ethnic and gender group advance, and large federal spending seemed to prove the point. Whether looking at group or region, they saw transformative change. Still, many historians have remained skeptical about the impact on either cities or regions. Southern historians hold that the war transformed their section, and many western historians accept the same transformation hypothesis for the West. Historians of groups, for the most part, do not agree. They do not find transformative change, but rather gradual change, the laying of foundations for future advances. Is there a middle ground? Probably not. Change was neither unprecedented, of Gold Rush proportions, nor transformative.

Since so many historians have followed the *San Francisco Chronicle* journalist who coined the phrase "Second Gold Rush," that comparison is the best place to begin. The historic Gold Rush struck an area that was almost totally nonurbanized. Early San Francisco had no parks for soldiers to bivouac in, no docks from which to load and unload, no mature government to run civil defense and keep order, no recreational department to amuse visiting servicemen, no schools to administer the ration system and educate workers for defense work, no modern waterworks to allow the creation of desert training grounds, no transportation terminals, no educated work force, no housing stock for in-migrant war workers, and very little else of military potential. In 1848, only the rusting, obsolescent cannons of the crumbling Spanish fort the Castillo del San Joaquin, protected San Francisco, with nothing to back them up. Other California pueblos were in the same state or worse. California in 1848 was a tabula rasa, upon which every aspect of urban life had to be written. It is fundamental to understand the conditions of the first Gold Rush before declaring World War II a second one, and it is essential to know the background of the Gold Rush in order to understand the role of the Bad City in the Good War.

The Gold Rush created something out of nothing. Americans, Europeans, Latin Americans, and Pacific peoples marched into an almost completely undeveloped state and created an outpost of western civilization. In the process, they dwarfed the California population of the state and callously muscled aside the Indian cultures too. Starting from scratch, they created, with astonishing speed, the full range of institutions present in the American Urban East and did so overnight. To put it quite simply, nothing approaching this change occurred during the Second World War.

Part of our misunderstanding of what happened during World War II stems from the underappreciation of the nature of urbanism. Cities have existed for centuries—depending on the findings of the latest archaeological digs, perhaps fifty or more. That is a long time in the history of the western world. Cities have seen empires, democracies, republics, oligarchies, and anarchies come and go, but they endure. Wars were won and lost; technologies were adopted and cast aside; epidemics raged, were conquered, and raged again; invading hordes came and went; settlement swept across this steppe and that plain; capitalism engulfed subsistence farming; national economies became global ones; ideologies rose and fell or were destroyed; colonies waxed and empires waned; but urbanism endured. The process of urbanization and the condition of urbanism are among the most profound continuities in the history of Western Civilization.

It is in this context of continuity that we should judge the fate of cities at war in the 1940s. Urban forms are enduring; their continuity vastly antedates the Second World War. Even in Europe, where the war devastated cities in the 1940s, they rose phoenix-like as pretty much what they had been before.[1] It is not realistic to suppose that something as ephemeral as the Second Great War would transform the process of urbanization or the condition of urbanism.

It is much more objective to view the war as an "heroic interlude." Men, women, and children stepped outside their normal roles into heroic ones for the duration. The war accelerated trends mostly underway for many years; it disrupted other trends ongoing for just as many years; it put people into unfamiliar roles; and it put everything into a heroic perspective. Everything had to be conceived, made, finished, and shipped overnight. People developed a higher degree of community; war marched into town in the form of gun emplacements, barrage balloons, sentries at the bridges, and longshoremen patrolling for fires. Cities mobilized their latent resources to bring victory. The war made patriots out of prisoners and democrats out of aristocrats. It put many women into factories and others into cottage industries making bandages and such. The Second Great War also modestly bootstrapped the cities' minorities and promised later immodest gains as well. The conflict minimally altered the ethnocultural composition of Urban California. It forced its own priorities on governments that would rather have pursued their own. And it literally took over the local economies and bent them to its will. Finally, the conflict boosted the population and economies of cities, though usually not to an unprecedented degree.

When the battles subsided, these trends resumed their accustomed antebellum manner. Community sentiment fell; the barrage balloons came down and the gun emplacements rusted; the inmates of San Quentin and Alcatraz went back to their normal careers; women left the factories, and the cottage industries shut down; minorities and women continued their fight for equality; the ethnocultural composition of the cities proceeded to move glacially onward; urban government rapidly resumed its upward trajectory;[2] and the federal government relaxed its hold on most local economies.[3] The cities' long-range trends were largely independent of the upheaval between the years 1939 and 1945. Except in the short run, the war did not disrupt the development of California cities. The only way to argue that the war brought unprecedented change to the Golden State is to disregard the earlier precedents. Furthermore, this emphasis tends to give the war a one-dimensional focus that neglects the decided impact of cities on war. The war did have an impact on cities, but cities had a tremendous effect on war as well. The influence was widespread and crucial.

APPENDIX: TABLES

Southland cities drew from a heterogeneous American native-white population, which added considerably to their diversity.

Table 6.1: U. S. Geographic origins of California urban populations, 1940.

Geog. Reg.	N Eng	M Atl	EN Cent	WN Cent	S Atl	ES Cent	WS Cent	Mount	Pacific	Other
Long Beach	02.46%	06.71%	15.97%	25.95%	02.85%	02.85%	07.85%	08.06%	26.13%	01.10%*
Los Angeles	02.38%	08.50%	16.29%	18.05%	02.31%	03.00%	09.22%	07.85%	31.09%	01.31%
San Diego	04.01%	08.12%	14.67%	17.79%	04.40%	03.22%	08.11%	07.16%	31.04%	01.48%
Oakland	01.93%	04.26%	08.71%	11.10%	01.34%	01.51%	04.46%	05.98%	58.22%	02.49%
Sacramento	01.26%	03.35%	07.90%	12.38%	01.19%	01.47%	04.29%	07.04%	60.15%	00.97%
San Francisco	01.82%	05.25%	07.19%	08.33%	01.50%	01.32%	02.85%	04.96%	64.35%	02.43%

Source: United States Department of Commerce, Bureau of the Census, *Sixteenth Census of the United States: 1940, Population*, no vol., *State of Birth of the Native Population*, (Washington, D. C.: U. S. Government Printing Office, 1944,), 59-65. *The category "other" includes people born in the United States who did not report a place of birth, citizens born abroad, and Americans born in "outlying possessions," 65.

Table 6.2 documents the African American population for the six cities except for Long Beach, for which the census does not provide totals. As the table demonstrates, the black population was far less diverse than the white, especially that of Northern California.

Table 6.2: Geographic origins of California black urban populations.

Geog. Reg	N Eng	M Atl	EN Cent	WN Cent	S Atl	ES Cent	WS Cent	Mountain	Pacific
Long Beach*	na	na	na	na	na	na	na	na	na
Los Angeles	00.25%	01.09%	02.92%	05.74%	06.78%	09.27%	34.65%	02.70%	36.55%
San Diego	00.67%	01.57%	02.29%	05.59%	08.77%	08.02%	30.58%	03.48%	38.99%
Oakland	00.28%	00.98%	02.37%	03.98%	05.00%	06.03%	32.47%	01.76%	47.09%
Sacramento	00.18%	00.64%	01.24%	03.27%	02.03%	03.18%	09.51%	02.21%	77.69%
San Fran.	00.25%	00.92%	01.48%	03.27%	02.76%	02.46%	09.03%	02.04%	78.54%

* 1940 figures not available.

Source: Bureau of the Census, *Census of Population: 1940*, (no vol.), *State of Birth of the Native Population*, (Washington, USGPO, 1944), 65.

The following tables illustrate the white ethnic dimension of the arsenals of democracy the year before the war engulfed them. The census provides a breakdown for only two California cities, but since the largest foreign-born colonies resided in Los Angeles and San Francisco, it is of some value. Tables 6.3 and 6.4 compare the percentages of the top five groups among those cities listed by the census.

Table 6.3: Five most numerous foreign stock groups, 1940, ordered by city.

San Francisco		Los Angeles		Chicago	
Italy	17.8%	Mexico	16.5%	Poland	19.2%
Germany	13.5%	Canada (oth)	11.9%	Germany	15.6%
Eire	12.1%	Germany	11.5%	Italy	9.9%
England	6.9%	Russia	10.5%	Russia	8.5%
Can (oth)	5.3%	England	8.9%	Eire	7.2%
Total	55.6%	Total	59.3%	Total	60.4%

Cleveland		Pittsburgh		St. Louis	
Poland	14.8%	Italy	17.5%	Germany	36.1%
Germany	12.4%	Germany	16.7%	Italy	10.5%
Czecho.	12.4%	Poland	13.1%	Eire	8.5%
Italy	11.6%	Eire	8.6%	Russia	7.3%
Hungary	9.5%	Russia	7.4%	Poland	5.3%
Total	60.7%	Total	62.3%	Total	67.7%

Minneapolis		Boston		New York City	
Sweden	26.6%	Eire	24.7%	Italy	22.7%
Norway	18.8%	Italy	18.8%	Russia	19.2%
Germany	12.7%	Russia	14.2%	Germany	10.3%
Canada oth	5.7%	Canada (oth)	9.5%	Eire	9.6%
Russia	5.0%	England	4.1%	Poland	8.5%
Total	68.8%	Total	70.3%	Total	71.3%

Philadelphia		Detroit		Providence	
Italy	21.8%	Poland	19.5%	Italy	35.8%
Russia	19.6%	Canada(Other)	16.3%	Eire	14.8%
Eire	11.4%	Germany	11.9%	Eng	8.6%
Germany	10.9%	Italy	8.3%	Russia	7.2%
Poland	8.0%	England	5.8%	Can (Fr.)	5.6%
Total	71.7%	Total	71.8%	Total	72.0%

Rochester		Newark		Milwaukee	
Italy	33.9%	Italy	32.7%	Germany	40.7%
Germany	16.8%	Russia	14.5%	Poland	19.6%
Can (oth)	9.4%	Poland	10.6%	Austria	5.4%
Eire	6.5%	Germany	9.5%	Russia	5.2%
England	6.3%	Eire	7.1%	Italy	4.4%
Total	72.9%	Total	74.4%	Total	75.3%

Jersey City		Buffalo		Baltimore	
Italy	26.5%	Poland	25.7%	Germany	21.6%
Poland	16.4%	Italy	18.7%	Rus-USSR	20.3%
Eire	16.2%	Germany	18.4%	Poland	15.6%
Germany	12.1%	Can(non Fr.)	9.5%	Italy	12.2%
Russia	6.2%	Eire	5.8%	Eire	5.9%
Total	78.1%	Total	77.4%	Total	81.1%

Source: *Census of the Population: 1940,* [no vol.; no part], *Special Report, Nativity and Parentage of the White Population, Country of Origin of the Foreign Stock* (Washington: USGPO, 1943), 76-80.

Table 6.4: Percent of total population in the five most numerous foreign stock groups in 1940 in ascending rank order.

San Francisco	55.6%	Minneapolis	68.8%	Rochester	72.9%
Los Angeles	59.3%	New York City	70.3%	Newark	74.4%
Chicago	60.4%	Boston	71.3%	Milwaukee	75.3%
Cleveland	60.7%	Philadelphia	71.7%	Jersey City	77.4%
Pittsburgh	62.3%	Detroit	71.8%	Buffalo	78.1%
St. Louis	67.7%	Providence	72.0%	Baltimore	81.1%

Source: Same as Table 3.

Table 6.5 indicates the percentage of foreign-derived residents, either foreign born or native born of foreign parentage, for both California cities and other major cities.

Table 6.5: Foreign white stock in 1940 as a % of the total population, in descending rank order.

1. New York City	64.81%	7. Jersey City	53.37%	13. Minneapolis	46.18%
2. Boston	62.30%	8. Rochester	51.17%	14. Philadelphia	41.76%
3. Providence	60.30%	9. Buffalo	50.90%	15. Pittsburgh	41.46%
4. Newark	57.67%	10. Detroit	50.21%	16. Los Angeles	37.28%
5. Cleveland	56.71%	11. San Francisco	49.79%	17. St. Louis	26.61%
6. Chicago	55.18%	12. Milwaukee	49.36%	18. Baltimore	22.24%

Source: *Sixteenth Census of the United States: 1940: Population, no. Vol., Nativity and Parentage of the White Population* (Washington: USGPO, 1943), 76-80; *Sixteenth Census of the U. S.: 1940, II, Characteristics of the Population*, pt. 1, U. S. Summary and Alabama-District of Columbia (Washington, DC: USGPO, 1943), 115.

Table 6.6 presents the non-white, non-black census category in 1940.

Table 6.6: Census category of other races, 1940, by city.

City	Total Pop.	Indian Pop.	%	Chinese Pop.	%	Japanese Pop.	%	Filipino Pop.	%	Other Pop.	%
Long Beach	164,271	52	0.03	80	0.04	241	0.01	241	0.01	1,079	0.65
Los Angeles	1,504,277	862	0.05	4,736	0.31	23,231	1.54	4,498	0.29	34,073	2.26
Oakland	302,163	121	0.04	3,201	1.05	1,790	0.59	627	0.21	5,765	1.90
Sacramento	105,958	81	0.07	1,508	1.42	2,879	2.71	152	0.14	4,682	4.41
San Diego	203,341	143	0.07	451	0.22	828	0.40	799	0.39	2,252	1.10
San Francisco	634,536	224	0.03	17,781	2.80	5,280	0.83	3,483	0.54	26,989	4.25
										Total 74,840	

Source: *Census of Population: 1940:* no vol., Second Series, *Sources of the Population of the United States: Summary* (Washington: USGPO, 1943), 108.

Table 6.7: Absolute and percent African American population rise by city.

City	1940 Pop	1950 Pop	Tot Inc. Pop	% Inc AA Pop	% of Tot 1940 Pop	% of Tot 1950 Pop	% Inc of Tot Pop
Cal.	124,306	462,576	338,270	271.64%	1.80%	04.40%	2.60%
L.B.	610	4,267	3,657	599.50%	0.037%	01.70%	1.34%
L.A.	63,774	171,209	107,435	168.46%	4.23%	09.56%	5.33%
Oak	8,462	47,562	39,100	462.06%	2.80%	12.37%	9.57%
S.D.	4,143	18,364	14,221	343.25%	2.03%	05.49%	3.46%
S.F.	4,846	43,502	38,656	797.68%	0.76%	05.61%	4.85%

Source: *Sixteenth Census of the United States, 1940: Population, II, Characteristics of the Population*, pt. 1, U. S. Summary and Alabama-District of Columbia (Washington, DC: USGPO, 1943), 204-07; *Census of Population: 1950, IV, Special Reports*, pt. 3, chap. B, Nonwhite Population by Race (Washington: USGPO, 1953), 57.

Table 6.8: Black population as a percent of the total population of consolidated metropolitan statistical areas over 1,000,000 in 1980, in descending order.

Rank	CMSA	% AA in 1980	Rank	CMSA	% AA in 1980	Rank	CMSA	% AA in 1980
1.	New Orleans	32.6%	12.	Cleveland	15.0%	23.	Pittsburgh	7.5%
2.	Norfolk	28.1%	13.	Miami-Ft. Lauderdale	14.9%	24.	H-ford-NB-Middletown	7.1%
3.	Washington, DC	26.8%	14.	Dallas-Ft. Worth	14.3%	25.	San Diego	5.6%
4.	Baltimore	25.5%	15.	Indianapolis	13.5%	26.	Denver	4.8%
5.	Atlanta	24.6%	16.	Kansas City	12.6%	27.	Boston	4.4%
6.	Chi-Gary-Lake Cty, In	19.6%	17.	Cincinnati	11.2%	28.	Seattle-Tacoma ·	4.2%
7.	Detroit	19.4%	18.	Columbus, Ohio	11.0%	29.	Phoenix	3.2%
8.	Houston	18.2%	19.	Buffalo-Niag Falls	9.2%	30.	Portland, Oregon	2.6%
9.	Philadelphia	18.2%	20.	Tampa-St Petersburg	9.2%	31.	Provi-Paw-Fall RI	2.3%
10.	St. Louis	17.2%	21.	LA-Anaheim-Riverside	9.2%	32.	Minneapolis	2.3%
11.	New York	16.1%	22.	SF-Oakland	8.7%			

Source: Bureau of the Census, *Statistical Abstract of the United States, 1986,* 106th ed. (Washington: USGPO, 1986), 21-24.

Table 6.9 illustrates the Mexican part of the Hispanic population.

Table 6.9: Foreign stock Mexicans as a part of total state and city populations and a percent of total state & city populations, 1940-1950.

	1940 Total Mex pop	1950 Total Mex pop	% 1940 Total State/City Pop	% Total 1950 State/City Pop
California	354,432	481,014	05.13%	04.54%
Long Beach*	-----	1,715	-----	00.68%
Los Angeles	92,680	115,572	06.16%	05.86%
Oakland*	-----	5,992	-----	01.55%
San Diego*	-----	11,236	-----	03.36%
San Francisco	9,149	13,578	01.44%	01.75%

*1940 figure not available.
Source: *Sixteenth Census of the United States: 1940, Population, Nativity and Parentage of the White Population, Country of Origin of the Foreign Stock* (Washington: USGPO, 1943), no vol., 52, 77-80; *Census of Population: 1950,* IV, *Special Reports,* pt. 3, Chapter A, Nativity and Parentage (Washington: USGPO, 1954), 3A-74 through 3A81; *Census of the Population: 1960,* I, *Characteristics of the Population,* pt. 6, section 3, *General Social and Economic Characteristics, California* (Washington, DC: USGPO, 1961), 232.

Table 6.10: "Spanish origin" population of the major metropolitan areas of the United States in 1980.

Rank	City	% Spanish origin	Rank	City	% Spanish origin
1.	Los Angeles	24.00%	17.	Seattle	02.10%
2.	Miami	23.50%	18.	Portland, Ore	02.00%
3.	San Diego	14.80%		Providence	02.00%
4.	Houston	14.50%	19.	Norfolk	01.60%
5.	Phoenix	13.20%		Detroit	01.60%
6.	SF-Oak-SJ	12.30%	20.	Cleveland	01.50%
7.	New York	11.70%	21.	Buffalo	01.30%
8.	Denver	10.70%	22.	Atlanta	01.10%
9.	Dallas-Fort Worth	08.50%	23.	Baltimore	01.00%
10.	Chicago	08.00%		Minneapolis	01.00%
11.	Tampa-St. Petersburg	05.00%	24.	St. Louis	00.90%
12.	Hartford	04.30%	25.	Indianapolis	00.80%
13.	New Orleans	04.00%	26.	Columbus, Ohio	00.70%
14.	Washington, D.C.	02.90%	27.	Boston-Law-Salem	00.60%
15.	Philadelphia	02.60%		Cincinnati	00.60%
16.	Kansas City	02.30%	28.	Pittsburgh	00.50%

Source: *Statistical Abstract of the United States, 1987,* 27-30.

Table 6.11: Origins and number of California population and percent rise 1940 & 1950.

	1930	1940	1950	Tot inc 1940s	% Increase
Europe					
Eng. & Wales	244,870	220,929	235,807	14,878	6.734%
Scotland	71,998	66,299	71,129	4,830	7.285%
N. Ireland	42,971	25,488	4,446*	??????	??????%
Eire	148,310	125,491	142,025	16,534	13.175%
Norway	48,566	49,064	66,080	17,106	34.681%
Sweden	108,602	100,759	113,807	13,048	12.949%
Denmark	60,815	57,966	66,523	8,557	14.762%
Netherlands	20,759	25,114	33,540	8,426	33.551%
Belgium	6,496	6,678	9,316	2,638	39.502%
Switzerland	49,698	43,788	47,753	3,965	9.054%
France	59,228	49,316	55,467	6,151	12.472%
Germany	310,409	273,967	300,516	26,549	9.690%
Poland	30,704	37,035	72,096	35,061	94.669%
Czechoslovakia	14,825	15,103	27,726	12,623	83.579%
Austria	31,383	40,380	62,213	21,833	54.068%
Hungary	13,348	18,321	34,658	16,337	89.170%
Yugoslavia	24,268	25,050	34,246	9,196	36.710%
U.S.S.R.	97,012	124,958	187,072	62,214	49.787%
Lithuania	3,296	5,210	12,241	7,031	134.952%
Finland	16,426	16,858	21,102	4,244	25.174%
Rumania	9,904	11,690	17,074	5,384	46.056%
Greece	20,364	23,741	30,965	7,224	30.428%
Italy	236,632	247,971	301,055	53,084	21.409%
Spain	27,273	27,985	30,015	2,030	7.253%
Portugal	64,981	60,144	54,337	-5,807	-9.655%
Other Europe	8,270	8,248	15,795	7,547	91.500%
				Total inc 360,683	
Asia	30,715	38,215	68,420		
Palestine & Syria	5,069	6,476	na	-------	------
Turkey in Asia	8,464	10,426	na	-------	------
Other Asia	17,182	31,312	na	-------	------
				Total inc 30,205	79.039%
America	597,526	599,817	793,209**	193,392	24.380%
Canada-French	22,642	22,936	22,005	-931	-4.059%
Canada-Other	201,714	204,205	255,595	51,163	25.054%
Mexico	358,171	354,432	481,014	126,582	35.714%
C. & S. America	11,540	13,535	-------		
Other America	3,459	4,709	34,595	29,886	734.657%
				Total 207,602	
All other					
Australia	10,802	9,184	na	------	------%
Azores	34,234	31,644	na	------	------%
All others not reported	8,430	20,580	71,785	51,205***	248.809%
				Total 51,205***	248.809%***
				Grand total 618,588	

* Census figure is obviously inaccurate. ** Central American figures missing. *** Australian and Azores figures missing.
Source: *U. S. Census of Population: 1950,* IV, *Special Reports,* pt. 3, chap. A, Nativity and Parentage (Washington, DC: USGPO, 1954); *U. S. Census of Population: 1950,* IV, *Special Reports,* pt. 3, Chapter C, Persons of Spanish Surname (Washington, DC: USGPO, 1953), 3A-71 through 3A-81.

Table 6.12: Foreign Stock numbers, absolute change, and percent of total California population, 1900-1960.

	1900	1910	1920	1930	1940	1950	1960
Cal	758,299	1,153,139	1,586,756	2,448,987	2,406,933	2,982,388	3,993,726
Change		394,840	433,617	862,231	-42,054	575,455	1,011,338
% FS	51.05%	48.50%	46.30%	43.13%	34.84%	28.17%	21.74%

Source: Same as table 6.11 & *Sixteenth Census of the United States: 1940*, no. vol., *Population, Nativity and Parentage of the White Population*, 52-53.

Table 6.13: Urban foreign stock in California, 1900-1960.

Cities	Years						
	1900	1910	1920	1930	1940	1950	1960
Long Beach							
For st	na	5,028	17,152	39,184	na	53,266	70,455
% tot pop	na	28.23%	30.85%	27.58%	na	32.42%	21.08%
Los Angeles							
For st	44,022	135,340	252,406	544,204	560,808	677,369	807,387
% tot pop	42.95%	42.40%	43.76%	43.95%	37.28%	34.37%	32.53%
Oakland							
For st	39,998	86,758	113,725	135,718	na	119,867	103,488
% tot pop	59.73%	57.77%	52.58%	47.77%	na	31.16%	38.15%
Sacramento							
For. st.	15,134	21,884	29,511	36,826	na	67,725	53,869
% tot pop	51.68%	48.96%	44.77%	39.28%	na	35.24%	28.10%
San Bernardino							
For. st	na	na	na	17,401	na	66,880	19,811*
% tot pop	na	na	na	46.26%	na	na	na
San Diego							
For st	7,698	15,915	31,041	47,091	na	78,408	122,696
% tot pop	43.49%	40.21%	41.56%	31.81%	na	23.44%	21.40%
San Francisco							
For st	241,820	284,655	322,843	367,358	315,971	312,603	321,802
% tot pop	70.54%	68.27%	63.71%	57.90%	49.79%	40.31%	43.46%
San Jose							
For st	10,766	14,878	20,772	28,268	na	48,650	59,060
% tot pop	50.07%	51.39%	52.39%	49.03%	na	54.54%	28.92%
Stockton							
For st	na	na	na	17,990	na	na	19,811
% tot pop	na	na	na	37.50%	na	na	21.55%

* Either the 1950 or 1960 figure for San Bernardino foreign stock is obviously inaccurate.

Source: *Fourteenth Census of the United States Taken in the year 1920*, vol. II, *Population: 1920: General Report and Analytical Tables* (Washington: USGPO, 1922), 53, 56, 58; *Fifteenth Census of the U. S., 1930, Population*, III, pt. 1, *Reports by States, Alabama-Missouri* (Washington: USGPO, 1932), 269-72; *Sixteenth Census of the United States: 1940: Population*, IV, pt. 3, *Nativity and Parentage of the White Population, Country of Origin of the Foreign Stock* (Washington: USGPO, 1943), 77-80; *Seventeenth Decennial Census of the US: Population*, IV, *Special Reports*, Pt. 3, Chap. A, Nativity & Parentage: Country of Origin of the Foreign Stock (Washington, DC: USGPO, 1954), 3A-78 through 3A-81; *Eighteenth Decennial Census of the United States, Population: 1960, Characteristics of the Population*, I, pt. 6, *California*, (Washington: USGPO, 1961), 6-377 through 6-385.

Table 6.14: Foreign stock diversity, 1950.

Foreign stock	Total	% of fs	Foreign stock	Total	% of fs	Foreign stock	Total	% of fs
San Francisco	312,603		**San Diego**	78,408		**Los Angeles**	677,469	
Italy	53,011	16.95%	Mexico	11,236	14.33%	Mexico	115,572	17.04%
Germany	36,639	11.72%	Germany	8,933	11.39%	U.S.S.R.	89,779	13.25%
Eire	35,511	11.35%	Canada-other	8,163	10.41%	Germany	63,902	09.43%
Eng. & Wales	18,950	6.06%	Eng. & Wales	7,986	10.18%	Eng. & Wales	50,331	07.42%
Canada-other*	18,316	5.85%	Italy	6,445	08.21%	Italy	47,240	06.97%
% fs, top 5 gps		51.93%	% fs, top 5 gps		54.52%	% fs, top 5 gps		54.11%
Oakland	119,867		**Long Beach**	53,266				
Italy	14,427	12.03%	Canada-other	7,736	14.52%			
Germany	12,615	10.52%	Eng. & Wales	7,634	14.33%			
Eng. & Wales	11,029	09.201%	Germany	7,505	14.08%			
Portugal	9,715	08.10%	Eire	3,092	05.80%			
Canada-other	9,570	07.983%	Sweden	2,979	05.59%			
% fs, top 5 gps		47.83%	% fs, top 5 gps		54.32%			

* Other than French.

Source: *United States Census of Population: 1950, Special Reports, Nativity & Parentage: 1950 Population Census Report P-E,* no. 3A (Washington: USGPO, 1954; reprint ed. of *United States Census of Population: 1950,* IV, pt. 3, chap. A, Washington: USGPO, 1953), 3A-79 through 3A-81.

Table 6.15: Percent in top five foreign stock groups, U. S. cities, 1950, ascending order.

1.	San Francisco	51.93%	8.	Detroit	62.01%	15.	Baltimore	72.59%
2.	Los Angeles	54.11%	9.	Pittsburgh	63.86%	16.	Rochester	72.75%
3.	Long Beach	54.32%	10.	St. Louis	66.81%	17.	Newark	73.58%
4.	San Diego	54.52%	11.	Minneapolis	68.30%	18.	Philadelphia	75.26%
5.	Oakland	57.41%	12.	New York City	70.04%	19.	Boston	76.75%
6.	Chicago	60.15%	13.	Milwaukee	71.73%	20.	Jersey City	77.68%
7.	Cleveland	60.83%	14.	Providence	72.03%	21.	Buffalo	87.01%

Source: *Census of Population: 1950: Special Reports, Nativity and Parentage,* 3A-74; *Sixteenth Census: 1940, Population, Nativity & Parentage of the White Population, Country of Origin of the Foreign Stock* (Washington: USGPO, 1943), 52.

Table 6.16: Most numerous foreign stock groups in California, 1930-1950

California, 1930	2,448,987		California, 1940	2,406,993		California, 1950	2,983,388	
Mexico	358,171	14.62%	Mexico	354,432	14.72%	Mexico	481,014	16.12%
Germany	310,409	12.67%	Germany	273,967	11.38%	Italy	301,045	10.09%
Eng. & Wales	244,870	09.99%	Italy	247,971	10.30%	Germany	300,516	10.07%
Italy	236,632	09.66%	Eng. & Wales	220,929	09.17%	Canada-other	255,594	08.56%
Canada-other	201,714	08.23%	Canada-other	204,205	08.48%	Eng. & Wales	235,753	07.90%
Total		55.17%	Total		54.05%	Total		52.74%

Source: Same as Table 6.15.

Table 6.17 shows the numerical fate of non-white groups—that is, Japanese, Chinese, Indians, and blacks—during the 1940s.

Table 6.17: Other races as a percent of the total city populations.

City	1910	1920	1930	1940	1950
Long Beach					
Ja	.71	.67	.40	na	.67
Ch	.14	.023	.0535	na	.0550
In	.0056	.0059	.0190	na	.0275
AA	.25	.24	na	.67	2.8
Los Angeles					
Ja	1.32	2.01	1.70	1.55	1.29
Ch	.61	.157	.243	.314	.409
In	.0251	.0327	.0497	na	.0485
AA	2.5	2.7	3.1	4.23	8.69
Oakland					
Ja	1.01	1.253	.752	.5293	.3250
Ch	2.40	1.253	1.073	1.059	.3250
In	.01331	.0273	.0341	na	.0436
AA	2.03	2.53	2.64	2.80	12.36
Sacramento					
Ja	3.2	2.998	3.570	.5923	2.0963
Ch	2.35	1.653	1.4570	1.4232	2.0970
In	.01342	.0273	.0906	na	.646
AA	1.102	1.15	1.38	3.33	6.3
San Bernardino					
Ja	na	na	.330	na	.0475
Ch	na	.128	.2481	na	.1490
In	na	.0240	.0800	na	.0475
AA	na	na	1.38	na	8.8
San Diego					
Ja	.040	1.033	.655	na	.3068
Ch	.87	.235	.3439	na	.2105
In	.02121	.0720	.0939	na	.0628
AA	1.33	1.83	2.03	4.40	6.0
San Francisco					
Ja	1.08	1.057	.985	.8321	.7195
Ch	2.53	1.221	2.5698	2.8023	3.2002
In	.01103	.0088	.0238	na	.0426
AA	.47	.599	.76	5.60	10.0
San Jose					
Ja	1.19	.809	.803	na	.9151
Ch	1.24	.622	.4735	na	.2015
In	.11727	.000	.0121	na	.0472
AA	.48	.41	na	na	1.0
Stockton					
Ja	2.01	2.084	.2889	na	1.2391
Ch	3.00	2.232	2.0661	na	2.5757
In	.00	.0124	.1105	na	.0546
AA	.83	.90	na	na	8.5

Source: *Census of the Population: 1930*, III, pt. 1, *Reports by States* (Washington: USGPO, 1932), 247-50, 266; *A Report of the Seventeenth Decennial Census of the United States*, II: pt. 5, California (Washington: U. S. Government Printing Office, 1952), 5-97 through 5-104, 5-179.

Table 6.18 illustrates the net gains or losses of native population (white and non-white) through interdivisional migration.

Table 6.18: Interdivisional migration per decade to Pacific Division.

Year	Net gain per decade	Total net gain	Percent gain per decade
1880	--------	+316,130	
1890	+294,458	+610,588	.9314%
1900	+139,215	+749,803	.2280%
1910	+826,033	+1,575,836	1.1016%
1920	+471,953	+2,047,789	.2994%
1930	+1,199,057	+3,246,846	.5855%
1940	+829,235	+4,076,081	.2553%
1950	+2,206,919	+6,283,000	.5414%
1960	+1,566,148	+7,849,148	.2492%

Source: *United States Census of Population: 1960: Subject Reports: State of Birth*
(Washington, D.C.: United States Government Printing Office, 1963), 4.

Table 6.19 presents comparable historical statistics for California, as opposed to the Pacific division, but only those from 1910 to 1970.

Table 6.19: California

Year	Net gain per decade.	Total net gain.	Percent gain per decade.
1900	na	------	------
1910	------	+762,625	------
1920	+460,102	+1,222,727	.6033%
1930	+1,178,561	+2,401,288	.9638%
1940	+774,250	+3,175,538	.3224%
1950	+1,776,832	+4,952,370	.5995%
1960	+1,703,371	+6,655,741	.3439%
1970	+346,345	+7,002,086	.0520%

Source: Same as Table 6.18, p. 9 and *Census of Population: 1970: Subject Reports*, II, pt. 2A-2C,
State of Birth (Washington, D.C.: United States Government Printing Office, 1973), 7.

Table 6.20 documents the proportions of people born inside and outside of California, in the United States or abroad.

Table 6.20

	1920	1930	1940	1950	1960
California					
Born in Calif.	37.0	34.1	36.6	36.9	39.9
Born in other U.S.	39.8	45.4	48.7	51.4	48.7
Born abroad	22.1	18.9	13.4	10.0	8.5*

* These percentages do not add up to 100 because of the omission of residual categories, such as American citizens born abroad, born in American overseas possessions rather than states, and so forth.
Source: *United States Census of Population: 1960: Subject Reports: State of Birth* (Washington, D.C.: United States Government Printing Office, 1963), 4; and *Census of Population: 1970: Subject Reports*, II, pt. 2A-2C, State of Birth (Washington, D.C.: USGPO, 1973), 7.

Table 7.1

Year	Work Force	Nonfatal injuries	Injuries per 1000	Fatal injuries	Injuries per 1000
1930	2,500,644	81,389	1 per 30.72	637	1 per 3,925.65
1940	2,953,257	85,043	1 per 34.72	536	1 per 5,509.80
1945	3,763,000	132,981	1 per 28.29	568	1 per 6,625.00
1950	4,245,000	136,123	1 per 31.18	691	1 per 6,143.27

Source: California, Department of Industrial Relations, *Handbook of California Labor, 1959-60* (San Francisco: California State Department of Industrial Relations, 1959), 88.

Table 8.1: Government spending in Californian cities. Figures are in thousands.

	Cities				
Years	LB	LA	OAK	SD	SF
1941-42	5,213	36,728	7,236	6,958	53,522
1942-43	5,683	36,074	7,253	7,820	40,652
1943-44	5,141	38,271	7,671	5,932	41,250
1944-45	6,045	42,675	8,306	6,470	43,986
1945-46	8,117	46,646	9,915	8,199	46,918
1946-47	11,198	65,156	13,272	12,019	54,089
1947-48	11,942	84,670	17,909	12,113	63,399
1948-49	16,038	114,794	19,724	16,689	72,791
1949-50	13,710	131,744	19,533	15,720	90,070
1950-51	27,642	204,862	21,733	22,563	126,588
1951-52	30,005	204,939	24,344	25,856	143,601
1952-53	35,358	246,244	25,546	30,058	141,634
1953-54	40,769	266,492	28,475	33,197	148,139
1954-55	43,822	277,965	26,967	32,449	144,052

Source: U.S. Bureau of the Census, *City Finances* (Washington, D.C.: U.S. Government Printing Office, 1944–1956).

NOTES

Introduction

1. *Los Angeles Times* (hereafter *LAT*), Jan. 16, 1942, sec. 2, p. 2.

2. For a similar assessment, see Beth Bailey and David Farber, *The First Strange Place: The Alchemy of Race and Sex in World War II Hawaii* (Baltimore: Johns Hopkins University Press, 1992), 17.

3. See William L. O'Neill, *A Democracy at War: America's Fight at Home and Abroad in World War II* (New York: Free Press, 1993); Paul D. Casdorph, *Let the Good Times Roll: Life at Home in America during World War II* (New York: Paragon House, 1989); Geoffrey Perrett, *Days of Sadness, Years of Triumph: The American People, 1939–1945* (New York: Coward, McCann and Geoghegan, 1973); Richard Polenberg, *War and Society: The United States, 1941–1945* (Philadelphia: Lippincott, 1972); Richard R. Lingeman, *"Don't You Know There's A War On?": The American Home Front, 1941–1945* (New York: G. P. Putnam's Sons, 1970).

4. That is not to say that the general field of World War II homefront history has been equally narrow. As the remaining chapters will indicate, those historians who have written general studies of the war have conceived them broadly: Bailey and Farber; Marilynn S. Johnson, *The Second Gold Rush: Oakland and the East Bay in World War II* (Berkeley: University of California Press, 1993); Marc Scott Miller, *The Irony of Victory: World War II and Lowell, Massachusetts* (Champaign: University of Illinois Press, 1988); Arthur C. Verge, *Paradise Transformed: Los Angeles during the Second World War* (Dubuque: Kendall/Hunt Publishing Co., 1993).

5. Richard Santillan, "Rosita The Riveter: Midwest Mexican American Women during World War II, 1941–1945," *Perspectives in Mexican American Studies* 2 (1989): 115–47; Deborah Scott Hirshfield, "Women Shipyard Workers in the Second World War: A Note," *International History Review* 11, no. 2 (May 1989): 478–85; Heather T. Frazer and John O'Sullivan, "Forgotten Women of World War II: Wives of Conscientious Objectors in Civilian Public Service," *Peace and Change* 5, nos. 2 and 3 (1978): 46–51; Eleanor F. Straub, "United States Government Policy toward Civilian Women during World War II," *Prologue* 5 (Winter 1973): 240–54; Cynthia Enloe, "Was It 'The Good War' for Women?" *American Quarterly* 37 (Fall 1985): 627–31; Susan M. Hartmann, "Prescriptions for Penelope: Literature on Women's Obligations to Returning World War II Veterans," *Women's Studies* 5,

no. 3 (1978): 223–39; Maureen Honey, "The Working-Class Woman and Recruit-ment Propaganda during World War II: Class Differences in the Portrayal of War Work," *Signs: Journal of Women in Culture and Society* 8, no. 4 (1983): 672–87; Esther MacCarthy, "Catholic Women and War: The National Council of Catholic Women, 1919–1946," *Peace and Change* 5, no. 1 (1973): 23–32.

6. This is obviously an interpretive statement that cannot be objectively prov-en. But from my reading of European and North American history for that period, the Second World War was infinitely more important than the wars of Louis XIV, or the wars of Dutch independence, or the wars of Italian unification, or those of German unification, or the invasion of Italy by Francis I. In these earlier wars often very small territories, such as Alsace, or a Dutch city, or Franche-Comte were at stake. In World War II, control of the Eurasian land mass and more was at stake. Of course, some earlier wars, such as the Ottoman conquest, were fought over more than a territory the size of Alsace, but only the First World War fully matches the importance of World War II. For earlier wars, see J. R. Hale, *War and Society in Renaissance Europe, 1450–1620* (Baltimore: Johns Hopkins University Press, 1985); William H. McNeill, *The Pursuit of Power: Technology, Armed Force, and Society since A.D. 1000* (Chicago: University of Chicago Press, 1982); Paul Kennedy, *The Rise and Fall of the Great Powers: Economic Change and Military Conflict, from 1500 to 2000* (New York: Random House, 1987).

1. Limping to Vallejo

1. Barbara Schillreff, "An Interview with Barbara Schillreff," Susan Painter, interviewer and ed., May 28, 1991, San Diego Historical Society Oral History Program (hereafter SDHSOHP), 2.

2. I am indebted to Arthur Verge for the suggestion to write about the everyday look and feel of the California cities at war. His own book, *Paradise Transformed: Los Angeles during the Second World War* (Dubuque: Kendall/Hunt Publishing Co., 1993), is a model study upon which I have tried to build; Roger W. Lotchin, *Fortress California, 1910–1961: From Warfare the Welfare* (New York: Oxford University Press, 1992); for American cities in the Civil War, see Shelby Foote, *The Civil War: A Narrative* (New York: Random House, 1958–74) 2, *From Fredericksburg to Meridian,* especially the chapters on the Siege of Vicksburg of 1863; and vol. 3, *From Red River to Appomattox,* the chapters on the Atlanta campaign of 1864, the Confederate thrust at Washington in 1864, and the Union Siege of Petersburg and Richmond in 1864–65.

3. Albert Eugene Trepte, "An Interview with Albert Eugene Trepte," Ruth Held, interviewer and ed., Jan. 29, 1991, SDHSOHP, 4; Howard B. Overton, comp. and ed., *The 19th Coast Artillery and Fort Rosecrans: Remembrances* (San Diego: National Park Service and Cabrillo Monument, 1993), 3; *San Francisco Chronicle* (hereafter *SFC*), Jan. 22, 1942, sec. 1, p. 3.

4. Vincent Battaglia, "An Interview with Vincent Battaglia," Robert G. Wright, interviewer, March 3, 1991, SDHSOHP; Leonard Ingrande, "An Interview with Leonard Ingrande," Robert G. Wright, interviewer, and Thomas E. Walt, ed., May 7, 1988, SDHSOHP.

5. Brian B. Chin, *Artillery at the Golden Gate: The Harbor Defenses of San Francisco in World War II* (Missoula, Mont.: Pictorial Histories Publishing Co., 1994), 8, 80, 91.

6. Peter Vogel, "The Last Wave from Port Chicago," *Black Scholar* 13, nos. 2 and 3 (1982): 30–47; Sheila Tropp Lichtman, "Women at Work, 1941–1945: Wartime Employment in the San Francisco Bay Area" (Ph.D. dissertation, University of California, Davis, 1981), 147; *SFC*, Apr. 17, 1942, sec. 1, p. 5; Philip A. Anderson, "The History and Development of the Coyote Point Merchant Marine Cadet School and Its Contribution toward America's Victory in World War II" (Ph.D. dissertation, California State University, Dominguez Hills, 1997), 1; Lichtman, 76. The foregoing description is heavily dependent on the magnificently complete Lawrence Kinnaird, *History of the Greater San Francisco Bay Region* (New York: Lewis Historical Co., 1966).

7. James Houlihan, *Western Shipbuilders in World War II* (Oakland: Shipbuilding Review Publishing Association, 1945), 23, 87.

8. *LAT,* Jan. 2, 1943, sec. 1, p. 10; Bruce R. Lively, "Naval and Marine Corps Reserve Center Los Angeles, *Southern California Quarterly* 69, no. 3 (1987): 241–73; Carlo D'Este, *Patton: A Genius for War* (New York: Harper Perennial, 1995), 408, 427; George W. Howard, "The Desert Training Center/ California-Arizona Maneuver Area," *Journal of Arizona History* 26, no. 3 (1985): 273–94; James O. Young, "The Golden Age at Muroc-Edwards," *Journal of the West* 30, no. 1 (1991): 69–79.

9. C. Bradford Mitchell, *Every Kind of Shipwork: A History of Todd Shipyards Corporation, 1916–1981* (New York: Todd Shipbuilding Corp,, 1981), 292–32, 153–54; Houlihan, 19–21.

10. *LAT,* Dec. 28, 1942, sec. 2, p. 1; Verge, *Paradise,* 96–97.

11. *LAT, Midwinter Edition,* Jan. 2, 1943, sec. 2, p. 11.

12. *LAT, Midwinter Edition,* Jan. 2, 1943, sec. 2, p. 8; Howard B. Overton, *Remembrances* (San Diego: The National Park Service Cabrillo National Monument, 1993), 17, 139, 198, 3, 9, 12, 16, 15, 194.

13. Mildred Finley Wohlford, "An Interview with Mildred Finley Wohlford," Cora Jane Jenkins, interviewer, and Philip M. Klauber and Jenkins, eds., Aug. 1987 [no other date given], SDHSOHP, 40; Overton, 181–82; Jane Randall Emerson, "An Interview with Jane Randall Emerson," Dr. Craig Carter, interviewer, and Thomas E. Walt, ed., Jan. 31, 1991, SDHSOHP, 1–11; Overton, 200, 207.

14. Overton, 122, 129; 122, 183; 143, 84, 2–3, 8.

15. Charles Forward, "An Interview with Charles Forward," Sylvia Arden, interviewer and ed., Apr. 29, 1975, SDHSOHP, 31.

16. Judy P. Schulman, "Camp Callan: From Glory to a Memory," *Journal of the Council on America's Military Past* 13, no. 1 (1984): 43–50; *LAT, Midwinter Edition,* Jan. 2, 1943, sec. 2, p. 8; *LAT, Midwinter Edition,* Jan. 2, 1943, sec. 1, p. 10; Overton, 81; J. Dallas Clark, "An Interview with J. Dallas Clark," Ruth Held, interviewer and ed., Oct. 30, 1991, SDHSOHPP, 11.

17. *LAT, Midwinter Edition,* Jan. 2, 1943, sec. 2, p. 8.

18. Effie Walling, "Interview with Effie Walling," Nancy Ledeboer, interviewer and ed., May 17, 1979, Regional Oral History Office (hereafter ROHO), Bancroft Library, 33; *SFC,* June 1, 1942, sec. 1, p. 1; June 7, 1942, sec. 1, p. 3; Frank An-

tonicelli, "An Interview with Frank Antonicelli," Craig Carter, interviewer, and Thomas E. Wald, ed., Nov. 20, 1985, SDHSOHP, 7; Herman I. Silversher, "An Interview with Herman I. Silversher," Susan Painter, interviewer and ed., May 24, 1990, SDHSOHP, 28.

19. *LAT, Midwinter Edition,* Jan, 2, 1943, 15; Mary Jean Potts, "Interview with Mary Jean Potts," Julie Denning, interviewer and ed., May 17, 1979, Regional Oral History Program (hereafter ROHP), Bancroft Library, 5–6.

20. Walling, interview, 33.

21. Wayne Padgett, "Orion Limps to Mare Island," *Naval History* 13, no. 4 (1999), 38–42.

22. Robert G. Wright, "An Interview with Robert G. Wright," Vincent Ancona, interviewer and ed., Nov. 8, 1990, SDHSOHP, 10; *LAT, Midwinter Edition,* Jan. 2, 1943, sec. 2, p. 8.

23. Potts, interview, 7, 20.

24. Sarah Buchanan, "Advertising during World War Two" (UNC History Department course paper, Dec. 3, 1997), 1–21; Jordan Braverman, *To Hasten the Homecoming: How Americans Fought World War II through the Media* (New York: Madison Books, 1996), 235–55; Overton, 215.

25. James H. Doolittle and Carroll V. Glines, *I Could Never Be So Lucky Again: An Autobiography* (New York: Bantam Books, 1991), 256–61.

26. *SFC,* Aug. 17, 1942, sec. 1, p. 1.

27. Walling, interview, 23; Potts, interview, 11, 31–32; *SFC,* Nov. 19, 1942, sec. 1, p. 17; Dec. 24, 1942, sec. 1, p. 6.

28. Wilsie Orjas, "An Account of Pearl Harbor Days, on and after December 7, 1941, 1942" (unpublished manuscript, Bancroft Library), 177.

29. Silversher, 25.

30. Overton, 65.

31. John Spencer Held, "An Interview with John Spencer Held," Ruth Held and Thomas E. Walt, interviewers and eds., Aug. 4, 1990, SDHSOHP, 28–29.

32. Verge, "Daily Life," 25; gold and silver stars were given to mothers whose sons were killed or wounded.

33. Phyllis Burns, "An Interview with Phyllis Burns," Ruth Held, interviewer and ed., Aug. 16 and 19, 1989, SDHSOHP, 31–35.

34. Forward, interview, 31; Kinnaird, sec. 2, p. 412.

35. Wright, interview, 6–7; Overton, 18.

36. Ruth Held and Thomas E. Walt, interviewers and eds., "An Interview with John Spencer Held," Aug. 4, 1990, SDHSOHP, 27–29.

37. *San Diego Union* (hereafter *SDU*), June 13, 1942, sec. A, p. 3; Gigi Sanders, "An Interview with Gigi Sanders," Robert G. Wright, interviewer, and Vincent Ancona, ed., Oct. 30, 1989, SDHSOHP, 11–13; Casdorph.

38. Bailey and Farber, 107.

39. Ronald D. Cohen, "Music Goes to War: California, 1940–1945," in *The Way We Really Were: The Golden State in the Second Great War,* ed. Roger W. Lotchin (Champaign: University of Illinois Press, 2000), 47–67; Marilynn Johnson, 138–40.

40. *SFC,* Oct. 30, 1942, sec. 1, p. 1; Held, interview, 33.

41. *LAT, Midwinter Edition,* Jan. 2, 1943, sec. 6, p. 4.

42. Edward Ortiz Jr., "An Interview with Edward Ortiz, Jr.," Craig Carter,

interviewer, and Joy Hayes, ed., Apr. 25, 1988, SDHSOHP, 4–5; Overton, 8; *LAT,* Jan. 1, 1943, sec. 2, p. 1.

43. *LAT,* Dec. 16, 1942, sec. 2, p. 14. Obviously the island is not contiguous to the mainland, but it was metropolitan because it functioned as a recreational suburb of the metropolis. See the 1950 census definition.

44. *LAT,* Jan. 27, 1943, sec. 1, p. 14; Jan. 1, 1943, sec. 2, p. 7; Dec. 28, 1942, sec. 2, p. 1; Overton, 127.

45. *LAT,* June 2, 1943, sec. 2, p. 127.

2. Dunkirk at the Marina

1. John U. Terrell, "War Comes to the Coast," *SFC,* Dec. 16, 1941, sec. 1, p. 1; Fletcher Bowron, "Radio Broadcast by Mayor Fletcher Bowron, Station KECA," Dec. 9, 1942, 7:30 P.M., 1–3; "Bad News but the Truth," editorial, *SDU,* Dec. 16, 1941, sec. 1, p. 17.

2. Allan R. Bosworth, *America's Concentration Camps* (New York: W. W. Norton, 1967), 33–85.

3. Editorial, *SDU,* July 7, 1941, sec. B, p. 2; Dec. 15, 1941, sec. B, p. 3; editorial, "Danger Is Real: Keep Yourself Prepared," *SFC,* sec. 1, p. 17; Fletcher Bowron, "Contributions to the War Effort of the City of Los Angeles," memo, March 23, 1943, Bowron Papers, Huntington Library (hereafter Bowron Papers).

4. Editorial, "Danger Is Real: Keep Yourself Prepared," *SFC,* sec. 1, p. 17; "Army Requests Cancellations," *SDU,* Dec. 15, 1941, sec. B, p. 3; "Patrol Arrests 13 Japanese on Fishing Boats," *SDU,* sec. B, p. 8; Bosworth, 36; "U.S. Relaxes Ban on Japanese," *SDU,* Dec. 16, 1941, sec. B, p. 1. Bosworth implies that the government froze all Japanese-American accounts and left them frozen. The *SDU* reported that only the accounts of Japanese nationals were frozen and then unfrozen as reported on December 16.

5. Potts, interview, 30.

6. *SFC,* March 4, 1942, sec. 1, p. 3; June 24, 1942, sec. 1, p. 6; Oct., 29, 1942, sec. 1, p. 1; May 29, 1942, sec. 1, p. 14; March 6, 1942, sec. 1, p. 1.

7. San Francisco Board of Supervisors, *Journal of the Proceedings* (hereafter SFBS, *Journal*) 37, June 8, 1942, p. 1376; Clark, interview, 10.

8. Clark, interview, 10.

9. Jack Smith, "The Great Los Angeles Air Raid," in *Los Angeles: Biography of a City,* ed. John and Laree Caughey (Berkeley: University of California Press, 1976), 364–66; for a discussion of the responsibility of Admiral Kimmel and General Short, see Gordon Prange, *At Dawn We Slept: The Untold Story of Pearl Harbor* (New York: McGraw Hill, 1981).

10. Potts, interview, 31; editorial, "Tell the Truth," *Southern California Business* (hereafter *SCB*) 3, no. 43 (Dec. 29, 1941): 1; editorial, "War and Business," *SCB* 3, no. 42 (Dec. 22, 1941): 1; Los Angeles Chamber of Commerce, "A Letter re Southern California's Position and Prospects in the War," *SCB* 3, no. 42 (Dec. 22, 1941): 1–2; "War Hysteria Hit for Loss of Tourist Trade," *SDU,* Dec. 24, 1941, sec. A, p. 4; editorial, "Persecution of Innocents Won't Win the War," *SFC,* Dec. 16, 1941, sec. 1, p. 17; editorial, "Cool Heads Win Through," Dec. 19, 1941, sec. 2, p. 19; Herb Caen, "It's News to Me," *SFC,* Dec. 22, 1941, sec. 1, p. 11.

11. Verge, *Paradise*, 22.

12. Verge, *Paradise*, 23. The estimates vary from six to twelve. Clark G. Reynolds, "Submarine Attacks on the Pacific Coast, 1942," *Pacific Historical Review* 33, no. 2 (1964): 191–92; Gerhard Weinberg, *A World at Arms: A Global History of World War II* (New York: Cambridge University Press, 1994).

13. *SFC*, June 22, 1942, sec. 1, p. 1. For a map of the aircraft industries and their subcontractors see chapter 1, p. 11; "866 L.A. Firms in Warplane Parts Work as Subcontracting Speeded," *SCB* 4, no. 50 (Jan. 25, 1943): 1. For similar fears of attack in Hawaii, where submarines shelled several islands after the air assault, see Bailey and Farber, 12–13; Reynolds, 191–92.

14. Reynolds.

15. Fletcher Bowron, "Remarks to the Secretaries of State Convention," Aug. 27, 1941, Bowron Papers.

16. SFBS, *Journal* 36, March 16, 1942, pp. 401–402; 37, June 15, 1942, pp. 1457–58. San Francisco, Civil Defense Council, "Bulletin for May 2, 1942," 1.

17. Michael Torigian, "National Unity on the Waterfront: Communist Politics and the ILWU during the Second World War," *Labor History* 30, no. 3 (1989): 409–32; William H. Harris, "Federal Intervention in Union Discrimination: FEPC and West Coast Shipyards during World War II," *Labor History* 11, no. 3 (1981): 325–47; Richard W. Steele, "'No Racials': Discrimination against Ethnics in American Defense Industry, 1940–42," *Labor History* 32, no. 1 (1991): 66–90; I am indebted to Arthur Verge for the phrase "Paradise Transformed."

18. SFBS, *Journal* 37, Nov. 23, 1942, p. 2596.

19. Fletcher Bowron, "Five Minute Radio Program: 11:25 to 11:30 A.M. from the steps of Los Angeles City Hall," Dec. 7, 1942, 1–3; Wright, interview, 10.

20. Editorial, *SDU*, sec. B, p. 2; Fletcher Bowron, "Speech to the Tournament of Roses Officials," Dec. 30, 1941; Bowron, "Speech to the New York Giants Football Team," Jan. 1, 1941, Bowron Papers. As late as August 23, 1943, the Los Angeles City Defense Council was trying to recruit 55,000 new fire guards in anticipation of a Japanese carrier-borne aircraft attack. Los Angeles County War Council, Los Angeles City Defense Council, "Bulletin No. 808," Aug. 23, 1943.

21. San Francisco authorities did not even call for volunteers until mid-November, and the East Bay did somewhat later. "A Call to Arms," *SFC*, Nov. 14, 1941, sec. 1, p. 5; "Blackout Lamp," *SFC*, Dec. 22, 1941, p. 8; "Raid Shelters Promised for S.D. Schools," *SDU*, Dec. 19, 1941, sec. A, p. 6; Los Angeles County, Civil Defense Council (hereafter LACCDC), "Guide Sheet no. 59," 1.

22. "Blackout: Fear—and Laughter in the Dark," *SFC*, Dec. 13, 1941, sec. 1, p. 4; "Longest Bay Area Blackout" and "I Will Be Responsible, Says Rossi," *SFC*, sec. 1, p. 1; "Dispute in Blackout Brings Court Lecture," *SDU*, Dec. 12, 1941, sec. A, p. 4.

23. "Shop Early," *SFC*, Dec. 17, 1941, sec. 1, p. 8; "Blackout Lamp," *SFC*, Dec. 22, 1941, sec. 1, p. 8; "Merchants to Close at 5 P.M. as Defense, Safety Measure," *SDU*, Dec. 12, 1941, sec. A, p. 1; "Churches Urged to Curb Night Gatherings," *SDU*, sec. A, p. 8; "Blackout of Weather Data Ordered for San Diego," *SDU*, Dec. 13, 1941, sec. A, p. 4.

24. "City's Seventh Blackout Lasts 19 Minutes," *SFC*, Feb. 19, 1942, sec. 1, p. 1; "Blackout Problems: Next Time Offenders Will Be Cited for Failure to Douse Lights," *SFC*, Feb. 20, 1942, sec. 1, p. 7; "Hundreds Guard San Diego by Keeping

Day-and-Night Watch for Hostile Planes," *SDU*, Jan. 1, 1942, sec. B, p. 10; Verge, *Paradise*, 25.

25. "Division, Battalion, and Sector Chiefs," *SFC*, Mar. 8, 1941, sec. 1, p. 5; LACCDC, "Bulletin No. 69," 1; "Guide Sheet No. 43–B," 1–2, 8; "Progress Report," March 20, 1942, p. 1; San Francisco Civilian Defense Council (hereafter SFCDC), "Bulletin of April 23, 1942," 1; "Bulletin of Jan. 6, 1942," 1.

26. LACCDC, "Guide Sheet No. 38," March 8, 1942, p. 20; SFCDC, "Bulletin for June 15, 1943," 1. The Army trained the air wardens to cope with gas out of doors in the Presidio and in special gas rooms. Civil defense authorities feared gas attacks enough to mandate that civil defense volunteers bear masks on their persons until well into 1942, when the Japanese threat faded and the masks began to wear out.

27. "Defense against Raids: Basement of Skyscraper Offers Almost Perfect Safety from Enemy's Bombs," *SFC*, Dec. 19, 1941, sec. 1, p. 8; "Committee Named to 'Tag' Children," *SFC*, Jan. 14, 1942, sec. 1, p. 8; LACCDC, "Guide Sheet No. 65," Feb. 4, 1942, p. 1; SFCCDC, "Bulletin for March 14, 1942," 1; "Bulletin for March 30, 1942," 2; "Raid Shelters Promised for S.D. Schools," *SDU*, Dec. 19, 1941, sec. A, p. 6.

28. SFCCDC, "Bulletin for April 22, 1942," 1–2; "Bulletin for April 24, 1942," 1–2.

29. "Mass Evacuation Program for S.D. Termed 'Silly'" *SDU*, July 2, 1942, sec. A, p. 8; Martin Middlebrook, *The Battle of Hamburg: Allied Bomber Forces against a German City in 1943* (New York: Scribner, 1981);"For a Defense-Minded City, a Thought—Let's FIGHT!" *SFC*, Mar. 10, 1942, sec. 1, p. 13.

30. "Rose Bowl," *SDU*, Jan 2, 1942, sec. B, p. 9; Jan. 6, 1942, sec. B, p. 3; SFCCDC, "Bulletin for March 18, 1942," 2; "All Amateur Radios Must Go Off Air," *SFC*, Jan. 10, 1942, sec. 1, p. 9.

31. "Bartenders Take Pledge: The Patrons Who Talk Too Much to Be Reported Immediately," Mar. 6, 1942, sec. 1, p. 8; "Education Needed to Zip Your Lip," March 7, 1942, sec. 1, p. 12; "Civic Opera Ballet Must Go On," Mar. 30, 1942, sec. 1, p. 10; "U.C. Asks Army about Commencement Crowd," Mar. 28, 1942, sec. 1, p. 10.

32. "Don't Run at First Raid, Coast Asked," *SFC*, Feb. 27, 1942, sec. 1, p. 13; LACCDC, "Guide Sheet No. 43–B," July 10, 1942, 1–2, 8.

33. SFCCDC, "Bulletin for March 10, 1942," 1; "Bulletin for June 30, 1942," 1; "Civilian Defense: More Than 25,000 Are Enrolled in Red Cross First Aid Classes," *SFC*, Feb. 14, 1942, sec. 1, p. 5; "Model Planes: 30,000 California School Kids Start Building for U.S. Monday," Feb. 18, 1942, sec. 1, p. 6.

34. "Know Your Neighbor," *SFC*, Jan. 30, 1942, sec. 1, p. 10; "Civil Defense . . . ," *SFC*, Feb. 3, 1942, sec. 1, p. 5.

35. Bill Simons, "In the Districts: Scavengers Do It Again—They Buy $10,000 in Defense Bonds," Feb. 6, 1942, sec. 2, p. 21; "Camouflage: Art Students Study Ways and Means of 'Flattening' Landmarks," Feb. 11, 1942, sec. 1, p. 9; "Kites Are Out; Chinese Will Concentrate on Building Model Airplanes This Year," Feb. 11, 1942, sec. 1, p. 14.

36. Bill Simons, "A Chance for Children to Do Their Bit—the Vickies," *SFC*, March 30, 1942, sec. 1, p. 20.

37. W. B. France, "Women Form 'Block Plan' Unit for Action in War Emergen-

cies," *SDU,* Feb. 8, 1942, sec. C, p. 3; Elliott M. Lewis, "In the Districts: 'Block Plan' Urged for Real Efficiency in Civilian Defense Effort," *SFC,* Jan. 1, 1942, sec. 2, p. 15; Frank Kelley, "In the Districts: 'Know Your Neighbor' Idea Spreads; the Block Clubs Grow in Number," Jan. 22, 1942, sec. 2, p. 22; Hazel Avery, "In the Districts: This Group Ready for Any Emergency," Feb. 2, 1942, sec. 1, p. 9.

38. SFBS, *Journal* 38, July 6, 1943, pp. 1710–12.

39. *LAT,* Dec. 21, 1942, sec. 1, p. 12; Dec. 28, 1942, sec. 2, p. 1.

40. *Long Beach Post Telegraph* (hereafter *LBPT*), May 7, 1943, p. B1.

41. *SFC,* Dec. 17, 1942, sec. 1, p. 4.

42. *LAT,* Jan. 2, 1943, sec. 1, p. 1.

43. For the concept of urban street theater, I am indebted to Susan Davis, *Parades and Power: Street Theatre in Nineteenth Century Philadelphia* (Philadelphia: Temple University Press, 1986).

3. Al Capone and Alcatraz

1. *SFC,* June 2, 942, sec. 1, p. 15.

2. Arnold S. Lott, *A Long Line of Ships: Mare Island's Century of Naval Activity in California* (Annapolis: United States Naval Institute, 1954), 211; *SFC,* Oct. 20, 1942, sec. 1, p. 9; *SFC,* Nov. 14, 1942, sec. 1, p. 10.

3. Robert K. Merton, "The Latent Functions of the Machine," in *Urban Bosses, Machines, and Progressive Reformers,* ed. Bruce M. Stave (Lexington, Mass.: D. C. Heath and Co., 1971), 27–36.

4. To my knowledge, there is no American history literature that considers the logistical and other advantages of urbanization to military operations.

5. For the war effort in Mobile, see Martha Mary Thomas, *Riveting and Rationing in Dixie: Alabama Women and the Second World War* (Tuscaloosa: University of Alabama Press, 1987).

6. Richard Walker, review of *Fortress California: From Warfare to Welfare,* by Roger W. Lotchin, *Economic Geography* 69, no. 2 (1993): 224–26.

7. I am indebted for the phrase "Improbable Los Angeles" to David L. Clark, "Improbable Los Angeles," in Richard M. Bernard and Bradley R. Rice, eds., *Sunbelt Cities: Politics and Growth since World War II* (Austin: University of Texas Press, 1983), 268. Many other scholars apply a similar term to L.A.; Stephen Ambrose, *D-Day, June 6, 1944: Climactic Battle of World War II* (New York: Simon and Schuster,1994), 320–80. Professor Ambrose notes that the enormous number of tanks and other vehicles landed at Omaha Beach created an acute traffic jam.

8. "Southern California Goes to War," *LAT, Midwinter Edition,* Jan. 2, 1943, sec. 1, p. 16; Fletcher Bowron, "Statement of Mayor Fletcher Bowron [On Housing] March 6, 1945," Bowron Papers.

9. Marilynn Johnson, 88–90; Charles S. Johnson, *The Negro War Worker in San Francisco: A Local Self-Survey* (San Francisco: Young Men's Christian Association, 1944), 29.

10. George Gleason, "Statement," 1–2, John Anson Ford Papers (hereafter Ford Papers), Huntington Library; Wright, interview, 6–7.

11. Fletcher Bowron to Senator Sheridan Downey, Apr. 27, 1943, Bowron Papers; *LAT,* Jan. 3, 1943, sec. 1, p. 21.

12. Gordon Wagenet, "Interview with Gordon Wagenet," Roger W. Lotchin, interviewer, May 31 and Aug. 18, 2000. p. 2; "Overnight Lodgings," *Hollywood Citizen News* (hereafter *HCN*), May 1, 1944; *LAT,* Jan. 5, 1942, sec. 2, p. 6; A. S. Campion, acting chief administrative officer of Los Angeles County to the L.A. County Board of Supervisors, Jan. 28, 1944, Ford Papers; Campion to Ford, Apr. 18, 1944; "JAF Housing Vote Record," Ford Papers.

13. For the building of the booster bowls such as the Rose Bowl and the Coliseum, see Steven A. Riess, *City Games: The Evolution of American Urban Society and the Rise of Sports* (Urbana: University of Illinois Press, 1991), 144–45; M. B. Pendleton to John Anson Ford, Jan. 3, 1944, Ford Papers; *SFC,* June 10, 1942, sec. 1, p. 6.

14. Harold Vatter, *The U.S. Economy in World War II* (New York: Columbia University Press, 1985), 15–19; *SFC,* June 12, 1942, sec. 1, p. 6; *SFC,* June 2, 1943, sec. 1, p. 15.

15. James N. Gregory, *American Exodus: The Dust Bowl Migration and Okie Culture in California* (New York: Oxford University Press, 1989), 172–90; Ruth Milkman, *Gender at Work: The Dynamics of Job Segregation by Sex during World War II* (Urbana: University of Illinois Press, 1987).

16. *LAT,* Jan. 5, 1942, sec. 2, p. 7; A. Russell Buchanan, *Black Americans in World War II* (Santa Barbara: Clio Books, 1977), 45–58.

17. Bureau of the Census, *County Data Book: A Supplement to the Statistical Abstract of the United States* (Washington, D.C.: U.S. Government Printing Office, 1947), 72, 354.

18. *SFC,* Nov. 23, 1942, sec. 1, p. 9; *SFC,* June, 12, 1942, sec. 1, p. 6; O'Neill, 361–62.

19. Joyce Maupin, "Working in War Industry: An Interview with Joyce Maupin," Julie Denning, interviewer and ed., 1976, ROHO, p. 21; Karen Anderson found the same phenomenon in Seattle, Detroit, and Baltimore. See *Wartime Women: Sex Roles, Family Relations, and the Status of Women during World War II* (Westport, Conn.: Greenwood Press, 1981), 91. She called the tales of children left in cars "scare stories."

20. *LAT,* Dec. 22, 1942, sec. 2, 1.

21. *SF Call Bulletin,* Jul. 21, 1945, [n.p.].

22. *SFC,* July 23, 1943, [n.p.]; Dec. 25, 1942, sec. 1, p. 14; *SF Examiner* (hereafter *SFE*), Oct. 16, 1944, [n.p.]; *SF News* (hereafter *SFN*), Dec. 7, 1943 [n.p.].

23. Houlihan, 51.

24. *LAT,* Dec. 22, 1942, sec. 2, p. 13. I compared the metropolitan counties of California, where migrants worked in war industries, with the entire states because Southwest migrants came from both city and country. See Gregory, 3–35; Bureau of the Census, *County Data Book,* 66, 74, 356.

25. Verge, *Paradise,* 111–12; "How Long Will Our Patience Last?," "Little Hope Seen for Strike End at Long Beach," "For Million Tram Riders: Pay Issue Still Undecided," *LAT,* May 7, 1944, sec. 1, p. 1; sec. 2, p. 4; Abraham Shragge, "Boosters and Bluecoats: The Civic Culture of Militarism in San Diego, California, 1900–1945" (Ph.D. dissertation, University of California at San Diego, 1998), 513–14.

26. Heather Freeman, "The Lives of Two Southern Housewives during World War II" (UNC undergraduate seminar paper, Dec. 6, 1996), 17.

27. Wagenet, 2.

28. Fletcher Bowron to Paul V. Betters, executive director, U.S. Conference of Mayors, Apr. 30, 1945, Bowron Papers; Kinnaird, sec. 2, p. 421.

29. For the harbor fights, see Mansel Blackford, *The Lost Dream: Businessmen and City Planning on the Pacific Coast, 1890–1920* (Columbus: Ohio State University Press, 1993), 63–97; Fletcher Bowron to the Board of Harbor Commissioners, City of Los Angeles, May 3, 1943, Bowron Papers; Kinnaird, sec. 2, p. 420.

30. Potts, interview, 5–6; "Southern California Goes to War," *LAT, Midwinter Edition,* Jan. 2, 1943, sec. 3, p. 15; for the role of airports in booster strategy see Lotchin, *Fortress California, 1910–1961,* 73, 247.

31. William L. Kahrl, *Water and Power: The Conflict over Los Angeles' Water Supply in the Owens Valley* (Berkeley: University of California Press, 1982), 149, 349; Norris Hundley Jr., *The Great Thirst: Californians and Water, 1770s–1990s* (Berkeley: University of California Press, 1992), 215, 228; *LAT,* Jan. 18, 1942, sec. 2, 1–2.

32. *LAT,* Jan. 19, 1942, sec. 1, p. 20; *County Data Book, 1947,* 72. Wartime population estimates vary all over the map. I have accepted those of the U.S. Bureau of the Census, for the period 1940–43.

33. General David C. Henley, "General Patton Memorial, Chiriaco Summit" (one-page handout, Patton Memorial); Carlo D'Este, *Patton: A Genius for War* (New York: HarperCollins, 1995), 408, 467, 427.

34. Kinnaird, sec. 2, 319–26; Hundley, 190.

35. Hundley, 187–90.

36. *SFC,* Feb. 11, 1942, sec. 1, p. 5; Forward, interview, 32; Schillreff, interview, p. 10; Antonicelli, interview, p. 7; Christine Killory, "Lost Opportunity of San Diego's National Defense Housing Projects," *Journal of San Diego History* 39, nos. 1 and 2 (1993): 33–50.

37. Kinnaird, sec. 2, 408.

38. Ortiz, interview, 4–5; *SFC,* Feb. 27, 1942, sec. 1, p. 16; Aug. 9, 1942, "Women's World," p. 7; and Aug. 30, 1942, sec. 1, p. 5.

39. *SFC,* July 30, 1942, sec. 1, p. 10; for the announcement and discussion of the program see *LAT,* Dec. 18, 1942, sec. 2, 1 and 7, and Dec. 20, 1942, sec. 2, p. 2, editorial; *LAT,* Jan. 26, 1942, sec. 2, p. 2; *LAT,* Dec. 21, 1942, sec. 1, p. 12; Albert C. Bilicke to the Civilian Protection Board, Aug. 24, 1942, CR-131, Bancroft Library.

40. *SFC,* Nov. 23, 1942, sec. 1, p. 9.

41. Elizabeth Rudel Gatov, "Grassroots Party Organizer to Treasurer of the United States," Malca Chall, interviewer, Nov. 1, 1975–May 11, 1976, published 1978, ROHO, 65; Catherine Ann Foster, "An Interview with Catherine Ann Foster," Thomas E. Walt and Betty Quayle, interviewers and eds., Oct. 3, 1988; Evelyn Harper Briggs, "An Interview with Evelyn Harper Briggs," Ruth Hampton, interviewer and ed., Nov. 2, 1983, SDHSOHP; Shirley Brandes, "An Interview with Shirley Brandes," Bernice Wall, interviewer, and Cora Janes Jenkins, ed., Jan. 16, 1985, SDHSOHP.

42. Betty Smith, *A Tree Grows in Brooklyn* (New York: Harper and Brothers, 1943); Jane Jacobs, *The Death and Life of Great American Cities* (New York: Vintage Books, 1963); David Nasaw, *Children of the City at Work and at Play* (New York: Oxford University Press, 1985), 88–100; *SFC,* May 16, 1942, sec. 1, p. 7; *LAT,* Dec. 21, 1942, sec. 2, p. 3.

43. The Essex numbers come from Francis E. McMurtrie, ed., *Jane's Fighting Ships, 1944/5* (New York: Arco Publishing Co., 1944), 360; *LAT*, Dec. 17, 1942, sec. 2, p. 12.

44. *SFC*, Nov. 29, 1942, sec. 2, p. 1; *SFC*, Oct. 17, 1942, sec. 1, p. 8.

45. Houlihan, 45.

46. Sherna Berger Gluck, ed., "Laughlin," in *Rosie The Riveter Revisited: Women, the War, and Social Change* (Boston: Twayne Publishers, 1987), 248–49.

47. Paul Kennedy rightly emphasizes the productive capacities of nations in war in his *The Rise and Fall of the Great Powers*; Vatter, 15–19.

48. Charles Wollenberg, *Marinship at War: Shipbuilding and Social Change in Wartime Sausalito* (Berkeley: Western Heritage Press, 1990), 97; Gerald Nash, *The American West Transformed: The Impact of the Second World War* (Bloomington: Indiana University Press, 1985), 201–16.

49. *LAT*, Jan. 24, 1942, sec. 2, p. 6.

50. Wollenberg, *Marinship*,), 97; Gerald Nash, *American West*, 201–16.

51. Three approaches to this problem may be found: Morton and Lucia White, *The Intellectual Versus the City* (Cambridge, Mass.: Harvard University Press and MIT Press, 1964); Thomas Bender, *Toward an Urban Vision: Ideas and Institutions in Nineteenth Century America* (Baltimore: Johns Hopkins University Press, 1975); Paul Boyer, *Urban Masses and Moral Order in America, 1820–1920* (Cambridge, Mass.: Harvard University Press, 1978); Carl Abbott, "Beautiful Downtown Burbank: Changing Metropolitan Geography in the Modern West," in *Journal of the West*, Special Edition on Western Cities, ed. R. W. Lotchin, 34, no. 3 (July 1995).

4. Tijuana Breakfast

1. Gluck, "Juanita Loveless," 124–50; Gretchen Lemke-Santangelo, *Abiding Courage: African American Migrant Women and the East Bay Community* (Chapel Hill: University of North Carolina Press, 1996), 107.

2. Gluck, "Loveless," 124–50.

3. Sheila Kishler Bennett and Glen H. Elder Jr., "Women's Work in the Family Economy: A Study of Depression Hardship in Women's Lives," *Journal of Family History* 4, no. 2 (1979): 153–76; *LAT*, Jan. 3, 1943, sec. 1 V, p. 5; Lichtman, 85, 168–83.

4. Gluck, "Helen Studer," 184; "Charlcia Neuman," 168; D'Ann Campbell, *Women at War with America: Private Lives in a Patriotic Era* (Cambridge: Harvard University Press, 1984), 202; Lichtman, 183, 318; Xiaojian Zhao, "Women and Defense Industries in World War Two" (Ph.D. dissertation, University of California at Berkeley, 1993), 117.

5. Natalie Marie Fousekis, "Fighting for our Children: Women's Activism and the Battle for Child Care in California, 1940–1965" (Ph.D. dissertation, University of North Carolina at Chapel Hill, 2000), 21–69, 50; Lichtman, 183, 310–30; Kimberly A. Hall, "Women in Wartime: The San Diego Experience, 1941–1945," *Journal of San Diego History* 39, no. 4 (1993): 272; Lemke-Santangelo, 118.

6. One hopes that a women-at-war book will someday be written about mothers who helped their families. Stumph's experience seemed quite typical, and their child care allowed the expansion of the workforce by freeing up their daugh-

ters to work in defense. Gluck, "Stumph," 64; "Studer," 189–90; "Marie Baker," 231. Karen Anderson, 50.

7. Gluck, "Laughlin," 248.

8. Wollenberg, *Marinship,* 60–61; *SFC,* March 16, 1942, sec. 1, p. 12; Gluck, "Loveless," 134; Maupin; Bernice Hubbard May, "A Native Daughter's Leadership in Public Affairs," Gabrielle Morris, interviewer, March 20–Nov. 7, 1974, ROHO, 76–80.

9. Wollenberg, *Marinship,* 64, 68; Gluck, "Conclusion," 259.

10. U.S. Bureau of Labor Statistics, "Industrial Injuries to Women Workers," *Monthly Labor Review* 60 (Feb. 1945): 311–17; "Work Injuries to Women in Shipyards, 1943–1944," *Monthly Labor Review* 60 (March 1945): 550–60; Gluck, "Laughlin," 247

11. Lichtman, 97–100, asserts the lack of training, oral testimony asserts the reverse. See Gluck, "Laughlin," 247.

12. May, 76–80.

13. Katherine Archibald thought that the dress code was "based fully as much on the principles of concealment and sexless propriety as on the purported aims of safety." Katherine Archibald, *Wartime Shipyard: A Study in Social Disunity* (Berkeley: University of California Press, 1947), 21; Potts, interview, 7; Walling, interview, 20–22.

14. Sanders, 7; Gluck, "Studer," 187; Walling, interview, 1–2, 34–35.

15. Potts, interview, 8; Gluck, "Studer," 187; Lichtman, 109.

16. Gluck, "Studer," 190; Karen Anderson found the same bias in favor of pretty women. Karen Anderson, 53; Archibald, 19; Walling, interview, 15; Sanders, interview, 5.

17. Wollenberg, *Marinship,* 65; Sanders, 4; Walling, interview, 13.

18. "Women Making Good on Long Beach Mail Routes," *Long Beach Press Intelligencer,* May 10, 1944, p. B3; Archibald, 15–41; Wollenberg, 58–59, 62–63; Gluck, "Laughlin," 243–55, 247; Men accepted them when it became evident that the female presence was "only for the duration." Gluck, "Laughlin," 249.

19. Virginia Snow Wilkinson, "From Housewife to Shipfitter," *Harper's,* Sept. 1943, pp. 331–36; Karen Anderson, 47–49, found more antipathy in Seattle, Detroit, and Baltimore; Lichtman, 169–88; Sanders, interview, 1–2; Walling, interview, 6, 8–9, 28, 31; Archibald, 17, 19; Gluck, "Studer," 172–97; "Beatrice Morales Clifton," 214; "Laughlin," 252–53; "Baker," 187, 233; Wollenberg, 67; *Monthly Labor Review* 60 (March 1945): 553; Campbell, 238; Sanders, interview, 5–6.

20. Archibald, 32. See Campbell, 126; Lichtman, 115, 117–30, 153, 188–211, 293.

21. Wollenberg, 65; Lichtman claims that women were *almost* as productive as men, 293, 188–211; Walling, interview, 27; Campbell, 136; Lichtman, 293.

22. Walling, interview, 4; Potts, interview, 21; Sanders, interview, 1–2, 11–12.

23. *SFC,* Aug. 9, 1942, "Women's World," p. 7; *LAT,* June 4, 1943, sec. 1, p. 1A; Gluck, " Studer," 189; Lichtman, 201; Overton, 223; *Monthly Labor Review* 60 (Feb. 1945), 313.

24. Campbell, 90–91; Elmer Bendiner, *The Fall of Fortresses: A Personal Account of the Most Daring—and Deadly—American Air Battles of World War II* (New York: G. P. Putnam's Sons, 1980), 218–33; Walling, interview, 31–32; Gluck, "Neuman," 169.

25. Gluck, "Laughlin," 253; " Studer," 192; Walling, interview, 28; Lichtman, 169, 96; Zhao, "Women and Defense," 8; Campbell, 238.

26. Federal Reserve Bank of San Francisco, *Monthly Review* (hereafter *Monthly Review*), Dec. 1, 1941, p. 63.

27. Zhao, "Women and Defense," 242–47, 260–64; Lemke-Santangelo, 107, stressed that East Bay black women kept their factory gains and did not fall back into domestic service.

28. See also Hall, 261; Wilkinson, 328. Lichtman, 86, argues the reverse, that money came first and patriotism and other matters second. See also Honey, 672–87; Joan M. Jensen and Gloria Ricci Lothrop, *California Women: A History* (Sparks, Nev.: Materials for Today's Learning, 1988), 105. The South may have had a comparable watershed.

29. This discussion relies heavily on Hall, 261–76.

30. Campbell, 15; Karen Anderson, 23–74, discusses many war topics, but almost all in the context of discrimination, as does Lichtman. See also Mary M. Schweitzer, "World War II and Female Labor Force Participation Rates," *Journal of Economic History* 40, no. 1 (1980): 89–95; Thomas R. H. Havens, "Women and War In Japan, 1937–1945," *American Historical Review* 80, no. 4 (1975): 913–34.

31. Karen Anderson, 27–30; Burns, interview, 29; Briggs, interview, 9; "Women Making Good"; Wilkinson, 337.

32. Santillan, 115–47; Wilkinson, 335.

33. O'Neill, 235–46.

34. *SFC*, May 1, 1942, sec. 1, p. 14; Apr. 24, 1942, sec. 1, p. 14; Apr. 30, 1942, sec. 1, p. 12.

35. *LAT*, Jan. 12, 1943, sec. 1, p. 8; *SFC*, May 14, 1942, sec. 1, p. 1; Apr. 24, 1942, sec. 1, p. 14; Aug. 16, 1942, sec. 1, p. 15; May 15, 1942, sec. 1, p. 9. Weight rules and laws were used by government to protect women and by unions to exclude them. Weight restrictions fell as the labor crisis demanded female workers. Lichtman, 185–86.

36. Seattle did not attain this breakthrough until October. Karen Anderson, 45–46; *SDU*, Jan. 24, 1942, sec. A, p. 9; *SFC*, May 16, 1942, sec. 1, p. 11; *SFC*, May 8, 1942, sec. 1, p. 11; Feb. 3, 1942, sec. 1, p. 5; March 2, 1942, sec. 1, p. 6; May 5, 1942, sec. 1, p. 21; Virginia Scharff, *Taking the Wheel: Women and the Coming of the Motor Age* (New York: Free Press, 1991), 165–75.

37. *LAT*, June 4, 1943, sec. 2, p. 5; *SFC*, Feb. 3, 1942, sec. 1, p. 5.

38. *LAT*, June 3, 1943, sec. 2, p. 4; June 4, 1943, sec. 2, p. 4.

39. *LAT*, Jan. 2, 1943, sec. 1, p. 6; Campbell, 47–61; Susan Hartmann, *The Home Front and Beyond: American Women in the 1940s* (Boston: Twayne Publishers, 1982), 105; *LAT*, June 3, 1943, sec. 2, p. 6.

40. Gatov, interview, 68; U.S. Congress, House, Committee on Naval Affairs, Subcommittee Investigating Congested Areas, *Investigation of Congested Areas: Hearings before a Subcommittee of the House Committee on Naval Affairs on H. Res. 30, 78th Cong., 1st sess.* (hereafter *Congested Areas*), 669.

41. *LAT*, June 3, 1943, sec. 2, p. 6.

42. *LAT*, Jan. 1, 1943, sec. 2, p. 6; Gluck, *Rosie*, 182; *SFC*, sec. 1, p. 11; *LAT*, June 6, 1943, sec. 2, p. 7.

43. *LAT*, Jan. 8, 1943, sec. 2, pp. 5–6.

44. Foster Rhea Dulles, *The American Red Cross: A History* (New York: Harper and Brothers, 1950), 381; *LAT,* June 4, 1943, sec. 2, pp. 6, 8; *SFC,* Feb. 6, 1942, sec. 1, p. 12; Russ Scargle, "Music and Men's Minds: A World War II Vignette," *Pacific Historian* 16, no. 1 (1972): 28–35.

45. *LAT,* June 3, 1943, sec. 2, p. 6; *LAT,* Jan. 8, 1943, sec. 2, pp. 5–6.

46. *SFC,* Apr. 4, 1942, sec. 1, p. 13, *LAT,* Jan. 1, 1943, sec. 1, p. 16; *SFC,* Apr. 29, 1942, sec. 1, p. 24.

47. *SFC,* Aug. 26, 1942, sec. 1, p. 12.

48. *SDU,* Aug. 1, 1942, sec. B, p. 10; Hartmann, *Home Front,* 135–36; *LAT,* Jan. 14, 1943, sec. 2, 1 and 3.

49. *LAT,* Dec. 26, 1942, sec. 2, p. 3.

50. Jacqueline R. Braitman, "Partisans in Overalls: New Perspectives on Women and Politics in Wartime California," in *The Way We Really Were: The Golden State in the Second Great War,* ed. Roger W. Lotchin (Champaign: University of Illinois Press, 2000), 215–36.

51. George Q. Flynn, *The Draft, 1940–1973* (Lawrence: University of Kansas Press, 1993), 51.

52. Wohlford, interview, 36–40.

53. *LAT,* Jan. 9, 1942, sec. 2, p. 6. For the participation of the many women in OPA work in other cities, see Karen Anderson, 87–88.

54. O'Neill, 395–96. There are strongly held opinions on both sides of the question of whether Truman succeeded. O'Neill has one; for the other, see the definitive Keith E. Eiler, *Mobilizing America: Robert P. Patterson and the War Effort, 1940–1945* (Ithaca: Cornell University Press, 1997), 231, and elsewhere; *LAT,* Jan. 12, 1943, sec. 2, p. 5; Hall, 270.

55. Braitman, 13–14.

56. *LAT,* Dec. 25, 1942, sec. 2, p. 5; Jan. 3, 1943, sec. 2, p. 1; Jan. 13, 1943, sec. 2, p. 5.

57. *LAT,* Jan. 4, 1943, sec. 2, p. 1.

58. William Chafe, *The American Woman: Her Changing Social, Economic, and Political Roles, 1920–1970* (New York: Oxford University Press, 1972), 246–54.

59. Zhao, "Women and Defense," 1–13.

60. Vatter, 19; Karen Anderson, 4–7; Alan S. Milward, *War, Economy and Society, 1939–1945* (Berkeley: University of California Press, 1977), 219–20; Schweitzer, 89–95; *LAT,* Jan. 2, 1943, sec. 1, p. 7. This conclusion is consistent with the "time bomb" theory of women's history. Following William Chafe, several women's historians have argued that World War II was a time bomb of feminism, which was set ticking during that conflict, but which did not explode into the women's rights movement until the 1960s. That would seem like a difficult question to document, but if it is true, it should be noted that the more affluent women who worked in volunteer activity during the Second World War were the same kind of women who led the women's rights movement in the 1960s. "Rosie the Riveter" women did not.

61. Campbell, 15; Karen Anderson, 56–60; Rebecca S. Greene, "The United States: Women in World War II," *Trends in History* 2, no. 2 (1981): 71–82; Enloe, 85–89; Hirshfield, 478–85; Hartmann, "Prescriptions," 223–39; Honey, 672–87; Michael Nash, "Women and the Pennsylvania Railroad: The World War II Years," *Labor History* 30, no. 4 (1989): 608–21; Milkman, 1–11: Lichtman, 87–95.

62. Most of the condemnation of the Axis powers in World War II has been

directed against Nazi Germany. The Nazis richly deserved all of the denunciation that has been leveled at them. However, one should never underestimate the malignity of Japanese fascism. For an example of this malevolence, see Iris Chang, *The Rape of Nanking: The Forgotten Holocaust of World War II* (New York: Basic Books, 1997). Chang argues that the massacres at this city were merely a down payment on the Imperial Japanese brutality, which may have cost the lives of 10 million Chinese in World War II. Not only were the Nanking and other deaths numerous, but they were inflicted in dreadful ways: medical experiments on humans; mass decapitations; an astonishing number of rapes; bayonet practice on live Chinese prisoners; wholesale violations of the Geneva Convention on the treatment of prisoners; other bestiality too gruesome to mention; and blatantly false denials of the atrocities from the Emperor on down. As Chang repeatedly documents, the Japanese considered the Chinese subhuman. See Chang, 35–60, and elsewhere.

63. Campbell, 237; Zhao, "Women and Defense," 1–13; Lichtman, 347–60; O'Neill, 235–46.

5. The Universal Double V

1. "White 'Superiority' Gone Forever," *SFC*, March 20, 1942, sec. 1, p. 16.

2. Charles Wollenberg, *Golden Gate Metropolis: Perspectives on Bay Area History* (Berkeley: Institute of Governmental Studies, 1985), 241–42.

3. Memo from Alfred Cohn to Fletcher Bowron, Jan. 21, 1942, in Bowron Papers.

4. "See Eleanor First for Action, Says Angeleno," *LAT*, Jan. 5, 1943, sec. 1, p. 10.

5. Bailey and Farber, 5.

6. Bill Hosokawa, *Nisei: The Quiet Americans* (New York: William Morrow and Co., 1969), 293, 295.

7. Ibid., 295.

8. Fletcher Bowron, Speech to the Army Day Luncheon, Apr. 6, 1942, Bowron Papers.

9. Hosokawa, 280–82.

10. Ibid., 276–77.

11. Ibid.

12. Ibid., 278.

13. "Time-Table: S. F. May Be Attacked at Any Moment, Deadly Accurate Book Says," *SFC*, March 17, 1942, sec. 1, p. 3; Hosokawa, 286.

14. Stephen C. Fox, "General John DeWitt and the Proposed Internment of German and Italian Aliens during World War II," *Pacific Historical Review* 57, no. 4 (1988): 407–38.

15. Interestingly enough, Great Britain, a nation very sensitive to the liberties of its inhabitants, did incarcerate German Jewish refugees temporarily living in their country during World War II. Art Barbeau, "Civilian Internment in World War II," *Journal of West Virginia Historical Association* 11, no. 1 (1989): 1–19.

16. Hosokawa, 258. Hosokawa points out that the shelling of the oil refinery at Goleta happened after the decision to relocate was reached, 294.

17. Margaret Leslie Davis, *Rivers in the Desert: William Mulholland and the Inventing of Los Angeles* (New York: HarperCollins Publishers, 1993), 196–211.

18. Judy Yung, *Unbound Feet: A Social History of Women in Chinatown*

(Berkeley: University of California Press, 1995), 250; speech of Fletcher Bowron at a celebration of the Chinese Republic, Oct. 10, 1942, Bowron Collection, Huntington Library. Ronald Takaki, *Strangers from a Different Shore: A History of Asian Americans* (New York: Little, Brown, 1989), chap. 10.

19. K. Scott Wong, "War Comes to Chinatown: Social Transformation and the Chinese of California," in *The Way We Really Were: The Golden State in the Second Great War,* ed. Roger W. Lotchin (Champaign: University of Illinois Press, 2000), 164–86; Yung, 241–48, 239–40, 235–37, 231, 223–49.

20. Yung, 271; Wong, 164–86.

21. Ibid., 272.

22. Xiaojian Zhao, "Chinese American Women Defense Workers in World War II," *California History* 75, no. 2 (1996): 112, 140; Marilynn Johnson, 65; "Chinese in War Work," *SFC,* Dec. 24, 1942, sec. 1, p. 6.; Zhao, "Chinese American Women," 146; Yung, 262, 269.

23. Dolly Rhee, "Chinese Home Front: East Joins West with One-Third of Chinatown on Defense Jobs," *SFC,* sec. 1, p. 6; Zhao, "Chinese American Women," 141, 149.

24. Wong, 164–86; Zhao, "Chinese American Women," 145–46; Yung, 251, 263, 268–69.

25. Rhee, 6; Yung, 267.

26. Wong, 164–86; Yung, 253, 254–55, 259; Zhao, "Chinese American Women," 140.

27. Wong, 164–86.

28. "Chinese in War Work," *SFC,* sec. 1, p. 6.

29. Assistant to John Anson Ford, entitled only "WD," to Ford, Aug. 2, 1944, Ford Papers, Box 74.

30. For the depth of anti-Chinese bias at an earlier date, see Willard Farwell, *The Chinese at Home and Abroad Together with the Report of the Special Committee of the Board of Supervisors of San Francisco, on the Condition of the Chinese Quarter of that City* (San Francisco: A. L. Bancroft and Co., 1885); Wong, 164–86.

31. The census categorized Mexicans as white, but obviously some were and some were not. The literature often categorizes them as people of color, which is equally ambiguous. Mario T. Garcia, "Americans All: The Mexican American Generation and the Politics of Wartime Los Angeles, 1941–1945," *Social Science Quarterly* 65, no. 2 (June 1984): 281–83.

32. Garcia, 278–89.

33. Los Angeles County Committee for Interracial Progress, Institute of Intergovernmental Studies, UC Berkeley (hereafter LACCIP), "Minutes of the Ninth Monthly Committee Meeting, November 13, 1944," 1–3; "Summary of a Paper Presented at the Meeting of the Committee on September 11, 1944," by Miss Ellis M. Tipton, Director of the Intercultural Center, Sam Dimas, California, 1–3.

34. Garcia, 283–85; Los Angeles County Grand Jury, Special Mexican Relations Committee, "Papers Read in a Meeting Held October 8, 1942," 33–37, Haynes Collection, Bureau of Governmental Research, University of California at Los Angeles.

35. Eric M. Mosier, "The Impact of World War II on the Mexican American Community in San Diego" (M.A. thesis, San Diego State University, 1998), 33–70, 107–29.

36. Garcia, 285–86.

37. Ibid., 287; Albert Camarillo, "A Research Note on Chicano Community Leaders: The G. I. Generation," *Aztlan: Chicano Journal of the Social Sciences and the Arts* 2, no. 2 (1971): 145–50; Mosier, 107–29.

38. Rose Doris Scherini, *The Italian American Community of San Francisco: A Descriptive Study* (New York: Arno Press, 1980), 191–92; Stephen Fox, *The Unknown Internment: An Oral History of the Relocation of Italian Americans During World War II* (Boston: Twayne Publishers, 1990), 22–40; Gary R. Mormino and George E. Pozzetta, "Ethnics at War: Italian Americans in California during World War II," in *The Way We Really Were: The Golden State in the Second Great War,* ed. Roger W. Lotchin (Champaign: University of Illinois Press, 2000), 143–62; Gloria Ricci Lothrop, "A Shadow on the Land: The Impact of Fascism on Los Angeles Italians," *California History* 75, no. 4 (1996–97): 347–48; Lothrop, "Unwelcome Aliens in Freedom's Land: The Impact of World War II on Italian Aliens in Southern California," *Southern California Quarterly* 81, no. 4 (1999): 507–44.

39. Fox, *Unknown Internment,* 1–40, 151–77; Fox, "General John DeWitt," 435; Mormino and Pozzetta, 143–62; Lothrop, "The Untold Story: The Effect of the Second World War on California Italians," *Journal of the West* 35, no. 1 (1996): 7–14.

40. Fox, *Unknown Internment,* 128; Mormino and Pozzetta, 7, 137; Lothrop, "Untold Story," 9–12; Lothrop, "Shadow," 338; Lothrop, "Unwelcome Aliens," 508–44; Deanna Paoli Gumina, "The Fishermen of San Francisco Bay," *Pacific Historian* 20, no. 1 (1976): 19.

41. Lothrop, "Untold Story," 13; Fox, *Unknown Internment,* 125–39; Mormino and Pozzetta, 9.

42. Quoted in Mormino and Pozzetta, 13; Fox, *Unknown Internment,* 1–21; Lothrop, "Shadow," 338–53; Lothrop, "Unwelcome Aliens," 508–44.

43. Mormino and Pozzetta, 19.

44. Fox, *Unknown Internment,* 1–21, 160; Mormino and Pozzetta, 13–17, 20–22.

45. Mormino and Pozzetta, 143–62; Lothrop, "The Italians of Los Angeles," *Californians* 5, no. 3 (1987): 42.

46. Harvard Sitkoff, "Racial Militancy and Interracial Violence in the Second World War," *Journal of American History* 58, no. 3 (1971): 661–81; Lee Finkle, "The Conservative Aims of Militant Rhetoric: Black Protest during World War II," *Journal of American History* 60, no. 3 (1973): 692–713; Albert Broussard, *Black San Francisco: The Struggle for Racial Equality in the West, 1900–1954* (Lawrence: University Press of Kansas, 1993): 144.

47. Keith Collins, *Black Los Angeles: The Maturing of the Ghetto, 1940–1950* (Saratoga, Calif.: Century Twenty One Publishing, 1980), 18–22; Wollenberg, *Marinship,* 71–72; Zhao, "Women and Defense," 100–10; Charles Johnson, 63; Broussard, 143, 154–55; "Cole's 'Muni' Training Is Balked Again," *SFC,* March 8, 1942, sec. 1, p. 1; March 12, 1942, sec. 1, p. 12 [letters to the editor]; March 3, 1942, sec. 1, p. 14. For a dimmer view of black progress see Patricia Rae Adler, "Watts: From Suburb to Black Ghetto" (Ph.D. dissertation, University of Southern California, 1977), 249–77.

48. James R. Wilburn, "Social and Economic Aspects of the Aircraft Industry in Metropolitan Los Angeles during World War II" (Ph.D. dissertation, UCLA,

1971), 171, 177; Collins, 20–21; LACCIP, "Minutes of the Fifteenth Monthly Committee Meeting, June 11, 1945," 2; Alonzo N. Smith, "Blacks and the Los Angeles Municipal Transit System, 1941–1945," *Urbanism Past and Present* 6, no. 1 (1980–81), 30; Josh Sides, "Battle on the Home Front: African American Shipyard Workers in World War II Los Angeles," *California History* 75, no. 3 (1996): 252.

49. Broussard, 150; Charles Johnson, 66; Archibald, 83–84; Collins, 21; Marilynn Johnson, 60–82. Collins, 56–58, held that fear on the part of bus, taxi, and trolley operators, and the consequent refusal to operate in South Central and Watts during late hours, caused the shortage. However, given that Los Angeles was one of the tightest labor markets in the country, it would seem that the city would have addressed the mass transit part of the problem. He also notes that frequent breakdowns on the Red Car lines due to worn-out equipment and the impossibility of getting spare parts in competition with war-related activities provided other obstacles to African American participation in the defense industries. He does not address the issue of possible work in the vast number of subcontractor enterprises that were spread all over the city.

50. Lawrence B. de Graaf, "Significant Steps on an Arduous Path: The Impact of World War II on Discrimination against African Americans in the West," *Journal of the West* 25, no. 1 (1996): 27; Broussard, 159–60, Archibald, 92; Charles Johnson, 69–73; Marilynn Johnson, 71–74; Wollenberg, *Marinship,* 76, 81.

51. Charles Johnson, 70, discovered a "tendency also for the Negro worker to ask for separate working gangs." Whether this was a majority sentiment is not known. Marilynn Johnson, 72–73; Broussard, 164–65; Collins, 21–22; Marilynn Johnson, 75; Delores Nason McBroome, *Parallel Communities: African Americans in California's East Bay, 1850–1963* (New York: Garland Publishing Co., 1993), 107; Shirley Ann Wilson Moore, *To Place Our Deeds: The African American Community in Richmond, California, 1910–1963* (Berkeley: University of California Press, 2000), 71–93.

52. Sides, "Battle," 262; Charles Johnson, 69; Archibald, 93–99; de Graaf, 27.

53. Wilburn, 173–76, 192, 234; "What Bishop McCucken Said," *LAT,* Aug. 14, 1944, sec. 2, p. 4; Sides, "Battle," 262, 254, 263.

54. Peter Vogel, "The Port Chicago Disaster: Was It a Nuclear Explosion?" *Black Scholar* 13, nos. 2 and 3 (1982): 46; McBroome, 116–21.

55. Marilynn Johnson, 96; Broussard, 65–69; "Blackouts of 1943, Lively, Funny Show," *LAT,* sec. 1, p. 15; editorial, "Only in a Democracy," *SDU,* March 28, 1942, sec. B, p. 2.

56. Collins, 24; Wilburn, 191, Broussard, 165; Adler, 261; Moore, 98–99.

57. Lemke-Santangelo, 76; Collins, p. 25; LACCIP, George Gleason, "The Housing Crisis in Los Angeles County, April 1, 1945," 2; Charles Johnson, 20–24; Adler, 262; Moore, 97.

58. Charles Johnson, 22.

59. Ibid., 3, 20–21.

60. Ibid., 22, 29–31; Broussard, 168–79; LACCIP, "Minutes . . . Jan. 8, 1945," 2.

61. Moore, 84–93; McBroome, 95; Marilynn Johnson, 105–109, 107, 109–11; Collins, 40–41.

62. Lemke-Santangelo, 78–79, 80, 84, 86, 90; Moore, 147–50.

63. Adler, 256; Marilynn Johnson, 111.

64. Adler, 254; Collins, 26–27, 40, 71–72.

65. de Graaf, 29–30; McBroome, 96–98; Collins, 69–71; Adler, 266–68.

66. Moore, 87–95; Archibald, 93; Wollenberg, *Marinship,* 84; Broussard, 180–87.

67. Broussard, 192–204.

68. McBroome, 99, 114; Marilynn Johnson, 170, 187–97; Lemke-Santangelo, 77.

69. Professor Sitkoff has made many important contributions to American history, but his thesis does not test out in Los Angeles. Roger W. Lotchin, "California Cities and the Hurricane of Change: World War II in the San Francisco, Los Angeles, and San Diego Metropolitan Areas," in *Fortress California at War: San Francisco, Los Angeles, Oakland, and San Diego, 1941–1945,* Special Issue, Roger W. Lotchin, guest ed., *Pacific Historical Review* 63, no. 3 (1994): 413–14; John Anson Ford to P. Price Cobbs, President of the Citizens Defense Committee, Aug. 5, 1942, Ford Papers; Sides, "Battle," 256, 260; Adler, 254.

70. *Eastside News,* Nov. 11, 1943, Ford Papers; Arthur F. Miley to Ford, July 8, 1943, Ford Papers; Ford, Helen Gahagan Douglas, and Bishop James Baker to a long list of people, Oct. 1942, Ford Papers; Raphael J. Sonenshein, *Politics in Black and White: Race and Power in Los Angeles* (Princeton: Princeton University Press, 1993), 101–113; Sides, "Battle," 259; de Graaf, 32.

71. E. Frederick Anderson, *The Development of Leadership and Organization Building in the Black Community of Los Angeles from 1900 through World War II* (Los Angeles: Century Twenty One Publishing, 1980), 81–104; de Graaf, 28, 32.

72. Gregory, 174.

73. Ibid., 174, 175–177.

74. Ibid., 172–82; Archibald, 48–49.

75. Archibald, 52–57; Gregory, 178, 181, 186–87.

76. Wilburn, 184, 187; LACCIP, "Minutes of the Eighth Monthly Committee Meeting—October 9, 1944," 1–4; LACCIP, "Minutes of the Eleventh Monthly Committee Meeting, Jan. 8, 1945," 1–3; "Police and Minority Groups—An Experiment," 1–8, undated, Kenny Papers, Bancroft Library; SFBS, *Journal* 38, Sept. 27, 1943, pp. 2193–2204.

77. Marilynn Johnson, 168–69; "Police and Minority Groups—An Experiment," 1–8; Collins, 27–31.

78. Mauricio Mazon, *The Zoot Suit Riots: The Psychology of Symbolic Annihilation* (Austin: University of Texas Press, 1984), 68; Marilynn Johnson, 160; Gregory, 143–49; Collins, 79; Charles Johnson, 33.

79. Mazon, 7–8, 15–53.

80. *LAT,* June 9, 1943, sec. 1, p. 1; the common charge of ethnic, racial, wartime, and other tensions is captured well throughout Archibald and Camp, and in Mazon, 15–53; Mazon, 9, 14, 26, 34, 53.

81. Dominic J. Capeci, *The Harlem Riot of 1943* (Philadelphia: Temple University Press, 1977), 69, 102.

82. LACCIP, "Minutes of the Sixteenth Meeting, July 1945," 3; LACCIP, "Minutes of the Twentieth Meeting, November 19, 1945," 1–3. For a contrary view that emphasized pluralism, see the excellent article by Philip Gleason, "Americans All: World War II and the Shaping of American Identity," *Review of Politics* 43, no. 4 (1981): 483–519. See also Nelson Lichtenstein, "The Making of the Postwar

Working Class: Cultural Pluralism and Social Structure in World War II," *Historian* 51 (1988): 42–63; Steele, 66–90.

83. LACCIP, "Minutes of the Twentieth Meeting, Nov. 19, 1945, 2.

84. "DeWitt Lists Alien Ouster Exemptions," *SFC*, March 30, 1942, sec. 1, p. 1; Valerie Matsumoto, "Japanese American Women during World War II," *Frontiers* 7, no. 1 (1984): 6–14.

85. LACCIP, "Minutes of the Nineteenth Meeting, Oct.8, 1945," 2–3.

86. LACCIP, "Minutes of the Eighteenth Meeting, Sept. 17, 1945," 2.

87. SFBS, *Journal* 36, March 16, 1942, pp. 401–402.

88. Eiler, 375–76.

89. Archibald, 59–60 and passim; Wilburn, 169; William Martin Camp, *Skip to My Lou* (Garden City, N.Y.: Doubleday, Doran and Co., 1945), 256–63; Zhao, "Women and Defense Industries," 101; McBroome, 94.

90. Mazon, 54–66; Collins, 26.

91. Archibald, 71.

92. Marilynn Johnson, p. 142.

6. War and the Sources of Urban Racial and National Diversity

1. Elliott Barkan, "Sunbelt Immigration" (paper presented to the Miami Conference on the Sunbelt, Nov. 1986).

2. Wollenberg, *Golden Gate Metropolis,* 242–43, 247–50.

3. For example, for the special attributes of Okie culture see Gregory, 139–248.

4. Beth Bailey and David Farber have written that "for most Americans local origin was still an essential part of one's identity." Bailey and Farber, 20–21.

5. In other words, the census asked if one was Mexican, spoke Spanish, had a Spanish name, or was of Spanish origin. I chose Mexican because that was the ethnic group that was most affected by the Second World War.

6. U.S. Bureau of the Census, *U.S. Census of Population: 1960,* Vol. I, Part 6, p. 489.

7. United States Bureau of the Census, *Seventeenth Decennial Census of the United States IV,* "Special Reports: Nativity and Parentage: No-White Population by Race: Persons of Spanish Surnames" (Washington, D.C.: U.S. Government Printing Office, 1953), 3A-71–81.

8. William Hagan, *American Indians* (Chicago: University of Chicago Press, 1961), 158–59.

9. K. Scott Wong, "War Comes to Chinatown: Social Transformation and the Chinese of America," in *The Way We Were: Daily Life in World War II California,* ed. Roger Lotchin (Champaign: University of Illinois Press, 1999) 164–86.

10. United States Department of Commerce, Bureau of the Census, *A Report of the Seventeenth Decennial Census of the United States II,* pt. 5, "California" (Washington, D.C.: U.S. Government Printing Office, 1952), 5–57.

11. Ibid. For the dramatic rise in Oakland and East Bay black populations, see also Marilynn Johnson, 30–59.

12. Marilynn Johnson is one of the few historians who discusses migrants other than minorities. See ibid., 30–60. So did Katherine Archibald, 40–109.

13. Charles Wollenberg correctly characterizes the war migration as a "massive influx of newcomers." See Wollenberg, *Golden Gate Metropolis,* 243.

14. United States Bureau of the Census, *United States Census of Population: 1960,* "Subject: State of Birth" (Washington, D.C.: U.S. Government Printing Office, 1963), 7.

15. Kevin Starr, *The Dream Endures: California Enters the 1940s* (New York: Oxford University Press, 1997), 244–84, 367–96.

16. Mormino and Pozzetta, 42–63; Gleason, 483–518.

17. I have elected to discuss population by decades for several reasons. There were counts between censuses done during the war, which estimated population from 1940 through November 1943 and which estimated it from 1940 to 1945. I have decided not to use these wartime censuses because we have no comparable figures for other decades. I could not compare growth from 1940 to 1945 with that from 1920 to 1930. At the same time, the decade figures for the 1940s would seem to give the transformation hypothesis more than its due. Some of the migrants to California after 1945 may have come because they had served there during the war and wanted to return or because their relatives had lured them out there based on the initial war boom. However, some of the postwar migrants came for other reasons. So using the decade figures gives maximum justice to the transformation hypothesis.

18. Marilynn Johnson, 130–76.

19. United States Bureau of the Census, *United States Census of Population: 1980,* sec. 1, pt. 6, "Characteristics of the Population, California" (Washington, D.C.: U.S. Government Printing Office, 1982), 6–8.

20. Ibid.

21. For a discussion of exurbia, settlements beyond the suburbs, but still tied to cities, see Blaine Brownell and David Goldfield, *Urban America: From Downtown to No Town* (Boston: Houghton Mifflin, 1979), 305, 382–85.

22. For a more extended and tabular discussion of this subject, see Lotchin, "California Cities," 393–420.

23. Walton Bean and James Rawls, *California: An Interpretive History,* 4th ed. (New York: McGraw-Hill, 1983), 364.

24. United States Bureau of the Census, *County Data Book,* 1947 (Washington, D.C.: U.S. Government Printing Office, 1947), 77–90 and passim; Roger W. Lotchin and David Long, "World War II and the Transformation of Southern Urban Society: A Reconsideration," *Georgia Historical Quarterly* 83, no. 1 (1999): 30–57.

7. Urban Economies in a Statist War

1. *Monthly Review,* Feb. 1, 1941, pp. 5–12; Sept. 1, 1941, p. 42; Sept. 1, 1942, pp. 41–43; Sept. 1, 1942, p. 43.

2. For example, "California refineries supply nearly all the petroleum products consumed in the western states, including products required for military operations in the Pacific area." *Monthly Review,* Apr. 1944, p. 15.

3. *Monthly Review,* Jan. 1, 1942, p. 1.

4. *Monthly Review,* Dec. 1, 1942, p. 59.

5. *Monthly Review,* Jan. 1, 1941, p. 1; May 1, 1941, p. 21; Oct. 1, 1941, pp. 49–50; Dec. 1, 1941, Supplement, p. 1.

6. Harold L. Platt, *The Electric City: Energy and the Growth of the Chicago Area, 1880–1930* (Chicago: University of Chicago Press, 1991), 195–97; John B. Rae, *Climb to Greatness: The American Aircraft Industry, 1920–1960* (Cambridge, Mass.: MIT Press, 1968), 1–101, 153–54. Banks continued to finance some operations. *Monthly Review,* Jan. 1, 1943, pp. 1–5.

7. Verge, *Paradise,* 85–106; Wilburn, 58–68, 87–88. Wilburn discussed the issue of airframe profits most comprehensively, including the various payment methods, rapid amortization, excess profits, postwar recapture, purchase of government financed plants, profits to sales, profits to investments, etc. His discussion does not indicate excess wartime profits. Neither does Eiler, 316–25, who believed that the payment practices of World War II, especially renegotiation of contracts, protected the public interest very effectively; *Monthly Review,* Jan. 1943, pp. 1–5; Rae, 142–44, 154–57, 159.

8. *Monthly Review,* Jan. 1942, p. 3; July, 1943, p. 45; Nov. 1945, p. 63; Feb.–March 1944, p. 5; June 1944, p. 26; Jan. 1945, p. 2.

9. Clifford M. Zierer, ed., *California and the Southwest* (New York: John Wiley and Sons, 1956), 294; Wilburn, 49, 54, 70; Gerald D. Nash, *World War II and the West: Reshaping the Economy* (Lincoln: University of Nebraska Press, 1990), 73–74; Rae, 52–53, 146; Verge, *Paradise,* 98; John S. Day, *Subcontracting Policy in the Airframe Industry* (Boston: Division of Research, Graduate School of Business Administration, Harvard University, 1956), 16–24; Senate Special Committee Investigating the National Defense Program, *Hearings Pursuant to S. Res. 55,* 79th Cong., 1st sess., *Hearings* (hereafter Truman Committee), pt. 31, 15460.

10. Wilburn, 50, 52; Rae, 153; Verge, *Paradise,* 100–101, 147–49.

11. Wilburn, 58–59; Verge, *Paradise,* 98–9, 100; Rae, 146; Douglas J. Ingells, *The McDonnell Douglas Story* (Fallbrook, Calif.: Aero Publishers, 1979), 59–81; Lockheed Corporation, *Lockheed Horizons,* Issue 12, *A History of Lockheed* (n.p.: Lockheed Corporation, 1983): 27–37.

12. Truman Committee, pt. 31, 15091–92, 15419, 15443–45, 15450; Rae, 149; *Monthly Review,* Oct.–Nov. 1945, p. 79; Aug.–Sept. 1945, p. 63; July 1945, p. 53; Wilburn, 57.

13. Bruce Catton, *The War Lords of Washington* (New York: Harcourt, Brace and Co., 1948), 304–13; Paul A. C. Koistinen, *The Military-Industrial Complex: A Historical Perspective* (New York: Praeger Publishers, 1980), 70; Carroll W. Pursell Jr., ed., *The Military-Industrial Complex* (New York: Harper and Row, Publishers, 1972), 5–6; Richard J. Barnet, *The Roots of War* (New York: Penguin Books, 1971), 35–37; Verge, *Paradise,* 87. Wilburn, 272, cites figures taken from company annual reports. *Monthly Review,* Jan. 1, 1942, p. 2, cites much higher figures.

14. Rae, 157–61; Stephen B. Adams, *Mr. Kaiser Goes to Washington: The Rise of a Government Entrepreneur* (Chapel Hill: University of North Carolina Press, 1997), 72.

15. *Monthly Review,* June 1, 1942, p. 30; Lotchin, *Fortress California, 1910–1961,* 135; Zierer, 294.

16. Wilburn, 66–68.

17. Samuel Eliot Morison, *The Atlantic Battle Won: May 1943–May 1945*

(Boston: Little, Brown and Co., 1956); Michael Gannon, *Black May* (New York: HarperCollins, Publishers, 1998); Frederic C. Lane, *Ships for Victory: A History of Shipbuilding under the U. S. Maritime Commission in World War II* (Baltimore: Johns Hopkins University Press, 1951), 9; Gerald Nash, *World War II*, 42.

18. *Monthly Review,* Dec. 1944, p. 59; Feb. 1, 1941, p. 5; June 1, 1941, p. 25; Feb. 1, 1942, p. 6; Feb. 1, 1943, p. 10.

19. *Monthly Review,* Dec. 1, 1942, p. 59.

20. Gerald Nash, *World War II*, 50; Lane, 240; Richard Finnie, comp. and ed., *Marinship: The History of a Wartime Shipyard Told by Some of the People Who Helped Build the Ships* (San Francisco: Marinship Corporation, 1947), 304, 312–13.

21. Finnie, 273–84, 301, 303.

22. Lane, 238; Wollenberg, *Marinship,* 29–31; Zhao, "Women and Defense," 59; *Monthly Review,* Dec. 1944, 61–2; Lott, 217; Finnie, 5; Gerald Nash, *World War II*, 52.

23. *Monthly Review,* Nov. 1943, p. 63; Feb.–Mar. 1944, p. 7; Apr. 1944, p. 14; July 1944, p. 29; Dec. 1944, p. 62.

24. Truman Committee, pt. 31, 15091–92; *Monthly Review,* Jan. 1945, p. 3; Jan. 1946, p. 2; Aug.–Sept. 1945, p. 63; Feb.–March 1946, p. 9; Lott, 236.

25. Wollenberg, *Marinship,* 19; *Monthly Review,* July 1945, p. 58; Lane, 5–6, 10, 39.

26. Lane, 34–35, 54, 58–59, 62, 64–66, 276, 618. The Six Companies actually learned their shipbuilding while participating in the Todd-Six Companies venture in shipbuilding in the Tacoma Shipbuilding venture. Mark Foster, *Henry J. Kaiser: Builder in the Modern American West* (Austin: University of Texas Press, 1989), 69; Mitchell, 153.

27. Finnie, 3; Wollenberg, *Marinship,* 23; Richard Prime Boyden, "The San Francisco Machinists from Depression to Cold War, 1930–1950" (Ph.D. dissertation, University of California at Berkeley, 1988), 277.

28. Lott, 217, 235. *Tang* succumbed when one of its own torpedoes reversed course and killed it. *Monthly Review,* Dec. 1944, p. 63.

29. Houlihan, 23; Zhao, "Women and Defense," 242–47. Zhao's discussion of shipbuilding is exemplary.

30. Houlihan, 43; Foster, 72; Verge, *Paradise,* 97; Lott, 214, 220; Finnie, 319.

31. *Monthly Review,* Dec. 1944, pp. 62–63; Lane, 1–3; Gerald Nash, *World War II*, 65–66; Eiler, 316–25; Wollenberg, *Marinship,* 26.

32. *Monthly Review,* May 1944, pp. 19–20.

33. Finnie, 402–403; Lott, 212–15; *Monthly Review,* May 1944, p. 21, put the figure at 25,000.

34. Finnie, 402–403; Houlihan, 1–160.

35. Houlihan, 41, 51, 62.

36. *Monthly Review,* May 1944, p. 21; Zierer, 307.

37. *Monthly Review,* May 1944, p. 21; Wollenberg, *Marinship,* 10.

38. *Monthly Review,* Feb. 1, 1942, p. 7; Dec. 1, 1942, pp. 59–60; Zierer, 300; Foster, 90–92; Lane, 315; Adams, 73.

39. Foster, 95; *Monthly Review,* Nov. 1, 1941, p. 53; May 1944, p. 21; Jan. 1946, p. 3.

40. Foster, 111; Zierer, 301.

41. *Monthly Review,* Sept. 1946, p. 39.

42. *Monthly Review,* Feb.–March 1945, p. 6.

43. *Monthly Review,* June 1, 1941, p. 25; Oct.–Dec. 1946, p. 50; May 1943, p. 31.

44. *Monthly Review,* Oct.–Dec. 1946, 49–51.

45. *Monthly Review,* Feb. 1, 1942, p. 16.

46. *Monthly Review,* Feb.–March 1946, pp. 7–8; Jan. 1946, p. 8.

47. *Monthly Review,* Feb. 1, 1941, p. 5; July 1, 1942, p. 33; Nov. 1, 1942, pp. 54–55; Dec. 1, 1942, p. 60; Wilburn, 69.

48. *Monthly Review,* May 1943, p. 35; Jan. 1945, p. 4; Jan. 1946, p. 3; Jan. 1946, p. 3.

49. *Monthly Review,* March 1, 1941, p. 13.

50. *Monthly Review,* Apr. 1, 1942, p. 20; March 1, 1941, p. 13; March 1, 1942, p. 13.

51. *Monthly Review,* Jan. 1945, p. 1; Verge, *Paradise,* 90.

52. *Monthly Review,* Jan. 1, 1942, p. 1; Verge, 88; Rae, 150–51.

53. Lane, 249, 259–67; Zhao, "Women and Defense," 70; *Monthly Review,* Oct. 1943, pp. 60–61; Aug. 1, 1941, p. 37; Aug. 1, 1942, p. 39; Feb. 1, 1943, p. 12; Dec. 1943, p. 73; Gerald Nash, *World War II,* 76; Wagenet, 1.

54. *Monthly Review,* Sept. 1943, p. 56; Feb. 1, 1943, p. 12, found split shifts; Lichtman, 177–81, argues the reverse; Archibald, 15–39; Verge, *Paradise,* 89; Lichtman, 72–73; Zhao saw the buildup after mid-1943, "Women," 84; Gerald Nash, *World War II,* 77; *Monthly Review,* Nov. 1943, p. 63; Feb.–March 1944, p. 7; March 1945, p. 27; Lane, 257; Lichtman, 85.

55. *Monthly Review,* March 1945, p. 27; Wilburn, 177.

56. *Monthly Review,* Sept. 1943, p. 56.

57. *Monthly Review,* March 1, 1943, p. 18; Rae, 150–51.

58. *Monthly Review,* Sept. 1943, pp. 55–58; Sept. 1943, p. 56.

59. Verge, *Paradise,* 90, 92; Gerald Nash, *World War II,* 77; Lichtman, 78–85, 96, 101–102; *Monthly Review,* Feb.–March 1944, p. 7; Verge, *Paradise,* 90; Eiler, 425–26.

60. *Monthly Review,* Apr. 1, 1942, pp. 17–18, 19–20.

61. Jeffrey E. Geiger, *German Prisoners of War at Camp Cooke, California: Personal Accounts, 1944–1946* (Jefferson, N.C.: McFarland Publishers, 1996), 76; *Monthly Review,* June 1944, p. 25.

62. *Monthly Review,* Feb.–March 1946, pp. 9–10.

63. *Monthly Review,* Apr.–May 1946, pp. 17–18.

64. *Monthly Review,* June–July 1946, pp. 24–25; Zierer, 308, found more skills buildup. For diluting skills in shipbuilding, see Frederic C. Lane's, excellent *Ships for Victory,* 238–41; Gerald Nash, *World War II,* 74–75, points out that even aircraft "design" was deskilled; *Monthly Review,* June–July 1946, pp. 24–25.

65. *Monthly Review,* June–July 1946, pp. 24–25; Oct.–Dec. 1946, p. 47; The war left other cities even more high and dry. In Lowell, Massachusetts, the war propped up a declining textile industry, but at war's end the business continued its long drift into decline; Miller. Lowell's experience reiterates the nonrevolutionary nature of the war's impact. In general, the conflict accelerated, but did not change the direction of, development. See also Neill R. McMillen, *Remaking Dixie: The Impact of World War II on the American South* (Jackson: University Press of Mis-

sissippi, 1997); Lotchin and Long.

66. See the works previously cited by McMillen, Lotchin and Long, Miller, Martha Thomas, and J. R. Hale, as well as Robert G. Spinney, *World War II in Nashville: Transformation of the Homefront* (Knoxville: University of Tennessee Press, 1998), and Alan Clive, *State of War: Michigan in World War II* (Ann Arbor: University of Michigan Press, 1979).

67. Paul Rhode, "The Nash Thesis Revisited: An Economic Historian's View," in *Fortress California at War: San Francisco, Los Angeles, Oakland, and San Diego, 1941–1945*, Roger W. Lotchin, guest ed., Special Issue, *Pacific Historical Review* 63, no. 3 (Aug. 1994): 363–92.

68. U.S. Bureau of the Census, *Statistical Abstract of the United States: 1986*, 106th ed. (Washington: U.S. Government Printing Office, 1986), 750–51; The information in this and succeeding discussions of manufactures is taken from tables compiled from the Bureau of the Census, *Sixteenth Census of the United States: 1940*, "Manufactures, 1939 III, Reports for States and Outlying Areas" (Washington: U.S. Government Printing Office, 1942), 80–127; *Census of Manufactures: 1947*, pt. 3, "Statistics by States" (Washington, D.C.: USGPO, 1950), 89–118.

69. Gerald Nash, *World War II*, 191.

70. U.S. Department of Transportation, *Highway Statistics: Summary to 1965* (Washington: U.S. Government Printing Office, 1967), 49.

71. Gerald Nash, *World War II*, 90.

72. Rae, 161–67; Theodor von Karman, with Lee Edson, *The Wind and Beyond: Theodore Von Karman: Pioneer in Aviation and Pathfinder in Space* (Boston: Little, Brown, 1967), 104; Truman Committee, pt. 31, 15580.

73. Truman Committee, pt. 31, 125437–38, 15396–418, 15436, 15578–614.

74. Nelson Lichtenstein, *Labor's War at Home: The CIO in World War II* (Cambridge: Cambridge University Press, 1982), 133; Lichtenstein, " Making of Postwar Working Class," 43. The discussion of strikes is based on California Division of Labor Statistics and Research, *Handbook of California Labor Statistics, 1949–50* (San Francisco: California State Printing Office, 1951), 82.

75. Boyden, 211; Truman Committee, pt. 4, 1121–251.

76. James R. Prickett, "Communist Conspiracy or Wage Dispute?: The 1941 Strike at North American Aviation," *Pacific Historical Review* 50, no. 2 (1981): 215–33; Boyden, 211; Torigian, 409–32; William Issel and James Collins, "The Catholic Church and Organized Labor in San Francisco, 1932–1958," *Records of the American Catholic Historical Society* 109, nos. 1 and 2 (1999): 81–112; Bridges's denial that he was a communist and his struggle to avoid deportation are well known. Recent discoveries in the Russian Archives document that he was indeed a member of the Communist Party U.S.A. Central Committee, at a time when the party was a Stalinist institution.

77. State of California, Div. of Labor, Statistics and Law Enforcement, *Labor in California, 1949–50* (Sacramento), 79; *1945–46*, 59.

78. Wilburn, 114–30, 137–38.

79. *Labor in California, 1945–46*, 52.

80. Wilburn, 132–35; Hugh Rockoff, "Indirect Price Increases and Real Wages during World War II," *Explorations in Economic History* 15, no. 4 (1978): 407–20.

81. *Labor in California, 1945–46*, 31, 44–45; *1949–50*, 50.

82. State of California, Div. of Labor, Statistics and Law Enforcement, *Labor in California, 1939–40,* (Sacramento), 12; *1949–50,* 20, 88–97.

83. *Labor in California, 1945–46,* 58–66; *Labor In California, 1949–50,* 79. United States Bureau of the Census, *United States Census of Population: 1950,* sec. 2, pt. 5, "California," 5–51.

84. Lane, 244–46.

85. Wilburn, 120; Lane, 287–310; Lichtman, 158–88.

86. *Labor in California, 1943–44,* 91.

87. Zierer, 308.

8. Government I

1. See Richard Lowitt, *The New Deal in the West* (Bloomington: Indiana University Press, 1984), 218–28.

2. *SFC,* June 1, 1943, sec. 1, p. 3.

3. John Anson Ford, "Comments on the Governmental Maze in Los Angeles County," Jan. 13, 1944, Ford Papers.

4. Vatter, 67–88, 170, is an excellent overall treatment of the economics of war; Arnold R. Hirsch, *Making the Second Ghetto: Race and Housing in Chicago, 1940–1960* (Cambridge: Cambridge University Press, 1983), 212–58; Marilynn Johnson, 83–112; Professor Johnson first applied the World War I phrase "Western Front" to the Second World War in California.

5. Kenneth T. Jackson, *Crabgrass Frontier: The Suburbanization of the United States* (New York: Oxford University Press, 1985).

6. John Morton Blum, *V Was for Victory: Politics and American Culture during World War II* (New York: Harcourt Brace Jovanovich, 1976), 230; "Federal Court Award Will Be Appealed," *LBPT,* May 8, 1943, sec. B, p. 1; *Congested Areas,* 494–96.

7. Verge, *Paradise,* 88, 118–19.

8. "Health Board Warns Public [of beach quarantine]" *LAT,* Dec. 7, 1942, sec. 2, p. 1; "The Taming of the Influent," *American City,* Jan. 1944, 52–53.

9. John Anson Ford, "Comments on Governmental Maze in Los Angeles County," Jan. 13, 1944, Ford Papers; Fletcher Bowron, radio addresses, KECA Los Angeles, Feb. 14, 1943 and July 14, 1943, speeches 10 and 11; Bowron to unnamed, Sept. 22, 1943, Bowron Papers.

10. "Civic Cooperation for Community Development," *Downtowner,* June 13, 1945, pp. 1–2; California Reconstruction and Reemployment Commission, "Richmond, California: A City Earns the Purple Heart," 6–9; City of Vallejo, Builders of the West, "Master Plan," Sept. 14, 1945, II-17.

11. "Warren Favors Deferment for City Employes [*sic*]," *LBPT,* May 10, 1944, sec. B, p. 3; Spinney, 148.

12. Thomas W. Hanchett, "Roots of the 'Renaissance': Federal Incentives to Urban Planning, 1941–1948," in *Planning the Twentieth-Century American City,* ed. Mary Corbin Sies and Christopher Silver (Baltimore: Johns Hopkins University Press, 1996), 305–30.

13. "Seven Million Increase in County Budget Proposed," *LAT,* May 2, 1945, sec. 2, p. 1; City and County of San Francisco, Citizens' Post War Planning Com-

mittee, "Report of the Subcommittee on Revenue and Taxation to the Citizens' Post War Planning Committee," June 15, 1945, 11–14.

14. "County Budget Tales Show Larger Requests," *LAT*, May 24, 1941, sec. 1, p. 11; "Seven Million Increase in County Budget Proposed," *LAT*, May 2, 1945, sec. 2, p. 1; "County Budget Cut $3,745,141 after Protests," *LAT*, June 8, 1948, sec. 1, p. 1.

15. Bureau of the Census, "San Francisco City Government Finances in 1945," *City Finances* 1, no. 10 (1945): 396–407; "Los Angeles City Government Finances in 1945," *City Finances* 1, no. 3 (1945): 192–204; "Oakland City Government Finances in 1945," *City Finances* 1, no. 19 (1945): 288–300.

16. Shragge, 486–555. I employed the "no more than" construction because *City Finances* rarely breaks down the "Contributions From Other Governments" category beyond specifying the amounts received from the state. The remainder, which includes federal contributions, is usually simply labeled "Other," which can include revenues from other governments such as county, district, cities besides that of the federal government.

17. John J. Gunther, *Federal-City Relations in the United States: The Role of the Mayors in Federal Aid to Cities* (Newark: University of Delaware Press, 1990), 133–44.

18. *Congested Areas*, 87, 1777–80, 1899–1901.

19. Bureau of the Census, *Historical Statistics of the United States: Colonial Times to 1970* (Washington, D.C.: U.S. Government Printing Office, 1970), 1117; Blum, 228–42; Henry C. Binford, *The First Suburbs: Residential Communities on the Boston Periphery, 1815–1860* (Chicago: University of Chicago Press, 1985), 223; U.S. Bureau of the Census, "Los Angeles City Government Finances in 1945," *City Finances* 1, no. 3 (1945): 192–93; "Oakland City Government Finances in 1945," *City Finances* 1, no. 19 (1945): 288–300; "San Francisco City Government Finances in 1945," *City Finances* 1, no. 10 (1945): 396–408.

20. That is true as recently as John Gunther's 1990 book, which discussed the mayors and the attempt to get federal funds, but not the impact of the war on cities. A recent book describes the relationship between state and federal governments as a competition rather than a partnership. That would seem a realistic way to describe a good part of the World War II relationship of city and national governments as well. See Thomas R. Dye, *American Federalism: Competition among Governments* (Lexington, Mass.: Lexington Books, 1990).

21. Editorial, "SF Will Not Have to Walk," *SFC*, Jan. 30, 1942, sec. 2, p. 14.

22. Shragge, 513–14; SFBS, *Journal* 38, Feb. 15, 1943, pp. 352–53; 37, Nov. 2, 1942, pp. 2468–69; 38, Feb. 8, 1943, p. 291; Mellier Scott, *The San Francisco Bay Area: A Metropolis in Perspective* (Berkeley: University of California Press, 1959), 250; "Solution Near for Problems of Commuter," *SFC*, Feb. 3, 1942, sec. 1, p. 11; "Defense Bottleneck: Committee to Untangle Local Transit Problems," Mar. 29, 1942, sec. 1, p. 12.

23. Ray Leavitt, "Supervisors: One-Way Street Plan, New Parking Restrictions Are Supported," *SFC*, May 5, 1942, sec. 1, p. 24; Leavitt, "Traffic: Down Town Group Urges Building 'Freeways,'" Feb. 20, 1942, sec. 1, p. 24.

24. "Bay Defense Workers' Transit Crisis," *SFC*, Mar. 21, 1942, sec. 1, p. 1; "Defense Bottleneck," March 29, 1942, sec. 1, p. 12; "Transportation: U.S. Urges Defense Workers to Swap Rides and Thus Save Tires," May 1, 1942, sec. 1, p. 14;

"Transportation: ODT Calls June First Meeting to Iron Our S. F. Traffic Problems," May 2, 1942, sec. 1, p. 4; *Congested Areas,* 497–98.

25. Alonzo Smith, 28; *Congested Areas,* pt. 3, 682; "Strike Cuts Transbay Bus Service," *SFC,* March 14, 1942, sec. 1, p. 1; editorial, "Speed and More Speed," May 13, 1942, sec. 1, p. 12; "Transit Crisis Postponed at Suggestion of Federal Conciliator," May 10, 1942, sec. 1, p. 1; "The Woman's Place Is in the War . . . Ban Is Lifted Municipal Railway Jobs," May 14, 1942, sec. 1, p. 1; Betty Turner, "Muni Conductoress: 2 Gongs Make a Dime . . . I Mean 'Go'—We Made It, Nobody Hurt," May 15, 1941, sec. 1, p. 15; SFBS, *Journal* 37, June 22, 1942, p. 22.

26. Much of the transportation crisis can be followed in *Congested Areas,* pt. 3, 968–73, 915–19, 782–83; pt. 2, 561–67, 443–45, 449–53; pt. 8, 1043–50.

27. The denouement of the transit crisis can be followed through the mayors' annual reports in the *Journal* and through the newspapers. See SFBS, *Journal* 34, June 8, 1942, pp. 1323–47; 35, June 22, 1942, pp. 1468–97; 38, Jan. 25, 1943, pp. 142–45; 39, Jan. 3, 1944, pp. 48–52; 50, Jan. 2, 1945, pp. 128–31; "San Francisco Will Not Have to Walk," *SFC,* Jan. 30. 1942, sec. 2, p. 14; "Railway Merger Market Line Receptive to Proposed Discussion of Lease Plan," May 3, 1942, sec. 1, p. 13; "Street Car Fares: Chamber of Commerce Asks about Uniform Transfer System," Apr. 18, 1942, sec. 1, p. 9.

28. Scott L. Bottles, *Los Angeles and the Automobile: The Making of the Modern City* (Los Angeles: University of California Press, 1987), 1–21; Alonzo Smith, 29–28; "How Long Will Our Patience Last?," "For Million Tram Riders Pay Issue Still Undecided," "Little Hope Seen for Strike End at Long Beach," *LAT,* May 7, 1944, sec. 1, pp. 1, 6; sec. 2, p. 4.

29. Bottles, 240–42.

30. *Congested Areas,* 1783–84, 1915–16; Bottles, 236–39; Marilynn Johnson, 99, 110, 145, 212.

31. *Congested Areas,* pt. 2, 561–67.

32. Ibid., 567.

33. Ibid., 1915–16, 561, 563, 783, 804, 932. The hearings gave two different figures, 400 percent and 500 percent. I relied on the figure given by the general manager of the San Diego electric system.

34. San Francisco, "Mayor's Annual Message," 1944, 57.

35. *Congested Areas,* 1874–87, 1966–70.

36. Peace Officers Association of the State of California, *Proc.,* 1942, p. 50; SFBS, *Journal* 40, Jan. 2, 1945, p. 53; U.S. Congress, Senate, Special Committee Investigating the National Defense Program, *Investigation of the National Defense Program: Hearings before a Special Committee Investigating the National Defense Program, Pursuant to S. Res. 71,* 77th Cong., 1st sess., 1941, pt. 6, 1813–25, 1828–32. The problem of undermanning arose before the war began. *Congested Areas,* pt. 2, 492–96, 404–15; pt. 3, 676–71, 759–70, 817–25, 870–80; pt. 8, 1811, 1837, 1863. The police manpower shortage is especially difficult to judge. On the one hand, mayors, police chiefs, and city officials bemoaned the loss of manpower to war industry and military services, but on the other hand, their own figures often show that they kept up with the losses. As will be seen below, San Diego actually gained 50 percent more men during the war and the Los Angeles department, despite the protests of the Fletcher Bowron, reported a slight gain in strength over the years 1941–1945. The force in that department advanced modestly every year

from 3,162 in 1941 to 3,335 in 1945, a 5 percent increase, counting both officers and civilian employees. Yet all public officials complained of a labor shortage in their departments. At this point it is impossible to determine if the figures for the Los Angeles department represent the actual numbers of active men and women or the authorized, but not realized, strength of the department. Los Angeles Police Department, *Annual Report*, p. 1.

37. POASC, *Proc.*, 28–29; *Congested Areas*, pt. 8, 776–82.

38. *Congested Areas*, 776–82, 21–24.

39. POASC, *Proc.*, 24–27, 28–29; *Congested Areas*, 871, 777.

40. *Congested Areas*, 677.

41. POASC, *Proc.*, 29, 32, 37; *Congested Areas*, pt. 3, 677.

42. POASC, *Proc.*, 36; *Congested Areas*, pt. 8, 1770–1773.

43. SFBS, *Journal* 39, Jan. 3, 1941, p. 42; 40, Jan. 2, 1945, p. 53.

44. SFBS, *Journal* 40, Jan. 2, 1945, pp. 53–54; 38, Jan. 25, 1945, pp. 136–37; POASC, *Proceedings*, 54–56. Historical crime statistics are notoriously treacherous, but for whatever it is worth, Los Angeles crime statistics, the most complete at my disposal, documented an overall rise of 9 percent in total crimes between 1940 and 1945. However, many types of violent crimes rose much more substantially—rape, 42 percent; felonious assault, 61 percent; murder, 26 percent. Crimes against property rose, too—robbery, 45 percent; grand theft, 69 percent; burglary, 21 percent. Petty theft (the most prevalent crime by a great deal), which rose by 21 percent, largely explains the modest overall rise of crime. On the other hand, traffic fatalities declined by 9 percent, which in absolute terms about equaled the added number of murders. Successful suicides declined 9 percent, while attempted suicides rose 13 percent. The overall danger of violent death through traffic fatalities, suicide, and murder declined. Thirty-two fewer people died of suicide; thirty-five fewer died in traffic accidents; and even though thirty-four more died of murder, there was a fall of just under 10 percent. If one leaves out suicides, the net decline of violent deaths due to accidents and murder is exactly one person. So the war made petty property safer, major property a lot less safe, persons a lot less secure from assault, women vastly more vulnerable to rape, and everyone a trifle less apt to suffer a violent death. Petty theft and loss of life, the two extremes of the crime spectrum, became less likely and everything in between more so. Los Angeles Police Department, *Annual Report* for 1945, 7, 13, 16, 18, and 20. No radical change here.

45. "Military Personnel Crime: Records Show Rise of Menace," *LAT*, Jan. 19, 1945, sec. 2, p. 1; "Curfew Cooperation," *SDU*, Oct. 15, 1943, sec. B, p. 2; "New Curfew Law Won't Hamper Proper Errands," Oct. 17, 1943, sec. B, p. 1; "National City Curfew Voted," Nov. 3, 1943, sec. A, p. 1.

46. Richard Donovan, "Gambling Joint: To the Click of Dice a City's Furtive Backroom Miniatures Come Alive," *SFC*, Jan. 22, 1942, sec. 2, p. 22; "Law Drawn Up to Put Ban on S.D. Cardrooms," *SDU*, Feb. 5, 1944, sec. A, p. 1; "Council Orders Cardroom Ban," Feb. 2, 1944, sec. A, p. 1; "Council Delays Cardroom Vote Another Week," Feb. 9, 1944, sec. A, p. 1; "Cardroom Ban Passed, 4 to 3," *SDU*, sec. A, p. 1; "Move to Block City's Ban on Cardrooms Shows Gain," *SDU*, sec. B, p. 1; "Actions Block Effectuation of Ordinance," *SDU*, March 24, 1944, sec. B, p. 1.

47. *Congested Areas*, 404; Bailey and Farber, 95–132, 108.

48. *Congested Areas,* 407–409.

49. *Congested Areas,* 599–605, 520–22.

50. *Congested Areas,* 676–71, 692–96.

51. San Francisco District Attorney (Edmund G. Brown), "Report of the Crime Prevention Department for 1944," 1–13.

52. Ibid.

53. Ibid.

54. Ibid.

55. Ibid.

56. *Congested Areas,* 1096; pt. 2, 492–96.

57. "Riots and Looting Mark Bay City's Celebration," *LAT,* Aug. 16, 1945, sec. 1, p. 8; "Celebration—Five Dead, 624 Injured," *SFC,* Aug. 16, 1945, sec. 1, p. 11; "'Peace' Rioting—11 S.F. Fatalities," Aug. 17, 1945, sec. 1, p. 1; *Congested Areas,* pt. 2, 423–30.

9. Government II

1. *Congested Areas,* pt. 3, 826–31.

2. *Congested Areas,* pt. 3, 1920–23.

3. SFBS, *Journal* 40, Jan. 2, 1945, pp. 57–61; Gerald Nash, *American West,* 98–99.

4. SFBS, *Journal* 40, Jan. 2, 1945, p. 150.

5. Ibid., pp. 18, 151; City of Vallejo, Builders of the West, *Master Plan,* Sept. 14, 1945, pt. IV, p. 6; *Congested Areas,* pt. 3, 841–53, 833–34, 1025; pt. 2, 530–35.

6. *Congested Areas,* pt. 8, 1971–79. The calculation of war housing units is complicated by the fact that federal authorities presented lower statistics than the local ones. See *Congested Areas,* pt. 3, 945–57. Wherever possible I have used the figures presented by the local people responsible for the daily management of the housing, on the assumption that they had greater familiarity with the situation than federal officials, in the Bay Area, the Southland, or Washington. Where one set of numbers survives, I have accepted that source.

7. *Congested Areas,* pt. 3, 945–57.

8. Vallejo, *Master Plan,* pt. 1, p. 17; Ray Leavitt, "Supervisors Study Project in Chinatown," *SFC,* March 6, 1942, sec. 1, p. 6. The San Francisco Chinatown housing project to spend $1.5 million for 232 units was one of those scrubbed.

9. E. P. Conser, Secretary-Manager, Apartment Association of Los Angeles County, Inc., to the Los Angeles Board of Supervisors, Oct. 9, 1945; Speech by Langdon W. Post, Regional Director of the Federal Public Housing Authority, before the Democratic Luncheon Club at Hotel Rosslyn, Los Angeles, Sept. 20, 1945, Ford Papers. Floyd Mashburn of the AFL building trades estimated that by early 1945, construction costs in the L.A. area had doubled. See his comments in Memo of Arthur F. Miley to Ford, Jan. 7, 1945, Ford Papers; *Congested Areas,* pt. 2, 593–97, 908–15.

10. *Congested Areas,* pt. 8, 1891–96, 1831–35; pt. 2, 568–72, 593–98; pt. 3, 9, 30–31; editorial, "Rent Profiteering," *SDU,* May 4, 1942, sec. B, p. 2; editorial,

"We Have Enough Rent Control," *LAT,* May 29, 1945, sec. 2, p. 4; SFBS, *Journal* 40, Jan. 11, 1945, pp. 76–77; 38, Aug. 2, 1943, pp. 1846–47.

11. A. H. Campion, to Ford, Jan. 27, 1944, Ford Papers.

12. *Congested Areas,* pt. 3, 927–28.

13. Jane Jacobs, *The Economy of Cities* (New York: Random House, 1969), 107–17; SFBS, *Journal* 40, Jan. 2, 1945, p. 10; 38, Aug. 2, 1943, pp. 1845–57; *Congested Areas,* pt. 3, 661–65.

14. *Congested Areas,* pt. 3, 768; *Congested Areas,* pt. 2, 508, 510; S.F. Civilian War Council, "Bulletin for Feb. 28, 1944," 1.

15. *Congested Areas,* pt. 3, 440–42; descriptions of the housing shortage can be found in LACCIP, "The Housing Crisis in Los Angeles County, April 1, 1945," 1–2; S.F. Planning and Housing Assn., "A Report on the Japanese Section," July 23, 1943, pp. 1–2; "Bay Area Needs Increased Housing," *Downtowner,* Feb. 24, 1943, p. 2; California Housing and Planning Assn., "Minutes of the Fresno Meeting," Apr. 11, 1942, p. 4; SFBS, *Journal* 37, Dec. 14, 1942, pp. 2693–94.

16. Memo from the Right Reverend Thomas J. O' Dwyer, President Los Angeles Citizens Housing Council, Ford Papers.

17. John Rickards Betts, Helen Meller, Dale Somers, Harold Seymour, David Q. Voights, Foster Rhea Dulles, Eugen Weber, Stephen Wiess, Melvin Adelman, and Geoffrey Perrett, *Days of Sadness,* 237–46, 379–97.

18. SFBS, *Journal* 39, Jan. 3, 1944, p. 59.

19. *Congested Areas,* pt. 8, 1912; "S.D. One of Six Ports Open for Sports Fishing," *SDU,* Feb. 3, 1942, sec. A, p. 3; "No Business: Hollywood Night Spot Folds as Result of War," *SFC* Jan. 14, 1942, sec. 1, p. 9; "Transportation for Vacations Won't Be Best," June 9, 1942, sec. 1, p. 19; "Sightseeing Tours Are Banned," May 22, 1942, sec. 1, p. 11; "'Ban Enemy Music,'" March 5, 1942, sec. 1, p. 6.

20. For the way curtailment of the auto encouraged a greater use of the parks, see the mayor's annual report. SFBS, *Journal* 40, Jan. 2, 1945, pp. 63–73.

21. Herb Caen, "It's News to Me: What Is New Year's Eve?," *SFC,* Jan. 2, 1942, sec. 1, p. 11; "Box-Office Boom Hits San Diego Movie Houses," *SDU,* Sept. 12, 1942, sec. A, p. 7; Joe Knefler, "Arcade 'Arts' Flourish: Galleries "Catch-all" for Boys on Leave," Jan. 2, 1944, sec. B, p. 1.

22. *Congested Areas,* pt. 3, 379; Long Beach, Recreation Commission, "Annual Report, 1940–41," 1–4; "Annual Report, 1942–43," 1–2; San Diego, Department of Playgrounds and Recreation, "Annual Report, 1940–1941," 1–2; *Congested Areas,* pt. 8, 1910–14.

23. SFBS, *Journal* 39, Jan. 3, 1944, pp. 59–71; 40, Jan. 2, 1945, pp. 63–73.

24. SFBS, *Journal* 39, Jan. 3, 1944, pp. 59–71; 40, Jan. 2, 1945, pp. 63–73.

25. SFBS, *Journal* 39, Jan. 3, 1944, pp. 9–71; 40, Jan. 2, 1945, pp. 63–73; *Congested Areas,* pt. 3, 696–98.

26. *Congested Areas,* pt. 8, 1910–14; "Orchestra Unit, Vocalists in Music Week Concert," *LBPT,* May 14, 1943, sec. A, p. 12; "City to Seek $500,000 for Beach Funds," May 4, 1943, sec. B, p. 1; *Congested Areas,* pt. 8, 732.

27. "And a Dance, Too," *SFC,* Nov. 17, 1941, sec. 2, p. 5.

28. *Congested Areas,* pt. 3, 882–84, 731.

29. "Schools as Rationing Centers," *SFC,* Feb. 27, 1942, sec. 1, p. 1; SFBS, *Journal* 39, Jan. 3, 1944, pp. 41–42.

30. *Congested Areas,* pt. 3, 789; SFBS, *Journal* 39, Jan. 3, 1944, pp. 40–42; 40, Jan. 2, 1945, pp. 136–46; "Schoolboys to Learn Shipfitting," *SFC,* May 9, 1942, sec. 1, p. 5; "10,018 Trained for War Work," *SDU,* Apr. 10, 1942, sec. A, p. 6; "Los Angeles School Board Drafts Student Labor Plan," Sept. 5, 1942, sec. A, p. 2; "Schools Open All Year," *LBPT,* May 5, 1943, p. B4.

31. SFBS, *Journal* 39, Jan. 3, 1944, pp. 41–42; 40, Jan. 2, 1944, pp. 136–46.

32. "Many Students Taking Part in Wartime Projects," *SDU,* Jan. 20, 1942, sec. B, p. 1; "Youth Army: Crack ROTC Units Put on a Spectacular Show at Kezar Stadium," *SFC,* June 11, 1942, sec. 1, p. 5.

33. "Los Angeles City School District Indexes," *SCB* 6, no. 26 (July 10, 1944): 3; SFBS, *Journal* 36, May 29, 1941, p. 1053 (budget for 1941–42); 39, June 1, 1944, p. 1276 (budget for 1944–45); "New Welding School to Open in Oakland," *SFC,* Nov. 11, 1941, sec. 1, p. 16; "S.D. Vocational School Ready for 7–Day Week," *SDU,* Dec. 29, 1941, sec. B, p. 1.

34. Perrett, 369–78.

35. The *SFC* carried the Rugg controversy almost day to day. Milton Silverman, "Education in S.F.: Debate on Textbook Ban Grows into Fight over Who Shall Control Schools," *SFC,* sec. 1, p. 1; "School Dispute: Board Calls for a Recess, Waits Written Testimony," June 18, 1942, sec. 1, p. 6; editorial, "Professor Rugg's Books," sec. 1, p. 14; "Books," June 19, 1942, sec. 1, p. 14; "Textbook Dispute: Objectors Quote Allegedly 'Subversive' Passages; Teachers Adamant," June 19, 1942, sec. 1, p. 1; "Rugg Textbooks; Pupils Prove Our Side of the Controversy, City's Teachers Say," June 20, 1942, sec. 1, p. 1; "The Textbook Dispute: Leaders of School System Denounce Attempts to Assist in Selections," June 21, 1942, sec. 1, p. 4; "Dictating Minorities Are Attacked," June 24, 1942, sec. 1, p. 1; "Textbooks," Teachings," "Rugg," June 24, 1942, sec. 1, p. 14.

36. "Textbook Dispute: Objectors Quote Allegedly 'Subversive' Passages; Teachers Adamant," *SFC,* June 19, 1942, sec. 1, p. 1.

37. "Board Passes the Buck on Rugg Books," *SFC,* July 29, 1942, sec. 1, p. 1.

38. *Congested Areas,* pt. 2, 538–40.

39. *Congested Areas,* pt. 3, 1063.

40. *Congested Areas,* pt. 3, 789–93.

41. *Congested Areas,* pt. 3, 886, 921–27.

42. *Congested Areas,* pt. 3, 991, 432, 654, 605, 1821, 1818–20.

43. *Congested Areas,* pt. 2, 453–55, 659, 1774.

44. Shragge, 513–38; *Congested Areas,* pt. 3, 657.

45. *Congested Areas,* pt. 2, 432; pt. 3, 789, 1773–77; pt. 8, 1819, 1777–80. On the other hand, the war was a national responsibility and not a state one.

46. *Congested Areas,* pt. 3, 1823–27, 832; pt. 2, 535–38, 609, 1820.

Conclusion

1. Josef W. Konvitz, *The Urban Millennium: The City-Building Process from the Early Middle Ages to the Present* (Carbondale: Southern Illinois University Press, 1985), 167–87.

2. After the war, city boosters crafted a large-scale program of public works,

which the public largely accepted, and therefore resumed its normal expansionary progress.

3. Given its defense importance, the aircraft industry remained an exception to this rule.

SELECTED
BIBLIOGRAPHY

Books

Abbott, Carl. *The New Urban America: Growth and Politics in Sunbelt Cities.* Chapel Hill: University of North Carolina Press, 1981.

Adams, Stephen B. *Mr. Kaiser Goes to Washington: The Rise of a Government Entrepreneur.* Chapel Hill: University of North Carolina Press, 1997.

Adelman, Melvin L. *A Sporting Time: New York City and the Rise of Modern Athletics, 1820–1870.* Urbana: University of Illinois Press, 1986.

Ambrose, Stephen. *D-Day, June 6, 1944: Climactic Battle of World War II.* New York: Simon and Schuster, 1994.

Anderson, E. Frederick. *The Development of Leadership and Organization Building in the Black Community of Los Angeles from 1900 through World War II.* Los Angeles: Century Twenty One Publishing, 1980.

Anderson, Karen. *Wartime Women: Sex Roles, Family Relations, and the Status of Women during World War II.* Westport, Conn.: Greenwood Press, 1981.

Archibald, Katherine. *Wartime Shipyard: A Study in Social Disunity.* Berkeley: University of California Press, 1947.

Bailey, Beth, and David Farber. *The First Strange Place: The Alchemy of Race and Sex in World War II Hawaii.* New York: Free Press, 1992.

Barnet, Richard J. *The Roots of War.* New York: Penguin Books, 1971.

Bean, Walton, and James Rawls. *California: An Interpretive History.* 4th ed. New York: McGraw-Hill, 1983.

Bender, Thomas. *Toward an Urban Vision: Ideas and Institutions in Nineteenth Century America.* Baltimore: Johns Hopkins University Press, 1975.

Bendiner, Elmer. *The Fall of Fortresses: A Personal Account of the Most Daring—and Deadly—American Air Battles of World War II.* New York: G. P. Putnam's Sons, 1980.

Bernard, Richard M., and Bradley R. Rice. *Sunbelt Cities: Politics and Growth since World War II.* Austin: University of Texas Press, 1983.

Betts, John Rickards. *America's Sporting Heritage.* Reading, Mass.: Addison Wesley, 1974.

Binford, Henry C. *The First Suburbs: Residential Communities on the Boston Periphery, 1815–1860.* Chicago: University of Chicago Press, 1985.

Blackford, Mansel. *The Lost Dream: Businessmen and City Planning on the Pacific Coast, 1890–1920.* Columbus: Ohio State University Press, 1993.

Blum, John Morton. *V Was for Victory: Politics and American Culture during World War II.* New York: Harcourt Brace Jovanovich, 1976.

Bosworth, Allan R. *America's Concentration Camps.* New York: W. W Norton, 1967.

Bottles, Scott L. *Los Angeles and the Automobile: The Making of the Modern City.* Los Angeles: University of California Press, 1987.

Boyer, Paul. *Urban Masses and Moral Order in America, 1820–1920.* Cambridge, Mass.: Harvard University Press, 1978.

Braverman, Jordan. *To Hasten the Homecoming: How Americans Fought World War II through the Media.* New York: Madison Books, 1996.

Broussard, Albert. *Black San Francisco: The Struggle for Racial Equality in the West, 1900–1954.* Lawrence: University Press of Kansas, 1993.

Brownell, Blaine, and David Goldfield. *Urban America: From Downtown to No Town.* Boston: Houghton Mifflin, 1979.

Buchanan, A. Russell. *Black Americans in World War II.* Santa Barbara: Clio Books, 1977.

Camp, William Martin. *Skip to My Lou.* Garden City, N. Y.: Doubleday, Doran and Co., 1945.

Campbell, D'Ann. *Women at War with America: Private Lives in a Patriotic Era.* Cambridge: Harvard University Press, 1984.

Capeci, Dominic J. *The Harlem Riot of 1943.* Philadelphia: Temple University Press, 1977.

Casdorph, Paul D. *Let the Good Times Roll: Life at Home in America during World War II.* New York: Paragon House, 1989.

Catton, Bruce. *The War Lords of Washington.* New York: Harcourt, Brace and Co., 1948.

Caughey, John, and Laree Caughey, eds. *Los Angeles: Biography of a City.* Berkeley: University of California Press, 1976.

Chafe, William. *The American Woman: Her Changing Social, Economic, and Political Roles, 1920–1970.* New York: Oxford University Press, 1972.

Chang, Iris. *The Rape of Nanking: The Forgotten Holocaust of World War II.* New York: Basic Books, 1997.

Chin, Brian B. *Artillery at the Golden Gate: The Harbor Defenses of San Francisco in World War II.* Missoula, Mont.: Pictorial Histories Publishing Co., 1994.

Clive, Alan. *State of War: Michigan in World War II.* Ann Arbor: University of Michigan Press, 1979.

Collins, Keith. *Black Los Angeles: The Maturing of the Ghetto, 1940–1950.* Saratoga, Calif.: Century Twenty One Publishing, 1980.

Crawford, Richard, ed. *War Comes to San Diego.* Special Edition on World War. *The Journal of San Diego History* 39, no. 1–2 (1993).

Davis, Margaret Leslie. *Rivers in the Desert: William Mulholland and the Inventing of Los Angeles.* New York: HarperCollins Publishers, 1993.

Davis, Susan. *Parades and Power: Street Theatre in Nineteenth Century Philadelphia.* Philadelphia: Temple University Press, 1986.

Day, John S. *Subcontracting Policy in the Airframe Industry.* Boston: Division of Research, Graduate School of Business Administration, Harvard University, 1956.

D'Este, Carlo. *Patton: A Genius for War.* New York: Harper Perennial, 1995.

Doolittle, James H., and Carroll V. Glines. *I Could Never Be So Lucky Again: An Autobiography.* New York: Bantam Books, 1991.

Duis, Perry, and Scott La France. *We've Got a Job to Do: Chicagoans and World War II.* Chicago: Chicago Historical Society, 1992.

Dulles, Foster Rhea. *The American Red Cross: A History.* New York: Harper and Brothers, 1950.

————. *A History of Recreation: America Learns to Play.* New York: Appleton-Century-Crofts, 1965.

Dye, Thomas R. *American Federalism: Competition among Governments.* Lexington, Mass.: Lexington Books, 1990.

Eiler, Keith E. *Mobilizing America: Robert P. Patterson and the War Effort, 1940–1945.* Ithaca: Cornell University Press, 1997.

Farwell, Willard. *The Chinese at Home and Abroad Together with the Report of the Special Committee of the Board of Supervisors of San Francisco, on the Condition of the Chinese Quarter of that City.* San Francisco: A. L. Bancroft and Co., 1885.

Finnie, Richard, comp. and ed. *Marinship: The History of a Wartime Shipyard Told by Some of the People Who Helped Build the Ships.* San Francisco: Marinship Corporation, 1947.

Flynn, George Q. *The Draft, 1940–1973.* Lawrence: University of Kansas Press, 1993.

Foote, Shelby. *The Civil War: A Narrative.* Vol. 2: *From Fredericksburg to Meridian;* Vol. 3: *From Red River to Appomattox.* New York: Random House, 1963, 1974.

Foster, Mark. *Henry J. Kaiser: Builder in the Modern American West.* Austin: University of Texas Press, 1989.

Fox, Stephen. *The Unknown Internment: An Oral History of the Relocation of Italian Americans during World War II.* Boston: Twayne Publishers, 1990.

Gannon, Michael. *Black May.* New York: HarperCollins Publishers, 1998.

Geiger, Jeffrey E. *German Prisoners of War at Camp Cooke, California: Personal Accounts, 1944–1946.* Jefferson, N.C.: McFarland Publishers, 1996.

Gluck, Sherna Berger, ed. *Rosie The Riveter Revisited: Women, the War, and Social Change.* Boston: Twayne Publishers, 1987.

Gregory, James N. *American Exodus: The Dust Bowl Migration and Okie Culture in California.* New York: Oxford University Press, 1989.

Gunther, John J. *Federal-City Relations in the United States: The Role of the Mayors in Federal Aid to Cities.* Newark: University of Delaware Press, 1990.

Hagan, William. *American Indians.* Chicago: University of Chicago Press, 1961.

Hale, J. R. *War and Society in Renaissance Europe, 1450–1620.* Baltimore: Johns Hopkins University Press, 1985.

Hartmann, Susan. *The Home Front and Beyond: American Women in the 1940s.* Boston: Twayne Publishers, 1982.

Hirsch, Arnold R. *Making the Second Ghetto: Race and Housing in Chicago, 1940–1960.* Cambridge: Cambridge University Press, 1983.

Hosokawa, Bill. *Nisei: The Quiet Americans.* New York: William Morrow and Co., 1969.

Houlihan, James. *Western Shipbuilders in World War II.* Oakland: Shipbuilding Review Publishing Association, 1945.

Hundley, Norris, Jr. *The Great Thirst: Californians and Water, 1770s–1990s.* Berkeley: University of California Press, 1992.

Ingells, Douglas J. *The McDonnell Douglas Story.* Fallbrook, Calif.: Aero Publishers, 1979.

Jackson, Kenneth T. *The Crabgrass Frontier: The Suburbanization of the United States.* New York: Oxford University Press, 1985.

Jacobs, Jane. *The Death and Life of Great American Cities.* New York: Vintage Books, 1963.

———. *The Economy of Cities.* New York: Random House, 1969.

Jensen, Joan M., and Gloria Ricci Lothrop. *California Women: A History.* Sparks, Nev.: Materials for Today's Learning, 1988.

Johnson, Charles S. *The Negro War Worker in San Francisco: A Local Self-Survey.* San Francisco: Young Men's Christian Association, 1944.

Johnson, Marilynn S. *The Second Gold Rush: Oakland and the East Bay in World War II.* Berkeley: University of California Press, 1993.

Kahrl, William L. *Water and Power: The Conflict over Los Angeles' Water Supply in the Owens Valley.* Berkeley: University of California Press, 1982.

Karman, Theodore von, with Lee Edson. *The Wind and Beyond: Theodore Von Karman—Pioneer in Aviation and Pathfinder in Space.* Boston: Little, Brown, 1967.

Kennedy, Paul. *The Rise and Fall of the Great Powers: Economic Change and Military Conflict, 1500 to 2000.* New York: Random House, 1987.

Kinnaird, Lawrence. *History of the Greater San Francisco Bay Region.* New York: Lewis Historical Co., 1966.

Koistinen, Paul A. C. *The Military-Industrial Complex: A Historical Perspective.* New York: Praeger Publishers, 1980.

Koppes, Clayton R. *JPL and the American Space Program: A History of the Jet Propulsion Laboratory.* New Haven: Yale University Press, 1982.

Lane, Frederic C. *Ships for Victory: A History of Shipbuilding under the U. S. Maritime Commission in World War II.* Baltimore: Johns Hopkins University Press, 1951.

Lemke-Santangelo, Gretchen. *Abiding Courage: African American Migrant Women and the East Bay Community.* Chapel Hill: University of North Carolina Press, 1996.

Lichtenstein, Nelson. *Labor's War at Home: The CIO in World War II.* Cambridge: Cambridge University Press, 1982.

Lingeman, Richard R. *"Don't You Know There's a War On?": The American Home Front, 1941–1945.* New York: G. P. Putnam's Sons, 1970.

Lockheed Corporation. *A History of Lockheed. Lockheed Horizons,* Issue 12. n.p.: Lockheed Corporation, 1983.

Lotchin, Roger W. *Fortress California, 1910–1961: From Warfare to Welfare.* New York: Oxford University Press, 1992.

Lotchin, Roger W., ed. *The Way We Really Were: The Golden State in the Second Great War.* Champaign: University of Illinois Press, 2000.

Lotchin, Roger W., guest ed. *Fortress California at War: San Francisco, Los Angeles, Oakland, and San Diego, 1941–1945.* Special Issue. *Pacific Historical Review* 63, no. 3 (1994).

———. *The Twentieth Century Urban West.* Special Edition on Urbanism. *Journal of the West* 34, no. 3 (1995).

Lott, Arnold S. *A Long Line of Ships: Mare Island's Century of Naval Activity in California.* Annapolis: United States Naval Institute, 1954.

Lowitt, Richard. *The New Deal in the West.* Bloomington: Indiana University Press, 1984.

Mazon, Mauricio. *The Zoot Suit Riots: The Psychology of Symbolic Annihilation.* Austin: University of Texas Press, 1984.

McBroome, Delores Nason. *Parallel Communities: African Americans in California's East Bay, 1850–1963.* New York: Garland Publishing Co., 1993.

McMillen, Neill R. *Remaking Dixie: The Impact of World War II on the American South.* Jackson: University Press of Mississippi, 1997.

McNeill, William H. *The Pursuit of Power: Technology, Armed Force, and Society since A.D. 1000.* Chicago: University of Chicago Press, 1982.

Meller, H. E. *Leisure and the Changing City, 1870–1914.* London: Routledge and Kegan Paul, 1976.

Middlebrook, Martin. *The Battle of Hamburg: Allied Bomber Forces against a German City in 1943.* New York: Scribner, 1981.

Milkman, Ruth. *Gender at Work: The Dynamics of Job Segregation by Sex during World War II.* Urbana: University of Illinois Press, 1987.

Miller, Marc Scott. *The Irony of Victory: World War II and Lowell, Massachusetts.* Champaign: University of Illinois Press, 1988.

Milward, Alan S. *War, Economy and Society, 1939–1945.* Berkeley: University of California Press, 1977.

Mitchell, C. Bradford. *Every Kind of Shipwork: A History of Todd Shipyards Corporation, 1916–1981.* New York: Todd Shipbuilding Corp., 1981.

Moore, Shirley Ann Wilson. *To Place Our Deeds: The African American Community in Richmond, California, 1910–1963.* Berkeley: University of California Press, 2000.

Morison, Samuel Eliot. *The Atlantic Battle Won: May 1943–May 1945.* Boston: Little, Brown and Co., 1956.

Nasaw, David. *Children of the City at Work and at Play.* New York: Oxford University Press, 1985.

Nash, Gerald D. *The American West Transformed: The Impact of the Second World War.* Bloomington: Indiana University Press, 1985.

———. *World War II and the West: Reshaping the Economy.* Lincoln: University of Nebraska Press, 1990.

Newton, Wesley Phillips. *Montgomery in the Good War: Portrait of a Southern City, 1939–1946.* Tuscaloosa: University of Alabama Press, 2000.

O'Neill, William L. *A Democracy at War: America's Fight at Home and Abroad in World War II.* New York: Free Press, 1993.

Overton, Howard B., comp. and ed. *The 19th Coast Artillery and Fort Rosecrans: Remembrances.* San Diego: National Park Service and Cabrillo Monument, 1993.

Perrett, Geoffrey. *Days of Sadness, Years of Triumph: The American People, 1939–1945.* New York: Coward, McCann, and Geoghegan, 1973.

Platt, Harold L. *The Electric City: Energy and the Growth of the Chicago Area, 1880–1930.* Chicago: University of Chicago Press, 1991.

Polenberg, Richard. *America at War: The Home Front, 1941–1945.* Englewood Cliffs, N.J.: Prentice Hall, 1968.

———. *War and Society: The United States, 1941–1945.* Philadelphia: Lippincott, 1972.

Prange, Gordon. *At Dawn We Slept: The Untold Story of Pearl Harbor.* New York: McGraw Hill, 1981.

Pursell, Carroll W., Jr., ed. *The Military-Industrial Complex.* New York: Harper and Row, 1972.

Rae, John B. *Climb to Greatness: The American Aircraft Industry, 1920–1960.* Cambridge, Mass.: MIT Press, 1968.

Riess, Steven A. *City Games: The Evolution of American Urban Society and the Rise of Sports.* Urbana: University of Illinois Press, 1991.

Scharff, Virginia. *Taking the Wheel: Women and the Coming of the Motor Age.* New York: Free Press, 1991.

Scherini, Rose Doris. *The Italian American Community of San Francisco: A Descriptive Study.* New York: Arno Press, 1980.

Scott, Mellier. *The San Francisco Bay Area: A Metropolis in Perspective.* Berkeley: University of California Press, 1959.

Seymour, Paul. *Baseball: The Early Years.* New York: Oxford University Press, 1960.

Sies, Mary Corbin, and Christopher Silver. *Planning the Twentieth-Century American City.* Baltimore: Johns Hopkins University Press, 1996.

Smith, Betty. *A Tree Grows in Brooklyn.* New York: Harper and Brothers, 1943.

Somers, Dale A. *The Rise of Sports in New Orleans, 1850–1900.* Baton Rouge: Louisiana State University Press, 1972.

Sonenshein, Raphael J. *Politics in Black and White: Race and Power in Los Angeles.* Princeton, N.J.: Princeton University Press, 1993.

Spinney, Robert G. *World War II in Nashville: Transformation of the Homefront.* Knoxville: University of Tennessee Press, 1998.

Starr, Kevin. *The Dream Endures: California Enters the 1940s.* New York: Oxford University Press, 1997.

Stave, Bruce M., ed. *Urban Bosses, Machines, and Progressive Reformers.* Lexington, Mass.: D. C. Heath and Co., 1971.

Takaki, Ronald. *Strangers from a Different Shore: A History of Asian Americans.* New York: Little, Brown, 1989.

Terkel, Studs. *"The Good War": An Oral History of World War Two.* New York: Ballantine Books, 1984.

Thomas, Martha Mary. *Riveting and Rationing in Dixie: Alabama Women and the Second World War.* Tuscaloosa: University of Alabama Press, 1987.

Vatter, Harold. *The U. S. Economy in World War II.* New York: Columbia University Press, 1985.

Verge, Arthur C. *Paradise Transformed: Los Angeles during the Second World War.* Dubuque: Kendall/Hunt Publishing Co., 1993.

Voights, David Quentin. *American Baseball: From Gentleman's Sport to the Commissioner System.* Norman: University of Oklahoma Press, 1968.

Weinberg, Gerhard. *A World at Arms: A Global History of World War II.* New York: Cambridge University Press, 1994.

White, Morton, and Lucia White. *The Intellectual versus the City.* Cambridge, Mass.: Harvard University Press and MIT Press, 1964.

Winkler, Allan M. *Home Front U. S. A.: America during World War II.* Arlington Heights, Ill.: Harlan Davidson, 1986.

Wise, Nancy Baker, and Christy Wise. *A Mouthful of Rivets: Women at Work in World War II.* San Francisco: Jossey-Bass, 1994.

Wollenberg, Charles. *Golden Gate Metropolis: Perspectives on Bay Area History.* Berkeley: Institute of Governmental Studies, 1985.

———. *Marinship at War: Shipbuilding and Social Change in Wartime Sausalito.* Berkeley: Western Heritage Press, 1990.

Yung, Judy. *Unbound Feet: A Social History of Women in Chinatown.* Berkeley: University of California Press, 1995.

Zierer, Clifford M., ed. *California and the Southwest.* New York: John Wiley and Sons, 1956.

Articles

Abbott, Carl. "Beautiful Downtown Burbank: Changing Metropolitan Geography in the Modern West." *Journal of the West* 34, no. 3 (1995): 8–18.

Barbeau, Art. "Civilian Internment in World War II." *Journal of West Virginia Historical Association* 11, no. 1 (1989): 1–19.

Barkan, Elliott. "Sunbelt Immigration." Paper presented to the Miami Conference on the Sunbelt, Nov. 1986, 1–25.

Bennett, Sheila Kishler, and Glen H. Elder Jr. "Women's Work in the Family Economy: A Study of Depression Hardship in Women's Lives." *Journal of Family History* 4, no. 2 (1979): 153–76.

Braitman, Jacqueline R. "Partisans in Overalls: New Perspectives on Women and Politics in Wartime California." In *The Way We Really Were: The Golden State in the Second Great War,* ed. Roger W. Lotchin, 215–36. Champaign: University of Illinois Press, 2000.

Buchanan, Sarah. "Advertising during World War Two." UNC History Department course paper, Dec. 3, 1997, 1–21.

Camarillo, Albert. "A Research Note on Chicano Community Leaders: The G. I. Generation." *Aztlan: Chicano Journal of the Social Sciences and the Arts* 2, no. 2 (1971): 145–50.

Cohen, Ronald D. "Music Goes to War: California, 1940–1945." In *The Way We Really Were: The Golden State in the Second Great War,* ed. Roger W. Lotchin, 47–67. Champaign: University of Illinois Press, 2000.

Elkind, Sarah S. "Public Oil, Private Oil: The Tidelands Oil Controversy, World War II, and Control of the Environment." In *The Way We Really Were: The Golden State in the Second Great War,* ed. Roger W. Lotchin, 120–42. Champaign: University of Illinois Press, 2000.

Enloe, Cynthia. "Was It 'The Good War' for Women?" *American Quarterly* 37 (1985): 627–31.

Finkle, Lee. "The Conservative Aims of Militant Rhetoric: Black Protest during World War II." *Journal of American History* 60, no. 3 (1973): 692–713.

Fox, Stephen C. "General John DeWitt and the Proposed Internment of German and Italian Aliens during World War II." *Pacific Historical Review* 57, no. 4 (1988): 407–38.

Frazer, Heather T., and John O'Sullivan. "Forgotten Women of World War II: Wives of Conscientious Objectors in Civilian Public Service." *Peace and Change* 5, nos. 2 and 3 (1978): 46–51.

Freeman, Heather. "The Lives of Two Southern Housewives during World War II." UNC undergraduate seminar paper, Dec. 6, 1996, 1–28.

Garcia, Mario T. "Americans All: The Mexican American Generation and the Politics of Wartime Los Angeles, 1941–1945." *Social Science Quarterly* 65, no. 2 (1984): 278–89.

Gleason, Philip. "Americans All: World War II and the Shaping of American Identity." *Review of Politics* 43, no. 4 (1981): 483–519.

Graaf, Lawrence B. de. "Significant Steps on an Arduous Path: The Impact of World War II on Discrimination against African Americans in the West." *Journal of the West* 25, no. 1 (1996): 24–33.

Greene, Rebecca S. "The United States: Women in World War II." *Trends in History* 2, no. 2 (1982): 71–82.

Gumina, Deanna Paoli. "The Fishermen of San Francisco Bay." *Pacific Historian* 20, no. 1 (1976): 8–21.

Hall, Kimberly A. "Women in Wartime: The San Diego Experience, 1941–1945." *Journal of San Diego History* 39, no. 4 (1993): 272.

Hanchett, Thomas W. "Roots of the 'Renaissance': Federal Incentives to Urban Planning, 1941–1948." In *Planning the Twentieth-Century American City,* ed. Mary Corbin Sies and Christopher Silver, 284–304. Baltimore: Johns Hopkins University Press, 1996.

Harris, William H. "Federal Intervention in Union Discrimination: FEPC and West Coast Shipyards during World War II." *Labor History* 11, no. 3 (1981): 325–47.

Hartmann, Susan M. "Prescriptions for Penelope: Literature on Women's Obligations to Returning World War II Veterans." *Women's Studies* 5, no. 3 (1978): 223–39.

Havens, Thomas R. H. "Women and War in Japan, 1937–1945." *American Historical Review* 80, no. 4 (1975): 913–34.

Hirshfield, Deborah Scott. "Women Shipyard Workers in the Second World War: A Note." *International History Review* 11, no. 2 (1989): 478–85.

Honey, Maureen. "The Working-Class Woman and Recruitment Propaganda during World War II: Class Differences in the Portrayal of War Work." *Signs: Journal of Women in Culture and Society* 8, no. 4 (1983): 672–87.

Howard, George W. "The Desert Training Center/California-Arizona Maneuver Area." *Journal of Arizona History* 26, no. 3 (1985): 273–94.

Issel, William. "New Deal and Wartime Origins of San Francisco's Postwar Political Culture: The Case of Growth Politics and Policy." In *The Way We Really Were: The Golden State in the Second Great War,* ed. Roger W. Lotchin, 68–92. Champaign: University of Illinois Press, 2000.

Issel, William, and James Collins. "The Catholic Church and Organized Labor in San Francisco, 1932–1958." *Records of the American Catholic Historical Society* 109, nos. 1 and 2 (1999): 81–112.

Killory, Christine. "Lost Opportunity of San Diego's National Defense Housing Projects." *Journal of San Diego History* 39, nos. 1 and 2 (1993): 33–50.

Leonard, Kevin Allen. "'Brothers under the Skin'?: African Americans, Mexican Americans, and World War II in California." In *The Way We Really Were: The Golden State in the Second Great War,* ed. Roger W. Lotchin, 187–214. Champaign: University of Illinois Press, 2000.

Lichtenstein, Nelson. "The Making of the Postwar Working Class: Cultural Pluralism and Social Structure in World War II." *Historian* 51, no. 1 (1988): 42–63.

Lively, Bruce R. "Naval and Marine Corps Reserve Center Los Angeles." *Southern California Quarterly* 69, no. 3 (1987): 241–73.

Lotchin, Roger W. "California Cities and the Hurricane of Change: World War II in the San Francisco, Los Angeles, and San Diego Metropolitan Areas." *Pacific Historical Review* 63, no. 3 (1994): 393–420.

Lotchin, Roger W., and David Long. "World War II and the Transformation of Southern Urban Society: A Reconsideration." *Georgia Historical Quarterly* 83, no. 1 (1999): 30–57.

Lothrop, Gloria Ricci. "The Italians of Los Angeles." *Californians* 5, no. 3 (1987): 28–43.

———. "A Shadow on the Land: The Impact of Fascism on Los Angeles Italians." *California History* 75, no. 4 (1996–97): 338–53.

———. "The Untold Story: The Effect of the Second World War on California Italians." *Journal of the West* 35, no. 1 (1996): 7–14.

———. "Unwelcome Aliens in Freedom's Land: The Impact of World War II on Italian Aliens in Southern California." *Southern California Quarterly* 81, no. 4 (1999): 507–44.

MacCarthy, Esther. "Catholic Women and War: The National Council of Catholic Women, 1919–1946." *Peace and Change* 5, no. 1 (1973): 23–32.

Matsumoto, Valerie. "Japanese American Women during World War II." *Frontiers* 7, no. 1 (1984): 6–14.

Mehr, Linda Harris. "The Way We Thought We Were: Images in World War II Films." In *The Way We Really Were: The Golden State in the Second Great War,* ed. Roger W. Lotchin, 30–44. Champaign: University of Illinois Press, 2000.

Mormino, Gary R., and George E. Pozzetta. "Ethnics at War: Italian Americans in California during World War II." In *The Way We Really Were: The Golden State in the Second Great War,* ed. Roger W. Lotchin, 143–63. Champaign: University of Illinois Press, 2000.

Nash, Michael. "Women and the Pennsylvania Railroad: The World War II Years." *Labor History* 30, no. 4 (1989): 608–21.

Padgett, Wayne. "Orion Limps to Mare Island." *Naval History* 13, no. 4 (1999): 38–42.

Prickett, James R. "Communist Conspiracy or Wage Dispute?: The 1941 Strike at North American Aviation." *Pacific Historical Review* 50, no. 2 (1981): 215–33.

Reynolds, Clark G. "Submarine Attacks on the Pacific Coast, 1942." *Pacific Historical Review* 33, no. 2 (1964): 191–92.

Rhode, Paul. "California in the Second World War: An Analysis of Defense Spending." In *The Way We Really Were: The Golden State in the Second Great War,* ed. Roger W. Lotchin, 93–119. Champaign: University of Illinois Press, 2000.

———. "The Nash Thesis Revisited: An Economic Historian's View." In *Fortress California at War: San Francisco, Los Angeles, Oakland, and San Diego, 1941–1945,* Roger W. Lotchin, guest ed. Special Issue. *Pacific Historical Review* 63, no. 3 (1994).

Rockoff, Hugh. "Indirect Price Increases and Real Wages during World War II." *Explorations in Economic History* 15, no. 4 (1978): 407–20.

Santillan, Richard. "Rosita The Riveter: Midwest Mexican American Women during World War II, 1941–1945." *Perspectives in Mexican American Studies* 2 (1989): 115–47.

Scargle, Russ. "Music and Men's Minds: A World War II Vignette." *Pacific Historian* 16, no. 1 (1972): 28–35.

Schulman, Judy P. "Camp Callan: From Glory to a Memory." *Journal of the Council on America's Military Past* 13, no. 1 (1984): 43–50.

Schweitzer, Mary M. "World War II and Female Labor Force Participation Rates." *Journal of Economic History* 40, no. 1 (1980): 89–95.

Sides, Josh. "Battle on the Home Front: African American Shipyard Workers in World War II Los Angeles." *California History* 75, no. 3 (1996): 222–97.

Sitkoff, Harvard. "Racial Militancy and Interracial Violence in the Second World War." *Journal of American History* 58, no. 3 (1971): 661–81.

Smith, Alonzo N. "Blacks and the Los Angeles Municipal Transit System, 1941–1945." *Urbanism Past and Present* 6, no. 1 (1980–81): 30.

Steele, Richard W. "'No Racials': Discrimination against Ethnics in American Defense Industry, 1940–42." *Labor History* 32, no. 1 (1991): 66–90.

Straub, Eleanor F. "United States Government Policy toward Civilian Women during World War II." *Prologue* 5, no. 4 (1973): 240–54.

Torigian, Michael. "National Unity on the Waterfront: Communist Politics and the ILWU during the Second World War." *Labor History* 30, no. 3 (1989): 409–32.

Verge, Arthur. "Daily Life in Wartime California." In *The Way We Really Were: The Golden State in the Second Great War,* ed. Roger W. Lotchin, 13–29. Champaign: University of Illinois Press, 2000.

Vogel, Peter. "The Last Wave from Port Chicago." *Black Scholar* 13, nos. 2 and 3 (1982): 30–47.

Walker, Richard. Review of *Fortress California: From Warfare to Welfare,* by Roger W. Lotchin. *Economic Geography* 69, no. 2 (1993): 224–26.

Weber, Eugen. "Gymnastics and Sports in Fin-de-Siecle France: Opium of the Classes?" *American Historical Review* 76, no. 1 (1971): 70–98.

Wong, K. Scott. "War Comes to Chinatown: Social Transformation and the Chinese of California." In *The Way We Really Were: The Golden State in the Second Great War,* ed. Roger W. Lotchin, 164–86. Champaign: University of Illinois Press, 2000.

Young, James O. "The Golden Age at Muroc-Edwards." *Journal of the West* 30, no. 1 (1991): 69–79.

Zhao, Xiaojian. "Chinese American Women Defense Workers in World War II." *California History* 75, no. 2 (1996): 112, 140, 145–146.

Theses and Dissertations

Adler, Patricia Rae. "Watts: From Suburb to Black Ghetto." Ph.D. dissertation, University of Southern California, 1977.

Anderson, Philip A. "The History and Development of the Coyote Point Merchant Marine Cadet School and Its Contribution toward America's Victory in World War II." Ph.D. dissertation, California State University, Dominguez Hills, 1997.

Boyden, Richard Prime. "The San Francisco Machinists from Depression to Cold War, 1930–1950." Ph.D. dissertation, University of California at Berkeley, 1988.

Fousekis, Natalie Marie. "Fighting for Our Children: Women's Activism and the Battle for Child Care in California, 1940–1965." Ph.D. dissertation, University of North Carolina at Chapel Hill, 2000.

Harris, Leroy. "The Other Side of the Freeway: A Study of Settlement Patterns of Negroes and Mexican Americans in San Diego." Ph.D. dissertation, Carnegie-Mellon University, 1974.

Lichtman, Sheila Tropp. "Women at Work, 1941–1945: Wartime Employment in the San Francisco Bay Area." Ph.D. dissertation, University of California, Davis, 1981.

Mosier, Eric M. "The Impact of World War II on the Mexican American Community in San Diego." M.A. thesis, San Diego State University, 1998.

Shragge, Abraham. "Boosters and Bluecoats: The Civic Culture of Militarism in San Diego, California, 1900–1945." Ph.D. dissertation, University of California at San Diego, 1998.

Sides, Josh A. "Working Away: African American Migration and Community in Los Angeles from the Great Depression to 1954." Ph.D. dissertation, UCLA, 1999.

Wilburn, James R. "Social and Economic Aspects of the Aircraft Industry in Metropolitan Los Angeles during World War II." Ph.D. dissertation, UCLA, 1971.

Zhao, Xiaojian. "Women and Defense Industries in World War Two." Ph.D. dissertation, University of California at Berkeley, 1993.

Oral History Interviews

Antonicelli, Frank. "An Interview with Frank Antonicelli." Craig Carter, interviewer, and Thomas E. Wald, ed. Nov. 20, 1985. San Diego Historical Society Oral History Program.

Asaro, Katie. "An Interview with Katie Asaro." Robert G. Wright, interviewer, and Thomas E. Walt, ed. March 24, 1990. San Diego Historical Society Oral History Program.

Battaglia, Vincent. "An Interview with Vincent Battaglia." Robert G. Wright, interviewer. March 3, 1991. San Diego Historical Society Oral History Program.

Bovet, Eva. "An Interview with Eva Bovet." Walter Fabert, interviewer and ed. Dec. 12, 1972. San Diego Historical Society Oral History Program.

Brandes, Shirley. "An Interview with Shirley Brandes." Bernice Wall, interviewer, and Cora Janes Jenkins, ed. Jan. 16, 1985. San Diego Historical Society Oral History Program.

Briggs, Evelyn Harper. "An Interview with Evelyn Harper Briggs." Ruth Hampton, interviewer and ed. Nov. 2, 1983. San Diego Historical Society Oral History Program.

Burns, Phyllis. "An Interview with Phyllis Burns." Ruth Held, interviewer and ed. Aug. 16 and 19, 1989. San Diego Historical Society Oral History Program.

Chana, William F. "An Interview with William F. Chana." Robert G. Wright, interviewer and ed. Oct. 26, 1989. San Diego Historical Society Oral History Program.

Clark, J. Dallas. "An Interview with J. Dallas Clark." Ruth Held, interviewer and ed. Oct. 30, 1991. San Diego Historical Society Oral History Program.

Curran, Frank. "An Interview with the Honorable Frank Curran." Robert Wright, interviewer and ed. March 26, 1983. San Diego Historical Society Oral History Program.

Dailard, Ralph C. "An Interview with Dr. Ralph C. Dailard." Ruth Hampton, interviewer, and Thomas E. Walt, ed. June 8, 1988. San Diego Historical Society Oral History Program.

Dishong, Barbara Jean. "An Interview with Barbara Jean Dishong." Robert G. Wright, interviewer, and Ruth Hampton, ed. Oct. 23, 1981. San Diego Historical Society Oral History Program.

Emerson, Jane Randall. "An Interview with Jane Randall Emerson." Dr. Craig Carter, interviewer, and Thomas E. Walt, ed. Jan. 31, 1991. San Diego Historical Society Oral History Program.

Famme, Joseph H. "An Interview with Joseph H. Famme." Robert G. Wright interviewer and ed., and Thomas E. Walt, ed., Nov. 6, 1989. San Diego Historical Society Oral History Program.

Forward, Charles. "An Interview with Charles Forward." Sylvia Arden, interviewer and ed. April 29, 1975. San Diego Historical Society Oral History Program.

Foster, Catherine Ann. "An Interview with Catherine Ann Foster." Thomas E. Walt and Betty Quayle, eds. Oct. 3, 1988. San Diego Historical Society Oral History Program.

Gatov, Elizabeth Rudel. "Grassroots Party Organizer to Treasurer of the United States." Malca Chall, interviewer. Interviewed between Nov. 1, 1975 and May 11, 1976, pub. 1978. Regional Oral History Office, University of California, Berkeley.

Grant, Donald Franklin. "An Interview with Donald Franklin Grant." Robert G. Wright, interviewer, and Thomas E. Walt, ed. Feb. 4, 1985. San Diego Historical Society Oral History Program.

Greene, Ethel. "An Interview with Ethel Greene." Betty Quayle, interviewer, and Thomas E. Walt, ed. Jan. 26, 1987. San Diego Historical Society Oral History Program.

Hastie, William L. "An Interview with Colonel William L. Hastie, U.S. Army Retired." Dr. Craig Carter, interviewer, and Thomas E. Walt, ed. Oct. 12, 1991. San Diego Historical Society Oral History Program.

Held, John Spencer. "An Interview with John Spencer Held." Ruth Held and Thomas E. Walt, interviewers and eds. Aug. 4, 1990. San Diego Historical Society Oral History Program.

Hinton, Sam. "An Interview with Sam Hinton." Dr. Craig Carter, interviewer, and . Nancy Fisk, ed. Feb. 1, 1990. San Diego Historical Society Oral History Program.

Ingrande, Leonard. "An Interview with Leonard Ingrande." Robert G. Wright, interviewer, and Thomas E. Walt, ed. May 7, 1988. San Diego Historical Society Oral History Program.

Kimbrough, Dr. Jack. "An Interview with Dr. Jack Kimbrough." Robert G. Wright, interviewer, and Thomas E. Walt, ed. Oct. 11, 1990. San Diego Historical Society Oral History Program.

Maupin, Joyce. "Working in War Industry: An Interview with Joyce Maupin." Julie Denning, interviewer and ed. 1976. Regional Oral History Office, University of California, Berkeley.

May, Bernice Hubbard. "A Native Daughter's Leadership in Public Affairs." Gabrielle Morris, interviewer. Interviews between March 20, 1974 and Nov. 7, 1974, pub. 1976. Regional Oral History Office, University of California, Berkeley.

McMullen, Jerry. "An Interview with Jerry McMullen." Robert G. Wright and Sylvia Arden, interviewers and eds. Sept. 21, 1980. San Diego Historical Society Oral History Program.

Muldrew, Oliver. "An Interview with Oliver Muldrew, Sergeant, Cavalry, U.S. Army." Dr. Craig Carter, interviewer, and Thomas E. Walt, ed. Oct. 12, 1991. San Diego Historical Society Oral History Program.

Muto, Marian. "An Interview with Marian Muto." Cora Jane Jenkins, interviewer and ed. Jan. 18, 1985. San Diego Historical Society Oral History Program.

Nicholson, Helen. "An Interview with Helen Nicholson." Mary Geran, interviewer and ed. Sept. 11, 1982. San Diego Historical Society Oral History Program.

Orjas, Wilsie. "An Account of Pearl Harbor Days, on and after December 7, 1941, 1942." Unpublished manuscript, Bancroft Library.

Ortiz, Edward, Jr. "An Interview with Edward Ortiz Jr." Craig Carter, interviewer, and Joy Hayes, ed. April 25, 1988. San Diego Historical Society Oral History Program.

Potts, Mary Jean. "An Interview with Mary Jean Potts." Julie Denning, interviewer and ed. May 17, 1979. Regional Oral History Office, University of California, Berkeley.

Ratner, Abraham. "An Interview with Abraham Ratner." Mary Fadem, interviewer, and Thomas E. Walt, ed. March 3, 1987. San Diego Historical Society Oral History Program.

Sanders, Gigi. "An Interview with Gigi Sanders." Robert G. Wright, interviewer, and Vincent Ancona, ed. Oct. 30, 1989. San Diego Historical Society Oral History Program.

Schillreff, Barbara. "An Interview with Barbara Schillreff." Susan Painter, interviewer and ed. May 28, 1991. San Diego Historical Society Oral History Program.

Segawa, Ben Satoshi. "An Interview with Ben Satoshi Segawa." Vincent Ancona, interviewer and ed. Sept. 13, 1990. San Diego Historical Society Oral History Program.

Segawa, Katherine (Tasaki). "An Interview with Katherine (Tasaki) Segawa." Vincent Ancona, interviewer, and Vincent Ancona and Thomas E. Walt, eds, Sept. 20, 1990. San Diego Historical Society Oral History Program.

Silversher, Herman I. "An Interview with Herman I. Silversher." Susan Painter, interviewer and ed. May 24, 1990. San Diego Historical Society Oral History Program.

Trepte, Albert Eugene. "An Interview with Albert Eugene Trepte." Ruth Held, interviewer and ed. Jan. 29, 1991. San Diego Historical Society Oral History Program.

Trevey, Helen. "An Interview with Helen Trevey." Ruth Hampton, interviewer, and Thomas E. Walt, ed. May 8, 1986. San Diego Historical Society Oral History Program.

Vetter, Yuri. "An Interview with Yuri Vetter." Cora Jane Jenkins, interviewer, and Thomas E. Walt, ed. July 25, 1985. San Diego Historical Society Oral History Program.

Wagenet, Gordon. "Interview with Gordon Wagenet." Roger W. Lotchin, interviewer. May 31 and Aug. 18, 2000.

Walling, Effie. "Interview with Effie Walling." Nancy Ledeboer, interviewer and ed. May 17, 1979. Regional Oral History Office, University of California, Berkeley.

Weiss, Mandell. "An Interview with Mandell Weiss." Sylvia Arden, interviewer, and Sylvia Arden and Thomas De. Walt, eds. Aug. 13, 20, 30; Sept. 4, 13, 1985. San Diego Historical Society Historical Society Oral History Program.

Wohlford, Mildred Finley. "An Interview with Mildred Finley Wohlford." Cora Jane Jenkins, interviewer, and Philip M. Klauber and Jenkins, eds. Aug. 1987. San Diego Historical Society Oral History Program.

Wright, Robert G. "An Interview with Robert G. Wright." Vincent Ancona, interviewer and ed. Nov. 8, 1990. San Diego Historical Society Oral History Program.

INDEX

ROGER W. LOTCHIN is Professor of History at the University of North Carolina, Chapel Hill. He has written widely on California and western history, American urban history, and the history of the U.S. home front in World War II. He is a jazz buff and an avid traveler, photographer, stonemason, and tennis player.